SETTINGS FOR
HEALTH PROMOTION

*This book is dedicated to Ron Draper (1934–1997),
pioneer and leader in health promotion, the
first Director-General of the Canadian Health
Promotion Directorate and consultant to the
World Health Organization on Healthy Cities.*

SETTINGS FOR HEALTH PROMOTION

Linking Theory and Practice

Blake D. Poland

Lawrence W. Green

Irving Rootman

Editors

Sage Publications, Inc.
International Educational and Professional Publisher
Thousand Oaks ▪ London ▪ New Delhi

For information:

Sage Publications, Inc.
2455 Teller Road
Thousand Oaks, California 91320
E-mail: order@sagepub.com

Sage Publications Ltd.
6 Bonhill Street
London EC2A 4PU
United Kingdom

Sage Publications India Pvt. Ltd.
M-32 Market
Greater Kailash I
New Delhi 110 048 India

Printed in the United States of America

Library of Congress Cataloging-in-Publication Data

Settings for health promotion: Linking theory and practice / edited by
Blake D. Poland, Lawrence W. Green, Irving Rootman.
    p. cm.
Includes bibliographical references.
ISBN 0-8039-7418-3 (cloth: acid-free paper)
ISBN 0-8039-7419-1 (pbk: acid-free paper)
  1. Health promotion. 2. Social medicine. I. Poland, Blake D. II. Green,
Lawrence W. III. Rootman, I.
RA427.8 .S48 2000
613—dc21   99-050471

This book is printed on acid-free paper.

00   01   02   03   04   05   06   7   6   5   4   3   2   1

Acquisition Editor: Margaret Seawell
Editorial Assistant: Brian Neumann
Production Editor: Sanford Robinson
Editorial Assistant: Victoria Cheng
Typesetter: Janelle LeMaster
Indexer: Julie Grayson
Cover Designer: Candice Harman

Contents

Foreword

David V. McQueen

Recently, there was an opening of a health promotion center at a community hospital affiliated with a prestigious New England University. The hospital was the setting for a participatory action approach to health promotion. Even to one long associated with health promotion, it may come as a bit of a shock to think of the hospital as a place for health promotion. Upon reflection, of course, it is a most appropriate place. Where else does one encounter an organization so predominantly focused on the theater of health and illness? Where better to play out the full drama, the full dimensions of health promotion? In its seeming antithesis of health promotion, the hospital reveals the power of settings as a place for health promotion.

The World Health Organization defines settings for health as the place or social context in which people engage in daily activities in which environmental, organizational and personal factors interact to affect health and well being. Thus, settings provide a critical proving ground for health promotion theory and practice. There is clearly a fundamental need for a book that examines the inter-action between settings and health promotion theory and practice. Poland, Green and Roadman have produced such a book.

This book, however, is not simply a summary of the state-of-the-art. By inter-weaving definitive chapters with critical commentary and discourse, it gives the reader a tremendous insight into the knowledge base revealed in the work that has taken place. It also reveals the depth and usefulness of the postmodern dis-course when juxtaposed with the concrete attempts to intervene in practice. It is this interplay throughout the work that gives it that added value.

The book also reveals all the issues around settings as the context in which evidence for health promotion success may be found. At first glance, settings ap-pear like a place bounded, controlled, and therefore subject to a certain rigor in intervention that will show how health promotion works. But this is illusory, be-cause the apparent bounded nature gives way to an incredibly rich complexity where interactions are multivariate, layered, dynamic, and synergistic. Thus set-tings reveal all the complexity with which health promotion must contend. This book takes us further down that complex path.

David V. McQueen
National Center for Chronic Disease
Prevention and Health Promotion
Centers for Disease Control and Prevention, Atlanta

ACKNOWLEDGMENTS

We wish to thank Linda Sagar, Joanne Taylor Lacey, and Veronica Dooley for their superb editing and clerical support and the Centre for Health Promotion, University of Toronto, Canada for making the contributions of Linda and Joanne possible.

We thank Dan Ruth, Sanford Robinson, and Linda Gray at Sage for their patience, faith, and continued enthusiasm for this project.

We thank our spouses and families for their loving support and understanding during the 2 years required to put this volume together.

As editors, we wish also to thank the many contributing authors to this vol-ume, without whom this project would not have been possible.

Blake D. Poland, *University of Toronto*
Lawrence W. Green, *University of British Columbia*
(*now at Centers for Disease Control and Prevention, Atlanta*)
Irving Rootman, *University of Toronto*

The Settings Approach
to Health Promotion

Lawrence W. Green

Blake D. Poland

Irving Rootman

This book is about the "settings approach" to health promotion. The concept of *setting* is fundamental to theory in health promotion because it delineates boundaries conceptually for the understanding of context as health promotion seeks to become more ecological and context sensitive. Setting has an equally fundamental place in practice as health promotion programs seek to be responsive to the particular needs and living circumstances of potential beneficiaries of health promotion, sometimes referred to as *target populations* or *audiences*. Setting defines the "subjects" of intervention (individually and collectively), the location of health promotion, and the frames of the setting itself as a target of intervention. Most health promotion activity is bounded in space and time within settings that provide the social structure and context for planning, implementing, and evaluating interventions.

To set the stage for consideration of the settings approach to health promotion, this chapter begins with a discussion of the development, conceptualization, and practice of health promotion. An explication of the rationale for a set-

AUTHOR'S NOTE: We would like to acknowledge Joan Eakin for contributions to some of the ideas elaborated in the section on a critical social science perspective on the settings approach and Michael Goodstadt for his contribution to the section on "What is Health Promotion?".

tings approach follows, together with a consideration of settings from an ecological perspective (including some of its disciplinary roots) and from a critical social science perspective. The chapter concludes with an overview of the contents of the remaining chapters.

WHAT IS HEALTH PROMOTION?

The past two decades have witnessed extensive and sometimes intense debate regarding the meaning and placement of health promotion in health policy and practice. We address these debates in three ways to set the stage for the discussion of settings for health promotion. First, we examine the origins, circumstances, and issues that led to recent notions of health promotion. Second, we review various definitions of health promotion offered or proposed. Last, we describe variations in practice that constitute health promotion in specific settings.

Recent Origins of Health Promotion

The idea of health promotion is not new. The prevailing methods and concepts of community health in the 19th century, before germ theory ushered in the "bacteriological era" of public health, had many of the political and ecological features of contemporary health promotion. Some of these features had precedents and intellectual roots in Ancient Chinese, Babylonian, Hebrew, and Greek civilizations (Green & Ottoson, 1999, pp. 7-18). Some attempts were made in the first half of this century to give health promotion prominence in public health (e.g., Sigerist, 1946; Winslow, 1920) and in the measurement of health (e.g., Dunn, 1977). The rise of health promotion as an organized, distinct field in health policy and practice can be traced to 1974. Marc Lalonde, the Canadian Minister of Health and Welfare at the time, released a monograph titled *A New Perspective on the Health of Canadians* (Lalonde, 1974). This is commonly and respectfully referred to as the "Lalonde Report," although it was based conceptually on the Health Field concept introduced a year earlier by Lalonde's deputy, Laframboise (1973). Globally, the Lalonde Report marked the first time that a national government policy document identified health promotion as a key strategy for improving the health of a population. This document stimulated international enthusiasm for health promotion as an approach to planning that could be potentially useful to governments, organizations, communities, and individuals, although it tended to be used most often to support a lifestyle focus within health promotion. The Lalonde Report provided the impetus for health promotion initiatives in other countries, including the United States (U.S. Department of Health, Education and Welfare 1979) and Australia (Commonwealth Department of Health, Housing, and Community Services, 1993). The surge in interest in health promotion was captured and endorsed at the First International Conference on Health Promotion in 1986, which issued the Ottawa Charter for Health Promotion (World Health Organization, 1986). The Ottawa Charter identified (a) a number of essential prerequisites for health (food, shelter, peace, income, stable ecosystem, sustainable resource use, social justice, and equity), (b) clearly framed health promotion as encompassing more than health care and lifestyles (focusing instead on well-being, broadly defined), and (c) identified five key strategies for health promotion:

1. Building healthy public policy

2. Creating supportive environments

3. Strengthening community action

4. Developing personal skills

5. Reorienting health services

The first three of these clearly focus activity on environments in which health is (and lifestyles are) created and sustained, providing support for a settings approach. The Ottawa Charter subsequently reinforced the development of health promotion throughout the world (Nutbeam, 1997).

Continued and renewed interest in health promotion resulted from the confluence of disparate forces. These have included the following:

- Growing emphasis on positive health and improved quality of life

- Recognition of the holistic nature of health—that is, the social, mental, and spiritual qualities of life

- Individuals' and communities' desire to exercise control over their lives, associated in part with a rise in the concept of the "consumer" in health care and in health policy

- Community development and communications movements that promoted grassroots, in contrast to top-down, initiatives

- Self-care and women's movements that required a shift in the distribution of power from "experts" to individuals and communities

- Limited effectiveness of traditional didactic education strategies

- Recognition that many health problems are related to individual lifestyles and that lifestyles do not occur in a vacuum but themselves have powerful socioeconomic and cultural determinants

- Evidence that increased investment in health care has produced decreasing marginal returns, as measured by improvements in health status

- Pressure imposed on social programs and high-tech medical care by deteriorating economic and environmental conditions around the world (Anderson, 1984; Green & Kreuter, 1991; Green & Raeburn, 1990; Macdonald & Bunton, 1992)

Finally, epidemiological research has documented the powerful influence of the broader determinants of health that extend beyond individual genetic and behavioral domains. These influences on health are strongly associated with socioeconomic conditions, culture, education, equity and access issues, national wealth, social support, and other structural and systemic factors (Evans, Barer, & Marmor, 1994; Evans & Stoddart, 1990; Green, Simons-Morton, & Potvin, 1996; Health and Welfare Canada, 1989; Martin & McQueen, 1989; Rose, 1992; Syme, 1991; Terris, 1994; Wilkinson, 1986, 1996). This evidence provides strong support for extending the domains of traditional prevention efforts and reorienting public health, thereby providing support for recent developments in health promotion.

Health promotion's breadth and mixed pedigree has given these more recent elements the appearance of a "new public health" (e.g., Macdonald & Bunton, 1992; Martin & McQueen, 1989), even though the specific components are not new. According to the new, wider perspective, public health concerns extend beyond health protection and prevention to include (a) reducing the negative impact of a broad range of social, political, and economic determinants of health; (b) giving attention to domains of health beyond the physical—including mental, social, and spiritual dimensions; (c) enhancement of health; (d) redistribution of power and control over individual and community health issues; (e) shifting the allocation of resources "upstream" toward prevention of problems before they occur; (f) taking an ecological approach to health that considers health the dynamic product of interactions between individuals and their environments (e.g., Chu & Simpson, 1994; Green, Richard, & Potvin, 1996; Kickbusch, 1989; McLeroy, Bibeau, Steckler, & Glanz, 1988; Stokols, 1996); and (g) recognizing community development and involvement as legitimate and effective strategies for maintaining and improving health.

These characteristics are reflected in the variety of definitions proposed for health promotion. Some defining features concern the goals of health promotion (b and c). Others concern the means by which these goals will be achieved (a, d, e, f, and g).

Definitions of Health Promotion

Table 1.1 summarizes key definitions of health promotion. We propose that the apparent discrepancies represent differences in perspective and emphasis rather than fundamental conflicts in meaning. A useful distinction has been

Table 1.1 Definitions of Health Promotion

Authors	Activities (programs, policies, etc.)	Processes (underlying mechanisms)	Objectives (instrumental outcomes)
Winslow (1920)	Organized community effort for the education of the individual in personal health and the development of the social machinery . . .		. . . to ensure everyone a standard of living for . . .
Sigerist (1946)			. . . by providing a decent standard of living, good labor conditions, education, physical culture, means of rest and recreation . . .
Lalonde (1974)	. . . informing, influencing and assisting both individuals and organizations . . .	. . . so that they (individuals and organizations) will accept more responsibility and be more active in matters affecting mental and physical health . . .	
Green (1979)	. . . any combination of health education and related organizational, political, and economic interventions designed to . . .		. . . to facilitate behavioral and environmental changes . . .
U.S. Office of Health Information and Health Promotion (Green, 1980)	. . . any combination of health education and related organizational, political, and economic interventions designed to . . .		

(Continued)

5

Table 1.1 Continued

Authors	Activities *(programs, policies, etc.)*	Processes *(underlying mechanisms)*	Objectives *(instrumental outcomes)*
Perry and Jessor (1985)	. . . the implementation of efforts to . . .		
WHO (1984, 1986), Epp (1986)		the process of enabling people to . . .	. . . to increase control over their health . . .
Goodstadt, Simpson, and Loranger (1987)	through the implementation of effective programs, services, and policies		
Kar (1989)			and the avoidance of health risks by achieving optimal levels of the behavioral, societal, environmental, and biomedical determinants of health
O'Donnell (1989)	the science and art of helping people choose their lifestyles to . . .		
Nutbeam (1997)		the process of enabling individuals and communities to increase control over . . .	. . . the determinants of health . . .
Green and Kreuter (1999)	any planned combination of educational, political, regulatory and organizational supports for actions and conditions of living conducive to . . .		
Labonte and Little (1992)	any activity or program designed to . . .		. . . to improve social and environmental living conditions

SOURCE: Adapted from Rootman, Goodstadt, Potvin, and Springett (1997).

made between health promotion as an outcome and health promotion as process, although in practice the two are intertwined. Kickbusch (1994) refers to health promotion in the latter context as "a process for initiating, managing, and implementing change . . . a process of personal, organizational, and policy development" (p. 13). The nature of the expected outcomes (goals and objectives) and strategies (processes and activities) distinguish health promotion from other approaches.

A definition of health promotion first proposed by the European Office of the World Health Organization (WHO) in 1984 and subsequently ratified by the First International Conference on Health Promotion was published in the Ottawa Charter for Health Promotion (WHO, 1986). The WHO definition, which has become preeminent in the field, suggests that health promotion is "the process of enabling people to increase control over, and to improve, their health" (p. i).

Nutbeam (1986) expanded this definition as follows: "the process of enabling individuals and communities to increase control over the determinants of health and thereby improve their health" (p. 114). The latter definition explicates a concern with both individuals and communities who are being enabled and makes explicit reference to a "causal" mechanism or process of health promotion—namely "increas[ing] control over the determinants of health."

The focus on individuals', and communities', level of control captures a key element of health promotion as understood and accepted by many people working in the field. In particular, it embodies a cardinal principle of health promotion—namely *empowerment.* That is, health promotion seeks to ensure that individuals and communities can exercise their rightful power in making decisions that can improve or damage their health. Thus, notwithstanding differences, there are substantial commonalities among conceptualizations of health promotion. Specifically, health promotion involves a diverse set of actions, focused on individuals and their environments, which increases control over, and ultimately improves, health or well-being.

The concept of empowerment presents many conceptual, operational, and evaluation challenges (e.g., Brown, 1991; Health Education Quarterly, 1994a, 1994b; Robertson & Minkler, 1994; Rissel, 1994; Wallerstein, 1992). It is especially problematic that many of the broader (social, cultural, political, and economic) determinants of health are beyond the control of individuals and communities, at least in the short term. However, health promotion can help people to work collectively to change those things which are beyond the control of individuals, small groups, or specific geographic communities, through broader-based coalitions and social movements.

Nevertheless, health promotion efforts can mitigate the negative influences of these determinants (e.g., through mutual aid among people with genetic disease or through community kitchens for low-income families). Moreover, health promotion seeks to reinforce or enhance the positive influences of determinants of health that people cannot control directly (e.g., by increasing social support). Finally, increasing a sense of personal "control" or self-efficacy can, in itself, be health enhancing (Landau, 1995; Marmot, Kogevinas, & Elston, 1991; Mirowsky & Ross, 1990).

Empowerment represents a primary criterion for identifying health promotion initiatives (Raeburn & Rootman, 1998; Robertson & Minkler, 1994). An initiative can be classified as a health promotion initiative if it involves the process of enabling or empowering individuals or communities. The absence of empowering activities should be a signal that an intervention does not fall within the rubric of health promotion. However, examination of the definitions contained in Table 1.1 and other literature suggests additional criteria for distinguishing health promotion from other approaches. These include (a) encouraging public participation by individuals and communities; (b) taking a social and cultural perspective in understanding and responding to health issues and problems; (c) emphasizing equity and social justice; (d) fostering intersectoral collaboration; (e) including physical, mental, social, and spiritual dimensions of health; and (f) focusing on enhancing health, not just on preventing problems (Downie, Fyfe, & Tannahill, 1990; Goodstadt, 1995; WHO, 1986).

Health Promotion in Practice

Health promotion initiatives are increasingly complex in their goals, content, approaches, and implementation. That is, health promotion activities frequently attempt to achieve broad environmental change as well as individual behavior change, and they employ the planning and implementation of a comprehensive mix of strategies to do so. In addition, current health promotion strategies favor multilevel (national, regional, community, and individual) action that employs multidimensional approaches (physical, social, mental, and spiritual aspects of health) to achieve and sustain impact.

Despite the ideals for health promotion expressed in the preceding section, a wide range of activities labeled "health promotion" by their practitioners would not qualify by most of the definitions. Richard, Potvin, Kishuck, Prlic, and Green (1996) examined 44 "health promotion" programs funded by the Canadian federal government. They coded the self-described interventions and settings of each project from telephone interviews to classify the degree to which the projects integrated an ecological approach. Single-setting, single-intervention, and individual-behavior-focused programs outnumbered ecologically oriented programs with multiple settings, interventions, and levels of organization.

In Canada, the following types of activities have been funded and carried out in the name of health promotion: (a) mass media campaigns to increase awareness of the dangers of smoking and drinking and driving; (b) comprehensive school-based health education programs; (c) mobilizing community concerns about heart health, low birth weight, and other prevention issues; (d) community development projects enabling disadvantaged mothers to enhance their parenting skills; (e) enabling workplaces to assess and deal with lifestyle and environmental issues; (f) building coalitions to respond to cutbacks in services; (g) lobbying for changes in smoking and other health-related policies; (h) enhancing the preventive practices of physicians and other health care workers; and (i) social support interventions for disadvantaged persons and caregivers.

Clearly, many activities carry the label "health promotion," whether they meet all or even some of the criteria derived from theoretical writings about health promotion. It is tempting to view only those activities that meet at least one of the criteria as falling under the rubric of health promotion. This, however, would exclude a wide range of interventions that nonetheless make a contribution to promoting health. Some of these, with relatively slight adjustments in their development and implementation, would legitimately meet the criteria for health promotion. By taking, for example, a more sociocultural perspective in identifying the problem of measles and in designing and implementing a measles vaccination program, several of the features defined as health promotion could be accommodated. Such was the intent of one of the earliest scientifically documented programs in health education (Rosenstock, Derryberry, & Carriger, 1959), which led in part to the development of the Health Belief Model (Rosenstock, 1974).

Much as it might be ideal to find every activity planned and conducted in the spirit and letter of the broader, ecological definitions of health promotion, practitioners and program managers know that this is impractical. What makes a community's or nation's many health promotion activities add up to an ecologically sound health promotion program is their combined effects. A community or state accomplishes the fullness of health promotion not by insisting that each activity achieve that fullness but by ensuring activities' mutual complementarity, their coverage of the full range of population groups in an equitable fashion, and their distribution of effort at many levels of intervention and in many settings (Green & Ottoson, 1999, p. 46).

The confluence of disparate forces during the past several decades has produced significant developments in the conception, implementation, and evaluation of health promotion. Drawing on the cumulative experience of public health in many spheres, health promotion emerges as an amalgamation of lessons from environmental protection, health services, and health education. For example, the field has concluded that empowerment represents a fundamental process of health promotion by which individuals and communities exercise the control they require to improve their health.

Consonant with the principle of empowerment, health promotion emphasizes public participation. It also seeks to address the more distal determinants of health, in addition to the more proximal risk factors and risk conditions. It places an emphasis on reducing inequities and social injustice. It works through inter-sectoral collaboration, and one of its goals, along with disease prevention, is the enhancement of health. Health promotion, however, is much more than a philosophy or ideology. It offers specific and concrete strategies for creating and building health at the individual, organizational, and community levels. As a consequence, a very wide variety of activities falls under the rubric of health promotion. Finally, health promotion is not an extension or repackaging of disease prevention, public health, or population health; health promotion overlaps, but does not fully encompass, both disease prevention and population health. Moreover, health promotion principles and strategies can be applied in all domains of health, including primary and secondary prevention, treatment, rehabilitation, and long-term care.

Given this breadth of roots and expectations, health promotion has pursued various approaches. One that has been most common is the *issue approach*. In this approach, the main point of intervention and the focus of activities is in relation to a particular issue of concern to individuals, communities, or gov-ern"ments. This includes issues such as alcohol or drug problems, AIDS, safety, or obesity. A second common approach has been the *population approach*. This approach identifies a population of concern, such as homeless people, seniors, or adolescents, and makes efforts to address their concerns, whatever they may be. A third approach, and one that has become more common recently, is the *settings approach*. This approach focuses on a particular setting such as schools, workplaces, or the community. This is the approach described in the next section and is the concern of this book.

RATIONALE FOR A FOCUS ON SETTINGS

One might have predicted from politics alone that the first bureaucratic offices of health promotion would organize themselves along lines compatible with their major constituencies. Health promotion had many potential constituencies, given its breadth of definition and the scope of health and other human services territory it would presume to cover. As Lavada Pinder (1994) noted in her excellent review of the Canadian federal history of health promotion, the Lalonde Report was produced with the integrity of a think tank product, but it was ensured acceptance even without consultation by "the fact that virtually every conceivable interest group, organization, and profession could find itself mentioned in the text" (p. 96).

The U.S. Office of Health Information and Health Promotion (later named the Office of Disease Prevention and Health Promotion) initially organized itself in the late 1970s around settings in which the major constituents, both professional and public, could be found. Staffing was based on the distribution of credentials, skills, and knowledge among medical care settings, school settings, workplace health promotion settings, and community or mass media (Green, 1980). The health education field from which American health promotion drew its frontline professional leadership had (and still has) subspecialties with professional training in patient education (for clinical settings), school health education (for educational settings), public health education (specializing in community settings), and increasingly, programs specializing in employee health promotion for workplaces. In the United Kingdom, health education has a similar tradition of organizing itself around settings (Tones & Tilford, 1994).

The World Health Organization, especially its Regional Office for Europe, has provided considerable leadership and momentum for the "settings approach" to health promotion. Building on the Ottawa Charter, the European Office of WHO initiated a small "Healthy Cities" project in 1987 which rapidly expanded beyond the original pilot cities to communities around the world (Tsouros, 1991). Meanwhile, parallel initiatives were being developed in schools, hospitals, workplaces, and other settings. These initiatives gained legitimacy and further momentum through the support of both WHO and some national governments such as the United Kingdom (Secretary of State for Health, 1992). The approach has featured prominently in subsequent international health promotion conferences organized by WHO. The Third International Conference on Health Promotion, held in Sundsvall, Sweden, in 1991, had as its theme "creating supportive environments for health" and among other things, resulted in the production of a handbook building on case study stories from around the world, and intended as a sourcebook of ideas and stimulus to action (Haglund et al., 1996). Similarly, the Fourth Conference, held in Jakarta, Indonesia, in 1997, strongly endorsed the "settings approach" to health promotion and recommended that WHO invest efforts in supporting this approach in all countries. WHO has subsequently expanded the settings approach to include other types of settings such as islands and regional groupings of countries (e.g., European Union).

The research agenda for the initial health promotion research centers also tended to be organized around settings, even though the funding for research was largely organized around health issues (Green, 1984). The organization of interest groups within the professional associations seeking to meet the expanding membership interests in health promotion also tended to be around the same grouping of settings (school, clinical, occupational, and community).

These were more than political expediencies and professional imperatives. Health promotion's implicit understanding that it needed to organize itself in relation to settings also seemed to recognize that organizational factors were powerful determinants of individual and group behavior. The setting-specific sub-disciplines found their strongest defense for maintaining their partitions in the argument that one could practice health promotion effectively in their setting only if one had a deep understanding of, and long experience in, the organizational culture of that setting. Nurses practicing health promotion in clinical settings, for example, found that defending their territory on grounds of substantive knowledge about clinical matters was less effective than defending it on grounds that they had organizational knowledge, experience, and credibility in health care settings.

Indeed, as health promotion professionals were increasingly employed by (and working in) specific settings, these became recognized loci of health promotion practice, literally where health promotion "takes place." The focus on "supportive environments for health" as one of the five key strategies of the Ottawa Charter, and its recognition of the fact that many determinants of health are setting specific, also provided an impetus and legitimizing discourse for a settings approach. In the words of the Ottawa Charter, "Health is created and lived by people within the settings of their everyday life; where they learn, work, play and love" (WHO, 1986, p. 2). The notion that health is created in the relationship between individuals and their environment reinforced the assertion that people are not definable solely by their "risk identities" (i.e., as smokers, hypertensives, etc.; see Kickbusch, 1995). We suspect that the settings approach also has powerful appeal for practitioners as a concrete, practical focus insofar as settings represent a pragmatic and manageable scale at which to direct change efforts. Settings come equipped with readily definable structures, routines, pathways of entrée and of change, are relatively stable over time, are less amorphous than community or "society," and are more easily operationalized than a focus on specific risk groups. As Mullen et al. (1995) describe them, settings are "major social structures that provide channels and mechanisms of influence for reaching defined populations."

SETTINGS AS AN ECOLOGICAL
FRAMEWORK FOR HEALTH PROMOTION

In addition to the pragmatic aspects of a focus on settings, and the legitimating rhetoric of the Ottawa Charter, one of the key factors behind the increased interest in the settings approach has been the ecological perspective of health promotion, demanding that individuals not be treated in isolation from the larger social units in which they lived, worked, and played. The essentially sociological perspective separated health promotion from the essentially psychological perspective or dominance of its forerunners in health education, social marketing, and behavior modification. The ecological perspective gained respectability and voice in health promotion, where it had been viewed with intellectual curiosity at best and suspicion at worst in earlier generations of health professionals addressing similar problems.

Health promotion is relatively young, but ecology is not. One finds several streams of thought and action from which ecological perspectives have influenced health promotion. Before that, they influenced public health education and before that, public health. These disciplines converged with various social and behavioral sciences and other professional perspectives to form the ecological and behavioral foundations of health promotion. These, in turn, form the foundation of the settings approach to health promotion practice.

Disciplinary Perspectives

Public Health

The earliest formulations and applications of public health employed ecological concepts (Bullough & Rosen, 1992; DeFries, 1940; Fee & Acheson, 1991; Green & Ottoson, 1999; Rogers, 1960; Winslow, 1920). The 19th-century development of biological, especially Darwinian, concepts of the "web of life" and the role of the environment and adaptation influenced public health science. Public health first sought to ensure the survival of the human species by controlling the physical environment. Epidemiologists celebrate John Snow's removal in 1854 of London's Broad Street pump handle to prevent people from using cholera-contaminated water as the first classic public health intervention based on a systematic epidemiological study. By mapping the sources of drinking water of those who died of cholera, Snow identified the environmental source of the illness 30 years before Koch isolated the cholera organism.

Epidemiology remained almost exclusively preoccupied with the physical, chemical, and biological environments until the 1960s. The refocusing of epidemiology on chronic diseases in the 1960s added a growing concern with behavioral determinants of health, accelerated in the 1980s with the advent of HIV and AIDS as the newest epidemic. As the behavioral emphasis narrowed the focus and the methodologies of epidemiology, health promotion sought to widen the focus to include social, economic, organizational, and political environments as determinants of health and points of intervention (Allegrante & Green, 1981; Brown & Margo, 1978; Freudenberg, 1978; Green, 1979).

Sociology

Park, Burgess, and McKenzie (1925) introduced the term "human ecology" in 1921 in an attempt to apply the basic theoretical scheme of plant and animal ecology to the study of human communities. The subdiscipline of demography arose earlier, with Malthus and others in the 19th century attempting to interpret population growth and movement in relation to environmental capacity to support the survival of populations. Rural sociology examined the patterns of social forces that could account for the diffusion and adoption of new farm practices and other innovations in social systems. These ecological concepts of diffusion and adoption of innovations in social systems influenced the breadth of early thinking about mass health education campaigns (Griffiths & Knutson, 1960; Lionberger, 1964; Lowry, Mayo, & Hay, 1958; Young, 1967), family planning (Green, 1970; Rogers, 1973), and chronic disease control in public health (Enelow & Henderson, 1975; Lionberger, 1964). Medical sociology also applied ecological and diffusion frameworks in its examination of the social and cultural contexts in which health conditions and health behavior developed and were distributed in populations (Andersen, 1968; Anderson, 1957; Croog, 1961; Friedson & Silver, 1960; Gray, Kesler, & Moody, 1966; Hollingshead & Redlich, 1958; Lambert & Freeman, 1967; Suchman, 1963).

Psychology

Even psychology, with its focus on individual behavior, has had an ecological awakening (Barker, 1965), even in its most behaviorist specialties, including behavior modification and behavior analysis (Baer, 1974; Rogers-Warren & Warren, 1977; Willems, 1974). Their "microecologies" offer perspectives on health promotion within settings that can be linked to the public health and sociological analyses of wider-ranging environments (macroecology). Within psychology, the subdisciplines of social psychology, community psychology, and environmental psychology have emerged to encompass ecological perspectives on individual behavior. Social psychology has been influential in health education since World War II in the formulation of theories about mass media influence through social networks (Flay, 1987; Hovland, Janis, & Kelley, 1953; Worden et al., 1988). It also contributed theories and methods for the use of group dynamics in resolving social conflict and bringing social forces into play in the decision-making process (Lewin, 1943; Morgan & Horning, 1940; Nyswander, 1942). Together with community psychology and environmental psychology, it has made more recent contributions to multilevel and multisetting health promotion in community organization, community development, and planned change (Altman et al., 1991; Bracht, 1990; Chavis & Wandersman, 1990; Elder, Hovell, Lasater, Wells, & Carleton, 1985; Jeffery, 1993; Lando, Loken, Howard-Pitney, & Pechacek, 1990; Lasater et al., 1991; Lefebvre, 1990; Pechacek, Lando, Northwehr, & Lichtenstein, 1994; Perry, Klepp, & Sillers, 1989; Rappaport, 1987; Sallis & Nader, 1988; Stokols, 1996; Wandersman, Florin, Friedmann, & Meier, 1987; Wells, DePue, Lasater, & Carleton, 1988; Zimmerman, Israel, Schulz, & Checkoway, 1992).

Education

Learning theory has always given prominence to the interaction of learner and environment (Miller, 1984). These have been elaborated in latter-day Social Learning Theory (now Social Cognitive Theory) and its core concept of reciprocal determinism between person and environment (Bandura, 1977; Clark, 1987; Parcel & Baranowski, 1981). Education formalized theories in which the role of the environment and its interdependency with the person were paramount considerations in the development of educational policies and programs (Dewey, 1946). These concepts extended into the development of the subspecialty of school health education. The broader field of school health encompassed health curriculum, school environment, school lunch programs, and school health services, among other elements in an ecological approach to the health of school children (Creswell & Newman, 1997). These integrating notions of school health have carried over into modern practice of school health promotion in which ecological notions of school-community coordination (Kolbe, 1986) and multilevel interventions with students, faculty, the school environment, school policy, and school districts have been studied (Parcel, Simons-Morton, & Kolbe, 1988).

Geography

Human geography and medical geography have given particular emphasis in the study of health to the importance of place. This has blended with health promotion concepts of setting specificity in the planning of interventions for schools, workplaces, neighborhoods, and clinical settings. Within the broader field of community health promotion, geography has provided critical analyses of the relation of environment and health (Hayes, Foster, & Foster, 1992). For example, geography has teamed with social work and other professions in the development and critique of indicators of healthy communities (Hayes & Manson Willms, 1990). Social theory has sometimes taken a back seat in geography's approach to health, but ecological analyses of the relationships between health characteristics and "the characteristics of the containing areas" (Litva & Eyles, 1995) have been a mainstay of human geography. Traditionally, "medical geography" has concentrated on either spatial accessibility of health care services (Joseph & Phillips, 1984) or disease ecology and disease diffusion studies (Mayer, 1982, 1983; Powell, 1995). More recently, geographers in the health field have drawn on interpretive and critical approaches in the examination of "salubrity of sites" (Rotenberg, 1993), the role of "place" in health experience (Kearns, 1993, 1995), geographies of the "deviant body" (Dorn & Laws, 1994), and the purification of public space as an objective and outcome of "healthy public policy" and "community participation" (Fischer & Poland, 1998; Poland,

1998). Critical and postmodern geographers have questioned the apparent "rationality" of the "geometric gaze," and the "spatial fetishism" and reification of space that they argue is inherent in disciplinary perspectives that treat "space" as a concrete causal force in social relations, as opposed to a context for them (Gregory, cited in Johnston, Gregory, & Smith, 1994; Soja, 1989; Werlen, 1993). Geography also sees the "respatialization" of social theory (the reinsertion of space alongside time) as key to understanding and theorizing the contingent nature of social relations (e.g., Giddens, 1984) and as a focus on the ways in which gender, class, and race are inscribed in (and constituted through) social space (Gregory & Urry, 1985; Smith, 1994).

That these many disciplines have contributed to health promotion has much to do with the inherently interdisciplinary nature of the field of health promotion (Green & Kreuter, 1999, p. 31; Macdonald & Bunton, 1992). The utility and effectiveness of their contributions has been measured through evaluations of practice within settings based on data pertaining to individual knowledge, attitudes, behavior, and health outcomes. The effectiveness of their contributions in the longer term could depend on the ecological perspectives each brings to bear on the actual work of health promotion, which must usually take place within practice settings. Ecological features within each discipline will be the connective tissue that enables each to relate to the other disciplines. But interdisciplinarity within settings will fall short of achieving what ecology has most to teach us—namely, that individuals are part of larger subsystems and that those subsystems are part of larger community, cultural, and societal systems. The effectiveness of the contributions of these disciplines to population health depends in part on the broader social, regional, and state or provincial planning for the integration of health promotion practice, which must occur largely outside or between settings.

The Implications of Ecology for Settings and Health Promotion

Organizational settings, from the ecological perspective of health promotion, provide a way to recast the focus from individual, behavioral risk factors to the more distal determinants of health beyond their personal control. Organizational settings provide a middle ground between individual behavior (the primary focus of past efforts) and higher levels of social organization beyond the grasp of practitioners, as a place to come to grips with the determinants of health. The ecological perspective presents health as a product of the interdependence between the individual and subsystems of the ecosystem. Subsystems for health promotion may include family, peer groups, organizations, community, culture, and physical and social environment (McLeroy et al., 1988).

Health practitioners working outside the clinical setting resonate with ecological perspectives because they distinguish their work from the one-to-one patient or client relationships of the more numerous clinical health professionals. Beside the descriptive aspects of ecology, what do the lessons of ecology have to say to health promotion practitioners? What implications do they hold for the settings approach to health promotion?

Unanticipated Effects

Human ecology cautions social reformers and practitioners against tampering with change in smaller systems without considering, before the intervention, their second- and third-order consequences, "not merely to rue them afterward" (Eisenberg, 1972). A similar caution of cultural and applied anthropology to the field of public health concerned the dangers of tampering with second-order systems (cultures) without considering the consequences for individuals and families (Foster, 1962; Paul, 1955).

Reciprocal Determinism

The ecological or transactional view of behavior holds that the organism's functioning is mediated by behavior-environment interaction. This has two implications for behavioral and social change:

1. Environment largely controls or sets limits on the behavior that occurs in it.

2. Changing environmental variables results in the modification of behavior.

These two points lead to the inexorable recognition that health promotion can achieve its best results by exercising whatever control or influence it can over the environment. But the reciprocal side of this equation also holds that the behavior of individuals, groups, and organizations also influences their environments. Hence, health promotion seeks to empower people by giving them control over the determinants of their health, whether these be behavioral or environmental. Ideally, people would exercise control by managing the interaction between behavior and environment. Taking greater control means adjusting their behavior to changing environmental conditions or adjusting their environments to changing behavioral conditions. It is generally thought that people can manage environments more feasibly at the second order of organization, where they work, play, or worship, than at third or higher levels of organization such as community, state, or national levels. But as discussed below, much depends not only on scale but on who controls these settings (viz., issues of power), for it may be that in some cases, workers find they have less control in the workplace than in the communities they live in.

Environmental Specificity

The same persons will behave differently in different environments (Sells, 1969). This principle has led to a recognition in health promotion that environment is a factor that predisposes, enables, and reinforces individual and collective behavior. Its implication for health promotion planning and evaluation is that there is nothing *inherently* superior or inferior in any health promotion method or strategy. The effectiveness of a method always depends on its appropriate fit with the people, the health issue at stake, and the environment in which it is applied (Green & Kreuter, 1999). Planning for a setting as a focus of health promotion can produce an outcome more adaptable and sensitive to particular traditions, cultural variations, and circumstances than planning for a multicultural community, state, provincial, or national level. (This book covers the more proximal settings of the home, workplace, and school as well as the community and state.)

The Necessity of Multilevel and
Multisectoral Intervention

The complex interdependencies of the elements making up an ecological web require planners to direct interventions to promote health at several levels within an organizational structure or system. They also require, for population health, that interventions be directed at multiple sectors (health, education, welfare, commerce, transportation) of a social system. This is where most descriptions of ecological approaches take us and where most of them leave us. Let us review now some of the limitations this places on broader ecological approaches and then seek a level of planning and intervention within settings that will be feasible for most health promotion practitioners.

Limitations of the Ecological View
for Health Promotion

For all its advantages in offering a broader perspective on planning and practice that might otherwise drift into a reductionist, person-centered, or victim-blaming orientation, ecological thinking has its own traps and pitfalls. Ecological approaches have not been worked out in great detail because of their complexity. Laurence Slobodkin (1988) complains that ecology is an intractable science, immature and not very helpful. Others have reproached ecologists for not producing testable hypotheses. The usual conclusion of such debates is that the scientific method requires the simplification of ecosystems, making artificial that which is inherently complex. Health promotion is drawn to ecology because it enlarges the spotlight from a sharper focus on behavior to a broader one that includes the environment. Reality forces us, however, to retreat to behavior at some level. "We will have to learn that we don't manage ecosystems, we manage our interaction with them" (Kay & Schneider, 1994, p. 39). Ecological approaches in health promotion are less amenable to traditional forms of evaluation than clinical interventions because the units of analysis do not yield easily to random assignment into experimental and control groups. Nor can scientists manipulate the independent variables with much control, given the interdependence of persons and environments. On the other hand, many of the assumptions behind these quantitative and postpositivist approaches to evaluation have been questioned (Guba & Lincoln, 1989; Poland, 1992).

Some particular limitations that ecological approaches will face in health promotion in the near future are as follows.

Emphasis on Observable Behavior and Environments

Ecology has historical roots in theories and methodologies that emphasize observability and de-emphasize what organisms feel, believe, perceive, or value about their environments. Historically, it represents a radically positivist tradition of science. This puts it potentially at odds with postmodernist methodological preference for phenomenological approaches to behavior, and the questions of how people perceive, appraise, and construct their environments.

Ecological Complexity Breeds Despair

The ecological credo of "everything influences everything else" carried to its logical extreme leaves health practitioners with little basis on which to set priorities. They have good reason to do nothing because the potential influence of or consequences to other parts of an ecological system are beyond comprehension, much less control. Some specific forms of this despair include the following (sometimes rhetorical) questions:

1. How much is enough? When trying to set the parameters around any given program, health planners, administrators, or practitioners must ask if they are doing enough to make a difference. They will always be subject to the criticism that they have not gone deeply enough to the root of the problem. For example, even after public health workers had disavowed more strictly educational approaches to alcohol control, Pittman (1993) challenged the field, stating,

Environmental factors that impact alcohol problems are broader than such questions as alcohol availability, advertising, and the alcohol beverage industry's marketing practices. . . . it is much easier to mandate warning labels . . . or propose further restrictions on alcohol advertising or alcohol availability than to address and enact legislation to reduce social inequality, racism, discrimination, and inadequate health care in the United States. (p. 169).

2. *Must everything that takes an educational approach or attempts to help indi-viduals be regarded as trivial and misguided?* Some of the health promotion rhetoric leaves health practitioners and teachers whose jobs are to help or edu-cate people in clinical, school, or workplace settings feeling that their efforts are a waste of time, even part of the problem. The most vituperative epitaphs for such work are "victim blaming" and "Band-Aid" treatment of the symptoms rather than the cause.

The Level of Analysis in an Ecosystem Hierarchy Is Observer Dependent

Both reductionist (small number, highly controllable) and holistic (large number, statistically described) approaches fail to describe an ecosystem be-cause neither captures the system-subsystem relationships. One must examine both the system as a whole and the component subsystems. The frustration and inevitable criticism come when one must acknowledge that the ecosystem within which one was examining the subsystems is itself a subsystem of a larger ecosystem. The observer must decide what to include and what to omit from the analysis—that is, where in the hierarchy of subsystems to take the slice for analysis (King, 1993). This necessarily subjective decision will invariably be too narrow or too broad for the tastes (or values) of some other observers. The dynamic rather than static nature of ecosystems also makes the chosen slice a time-dependent set of observations. These problems leave one, unavoidably, with a case study of limited generalizability.

Limits of Medical and Epidemiological Methods of Program Evaluation

Setting-based health promotion and prevention programs give the ecological approach a chance to be demonstrated in public health, but the task of evaluating these programs presents formidable challenges and puzzles. The medical and epidemiological approach to evaluation implemented in most setting-based pro-gram evaluations advocates the use of an experimental or quasi-experimental design. Because such programs are complex and unique for their settings, com-parison groups outside the setting may be prohibitive or simply inappropriate (poorly matched). Typically, a small number of subjects is enrolled in a pilot, ef-ficacy trial of a health promotion program in one setting, and a smaller number of sites, if any, serve as controls (e.g., Farquhar et al., 1985). For the model to work optimally, as in any drug trial, the experimenter should have control over the treatment and major external influences, either through random assignment or controlled environment. By their very nature, ecological, organizationally based health promotion programs often do not allow a researcher or evaluator to use either of these means of experimental or quasi-experimental control of the ongoing "experiment."

Even if the experimental and control subjects or sites could be selected by the researcher, he or she would not have control over the individuals exposed to the program. Typically, people self-select themselves for various components of a program.

The mere use of a control site does not necessarily solve the problem of comparison. As organizations are open systems, evolving in a constantly changing environment, one cannot assume that a control community will remain in stasis or free of influence by national campaigns or events occurring in the experimental communities (see Hayes & Manson Willms, 1990; Zanna et al., 1994). In the control communities of the Pawtucket and Minnesota Heart Health Programs, for example, researchers observed that knowledge and behaviors regarding heart health changed faster than the secular trends would have predicted (Green & Richard, 1994). Nutbeam, Smith, and Catford (1990) noted that the control communities in the Heartbeat Wales project had a rapid uptake of heart disease prevention activities, so much so that they jeopardized the results of the outcome evaluation. Obviously, neither experimental nor control communities evolve in a vacuum.

A systems theory approach to ecological analysis may be able to overcome some of these experimental limitations of setting-specific evaluation based in complex organizations by conceptualizing health promotion programs in organizational settings as systems implemented within ecosystems to improve the health of populations (Florin, Mitchell, & Stevenson, 1993; Francisco, Paine, & Fawcett, 1993; Goodman, Wandersman, Chinman, Imm, & Morrissey, 1996; Green, Richard, et al., 1996; Richard et al., 1996; Stokols, Pelletier, & Fielding, 1996; Walsh & McPhee, 1992). In this regard, it is noteworthy that a number of questions for research on and evaluation of settings in health promotion have been proposed by a consensus group (Mullen et al., 1995).

A CRITICAL SOCIAL SCIENCE PERSPECTIVE ON THE SETTINGS APPROACH

This section examines the theory and practice of the settings approach using a critical social science perspective on health promotion. As articulated by Eakin, Robertson, Poland, Coburn, and Edwards (1996), a critical social science perspective encompasses a number of key dimensions of reflexivity in an attempt to reveal the sociopolitical construction of research and practice "problems" and "solutions" in health promotion. The purpose of making the implicit explicit is so that it can be debated and contested, for as long as what is taken for granted remains hidden, it cannot be challenged. For many critical theorists (e.g.,

Habermas, 1973) and proponents of critical pedagogy (e.g., Freire, 1973, 1990, 1995), emancipation begins with the unmasking of hegemony (see Gramsci, 1932/1975; Thomas, 1993). They seek this unmasking through the emergence of a renewed critical awareness of how taken-for-granted ideas are socially constructed, embedded in power relations, and supportive of the status quo. This awareness, which opens up new possibilities of thought and action, is seen as a prerequisite for change.

The adoption of a critical social science perspective would lead us to pose certain types of questions about the settings approach. The notion of "settings" would be problematized so as to uncover its hidden assumptions. The role of power in social relations within settings would be examined. The contingent nature of human experience and the sociopolitical and historical location of settings, as well as the dialectical relationship between individuals and organizational or social structures, would be more fully appreciated, together with the paradoxes or contradictions that arise in theory and practice within a settings approach.

Assumptions

A critical social science perspective requires that we unpack (deconstruct) the apparently self-evident concept of *setting*. It begins by arguing against a purely instrumental view of settings as arenas of practice, as places in which "captive audiences" can most conveniently be found for behavior modification programming. It argues against conceptualizing (or acting on) settings as containers or vessels containing ready-made "target audiences" and as relatively homogeneous and self-contained environments that are neutral with respect to the agenda of the health professional. Instead, an ecological and critical perspective on settings for health promotion recognizes that settings vary considerably, even within categories of settings (e.g., diversity of workplace environments). Such a perspective would view the boundaries between settings as permeable (settings do not exist in a vacuum; people move in and out of many different settings in the course of their daily routines). It would acknowledge preexisting social relations in the setting (e.g., management-labor relations) that can influence how health promotion initiatives are framed and perceived by different players in the setting, how well they are supported (and by whom), and what their impact will be in the short and long term.

We feel that it is also crucial to recognize and act on opportunities to enhance the healthfulness of settings themselves as environments conducive to health, in addition to opportunities that may arise for using settings as a medium for reaching those who are "contained" within them. This focus on environments supportive of health, very much in keeping with the 1991 Sundsvall declaration (*Supportive Environments,* 1998), entails not only those environmental changes that seek to alter the behavior of setting participants (e.g., regulations on use of safety equipment or on smoking in the workplace) but also changes to factors in the setting that may more directly influence health (e.g., reduction in exposure to harmful substances, improvements in ergonomics, enhanced worker control and participation).

Settings can be conceptualized as both (a) physically bounded space-times in which people come together to perform specific tasks (usually oriented to goals other than health) and (b) arenas of sustained interaction, with preexisting structures, policies, characteristics, institutional values, and both formal and informal social sanctions on behavior. This corresponds with Fuhrer's (1990) concept of "behavior settings" or Thrift's (1983) "interactional settings." They view settings as culturally constructed but individually mediated interactional and activity microenvironments (a) with their own cultural codes of conduct, (b) infused with situational characteristics, and (c) subject to temporal variations in rhythms of social interaction (day vs. night, weekday vs. weekend) and in the longer term (Poland, 1998). Settings are more than simply locations in space-time: They are both the medium and the product of human social interaction. To quote Gregory and Urry (1985), "Spatial structure is now seen not merely as an arena in which social life unfolds, but rather as a medium through which social relations are produced and reproduced" (p. 3).

Even this expanded view of the settings approach requires careful examination, however. One assumption that is typically made (and reflected in the conceptualizations discussed above) is that settings are characterized by face-to-face interaction. The implications for a settings approach of the current proliferation of "virtual settings" (facilitated through information technology, whether "real time" or not) is not clear, although these share many of the characteristics of physically bounded settings outlined above. And what are we to make of the disintegration (or increasing permeability) of spatial boundaries and "locatedness" of traditionally spatially well-defined settings such as work and school, as people in larger numbers begin working from home, engaging in distance education, and so forth?

Implicit in the settings approach is, also, the assumption that settings are relatively amenable to professional efforts directed at shaping them to be more conducive to health. Wenzel (1997) argues that an instrumental view of settings portrays them as more easily manipulated by the professional (as change agent or catalyst) than is often the case. The extent to which specific historical, economic, political, and cultural contexts, processes, and imperatives have shaped and will continue to shape particular settings is underestimated in the strictly instrumental approach. Much is made of the power of organizational and policy levers as tools that allow health professionals to do this because they can mandate changes within settings across entire categories of settings without the need to enter into the "messy politics" of engaging participants in change efforts within particular sites. For all the confidence placed in policy changes, relatively little research has examined how such policies are resisted or modified within organizations during implementation (Ottoson & Green, 1987).[1]

Wenzel (1997) questions the theoretical roots of a settings approach and the degree to which it is tactical or rhetorical in nature as opposed to designating a significant change in practice. According to Wenzel, a settings approach designates arenas of practice (geographical sites as targets of health promotion) rather than a meaningful shift in the nature and sophistication of its practice. Despite the rhetorical distancing of health promotion from health education that is implied in a settings approach, Wenzel contends that in practice it often narrows to the application of lifestyle modification programming in particular settings. In a response to Wenzel's editorial, Mittlemark (1997) charges that this paints an unduly harsh and unflattering picture of health promoters as naïve. He feels they are well aware of the multiple layers of impact of settings on behavior (indeed, this is central to the concept of "healthy environments" in the Ottawa Charter). However, an alternative interpretation revolves not around the sophistication of the concepts or the ability of their proponents or of health promotion practitioners to comprehend their depth and significance; rather, it hinges on the very real limitations imposed on practice by the competing interests, agendas, and interpretations of key "gatekeepers" who hold the balance of power in specific settings (e.g., employers) and who do not wish to see health promotion framed too broadly because it may call into question the status quo on which their power and material success rests. In this regard, for example, stress reduction workshops in the workplace are typically perceived by management as much less threatening than efforts to increase worker control (Eakin, Cava, & Smith, 1997).

Power

Despite the considerable emphasis on empowerment in the health promotion literature, it is striking how little attention is sometimes paid to power relations in the settings in which health promotion programs have been developed. For example, the literature frequently encourages health professionals to work collaboratively with management to gain entrée to the workplace or school, yet little is said about the implications for subsequent practice with students or employees of an explicit (or perceived) alignment with management or school administration (Green & Kreuter, 1999, pp. 199-207; MacDonald, 1998). If change efforts are unsuccessful, students or workers may be labeled as "resistant to change" or "hard to reach." Little reflexive attention is brought to bear on the ways in which the health promotion practitioner may have inadvertently played into existing power relations and alliances within the setting. More attention has been given to the ways in which the practitioner's language, demeanor, or approach might reinforce internal divisions along existing class, race, or gender lines, but this literature has centered on the use of indigenous workers or para-professionals or on participatory approaches to planning and research (Green et al., 1995; Wallerstein & Freudenberg, 1998). By aligning with powerful gate-keeper interests in these settings (workplace management, school administration), whether for strategic or other reasons, those students or workers most alienated by or resistant to authority (those sometimes labeled "hard to reach") are likely to be the least receptive to health promotion efforts in their settings. Thus, settings present practitioners with something of a paradox: On the one hand, the approval of key gatekeepers may be required to gain entry and access; on the other hand, this may jeopardize the ability of the health promotion practitioner to gain the trust and support of those with whom she or he wishes to work in that setting. Part of an emancipatory stance toward power relations in settings, therefore, may well require the discovery (and empowerment) of "voices" (experiences, perspectives, interests) not traditionally heard or legitimized in that setting. Part of this emancipatory project could include a sort of local political economy of different settings.

The issue of who is left out of a settings approach also matters. Viewed from this angle, the settings approach has the purported strength of overwhelming numbers of people who spend time at school or in a workplace, who are residents of definable communities, who see a physician on a regular basis, who are subject to the regulative powers of the legislative arm of the state—in short, who are "reachable" through a settings approach. This also becomes its weakness, for the settings in which one is to find the unemployed, the homeless, the disenfranchised youth, the illegal immigrants, and so forth are not as well defined. Indeed, there is considerable selectivity in what settings are addressed (even in this book); health promotion has chosen to privilege some settings (e.g., workplaces, schools, communities) as being more "legitimate" sites of practice than others (e.g., bingo halls, nightclubs, street corners, public washrooms, and other "sites of resistance"). Kickbusch (1995) argues that we need to move toward considering these "less obvious" settings, beyond hospitals, corporations, prisons, or other "total institutions." The unconventional settings for health promotion are in many cases those (a) in which the health-adverse behaviors that have traditionally been of concern to health professionals are perhaps most common; (b) that are the least "formal" in terms of the social organization of interaction (and therefore the least amenable to bureaucratic intervention and control, possessing few of the formal channels of power of formalized institutions; i.e., they are more fluid in structure and therefore less amenable to formal regulation, which is predicated on clearly delineated jurisdictional space); and (c) that are most likely to challenge the historically middle-class, rational actor, deferred gratification, health-as-superordinate-goal, professional, expertise-oriented bias characteristic of much (though certainly not all) health promotion. We would argue that there is a critical role and need for health promotion "at the margins," but with the proviso that it remains reflexive about its own potential to become a mechanism of social control by virtue of the unintended consequences of its well-intentioned discourses and practices of "risk management" (see Bunton & Macdonald, 1992; Fischer & Poland, 1998; Poland, 1992, 1998).

Contradiction and Paradox

The paradox of the practitioner who must rely on the approval of powerful gatekeepers to secure access to a setting, yet for whom that alliance becomes a liability in the course of working with others located in that setting, was acknowledged above. Much of the literature on the settings approach contains the tacit assumption that consensus is both desirable and more achievable by virtue of the ostensible cohesiveness or self-contained "community" nature of many settings that presumably arises from shared experiences over time among participants in each setting. The summary report from a recent WHO-sponsored conference on the settings approach, for example, is replete with references to "consensus" as a natural by-product of a settings approach and with exhortations to find or create consensus around common aims, framed in terms of alliances, partnerships, cohesion, innovation, flexibility, trust, openness, and so forth (St. Leger, 1997; Theaker & Thompson, 1995). The benefits of consensus notwithstanding, there can be a certain tyranny implied in the assertion or creation of consensus by key stakeholders insofar as certain voices may be silenced (intentionally or inadvertently) in the process of "manufacturing consent" (Hawe, 1996). A critical social science perspective, as articulated by Eakin et al. (1996), sees merit in dissensus, too, and in resisting the temptation to "resolve" contradictions or paradoxes that may contain powerful insights about the political nature of health and health promotion and about the irreducibility of human experience.

Dialectical Relationship of
Structure and Agency

A dialectical view inherent in a critical social science perspective highlights the reciprocity of influence between persons in settings (referred to in the sociological literature as "agency") and the characteristics and nature of that setting (referred to in the sociological literature as social "structure"). A dialectical (reciprocal) relationship exists also between social and physical space. This needs to be taken into account insofar as it sets a context for practice; for example, the spatial structuring of social class in an urban environment (i.e., the segregation of "haves" and "have nots" into distinct neighborhoods) has profound implications for community development approaches to health promotion. The term *dialectic* is intended in both cases to point away from *either/or* distinctions between the individual and the setting, to encompass a variety of *both/and* types of propositions about their mutual interdependence. For example, individuals, through their actions (intentionally or otherwise), assist in shaping and reproducing the organizational structures of the setting as surely as the setting, with all its cultural and institutional baggage, frames the expected parameters of individual action. In myriad social actions and interactions, these can be reinforced (taken-for-granted assumptions on which interactions are based) and/or resisted (to varying degrees, even in their reproduction).

One of the "spaces" of inquiry that such a perspective opens up is that which seeks to understand how people interpret and make sense of particular settings. This is analogous to a methodology that Stones (1991), drawing on Giddens (1979, 1984) and Cohen (1989), has termed "strategic context analysis": exploring the lay knowledgeability of boundaries and constraints on action in a given situation or context. Such an understanding would greatly enhance our appreciation of the influence of settings on the actions of individuals and groups in those settings, as well as the ways in which changes are wrought, intentionally or otherwise, on those settings. Bronfenbrenner (1979, cited in Wenzel, 1997), one of the "grandfathers" of social ecology, goes further than this, arguing that the process of learning about and becoming adept at managing social interaction in settings is fundamental to human development:

> Human development is the process through which the growing person acquires a more extended, differentiated, and valid conception of the ecological environment, and becomes motivated and able to engage in activities that reveal the properties of, sustain, or restructure that environment at levels of similar or greater complexity in form and content.

Such a perspective also opens a space for investigating the nature of resistance to pressures and normative rules of conduct characterizing particular settings. It lends itself as well to research on the circumstances in which some things are resisted and others not (and how that resistance is carried out and perceived by self and others). Together, these research questions produce a basis for understanding how changes in the "normative culture" of a setting occur and, more practically, how they can be brought about with minimal harm.

Contingency

The embeddedness of behavior in a "nested arrangement of concentric structures" (Bronfenbrenner, 1979, cited in Wenzel, 1997) points to the fifth dimension of a critical social science perspective, as articulated by Eakin, Robertson, Poland, Coburn, and Edwards (1995)—that of contingency. The notion of contingency calls to attention the uncertainty of phenomena (including causal relations) by virtue of their "locatedness" in a specific social, historical, and/or political context. The rather straighforward observation that certain things hold true under some circumstances but not others, when taken seriously, challenges postpositivist assumptions about the generalizability of observed relationships (or settings). The ecological perspective addresses the social and structural locatedness and embeddedness, but not necessarily as effectively the historical and political contingency of settings and interventions.

Theories that remain essentially contextual in nature thus differ significantly from those predicated on the generalization of observations across settings. To quote Gregory (1994), contextual theory is "an approach which regards the time-space settings and sequences of human activity as essential to its constitution," that "[depends] upon identifying relations of coexistence, connection or 'togetherness,' rather than the relations of 'similarity' that characterize compositional theory" (p. 90), which "[removes] different classes of being from their habitats and [places] them in a classification system" (Hagerstrand, 1984, cited in Gregory, 1994, p. 90). Rather, the emphasis in contextual theory is on the configuration of unique conditions of time and space that bear on human activity, which itself creates a new situated configuration for subsequent actions, and so on. This is not to deny the existence of strong "internal" relationships, or what Sayer (1984) refers to as "necessary" (as opposed to contingent) relations such as "landlord-tenant," where the one (landlord) essentially presumes the other (tenant). But even "necessary" relations such as landlord-tenant take on particular meanings or nuances in specific contexts, because not all landlord-tenant relations are the same.

Thus, we would assert that to understand human action we must still be acutely aware of its socially contingent nature. Simonsen (1991) writes about the importance of situated life stories (biographies of human agents bounded in time and space) as a crucial methodology for accessing these aspects of reality. For contextualists, space (place) becomes "both 'condition' and 'consequence' of human activity" (Gregory, 1994, p. 92). Taking contingency seriously implies concretizing abstract concepts such as "power" in terms of their manifestation in time and space in the practices of situated actors in relationship with one another. It also means being sensitive to the importance of particular confluences of factors for the shaping of social forces, including those that characterize different categories of settings.

ABOUT THIS BOOK

Focus of the Book

Contributing authors were asked to identify innovations in theory and practice in the application of health promotion to the category of settings under consideration, as well as to provide a historical perspective on these developments. We asked them to identify what they felt to be the state of the art in the field, together with evidence supporting such claims, with respect to "what works" and why (how success might be defined and evaluated). We also asked contributing authors to consider the following:

- What are the assumptions usually made about this setting? What is taken for granted? Under what circumstance are these assumptions warranted?

- What changes can be identified in how this category of settings has been conceptualized over time?

- What features of the setting "make a difference," including barriers and facilitating factors in the successful application of health promotion (e.g., internal politics, power relations, organizational structure)?

- How should awareness of context and setting influence intervention design and implementation?

- What cross-cultural and national differences might exist between similar settings?

- What is the cumulative experience with contextual factors affecting practice?

- Identify gaps in knowledge and practice.

- Address possible contradictions that arise in practice or between theory and practice in the application of a settings approach.

Intended Audience

We have produced this volume in the anticipation that it will be the most appealing and useful to the following three groups. First, we feel it will be a valuable resource for professionals who are engaged in the design, implementation, and/or evaluation of health promotion interventions in particular settings. Second, it is intended to be of assistance in the training of health professionals at the postgraduate level in health promotion and the allied health sciences, including nursing, occupational health, and community health. Third, we think it will be of considerable interest to academic scholars in the health sciences with an interest in health promotion.

We have structured the book so that it will be of interest to these audiences in Canada and the United States and also in Europe, Australia, and New Zealand.

A Unique Contribution to the Settings Approach in Health Promotion

Our review of the literature suggests that there are no similar texts on the settings approach to health promotion. Some texts devote chapters to settings, but these have been for the purpose of illustrating applications of theories and models for health education or health promotion planning, implementation, or evaluation (e.g., Green & Kreuter, 1999; Naidoo & Wills, 1994; National Forum on Health, 1998; Tones & Tilford, 1994). Despite extensive use of the concept in the field, the nature, characteristics, and implications for theory and practice of a settings approach do not appear to have generated much sustained debate, commentary, or examination in the literature. This suggested to us that a solid and well-rounded treatment of these issues in a manner accessible to practitioners was overdue. This is what we set out to accomplish in producing this book.

We believe that an international focus is a key strength of this volume. We sought to engage contributing authors from as many countries in the English-speaking industrialized world as possible, and the result is a diversity of opinions from Canada, the United States, the United Kingdom, Europe, and New Zealand. To maintain a focus on issues facing health promotion in using a settings approach in so-called developed countries, we have ignored the rich and diverse experiences of health promoters in developing countries and newly industrialized countries.

We have brought together a distinguished group of some of the leading thinkers in health promotion from Canada, the United States, the United Kingdom, and elsewhere to deliberate on the state of the art in health promotion in specific categories of settings and to comment on each other's work. Contributing authors were identified specifically for their internationally recognized expertise in a particular setting or category of settings.

Indeed, another distinguishing feature of this volume is that each primary chapter (devoted to a specific category of settings) was sent to other leading thinkers in the field, who were asked to write a commentary response. Thus, each chapter is followed by two commentary pieces written in response to the primary pieces.

Outline of the Book

A multiplicity of settings could have been covered in a book such as this. We have chosen to focus on those settings that are central to health promotion at this time, but we recognize that these are selective and will change over time. They are ordered roughly according to scale and comprise the following: home, school, workplace, health care institution, clinical general practice, community, and state.

In Chapter 2, Hassan Soubhi and Louise Potvin review what is known about the family as a microsocial context and setting for health promotion. They examine several normative, developmental, and cognitive models of family health interaction and propose an integrated ecological model of family health promotion that encompasses member characteristics, interaction patterns, internal processes and structures, and external environmental influences. The authors also review a number of different approaches to the promotion of health within families, concluding that multicomponent interventions that also encompass the school and community settings tend to be the most effective. In his commentary on this chapter, Larry Fisher proposes a broader definition of *family* that emphasizes that shared social reality in small social units can encompass a number of nontraditional forms and suggests that the individual cannot easily be separated from the family context. Fisher argues that a family-centered model implies that the family remains at the core of health promotion's efforts in other settings that represent other points of intersection for influencing the individual/family nexus. Furthermore, he advances a set of suggestions vis-à-vis family health promotion that include (a) recognizing that interventions must be tailored to the needs of individual families, (b) reframing the intervention to include indirect goals, (c) targeting relationships within families rather than individuals, (d) focusing change efforts on those members with the most power within the family system, and (e) expanding the definition of appropriate interventions and outcomes to include positive changes in the family system itself, in terms that are meaningful to all family members. In her commentary on Soubhi and Potvin, Ilze Kalnins focuses on the ways in which the home as a physical dwelling (e.g., dampness, potential for child injury) and its neighborhood location (overall safety, neighborhood social cohesion, access to green space, proximity to dense traffic, recreational and educational opportunities, etc.) are determinative of health. These aspects of the home environment (and not simply the family as a social unit) can be important targets of intervention in their own right, argues Kalnins. In the second part of her commentary, she also focuses on the tremendous opportunities, risks, and implications of the "invasion" of the home environment by new (and existing) information technologies, particularly given their loosely regulated and increasingly corporatist nature (especially in regard to the advertising of junk food and other items linked in increasingly novel and subtle ways to "information sites" on the World Wide Web, for example). This provides a clarion call for health promoters to become increasingly sophisticated in their understanding and application of new information technologies.

In Chapter 3, Guy Parcel, Steven Kelder, and Karen Basen-Engquist examine the state of the art in school health promotion. They review knowledge-based, affective, behavioral, and youth empowerment models of intervention, as well as multiple-component approaches (which typically focus on youth in schools, their parents, and the community context). Several innovative multiple component health promotion intervention projects are described and reviewed, including the Child and Adolescent Trial for Cardiovascular Health (CATCH), Project Northland (alcohol use), Safer Choices (pregnancy, HIV, and STD prevention), and Students for Peace (violence prevention). In each case, the projects are well described, and evaluation data are reviewed. The chapter closes with a number of helpful suggestions regarding the implementation of school health promotion programs. In her commentary on this chapter, Cheryl Perry focuses on the factors that enable multiple component interventions to be particularly effective, including complementarity of components, breadth and coordination, and degree of "fit" with existing policies, practices, and structure of the setting. Perry also identifies several "burning questions" in school health promotion. One of these relates to the relative emphasis on complex, expert-driven, multiple component interventions versus grassroots student- and teacher-led "bottom-up" approaches. The contribution and role of theory to intervention design, implementation, and evaluation is also discussed. In their commentary on Parcel et al., Peter McLaren, Zeus Leonardo, and Xóchitl Pérez take a radically different stand on the role and purpose of health promotion in the school. As if to answer, in part, Perry's query regarding the appropriate balance of top-down and bottom-up strategies (although it is about much else besides), these commentators argue that if health promotion is about fostering and enabling self-emancipation, it must relinquish technocratic management approaches to health promotion in schools. It must, they contend, enable the self-actualization of the student as a critical citizen, rather than fostering dependency on expertise as a basis for knowledge of self. This is to be achieved or begun, in part, through working to expose social needs and working in solidarity to meet them; this will arise from a collective ethical obligation to social justice. This solidarity arises, they argue, to the extent that we can own our own hurt and disease and imminent death, as opposed to the "othering" of the unhealthy (and those who do not enhance health as we define it) that is embodied in a discourse of "risk" and "risk management." Their radical critique of the technocratic management of human behavior and of settings, then, extends well beyond the school as a setting of health promotion, to the core assumptions, practices, and values of the discipline.

In Chapter 4, Michael Polanyi, John Frank, Harry Shannon, Terry Sullivan, and John Lavis examine the strengths and limitations of three key approaches to workplace health promotion: (a) occupational health and safety, with its focus on the physical healthfulness of the setting; (b) workplace health promotion, targeting the lifestyles of the workforce; and (c) the promoting workplace determinants (PWD) of health approach, targeting the psychosocial work environment in particular. The authors favor the latter approach in particular for its potential (as yet largely unexplored, but nonetheless promising) to address powerful psychosocial workplace determinants of health such as the organization of work in psychological demands, decision latitude, status hierarchy, job satisfaction, and morale. Polanyi et al. also identify and discuss a number of challenges facing those who would seek to implement a PWD approach to health promotion in the workplace, as well as the steps that might be taken (using participatory action research, for example) to begin the process of incorporating PWD into the workplace. In his commentary on this chapter, Robert Bertera focuses on the need for integration of categorical and programmatic efforts to deliver health services to workers, using a detailed case study of the DuPont Company as an exemplar. Joan Eakin, in her commentary, suggests that the limitations of each of the approaches to the promotion of health in the workplace reviewed by Polanyi et al. are strikingly similar and pertain to the nature of the workplace *as a setting*. In particular, she draws attention to the political and ideological environment of the workplace, which can constrain and shape the practice of health professionals who seek to use the workplace as a location for or as a target of health promotion. She suggests that some of these limitations might be overcome by selecting, as foci of intervention, determinants of health that straddle settings (e.g., home and work), so as to "share the blame" and thereby deflect (and manage) the objections of gatekeepers.

Joy Johnson opens her examination of the health care institution (specifically, the hospital) as a setting for health promotion (Chapter 5) with a historical overview of the development of hospitals and the forces that have shaped them to be what they are today. She examines the nature of health promotion offered within and by hospitals, including patient education, clinical rehabilitation, and community and corporate wellness. Johnson discusses the prevailing culture of health care institutions (bureaucratization, values, role definitions) as a context for health promotion, steps that health promoters could be recommended to take to maximize their chances of success in this setting, and the ways in which such success might be measured and evaluated. In closing, she identifies a number of challenges and trends that shape the opportunities for health promotion in health care institutions. Jane Lethbridge picks up where Joy Johnson leaves off by anticipating the trends that will shape the delivery of health care over the next 15 to 20 years and the implications this will have for health promotion in the hospital setting. Although they do not disagree with Johnson regarding the opportunities for community health promotion, Patricia Dolan Mullen and L. Kay Bartholomew argue that the public's health would be better served if hospitals concentrated their health promotion efforts "closer to home," with patients and their families. Using the examples of diabetes and asthma management, they demonstrate that even when well-established protocols exist to guide patient education, considerable room for improvement remains in terms of the proportion of patients and their families who are exposed to (and benefit from) such interventions. Both sets of authors point to trends that simultaneously enable and, in other cases, act as barriers to the enhancement of health promotion efforts within the hospital setting. These include the aging of the population, downsizing, decentralization of health care, changes in financing arrangements (e.g., capitation), increasingly solid evidence of the effectiveness of patient health promotion, reduced lengths of stay, and devolution of care to less-well-trained providers.

In Chapter 6, Vivek Goel and Warren McIsaac examine clinical general practice as a setting for health promotion. They indicate that despite considerable potential for health promotion in clinical practice, much of this remains unexplored. Factors that act as barriers (and facilitators) to the use of health promotion opportunities in clinical practice are explored by the authors; in particular, those relating to the physician (training, expectations, practice style, other characteristics), the patient (especially in terms of expectations), and the practice setting (pace of work, fee schedules, reminder systems, focus on presenting problem). Goel and McIsaac also address the potential for physicians to engage in health promotion outside of clinical practice, in terms of drawing attention to the health impacts of social and economic policies (child welfare, homelessness, gun control), and advocating for healthy public policy (e.g., smoking). In his commentary on Goel and McIsaac, David Butler-Jones reminds the reader that there is much to commend the fine art of the "teachable moment" in clinical practice. Focusing primarily on the role of physicians in primary care settings, he recommends a series of practical strategies that can enhance the role of health promotion and reviews a number of potential roles for physicians in this regard, stressing (as do others in this volume) the benefits of synergy with interventions in other settings, for which there may also be a role for the physician, particularly as the evidence regarding the broader determinants of health (beyond health care and lifestyles) becomes better known. In her commentary on Chapter 6, Jane Zapka discusses the difficulties involved in assessing current health promotion practice in clinical settings and argues for its conceptualization in terms of primary, secondary, and tertiary prevention. Her consideration of the barriers to and opportunities for health promotion in clinical settings echoes (and builds on) several points made by Goel and McIsaac (regarding physician training, patient expectations, and context of clinical practice). Her commentary ends with a number of specific recommendations for ways in which the incremental incorporation of health promotion into clinical practice can be enhanced.

The next set of contributions focuses on a qualitatively rather different type of setting, in that the community can be seen as encompassing the settings discussed in the preceding chapters as well as having many unique features of its own as a setting for health promotion. In Chapter 7, Marie Boutilier, Shelley Cleverly, and Ron Labonte begin their examination of this setting by noting the emergence of "community" as being of increasing importance to health promotion as a locus of activity and by problematizing the term *community* with respect to the political agendas that it has served. They proceed to examine three ideal-typical approaches to community development, both as discussed in the literature and as exemplified in a number of North American case examples. The differing understandings implicit or explicit in each model of power relations (especially between the community and the community development worker and his or her sponsoring institution) are emphasized. The authors close with a discussion of the organizational and personal conditions that appear to be supportive of empowering community development practice. In his commentary, John Raeburn defends "idealized" or "romanticized" visions of locality-based community on the part of community members and community workers as a vital life force in community development and the building of community (rooted in place) as a key focus of health promotion. Evelyne de Leeuw, on the other hand, argues that in light of the impacts of information technologies and the proliferation of "virtual" communities and other non-locality-based communities, communities ought to be seen as unique communication arrangements that are increasingly divorced from spatial ties. The observation that community action initiatives are frequently not sustained leads deLeeuw to examine the potential for such projects to "live on" in part through their ability to be incorporated into social and economic policy at the local level. The balance of her contribution is therefore devoted to examining the nature of emerging decentralized forms of policy development in which communities can and are playing an increasing role. In an addendum to Chapter 7, Blake Poland explores the similarities and differences between the concepts of social capital, social cohesion, community capacity, and community empowerment as they pertain to the community as a setting for health promotion.

A focus on policy is maintained by John Lavis and Terry Sullivan in Chapter 8, on the grounds that it represents one of the key mechanisms available to the state to promote (or prevent) change. Their chapter, which focuses on the role of the state as a setting for health promotion at the national and provincial or state level, zeros in on innovative new theories concerning the impacts of health policy and policy in nonhealth sectors on subsequent policy-making activity (what they call "policy legacies"), which they argue pose special challenges to the ability of the state to reframe its approach to health in terms of population health and healthy public policy at the extralocal level. In particular, they argue that prior attempts to address the determinants of health within (and through the further development of) state health bureaucracies has paradoxically made it more difficult to adequately address the health consequences of nonhealth social and economic policies in ways consonant with a population health approach. In closing, Lavis and Sullivan also present a number of key conditions that they feel are required for overcoming these policy legacies. In his commentary on this chapter, Marshall Kreuter argues that a crucial task facing those at the state and federal level dedicated to overcoming policy legacies is to successfully communicate a "coherent and inspiring vision of population health," so as to generate a broad base of public support (and thus political pressure) for public health and for the integration of health consequences into public policy (not to mention creating a broader awareness of how fundamentally linked the two are).

In the concluding chapter (Chapter 9), we review a number of themes and issues raised by the contributing authors to this volume and consider their implications for the theory and practice of a settings approach to health promotion. We also offer suggestions for future research.

NOTE

1. One potential paradox that emerges in this context is the desire to regulate change through legislative measures on the one hand (often with a top-down, punitive tone) and, on the other hand, considerable emphasis in health promotion on the importance of grass-roots participation and empowerment.

REFERENCES

Allegrante, J. P., & Green, L. W. (1981). When health policy becomes victim blaming. *New England Journal of Medicine, 305,* 1528-1529.

Altman, D., Endres, J., Linzer, J., Lorig, K., Howard-Pitney, B., & Rogers, T. (1991). Obstacles to and future goals of ten comprehensive community health promotion projects. *Journal of Community Health, 16,* 299-314.

Andersen, R. (1968). *A behavioral model of families' use of health services.* Chicago: University of Chicago Press.

Anderson, O. W. (1957). Infant mortality and social and cultural factors: Historical trends and current patterns. In E. G. Jaco (Ed.), *Patients, physicians and illness* (pp. 10-24). Glencoe, IL: Free Press.

Anderson, R. (1984). Health promotion: An overview. In L. Baric (Ed.), *European monographs in health education research.* Edinburgh: Scottish Health Education Group.

Baer, D. M. (1974). A note on the absence of a Santa Claus in any known ecosystem: A rejoinder to Willems. *Journal of Applied Behavior Analysis, 7,* 167-170.

Bandura, A. (1977). *Social learning theory.* Englewood Cliffs, NJ: Prentice Hall.

Barker, R. G. (1965). Explorations in ecological psychology. *American Psychologist, 20,* 1-14.

Bracht, N. (Ed.). (1999). *Health promotion at the community level* (2nd ed.). Thousand Oaks, CA: Sage.

Brown, E. R. (1991). Community action for health promotion: A strategy to empower individuals and communities. *International Journal of Health Services, 21*(3), 441-456.

Brown, E. R., & Margo, G. E. (1978). Health education: Can the reformers be reformed? *International Journal of Health Services, 8,* 3-25.

Bullough, B., & Rosen, G. (1992). *Preventive medicine in the United States, 1900–1990: Trends and interpretations.* Canton, MA: Science History.

Bunton, R., & Macdonald, G. (Eds.). (1992). *Health promotion: Disciplines and diversity.* London: Routledge.

Chavis, D. M., & Wandersman, A. (1990). Sense of community in the urban environment: A catalyst for participation and community development. *American Journal of Community Psychology, 18,* 55-81.

Chu, C., & Simpson, R. (1994). *Ecological public health: From vision to practice.* Toronto: Centre for Health Promotion.

Clark, N. M. (1987). Social learning theory in current health education practice. In W. B. Ward, S. K. Simonds, P. D. Mullen, & M. H. Becker (Eds.), *Advances in health education and promotion* (Vol. 2, pp. 251-275). Greenwich, CT: JAI.

Cohen, I. J. (1989). *Structuration theory: Anthony Giddens and the constitution of social life.* London: Macmillan.

Commonwealth Department of Health, Housing, and Community Services. (1993). *Toward health for all and health promotion: The evaluation of the National Better Health Program.* Canberra: Australian Government Publishing Service.

Creswell, W., Jr., & Newman, I. M. (1997). *School health practice* (10th ed.). St. Louis: Times Mirror/Mosby.

Croog, S. H. (1961). Ethnic origins, educational level, and responses to a health questionnaire. *Human Organization, 20,* 65-69.

DeFries, R. D. (Ed.). (1940). *The development of public health in Canada.* Ottawa, Ontario: Canadian Public Health Association.

Dewey, J. (1946). *The public and its problems: An essay in political inquiry.* Chicago: Gateway.

Dorn, M., & Laws, G. (1994). Social theory, body politics, and medical geography: Extending Kearns' invitation. *Professional Geographer, 46*(1), 106-110.

Downie, R. S., Fyfe, C., & Tannahill, A. (1990). *Health promotion: Models and values.* Oxford: Oxford University Press.

Dunn, H. L. (1977). *High level wellness.* Thoroughfare, NJ: Charles B. Slack.

Eakin, J., Cava, M., & Smith, T. (1997). *Playing it safe: Power and contradiction in a public health department stress reduction program for small business.* Unpublished manuscript, University of Toronto, Ontario.

Eakin, J., Robertson, A., Poland, B., Coburn, D., & Edwards, R. (1995). *Young girls smoking: A critical social science perspective* (Ontario Tobacco Research Unit Working Papers Series No. 4). Toronto: Ontario Tobacco Research Unit.

Eakin, J., Robertson, A., Poland, B., Coburn, D., & Edwards, R. (1996). Toward a critical social science perspective on health promotion research. *Health Promotion International, 11*(2), 157-165.

Eisenberg, L. (1972). The human nature of human nature. *Science, 176,* 123-128.

Elder, J., Hovell, M., Lasater, T., Wells, B., & Carleton, R. (1985). Applications of behavior modification to community health education: The case of heart disease prevention. *Health Education Quarterly, 12,* 151-168.

Enelow, A. J., & Henderson, J. B. (Eds.). (1975). *Applying behavioral science to cardiovascular risk.* New York: American Heart Association.

Epp, J. (1986). *Achieving health for all: A framework for health promotion.* Ottawa, Ontario: Health and Welfare Canada.

Evans, R. G., Barer, M. L., & Marmor, T. R. (Eds.). (1994). *Why are some people healthy and others not? The determinants of health of populations.* New York: Aldine de Gruyter.

Evans, R. G., & Stoddart, G. L. (1990). Producing health, consuming health care. *Social Science and Medicine, 31*(12), 1347-1363.

Farquhar, J. W., Fortmann, S. P., Maccoby, N., Haskell, W. L., Williams, P. T., Flora, J. A., Taylor, C. B., Brown, B. W., Solomon, D. S., & Hulley, S. B. (1985). The Stanford Five-City Project: Design and methods. *American Journal of Epidemiology, 122,* 323-334.

Fee, E., & Acheson, R. M. (Eds.). (1991). *A history of education in public health: Health that mocks the doctors' rules.* London: Oxford University Press.

Fischer, B., & Poland, B. (1998). Exclusion, "risk," and social control: Reflections on community policing and public health. *GeoForum, 29*(2), 187-197.

Flay, B. R. (1987). Social psychological approaches to smoking prevention: Review and recommendations. In W. B. Ward & P. D. Mullen (Eds.), *Advances in health education and promotion* (Vol. 2, pp. 121-180). Greenwich, CT: JAI.

Florin, P., Mitchell, R., & Stevenson, J. (1993). Identifying technical assistance needs in community coalitions: A developmental approach. *Health Education Research, 8,* 403-416.

Foster, G. M. (1962). *Traditional cultures and the impact of technological change.* New York: Harper.

Francisco, V. T., Paine, A. L., & Fawcett, S. (1993). A methodology for monitoring and evaluating community health coalitions. *Health Education Research, 8,* 403-416.

Freire, P. (1973). *Education for critical consciousness.* New York: Seabury.

Freire, P. (1990). *Pedagogy of the oppressed.* New York: Continuum.

Freire, P. (1995). *Pedagogy of hope.* New York: Continuum.

Freudenberg, N. (1978). Shaping the future of health education: From behavior change to social change. *Health Education Monographs, 6,* 372-377.

Friedson, E., & Silver, G. A. (1960). Social science in family medical care. *Public Health Reports, 75,* 489-493.

Fuhrer, U. (1990). Bridging the ecological-psychological gap: Behavior settings as interfaces. *Environment and Behavior, 22*(4), 518-537.

Giddens, A. (1979). *Central problems in social theory: Action, structure and contradiction in social analysis.* London: Macmillan.

Giddens, A. (1984). *The constitution of society.* Berkeley: University of California Press.

Goodman, R. M., Wandersman, A., Chinman, M., Imm, P., & Morrissey, E. (1996). An ecological assessment of community-based interventions for prevention and health promotion: Approaches to measuring community coalitions. *American Journal of Community Psychology, 24,* 33-61.

Goodstadt, M. S. (1995, February). *Health promotion and the bottom line: What works?* Paper presented at the Seventh National Health Promotion Conference, Brisbane, Australia.

Goodstadt, M. S., Simpson, R. I., & Loranger, P. O. (1987, Winter). Health promotion: A conceptual integration. *American Journal of Health Promotion, 1*(3), 58-63.

Gramsci, A. (1975). *Letters from prison: Antonio Gramsci* (L. Lawner, Ed.). New York: Harper Colophon. (Original work published 1932)

Gray, R. M., Kesler, J. P., & Moody, P. M. (1966). The effects of social class and friends' expectations on oral polio vaccination participation. *American Journal of Public Health, 56,* 2028-2032.

Green, L. W. (1970). Identifying and overcoming barriers to the diffusion of knowledge about family planning. *Advances in Fertility Control, 5,* 21-29.

Green, L. W. (1979). National policy in the promotion of health. *International Journal of Health Education, 22,* 161-168.

Green, L. W. (1980, March/April). Current report: Office of Health Information, Health Promotion, Physical Fitness and Sports Medicine. *Health Education, 11,* 28.

Green, L. W. (1984). Health promotion research and development. *Alabama Journal of Medical Science, 21*(2), 217-219.

Green, L. W., George, A., Daniel, M., Frankish, C. J., Herbert, C. P., Bowie, W., & O'Neill, M. (1995). *Study of participatory research in health promotion.* Ottawa, Ontario: Royal Society of Canada.

Green, L. W., & Kreuter, M. W. (1991). *Health promotion planning: An educational and ecological approach* (3rd ed.). Mountain View, CA: Mayfield.

Green, L. W., & Ottoson, J. M. (1999). *Community and population health* (8th ed.). New York: McGraw-Hill.

Green, L. W., & Raeburn, J. (1990). Contemporary developments in health promotion: Definitions and challenges. In N. Bracht (Ed.), *Health promotion at the community level.* Newbury Park, CA: Sage.

Green, L. W., & Richard, L. (1994). The need to combine health education and health promotion: The case of cardiovascular disease prevention. *International Journal of Health Promotion and Education, 1,* 11-17.

Green, L. W., Richard, L., & Potvin, L. (1996). Ecological foundations of health promotion. *American Journal of Health Promotion, 10,* 270-281.

Green, L. W., Simons-Morton, D., & Potvin, L. (1996). Education and lifestyle determinants of health and disease. In W. W. Holland, R. Detels, & G. Knox (Eds.), *Oxford textbook of public health.* London: Oxford University Press.

Gregory, D. (1994). Contextuality theory. In R. J. Johnston, D. Gregory, & D. M. Smith (Eds.), *The dictionary of human geography* (3rd ed.). Cambridge, MA: Basil Blackwell.

Gregory, D., & Urry, J. (1985). *Social relations and spatial structures.* London: Macmillan.

Griffiths, W., & Knutson, A. L. (1960). The role of mass media in public health. *American Journal of Public Health, 50,* 515-523.

Guba, E., & Lincoln, Y. S. (1989). *Fourth generation evaluation.* Newbury Park, CA: Sage.

Habermas, J. (1973). *Legitimation crisis.* Boston: Beacon.

Haglund, B. (1992). *We can do it! The Sundsvall handbook.* Stockholm: Karolinska Institute.

Hawe, P. (1996). Needs assessment must become more needs focused. *Australian and New Zealand Journal of Public Health, 20,* 473-478.

Hayes, M. V., Foster, L., & Foster, H. (1992). *Community environment and health.* Victoria, BC: University of Victoria Press.

Hayes, M. V., & Manson Willms, S. (1990). Healthy community indicators: The perils of the search and the paucity of the find. *Health Promotion International, 5,* 161-166.

Health Education Quarterly. (1994a). Community empowerment, participatory education, and health—Part I. *Health Education Quarterly, 21*(2), entire issue.

Health Education Quarterly. (1994b). Community empowerment, participatory education, and health—Part II. *Health Education Quarterly, 21*(3), entire issue.

Health and Welfare Canada. (1989). *Knowledge development for health promotion: A call for action.* Ottawa: Author.

Hollingshead, A. B., & Redlich, F. C. (1958). *Social class and mental illness: A community study.* New York: John Wiley.

Hovland, C., Janis, I. L., & Kelley, H. H. (1953). *Communication and persuasion.* New Haven, CT: Yale University Press.

Jeffery, R. (1993). Minnesota studies on community-based approaches to weight control. *Annals of Internal Medicine, 119*(7, Part 2), 719-721.

Johnston, R. J., Gregory, D., & Smith, D. M. (1994). *The dictionary of human geography* (3rd ed.). Oxford, UK: Basil Blackwell.

Joseph, A. E., & Phillips, D. R. (1984). *Accessibility and utilization: Geographical perspectives on health care delivery.* New York: Harper & Row.

Kar, S. B. (Ed.). (1989). *Health promotion indicators and actions.* New York: Springer.

Kay, J. J., & Schneider, E. (1994). Embracing complexity: The challenge of the ecosystem approach. *Alternatives, 20*(3), 32-39.

Kearns, R. A. (1993). Place and health: Toward a reformed medical geography. *Professional Geographer, 45*(2), 139-148.

Kearns, R. A. (1995). Medical geography: Making space for difference. *Progress in Human Geography, 19*(2), 251-259.

Kickbusch, I. (1989). Approaches to an ecological base for public health. *Health Promotion International, 4,* 265-268.

Kickbusch, I. (1994). Introduction: Tell me a story. In A. Pederson, M. O'Neill, & I. Rootman (Eds.), *Health promotion in Canada: Provincial, national and international perspectives.* Toronto: W. B. Saunders.

Kickbusch, I. (1995). An overview to the settings based approach to health promotion. In T. Theaker & J. Thompson (Eds.), *The settings-based approach to health promotion: Report of an international working conference.* Hertfordshire, UK: Hertfordshire Health Promotion.

King, A. W. (1993). Considerations of scale and hierarchy. In S. Woodley, J. J. Kay, & G. Francis (Eds.), *Ecological integrity and the management of ecosystems* (pp. 19-46). Delray, FL: St. Lucie.

Kolbe, L. J. (1986). Increasing the impact of school health promotion programs: Emerging research perspectives. *Health Education, 17*(5), 47-52.

Labonte, R., & Little, S. (1992). *Determinants of health: Empowering strategies for nurses.* Vancouver: Registered Nurses Association of British Columbia.

Laframboise, H. (1973). Health policy: Breaking the problem down into more manageable segments. *Canadian Medical Association Journal, 108,* 388-391.

Lalonde, M. (1974). *A new perspective on the health of Canadians.* Ottawa: Ministry of Supply and Services.

Lambert, C. Jr., & Freeman, H. E. (1967). *The clinic habit.* New Haven, CT: College and University Press.

Landau, R. (1995). Locus of control and socioeconomic status: Does internal locus of control neglect real resources and opportunities of personal coping abilities? *Social Science and Medicine, 41*(11), 1499-1505.

Lando, H., Loken, B., Howard-Pitney, B., & Pechacek, T. (1990). Community impact of a localized smoking cessation contest. *American Journal of Public Health, 80,* 601-603.

Lasater, T., Sennett, L., Lefebvre, R., Dehart, K., Peterson, G., & Carleton, R. (1991). Community-based approach to weight loss: The Pawtucket "weight-in." *Addictive Behaviors, 16,* 175-181.

Lefebvre, R. (1990). Strategies to maintain and institutionalize successful programs. In N. Bracht (Ed.), *Health promotion at the community level* (pp. 209-228). Beverly Hills, CA: Sage.

Lewin, K. (1943). Forces behind food habits and methods of change. *Bulletin of the National Research Council, 108,* 35-65.

Lionberger, H. F. (1964). *Application of diffusion research in agriculture to heart disease control.* Berkeley: California State Department of Public Health.

Litva, A., & Eyles, J. (1995). Coming out: Exposing social theory in medical geography. *Health and Place, 1,* 5-14.

Lowry, S. G., Mayo, S. C., & Hay, D. G. (1958). Factors associated with the acceptance of health care practices among rural families. *Rural Sociology, 23,* 198-202.

Macdonald, G., & Bunton, R. (1992). Health promotion: Discipline or disciplines. In R. Bunton & G. Macdonald (Eds.), *Health promotion: Disciplines and diversity.* London: Routledge.

MacDonald, M. (1998). *Reconciling concept and context: An evaluation of the British Columbia School-Based Prevention Program.* Unpublished doctoral dissertation, Institute of Health Promotion Research, University of British Columbia, Vancouver.

Marmot, M. C., Kogevinas, M., & Elston, M. A. (1991). Socioeconomic status and disease. In B. Badura & I. Kickbusch (Eds.), *Health promotion research: Toward a new social epidemiology* (pp. 113-146). Copenhagen: WHO Regional Publications.

Martin, C. J., & McQueen, D. V. (Eds.). (1989). *Readings for a new public health.* Edinburgh: Edinburgh University Press.

Mayer, J. D. (1982). Relations between two traditions of medical geography: Health systems planning and geographical epidemiology. *Progress in Human Geography, 6*(2), 216-230.

Mayer, J. D. (1983). The role of spatial analysis and geographic data in the detection of disease causation. *Social Science and Medicine, 17*(16), 1213-1221.

McLeroy, K. R., Bibeau, D., Steckler, A., & Glanz, K. (1988). An ecological perspective on health promotion programs. *Health Education Quarterly, 15*(4), 351-377.

Miller, N. E. (1984). Learning: Some facts and needed research relevant to maintaining health. In J. D. Matarazzo, S. M. Weiss, J. A. Herd, & N. E. Miller (Eds.). *Behavioral health: A handbook of health enhancement and disease prevention* (pp. 199-208). New York: John Wiley.

Mirowsky, J., & Ross, C. (1990). Control or defense: Depression and the sense of control over good and bad outcomes. *Journal of Health and Social Behavior, 31,* 71-86.

Mittlemark, M. B. (1997, May 6). Health promotion settings. *Internet Journal of Health Promotion.* Retrieved from the World Wide Web June 16, 1999, at http://www.monash.edu.au/health/IJHP/1997/1

Morgan, L. S., & Horning, B. G. (1940). The community health education program. *American Journal of Public Health, 30,* 1323-1330.

Mullen, P. D., Evans, D., Forster, J., Gottlieb, N. H., Kreuter, M., Moon, R., O'Rourke, T., & Strecher, V. J. (1995). Settings as an important dimension in health education/promotion policy, programs, and research. *Health Education Quarterly, 22,* 329-345.

Naidoo, J., & Wills, J. (1994). *Health promotion: Foundations for practice.* Toronto: Bailliere Tindall.

National Forum on Health (1998). *Determinants of health: Settings and issues.* Canada Health Action: Building on the Legacy. Papers commissioned by the National Forum on Health. Vol. 3. Sante-Foy, Quebec: Editions MultiMondes.

Nutbeam, D. (1986). Health promotion glossary. *Health Promotion, 1*(1), 113-127.

Nutbeam, D. (1997). *Health promotion glossary.* From the 4th International Conference on Health Promotion, Jakarta, Indonesia.

Nutbeam, D., Smith, C., & Catford, J. (1990). Evaluation in health education: A review of possibilities and problems. *Journal of Epidemiology and Community Health, 44,* 83-89.

Nyswander, D. B. (1942). *Solving school health problems.* New York: Oxford University Press.

O'Donnell, M. P. (1989). Definition of health promotion: Part III: Expanding the definition. *American Journal of Health Promotion, 3*(3), 5.

Ottoson, J. M., & Green, L. W. (1987). Reconciling concept and context: Theory of implementation. In W. B. Ward & M. H. Becker (Eds.), *Advances in health education and promotion* (Vol. 2, pp. 353-382). Greenwich, CT: JAI.

Parcel, G. S., & Baranowski, T. (1981). Social learning theory and health education. *Health Education, 12*(3), 14-18.

Parcel, G. S., Simons-Morton, B. G., & Kolbe, L. J. (1988). Health promotion: Integrating organizational change and student learning strategies. *Health Education Quarterly, 15,* 435-450.

Park, R. E., Burgess, E. W., & McKenzie, R. D. (Eds.). (1925). *The city.* Chicago: University of Chicago Press.

Paul, B. D. (Ed.). (1955). *Health, culture and community.* New York: Russell Sage Foundation.

Pechacek, T., Lando, H., Northwehr, F., & Lichtenstein, E. (1994). Quit and win: A community-wide approach to smoking cessation. *Tobacco Control, 3,* 236-241.

Perry, C., Klepp, K., & Sillers, C. (1989). Community-wide strategies for cardiovascular health: The Minnesota Heart Health Program youth program. *Health Education Research, 4,* 87-101.

Perry, C. L., & Jessor, R. (1985). The concept of health promotion and the prevention of adolescent drug abuse. *Health Education Quarterly, 12*(2), 169-184.

Pinder, L. (1994). The federal role in health promotion: Art of the possible. In A. Pederson, M. O'Neill, & I. Rootman (Eds.), *Health promotion in Canada: Provincial, national and international perspectives.* Toronto: W. B. Saunders Canada.

Pittman, D. J. (1993). The new temperance movement in the United States: What happened to macrostructural factors in alcohol problems? *Addiction, 88,* 167-170.

Poland, B. (1992). Learning to "walk our talk": The implications of sociological theory for research methodologies in health promotion. *Canadian Journal of Public Health, 83*(Suppl. 1), S31-S46.

Poland, B. (1998). Smoking, stigma, and the purification of public space. In R. Kearns & W. Gesler (Eds.), *Putting health into place: Making connections in geographical research.* Syracuse, NY: Syracuse University Press.

Powell, M. (1995). On the outside looking in: Medical geography, medical geographers and access to health care. *Health and Place, 1*(1), 41-50.

Raeburn, J., & Rootman, I. (1998). *People-centered health promotion.* Toronto: John Wiley.

Rappaport, J. (1987). Terms of empowerment, exemplars of prevention: Toward a theory for community psychology. *American Journal of Community Psychology, 15,* 121-148.

Richard, L., Potvin, L., Kishuck, N., Prlic, H., & Green, L. (1996). Assessing the integration of an ecological approach in health promotion programs. *American Journal of Health Promotion, 10,* 318-328.

Rissel, C. (1994). Empowerment: The holy grail of health promotion? *Health Promotion International, 9*(1), 39-47.

Robertson, A., & Minkler, M. (1994). New health promotion movement: A critical examination. *Health Education Quarterly, 21*(3), 295-312.

Rogers, E. M. (1973). *Communication strategies for family planning.* New York: Free Press.

Rogers, E. S. (1960). *Human ecology and health: An introduction for administrators.* New York: Macmillan.

Rogers-Warren, A., & Warren, S. F. (1977). *Ecological perspectives in behavior analysis.* Baltimore, MD: University Park Press.

Rootman, I., Goodstadt, M., Potvin, L., & Springett, J. (1997). *Toward a framework for health promotion evaluation.* Copenhagen: European Office of the World Health Organization.

Rose, G. (1992). *The strategy of preventive medicine.* New York: Oxford University Press.

Rosenstock, I. M. (1974). The historical origins of the Health Belief Model. *Health Education Monographs, 2,* 354-395.

Rosenstock, I. M., Derryberry, M., & Carriger, B. (1959). Why people fail to seek poliomyelitis vaccination. *Public Health Reports, 74,* 98-103.

Rotenberg, R. (1993). On the salubrity of sites. In R. Rotenberg & D. McDonogh (Eds.), *The cultural meaning of urban space.* Westport, CT: Bergin & Garvey.

Sallis, J., & Nader, P. (1988). Family determinants of health behaviors. In D. Gochman (Ed.), *Health behavior: Emerging research perspectives* (pp. 107-124). New York: Plenum.

Sayer, A. (1984). *Method in social science: A realist approach.* London: Hutchinson.

Sells, S. B. (1969). Ecology and the science of psychology. In E. P. Willems & H. L. Raush (Eds.), *Naturalistic viewpoints in psychological research* (pp. 15-30). New York: Holt, Rinehart & Winston.

Sigerist, H. M. (1946). *The university at the crossroads.* New York: Henry Schuman.

Simonsen, K. (1991). Toward an understanding of the contextuality of social life. *Environment and Planning D: Society and Space, 9,* 417-432.

Slobodkin, L. B. (1988). Intellectual problems of applied ecology. *Bioscience, 38,* 337-342.

Smith, D. M. (1994). *Geography and social justice.* Cambridge, MA: Blackwell.

Soja, E. (1989). *Postmodern geographies.* New York: Verso.

St. Leger, L. (1997). Health promoting settings: From Ottawa to Jakarta. *Health Promotion International, 12,* 99-102.

Stokols, D. (1996). Translating social ecological theory into guidelines for community health promotion. *American Journal of Health Promotion, 10,* 282-298.

Stokols, D., Pelletier, K. R., & Fielding, J. E. (1996). The ecology of work and health: Research and policy directions for the promotion of employee health. *Health Education Quarterly, 23,* 137-158.

Stones, R. (1991). Strategic context analysis: A new research strategy for structuration theory. *Sociology, 25*(4), 673-695.

Suchman, E. A. (1963). *Sociology and the field of public health.* New York: Russell Sage.

Supportive environments for health: Sundsvall statement. (1998). Geneva: World Health Organization, Division of Health Promotion, Education and Communication.

Syme, S. L. (1991). Control and health: A personal perspective. *Advances, 7*(2), 16-27.

Terris, M. (1994, Spring). Determinants of health: A progressive political platform. *Journal of Public Health Policy,* 5-17.

Theaker, T., & Thompson, J. (1995). *The settings-based approach to health promotion: Conference report.* Welwyne Garden City, UK: Hertfordshire Health Promotion.

Thomas, J. (1993). *Doing critical ethnography.* Newbury Park, CA: Sage.

Thrift, N. (1983). On the determination of social action in space and time. *Environment and Planning D: Society and Space, 1,* 23-57.

Tones, K., & Tilford, S. (1994). *Health education: Effectiveness, efficiency and equity* (2nd ed.). London: Chapman & Hall.

U.S. Department of Health, Education and Welfare. (1979). *Healthy people: The Surgeon General's report of health promotion and disease prevention.* Washington, DC: Author.

Wallerstein, N. (1992). Powerlessness, empowerment, and health: Implications for health promotion programs. *American Journal of Health Promotion, 6*(3), 197-205.

Wallerstein, N., & Freudenberg, N. (1998). Linking health promotion and social justice: A rationale and two case stories. *Health Education Research, 13,* 451-457.

Wandersman, A., Florin, P., Friedmann, R., & Meier, R. (1987). Who participates, who does not and why? An analysis of voluntary neighborhood organizations in the United States and Israel. *Sociological Forum, 2,* 534-555.

Wells, B., DePue, J., Lasater, T., & Carleton, R. (1988). A report on church site weight control. *Health Education Research, 3,* 305-316.

Wenzel, E. (1997, May 6). A comment on settings for health promotion (editorial). *Internet Journal of Health Promotion.* Retrieved June 16, 1999, from the World Wide Web at http://www.monash.edu.au/health/IJHP/1997/1

Werlen, B. (1993). *Society, action and space: An alternative human geography.* New York: Routledge.

Wilkinson, R. G. (1986). *Class and health.* London: Tavistock.

Wilkinson, R. G. (1996). *Unhealthy societies.* Boston: Routledge.

Willems, E. P. (1974). Behavioral technology and behavioral ecology. *Journal of Applied Behavior Analysis, 7,* 151-165.

Winslow, C. E. A. (1920). The untilled fields of health promotion [Abstract]. *Science, 51,* 23.

Worden, J. K., Flynn, B. S., Geller, B. M., Chen, M., Shelton, L. G., Secker-Walker, R. H., Solomon, D. S., Solomon, L. J., Couchey, S., & Costanza, M. C. (1988). Development of a smoking prevention mass-media program using diagnostic and formative research. *Preventive Medicine, 17,* 531-558.

World Health Organization. (1984). *Discussion document on the concept and principles of health promotion.* Copenhagen: European Office of the World Health Organization.

World Health Organization. (1986). Ottawa charter for health promotion. *Health Promotion, 1*(4), i-v.

Young, M. A. C. (1967). Review of research and studies related to health education communication: Methods and materials. *Health Education Monographs, 1*(25), 18-24.

Zanna, M., Cameron, R., Goldsmith, C. H., Poland, B., Lindsay, E., & Walker, R. (1994). Critique of the COMMIT study based on the Brantford experience. *Health and Canadian Society, 2*(2), 319-336.

Zimmerman, M. A., Israel, B. A., Schulz, A., & Checkoway, B. (1992). Further explorations in empowerment theory: An empirical analysis of psychological empowerment. *American Journal of Community Psychology, 20,* 707-727.

2

Homes and Families as Health Promotion Settings

Hassan Soubhi

Louise Potvin

The Ottawa Charter for Health Promotion (World Health Organization [WHO], 1986) defines health promotion as "the process of enabling people to increase control over and improve their health" (p. iii). In this perspective, health promotion programs are generally conceived of as a series of activities planned over a definite time period and aimed at fostering the general development of communities and individuals by facilitating their empowerment, leading to better health and well-being (Green & Kreuter, 1999). Designed as a schedule of related events aimed at achieving specific social goals, social programs, including health promotion programs, may also be conceptualized as social systems (Klein, 1991). The ability of such systems to produce changes in individuals or groups of individuals is partly determined by the effectiveness of the changes produced in the social settings where these individuals evolve (Syme, 1986).

The home is such a social setting where simultaneous individual and group processes and actions occur. It is also an organized physical space to which its occupants attribute meaning. As a private setting, it provides its occupants with specific environmental cues, opportunities, and obligations. Underlying the concept of home, we find an interdependency between the ecological environment of the home and the people living in it (Perkins, Burns, Perry, & Nielsen, 1988). Part of what makes this environment a "home" comes from the power of its occupants to organize it according to their needs. Thus, an important challenge for health promotion practitioners is to identify how home members create or select health-related conditions and processes in a given set of constraints and opportunities provided by the home environment and the general social context. Health promotion action conceived as an integrative move toward health would then increase its efficiency by taking advantage of and integrating the health resources and strengths of the home setting. Indeed, it is in the home that health behaviors are learned and maintained. It is within the home that young children develop most of their strategies for interacting with the environment, including their health-related habits. It is also here that adults make important decisions regarding their health, including specific health-related behaviors such as dietary habits and taking time for physical exercise.

Within the home, we may distinguish between at least two kinds of living arrangements: Members who live in the home as families defined in the usual sense, whereby the relationships between members are established by marriage, adoption, or biological links, and family-like systems (Broderick, 1993) that mimic to some extent traditional family members' relationships (mates, live-in lovers, etc.). Many factors converge to extending the concept of home to other living arrangements than that of the traditional family. Indeed, gay and lesbian couples raise children, and in many modern families, biological links are not primarily what determine living arrangements. We believe that the hypotheses that can be drawn about these various living arrangements are best derived from the theoretical and empirical knowledge that has been accumulated about the family.

In this chapter, we suggest a framework for thinking about the interaction between health promotion programs and the families in their home environment. The first section defines the family as a functional unit and lays out the different processes that shape the patterns of interactions of family members within the home and with the external environment. Building on the systemic perspective advocated by many authors, the family context is presented as a dynamic social system encompassing a set of multidirectional influences stemming from the interplay of different home settings and family processes: environmental, psychosocial, developmental, and cognitive. In the second section, we devote specific attention to recent studies on the relationship between family an   health. We also review the concepts and the assumptions underlying different family health promotion models. In the third section, we present our framework for an integrative view of the interactions between health promotion programs and the family. In the last section, we review some of the implications of this framework for health promotion and the available evidence in support of the framework.

THE FAMILY AS A DYNAMIC CONTEXT FOR HEALTH

The Family as a Functional Unit

The increasing frequency of new living arrangements, as well as profound changes in Western societies, have made it difficult to define families using structural characteristics alone. This calls for extending the focus to the functional and relational aspects of family life in the home (including those of familylike living arrangements) rather than simply on its structure. These functional aspects include the exchange of support between members, sharing of responsibility, and the meeting of individual needs. Also included is the family's ability to fulfill basic needs of its members within an interdependent relationship, regardless of whether or not this relationship was set by legal or biological means. Also implied are the processes by which the members express and communicate their needs and the processes involved in the provision and use of internal and external family resources.

Many authors (e.g., Beavers, 1982; Curran, 1983; Lewis, 1979; Pratt, 1976) have in some way used this focus on family members' relationships to study what makes up a healthy family. Beavers (1982), for example, defined optimal healthy families as the most functional in contrast to adequate, midrange, and severely dysfunctional families. This acknowledges the fact that families do vary along a continuum, with different degrees of dysfunction at different levels and probably involving different underlying processes. In the context of community-based health promotion programs, the frequency of severely dysfunctional families is expected to be low. This, however, does not mean the absence of violence and abuse in nonpathological (or non-identified-as-such) families. For example, according to Ammerman (1990), only 10% to 15% of child-abusing parents have a psychiatric condition.

Attention to the functional aspects of home members' relationships suggests that health promotion programs should be designed with a specific focus on predefined functional dimensions of the family unit according to the objectives pursued. These functional dimensions may refer to the patterns of interaction within the home and between the family members and the surrounding environment. For example, interventions targeting children's health behaviors should not only take into account the patterns of interaction between the child and other family members but also the patterns of relationships these members have with other systems, such as the school. In this case, the functional unit of interest encompasses the home unit and the links between the home and the school. Structural definitions of the family may not allow for enough flexibility in target definition.

The relationships between family members provide for dynamic and persistently renewed interactions. These interactions form a specific variety of social interactions, the patterns of which are shaped by biological and psychological individual attributes, family dynamic structural composition, and the surrounding social environment (Broderick, 1993). These interactions are patterned also by regularly occurring experiences (e.g., families convening at the dinner table, watching television, visiting other family members) that form part of the family ritual process, conveying to its members a sense of identity and uniqueness (Wolin & Bennett, 1984). Several theoretical models have been developed to explain these patterned interactions in the family system. These models help point to different sources of influence that shape the family context for health.

Shaping the Family Context for Health

Broderick (1993) reviewed several models explaining family patterns of interactions. These models account for the influence of four sets of processes that shape the patterns of interactions and behaviors among family members. They are environmental processes, psychopolitical and reflexive processes, developmental processes, and cognitive processes.

Environmental Processes

Two categories of models in Broderick's review stress the influence of the environment: the opportunistic models and the normative models. The first category, "opportunity structure models," emphasizes the influence of resources, opportunities, and situational constraints on the environment. In the family, fundamental environmental units can be defined by physical and temporal boundaries in which regular patterns of behavior or interactions occur. We may take as examples the kitchen or the living room. In these environmental units, regular interactions between members occur at specific times and duration. These are the "stable, regularly occurring place-activity" of behavior-setting theory (Perkins et al., 1988, p. 356). In turn, these environmental units or home settings are also part of the opportunity structure (Broderick, 1993). This structure is the result of the interactions between four components: (a) the characteristics of the physical environment of the home, such as the provision for sufficient conditions for privacy and the protection from various hazards and pollutants; (b) the temporal patterning shaped by regular events such as different family rituals, meals, or outings; (c) the material milieu described by the availability of material objects such as home safety requirements, sports equipment, food, toys, and books; and (d) the social milieu, which may be described as the presence or absence of different social categories of individuals. At the family level, because each member is also involved in other settings outside the home, members' opportunity structures may complement or counteract each other's. From a health promotion perspective, attention to the interaction of individual members' opportunity structures would, for example, help take into account the way these structures strengthen the links between family members, the expression and communication of individual needs, and the provision and use of family internal and external resources. As they are conveyed and expressed through the members, the effects of the interaction of individual members' opportunity structures reflect the effects of the settings in which the members are involved.

Normative models reflect the regulating influence of the environment through the social norms as they may originate from the general community or be part of the family set of rules and boundaries. Different settings in the home can be described as subsystems within the family system, and each subsystem is regulated by implicit or explicit rules. In turn, some of these rules define the boundaries of the subsystems. These boundaries may, for example, exclude specific individual members (e.g., the marital subsystem is more or less child-proof). It is usually through the socialization process that the normative influence of the general social environment is transmitted to family members. The family system, however, may have its own rules involving the idiosyncrasies of individual members (Broderick, 1993). Individual members do have their own perceptions, judgments, and political influences within the family system, and this is addressed by the next model.

Psychopolitical and Reflexive Processes

Psychopolitical processes reflect the fact that family members have their own idiosyncratic needs and agendas. Consensus among members is therefore often achieved through conscious negotiations. At play in these negotiations are individuals' subjective judgments and political and strategic resources. Because these resources are unevenly distributed among members, issues of differential power between members are of central importance. They help explain how decision-making processes can be heavily influenced by one member or a coalition of members in the family. This is, for example, a relevant issue for health-related behavior dissemination among family members. Power differentials provide also a plausible explanation (along with the biological and social ones) for the gender differences in communication (Steen & Schwartz, 1995). These differentials are part of the dynamics of power that have been related to the social and political contexts by the feminist movement, emphasizing the influence on health and well-being of hierarchically structured and male-oriented social arrangements (Brown, 1981; Fox & Luxton, 1993).

The psychopolitical processes emphasize conscious and deliberate negotiations; the reflexive spirals processes, on the other hand, provide an explanation for the "unmediated, reflexive interaction between members" (Broderick, 1993, p. 72). These interactions bring into play the more or less conscious reactions occurring among family members in different situations and explain, for example, the escalating spirals of tension and resentment that any family may experience from time to time.

The psychopolitical processes, along with the reflexive spirals processes, account for the fact that different family members may have different influences on the family as a whole. All these influences work toward a family goal that may or may not be deliberate. These processes point also to the fact that individual priorities reflect the influence of the general environment (which includes health promotion programs' influence), as well as the influence of the more immediate environment, composed of the family and its members.

Family Developmental Processes

Although accounting only for major changes in family situation, these processes provide a dynamic view of the family system. Developmental models (Combrinck-Graham, 1985) present the family system's directionality as a result of the ever-changing pressures of both individual developmental needs and changing environmental norms and constraints. Different stages in the family life cycle can be distinguished (Carter & McGoldrick, 1980): newly married couples, families with newborn babies or preschool or school-age children, families with adolescents, families in which mature young adults are leaving the home (launching period), and the aging family. As the family evolves through these stages, societal norms and expectations, as well as the family's own rules and expectations, evolve. Each of these stages helps take into account the temporal variation of the availability of different families' resources and potentialities, as well as their vulnerabilities.

Attention to the developmental stages of the family may help account for the differential effects of health promotion programs when applied to families in different stages of their life cycle. The best potential for success seems to be in the first years of family life. Steinglass (1992) states that families at this stage are concerned with their identity and boundary definition, goals, and selection of values and priorities. This stage refers to the primary years where shared family values and beliefs about the world and life are shaped. These first years could be marked by the arrival of a child, and long-lasting health effects could be expected for successful health promotion programs (e.g., via parent's modeling and/or opportunity structure effects). As family influence decreases in the adolescence and launching period (Sallis & Nader, 1988), health promotion programs would gain from a greater focus on extrafamilial environments, such as school and worksite. This does not mean that it is not possible to influence the family at this stage. Children may still influence their parents' health behaviors and attitudes by bringing home new health-related information and skills. This is, in fact, an argument for more systematic linkages between health promotion programs conducted in other settings and the family system. Finally, the postlaunching period calls for specific health promotion programs designed for aging parents (need for physical, social, and economic resources).

It appears, then, that health promotion inputs and the potential participants in these inputs and resources would vary according to the configuration of the family's own resources, potentialities, and vulnerabilities, through its temporal development and through the preexisting links (if any) between the family system and other social contexts.

Cognitive Processes

Each of the process categories described above provides a different perspective on the interactions among family members. Each also identifies relevant sources of influence within the family. These influences are, however, mediated by individual cognitive processes, including those that contribute to the elaboration of a set of meanings that the family members attribute to the events and components of their environment. It has been shown also that some of these meanings are shared among family members. These are part of what Reiss (1981) defined as the family paradigm, or a long-lasting fundamental set of assumptions the family develops about its surrounding world. The literature describes different mechanisms by which this set of assumptions is shared by family members (e.g., Broderick, 1993). There has also been extensive research on how these "constructions" shape the reactions that families may have in the face of stress and with their interactions with health professionals (e.g., Reiss & De-Nour, 1989).

Family members have a set of values, beliefs, expectations, and attitudes toward health that shape overall family health patterns through a family's temporal development. These "health cognitions" (Gochman, 1992, p. 23) are part of what makes the family system a social structure. All the experiences that occur within the family, including those around health and illness, become anchored or crystallized in material and symbolic components of the family environment and get linked to specific meanings, sometimes leading to unique patterns of reactions to environmental stimuli (Doherty, 1992; Katz & Kahn, 1966). Doherty (1992) called "family appraisal" of the system that by which family members create meanings in and about their environment and act according to these meanings. This system includes the process by which the family attributes meaning to its everyday and long-range experiences, including the challenges health and illness may impose on family members.

So far, we have described some of the processes that shape family patterns of interaction. The family has been presented as a dynamic and adaptive system, a complex set of environmental, psychopolitical, and developmental processes to which the family members attribute specific meanings whether individually or collectively. This family context shapes emergent patterns of family members' interactions and transactions within the home and with the surrounding environment, which can be unique. It is interesting to conceive the focus of health promotion programs as being the dynamic interactions between all these sources of influence and their impact on family health and family health promotion. The next section documents how family processes influence family health and family members' health-related behaviors. Some of these studies deal with the child's socialization process and with features of the physical, sociocultural, and normative environment that make it easier to adopt healthy behaviors and to build support structures to reinforce them. Other studies document the relationship between the family system and health. All these studies help explain how family patterns of interaction within the home and with the external environment help shape the way the family promotes its health.

Family and Health-Related Behaviors

Sallis and Nader's (1988) model of the mechanisms of family influence on health-related behaviors is a good example of a model that links various home contextual processes to the patterns of interactions of family members and, ultimately, to their health-related behaviors. This model offers the most elaborate and integrative way of describing family mechanisms of influence on health behaviors. Based on Bandura's cognitive-social learning theory and on conditioning learning principles, this model integrates the influence of different features of the family environment (structure, organization, roles, and communication patterns), along with family events that either cue behaviors or support them. Central to this model is the concept of modeling influences that trigger learning; reinforce behavior practice, timing, and frequency; and set self-regulating standards for behavior performance. This model also takes into account the influence of developmental stages of the family. External influences from other systems are part of the model, although the mechanisms through which they exert their influence are not explicitly defined.

At the empirical level, many studies have examined how characteristics of the family (physical, normative, and social environments), socialization, and interactional processes are associated with health-related behavior. Social stimuli such as house rules, encouragement from family members, emotional support, and positive and negative reinforcement are among the most powerful determinants of health-related behavior acquisition in children (Sallis & Nader, 1988). Epright, Fox, Fryer, Lamkin, and Vivian (1969) report that parents use food to reward or punish their children. Parents also behave differently depending on children's weight (Waxman & Stunkard, 1980). Klesges and colleagues (Klesges et al., 1983; Klesges, Malott, Boschee, & Weber, 1986) report positive correlations between children's weight and how frequently their parents encourage them to eat. Obese children are three times less likely to receive parental encouragement to be active, as compared with their nonobese brothers and sisters.

Other authors suggest that parental support favors young peoples' participation in sport activities (Overman & Rao, 1981). Influence is exerted also through parents' attitudes toward the adoption of certain behaviors. According to Nolte, Smith, and O'Rourke (1983), the children whose parents disapprove of smoking are five times less likely to become smokers than those whose parents have no objection. Pratt (1973) has demonstrated that family environments that enable children to develop autonomy and a sense of responsibility lead them to adopt healthier lifestyles. This effect was maintained even after controlling for socioeconomic status. In a review of the literature about children's food patterns, Hertzler (1983) reports that families offering a lot of verbal exchanges and emotional support seem to enjoy healthier diets. The influence of socioeconomic status was not, however, clearly documented in this review. Pratt (1976) has also demonstrated that couples characterized by shared decision making, flexible division of tasks, and participation in common activities also have healthier lifestyles, regardless of socioeconomic status. More recently, Harkness and Super (1994) suggested that specific features of the household physical and social settings are associated with health outcomes.

Several studies document the multidirectional nature of family influences on health-related behaviors (Brim, 1968; Hoffman, 1975; Sallis & Nader, 1988). Baranowski's findings reveal that adolescents influence their parents' use of leisure time and the planning of meals. The target of these pressures is more often the mother than the father (Baranowski & Nader, 1985). Parents give in to their children's demands concerning brands of cereal, snacks, and candy (Ward & Wackman, 1972). A review of the literature on school-based prevention campaigns notes the influence young people may exert on their parents (Perry et al., 1989); for example, awakening their interest in sports (Snyder & Purdy, 1982).

Family and Health

Evidence from family and health studies shows that some family environments are more likely to promote the health and health-related behaviors of their members. Families with these environments are notably differentiated by the nature of the processes of socialization and exchanges existing among their members. Different typologies developed in the literature have been linked with health (Fisher & Ransom, 1995; Ransom & Fisher, 1995). These studies show that processes favoring exchanges among members, autonomy, and openness to the outside world are more conducive to health than processes limiting interactions and reinforcing conformity and dependence. It is very likely that those families whose characteristics are more compatible with health would be more open to the information and resources provided by health promotion programs.

In this perspective, the family would be a mediator between health promotion programs and health at the individual level.

Family beliefs, structures, and functioning styles have been associated with several health-related outcomes: compliance with medical regimens (Rissman & Rissman, 1987), frequency of hospitalization (Doane, Falloon, Goldstein, & Mintz, 1985), use of health care facilities (Schor, Starfield, Stidley, & Hanks, 1987), and postillness recovery (Medalie & Goldbourt, 1976). In general, the following variables, reflecting specific patterns of interaction between family members within the home and with their surrounding environment, have received the greatest attention and have demonstrated the most consistent links with family members' poor health: low family cohesion, high family conflict, too rigid or too permeable family boundaries, low levels of family organization, distant or hostile family affiliative tone, critical attitudes, lack of clear communication, and poor spousal support (Fisher, Ransom, Terry, Lipkin, & Weiss, 1992).

A recent research program examined more closely the relationships between family variables and health (Fisher, Nakell, Terry, & Ransom, 1992; Fisher, Ransom, & Terry, 1993a, 1993b; Fisher, Ransom, Terry, & Burge, 1992; Fisher, Ransom, Terry, Lipkin, et al., 1992). In a series of cross-sectional studies with a community-based sample of families, the authors demonstrated associations between three groups of family variables and the personal health and well-being of adult male and female family members (Fisher, Nakell, et al., 1992; Fisher, Ransom, Terry, & Burge, 1992; Fisher, Ransom, Terry, Lipkin, et al., 1992; Ransom, Fisher, & Terry, 1992; Ransom, Locke, Terry, & Fisher, 1992). The first group of variables, "organized cohesiveness," refers to the clarity of the family structure as expressed in roles, rules, and family ties. The second group, "world view," reflects family beliefs and attitudes toward its surrounding world that have been linked with health (Antonovsky, 1979, 1987). The last group, "emotion management," is composed of the couple's emotional interaction around intimacy and conflict issues.

These studies suggest that conflict and avoidance of intimacy are linked to negative health for wives but not for husbands, whereas poorer health in husbands is associated with overt anger and hostility. Other interactions between gender and variables reflecting family relationships with the outside world, intrafamilial issues (differentiated sharing), and health status have also been identified. Differences in health variables were related to mood and self-appraisal for wives and drinking or smoking and work satisfaction and productiveness for husbands. These differences lead the authors to suggest "that the family is not a homogeneous vector that affects husbands and wives in the same way" (Fisher et al., 1993b, p. 80).[1] This view reflects the family system's perspective, suggesting circular and nonlinear effects of family interactions among members and between the members and their environment. Among these effects are merging patterns of family functioning that provide the family system with health-enhancing capabilities or that limit family resources and hamper the family's ability to foster its own health, growth, and development. The next section examines how family health can be defined and explores how the family can function as its own health-promoting agency (Ransom, 1992).

FAMILY HEALTH PROMOTION

Defining Family Health

Family health is a concept that may be used as an attribute of the family as a whole. It is more than just the health of its individual members or the sum of its members' health. Different perspectives can be used to define family health (Doherty, 1992). Family therapists would focus their definition on the presence or absence of psychopathology and family dysfunction (Minuchin, Rosman, & Baker, 1978). Stress theory would put more emphasis on the way families adjust and adapt to different environmental stresses (Hill, 1958; Patterson & Garwick, 1994). Developmental theorists would see as healthy those families that perform normal tasks at the right time of their developmental stage (Duvall, 1977; Steinglass, 1992). Each of these perspectives taken alone cannot account for the complex influences that shape a family's health.

Using specific dimensions of the health concept, Loveland-Cherry (1989) proposed four categories of family health models. The first category is represented by clinical models based on the negative perspective of health as the absence of disease or social dysfunction. The second category emphasizes the positive aspect of health as a resource allowing for the performance of family functions and developmental tasks. The third category stresses the family's ability to adapt and change its structural and functional patterns, allowing it to grow and to evolve along its developmental life cycles. The fourth group of models describes family health as the way the family engages in the "ongoing provision of resources, guidance and support for the realization of family members' maximum well-being and potential throughout the family life span" (p. 14). These resources can be financial, personal (self-esteem, knowledge, skills), familial (communication, cohesion, organization, problem-solving skills) or available in the community (social support, schools, churches, health centers).

This fourth category of model is the most compatible with the generally accepted definitions of health promotion that focus on the enabling process. It is also very much in line with the functional focus on family life we presented in the first section of this chapter. With this model of family health in mind, we now turn to a review of family health promotion models.

Family Health Promotion Models

Different definitions have been developed for family health promotion. In all of them, families are conceptualized as generally proactively seeking health and well-being. Bomar (1990), for example, defines family health promotion as "family behaviors that are undertaken to increase the family's well-being or quality of life" (p. 1). Various efforts have also been made to describe how a family could be health promoting or health damaging. These efforts are illustrated in different typologies of families' internal processes and their relationships with health (Fisher & Ransom, 1995; Pratt, 1976; Reiss, 1981). Pratt's (1976) model of the "energized" family seems to be the most illustrative of how the family system can be health promoting or health damaging.

In the energized family, members have rich and regular interactions, leading to a steady exchange of stimuli and information. Showing a good sense of life mastery, members in this type of family maintain extensive and diversified contacts with different community settings. They are flexible in their family organization. They share power in decision making and they maintain continuous efforts to support family members' health and growth. In terms of health behaviors, these families promote good health habits by sound child-rearing practices that promote autonomy and personal development.

More recently, Berman, Kendall, and Bhattacharyya (1994) introduced an integrating concept, the "household production of health." It is defined as "a dynamic behavioral process through which households combine their (internal) knowledge, resources, and behavioral norms and patterns with available (external) technologies, services, information, and skills to restore, maintain, and promote the health of their members" (p. 206). This concept is derived from recent works in household economics, anthropology, and public health. It implies that health promotion processes in the family have behavioral components. It also states that family health is promoted through the provision and use of internal and external resources.

These models and empirical findings lead to defining family health promotion as an ongoing and adaptive process of production and mobilization of family resources toward family health and well-being. Underlying this definition are the following assumptions:

1. The family as a unit has its own health and illness appraisal system.

2. The family milieu is a learning environment in which health-related beliefs and behaviors are developed.

3. This learning ability allows the family system to adjust and adapt when facing new challenges and stress, taking advantage of past experiences.

4. Family health promotion behaviors are part of more enduring and recurrent patterns of family members' interaction within the home and with their environment that can be health enhancing or health damaging.

5. These behaviors rest on ongoing processes of decision making regarding the import, use, and exchange of resources inside and outside the family system.

6. Families are linked to their environment. They are at the center of a complex web of interactions connecting individual members to other environments. Families are therefore permeable to outside influences through each of the other social systems to which family members belong.

Awareness of these assumptions helps direct attention to relevant views on the family system and its health-related processes, which lead ultimately to its health. These views are the starting point for an effective practice of health promotion within the family. We have seen that the family system can be conceived of as a milieu that integrates a myriad of influences on health and health-related behaviors. Within the family, genetic, biological, behavioral, developmental, and social factors are at play, along with external influences such as those of the social, economic, and political environments. This view calls for an integrative theoretical perspective for examining the interactions between the family system and health promotion programs.

AN INTEGRATIVE VIEW OF HEALTH PROMOTION AND THE FAMILY

Green and Raeburn (1990) proposed enablement and community as two integrative concepts for health promotion actions. In this perspective, the health promotion process fosters both individual and group autonomy. The effectiveness and sustainability of this process presupposes continued transactions among individuals, the social networks and the groups to which they belong, and health promotion programs. According to systems theory, these transactions consist of a modulated exchange of information and energy, allowing for the continuing development of community, family, and individual aptitudes (Klein, 1991). Thus, health promotion programs conceptualized as social systems generate actions to influence or redirect the distribution of health-related information and other resources within the community.

Richard, Potvin, Kishchuk, Prlic, and Green (1996) have defined two categories of relationships that a program can establish with its targets: a direct action aimed at transforming one or many aspects of a given target, be it an individual, an organization, or a community, and the creation of conditions that facilitate networking among two or many targets. Taking the family as a unit of intervention, health promotion programs could act according to any of the following three strategies: (a) directly target family members within their homes (mostly through health education and information transfer aimed at increasing knowledge or improving practical health skills); (b) bring about changes in the social and community contexts that would in turn affect the family (e.g., changes in influential decision makers regarding social policies that have a bearing on the family); (c) help create and/or strengthen the links between the family system and other social systems (school, day care, neighborhood, worksite, etc.); these links would improve the family's access to necessary resources to promote and sustain its health. In the last two strategies, health promotion interventions would more indirectly reach their target by increasing the social and family environments' capacity to sustain healthy development.

Programs of the first type directly target behavior changes at the individual level. Mass media campaigns and training sessions are examples of such programs. They will be referred to in the following section as behavioral approaches. They fit more into the traditional health education model emphasizing intrapersonal factors. Most training sessions have the advantage of targeting specific members in the family, although their effect may be mitigated by high dropout rates and low attendance (e.g., Farris, Frank, Webber, & Berenson, 1985).

The second type of program would be part of a social and structural strategy that seeks change in the social and community contexts. Health promotion actions generated according to this strategy would be based on the ecological model of health promotion in which health is partly determined by the components of the individual's ecosystem (family, community, culture, and physical and social environment) (WHO, 1986). In order to promote health, this ecosystem must procure economic and social conditions compatible with health and healthy lifestyle. For example, air pollution must be kept to a minimum level and housing must fulfill the requirements offering warm and safe shelter. These environments must also provide information and life skills so that people can make decisions that may sustain health. Finally, healthy choices among goods and services offered must be available (Kickbusch, 1986; WHO, 1984).

Interventions based on the social and structural strategy would be composed of a set of actions that increase the availability of healthful resources in the family environment. As family health promotion processes provide for a continued provision of resources and support leading to individual members' well-being throughout their lives, the concept of enabling appears as an integrating junction between health promotion programs and the family. In this view, the family becomes a necessary participant and contributor to health promotion processes. In this context, social and family policies would seek to complement family health promotion processes by increasing the access of families to healthful resources and improving the educational and economic positioning of the family. These policies would enhance the socialization and developmental processes in which the family acts as a powerful participant.

Programs of the third type involve networking. We view networking as a strategy that seeks the creation or reinforcement of the links between the family and different systems that bear a direct or indirect influence on family members. This view parallels that of Bronfenbrenner (1986) on the potential influence of mesosystems, defined as links between different settings, relating the family to different social contexts such as the school or day care, the worksite, and so on. These links may be represented by the social interactions between settings or by the attitudes and expectations that the occupants of the settings have about each other. In an extensive review of research on the influence of external environments on family functioning, Bronfenbrenner (1986) stresses, for example, the importance for child development of the nature and strength of the linkages between the family and its surrounding settings. It has been shown also that the strength and diversity of the links between these different social contexts or microsystems increase their influence on the individuals involved (Bronfenbrenner, 1986; Tietjen, 1989). The links between microsystems provide adequate feedback, information, and other resources to the family. These links would function as vehicles for the empowerment of families, increasing their capacity to extract and use the health promoting resources in their environment.

Figure 2.1 lays out the different components of what we view as the social context of family health. This view draws attention to the patterns of interaction and interdependency between different components of the family system and its environment. Strategies targeting the behavior of an individual home member would seek to influence the home and family contextual processes (e.g., family cognitive processes and home environmental processes) by modifying family members' perceptions and skills. Strategies aimed at increasing the social network of the family would take into account the bidirectional influence between the family members' patterns of interaction within the home and with their environment. These strategies would also take advantage of the network of relationships in which each individual member is involved in multiple microsystems (school, worksite, community organizations, etc.), thus improving the family's access to various resources. Health promotion actions targeting the individuals in these social systems would be channeled to the family through the individuals involved. Finally, strategies aimed at the general social and structural contexts would improve the environmental conditions and processes that converge to produce family and individual well-being (Zimmerman, 1992). In the next section, we review some of the implications and available evidence that may fit into these three strategies.

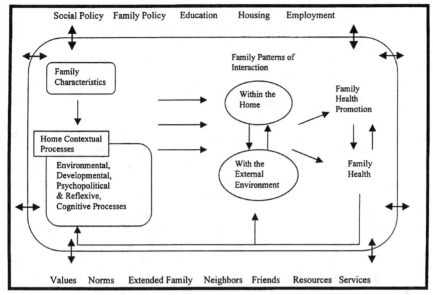

Figure 2.1. Social Context of Family Health

HEALTH PROMOTION PROGRAMS FOR THE FAMILY

Behavioral Approaches

Most health promotion interventions that link health promotion to the family are designed on the assumption that the family system is a learning environment. Studies consistently show that the application of behavioral approaches is feasible and effective in producing health-related changes in family members, mostly through informational input or actions directed to different family processes and contexts, such as family patterns of interaction within the home (e.g., communication patterns) or the normative and belief context of the family (family paradigm and related cognitive processes).

Health promotion interventions in the family provide interesting evidence for a comprehensive effect of the family system on the health of its members. This effect can be drawn from studies that show some level of "aggregation" (similarity) of health-related behaviors among family members after health promotion intervention. Patterson et al. (1989) have shown that interventions targeting physical activity and dietary behaviors can lead to changes within the same family in the frequency and intensity of physical activity among members and in dietary fat and sodium consumption. The change was more strongly related among members within the same generation. The concept of aggregation is indicative of the influence of the family as a unit on health and suggests circular effects of the interaction between members.

Modeling processes have been suggested to explain these aggregated changes (Sallis & Nader, 1988). Once one family member initiates a change, others might follow and, in turn, influence and reinforce the change initiator. Other explanations might involve the changes in the opportunity structure of the home. A study by Shattuck, White, and Kristal (1992) provides evidence that elements of the family environment that are specific to low-fat diet are amenable to change following efforts by one family member to change his or her own behavior. Husbands whose wives were involved in a health trial changed their eating patterns compared with husbands whose wives were in the control group. However, their own attitudes and knowledge toward food were not correlated with their fat intake. The authors hypothesize that because of changes in food availability in the house and modifications in the norms regarding eating habits within the family (as illustrated by the women's changes in attitude), husbands who were not directly involved in the experiment passively changed their diet in response to changes in features of their family environment. It appears that in this case, these changes were reinforced by the fact that the wives were primarily responsible for food purchase and preparation.

Social and Structural Strategies

Action on the general community and social context would lead to the improvement of the community's opportunity structure, which emerges from the interaction of the physical, economic, social, and temporal patterning of community life and functioning. Part of this patterning is driven by broad social, economic, and cultural processes and structures that lead to an inequitable distribution of basic necessities, such as the housing stock, food, and sanitation (Ransom, 1991; Smith, 1991). Concerted social and political actions aimed at improving the family's educational and economic positioning in the social system, as well as the family's capacity to function effectively, should take into account this patterning, on the one hand, and the sustained changes and instability in the family's structure that characterize most of our Western societies, on the other. As Schor and Menaghan (1995) suggest, the latter changes should be mirrored by equivalent changes in the social institutions that influence the functioning of home members. This calls for a complete rethinking of the role of community and social institutions in the day-to-day functioning of the home.

Networking Strategies

Actions targeting a change in individual behavior call for combined actions on multiple sites, including the family. Strategies involving behavior change are usually intensive and resource consuming. They include the acquisition or improvement of specific behavior skills and family social support enhancement and, therefore, the involvement of many family members. Education and information transfer to other family members influences the individual's cognitive and belief system, thus enhancing the effectiveness of health promotion programs.

On a more empirical level, it was suggested, for example, by Sallis and McKenzie (1991) that, for better effectiveness, parents should be involved in school-based programs. This involvement is feasible, but careful attention should be paid to the method used to ensure parents' participation. Behavioral training or counseling of parents have been found effective in producing dietary changes in children and their family members (Nader et al., 1983) and in improving weight status in overweight children (Israel, Stolmaker, & Andrian, 1985). Epstein, Wing, Koeske, and Valoski (1987) showed greater weight reduction and maintenance in overweight children in a program involving both children and their parents, compared to programs in which only the child was the target or where there was no specific target. Studies of family-based interventions for high cardiovascular risk populations show also that classes or evening sessions for parents do enhance the intervention's effectiveness, despite high dropout rates and low attendance (Farris et al., 1985).

Another way to insure parents' involvement was through some form of systematic linkage (newsletter, mail, written material sent home, etc.) between the school and the home setting. These linkages were part of the program, and through them, parents were provided with the necessary knowledge and resources that could help them support their children's efforts to implement healthy behaviors. Evaluation of the Minnesota Heart Health Program school-based interventions showed that parents were mostly influenced through (a) written information brought home by the child, (b) child-initiated discussions with a parent about health issues and intervention-related content, and (c) belief among parents in their child's ability to make healthy decisions (Crockett, 1987).

Interventions targeting smoking in schoolchildren that involved other family members significantly improved children's attitudes and knowledge about smoking (Bonaguro & Bonaguro, 1989; Nader et al., 1996). In interventions targeting weight reduction in obese children, percentage of excess weight loss is significantly higher (and may last up to 5 years) in children whose parents were involved in the program, compared with those whose parents were not. In some cases, parents also lost weight. This loss was highly correlated to their children's weight loss (Epstein et al., 1987; Kirschenbaum, Harris, & Tomarken, 1984).

The provision of linkages between the family and other settings and their impact on children's behavior and development has been explored in a few studies. In the case of the school-based programs, some studies have explored the effects of involving parents and of fostering interactions between family and classroom processes on children's attitudes and scholastic achievement. Children from families or schools that encourage communication and autonomy in decision making show greater independence and school achievement. Noteworthy is the finding that the influence of the family was greater than that of the school. Moreover, the effects of family and school processes on school achievement were greater than those of socioeconomic status or race (Bronfenbrenner, 1986).

More effort should, then, be invested in improving the techniques allowing for informed and genuine involvement by family members in health promotion programs (e.g., through television, written media, etc.). However, it is of utmost importance to explore family health promotion processes in conjunction with those that are triggered in the general social and community context, which may include those of health promotion programs occurring in other settings. Better outcomes can be expected from a concerted effort to act on family patterns of communication, family beliefs, and family values, along with the provision of environmental cues to facilitate practice of the targeted change inside and outside the home. This calls for action to be implemented on the norms and the family environment and implies that interventions aimed at the more general environment should occur through healthy public and family policies.

CONCLUSION

In some ways, the family system can be compared to an ecological social system that "organizes" the influence of health and illness factors (Akamatsu, 1992). The influence of genetic constraints and developmental and socialization processes are subsumed in this ecosystem, which in turn integrates external economic, cultural, and political influences. Among these influences could be those of health promotion programs, which are expected to tap into multiple mechanisms and processes and trigger multiple outcomes. This chapter has provided some rationale for an integrative approach to health promotion in the family through the concept of "enabling." The enabling approach leads to the concept of providing power, technology, knowledge, skills, and other resources to individuals, families, and whole populations (Green & Raeburn, 1990). In this context, empowerment of communities would be used to foster empowerment of families, which is the most immediate and private system of influence on the individual. The provision of needed resources to the family or reinforcement of the family's own resources is a matter of creating or strengthening the linkages between the family system and other settings (school, worksite, health care system, etc.). Strengthening these linkages would result in increasing the degree of social embeddedness and integration of the family. In an ecological and integrative approach to health promotion in the family, health professionals would also advocate for economic and social conditions compatible with healthy families. Given their integrative influence, horizontal packages seem more appropriate for meeting family needs in diverse areas such as housing, education, development, and health. These packages would be part of the family's opportunity structure, shaping and guiding family members' interactions and behaviors toward their own well-being.

Some gaps in knowledge remain to be filled. Because they call for mixed and complex methodologies, family internal and external transactions and exchanges in natural settings are still poorly documented. They nevertheless hold fruitful prospects for a better understanding of resource exchanges and their differential distribution among family members. Only a few studies have explored the effects on family members of family linkages with their surrounding environment. There is also a need to categorize families according to their health promotion capacities and activities. Focusing on resource mobilization, health promotion programs would gain from a better categorization of family resources as they evolve over time. There is also a need in this context for health promotion programs to consider the family interactions and behaviors by which the members actualize and develop their own potential. Despite these gaps in knowledge, involving the family in any health promotion action appears an increasingly successful avenue.

NOTE

1. The authors interpret the differences and similarities in family correlates of husbands' and wives' health in the context of gender-related marital roles and role expectations.

REFERENCES

Akamatsu, T. J. (1992). Family health psychology: Defining a new subdiscipline. In T. J. Akamatsu, M. A. P. Stephens, S. E. Hofboll, & J. H. Crowther (Eds.), *Family health psychology* (pp. 239-250). Washington, DC: Hemisphere.

Ammerman, R. T. (1990). Etiological models of child maltreatment. *Behavior Modification, 14,* 230-254.

Antonovsky, A. (1979). *Health, stress, and coping: New perspectives on mental and physical well-being.* San Francisco: Jossey-Bass.

Antonovsky, A. (1987). *Unraveling the mystery of health: How people manage stress and stay well.* San Francisco: Jossey-Bass.

Baranowski, T., & Nader, P. R. (1985). Family health behaviour. In D. C. Turk & R. C. Kerns (Eds.), *Health, illness and families* (pp. 51-80). New York: Wiley-Interscience.

Beavers, W. R. (1982). Healthy, midrange, and severely dysfunctional families. In F. Walsh (Ed.), *Normal family processes* (pp. 45-66). New York: Guilford.

Berman, P., Kendall, C., & Bhattacharyya, K. (1994). The household production of health: Integrating social science perspectives on microlevel health determinants. *Social Science and Medicine, 38,* 205-215.

Bomar, P. J. (1990). Perspectives on family health promotion. *Family and Community Health, 12*(4), 1-11.

Bonaguro, E. W., & Bonaguro, J. A. (1989). Tobacco use among adolescents: Directions for research. *American Journal of Health Promotion, 4*(1), 37-41.

Brim, O. (1968). *Adult socialization: Socialization and society.* Boston: Little, Brown.

Broderick, C. B. (1993). *Understanding family process: Basics of family systems theory.* Newbury Park, CA: Sage.

Bronfenbrenner, U. (1986). Ecology of the family as a context for human development: Research perspectives. *Developmental Psychology, 22*(6), 723-742.

Brown, C. (1981). Mothers, fathers, and children: From private to public patriarchy. In L. Sargent (Ed.), *Women and revolution* (pp. 239-267). New York: South End.

Carter, E. A., & McGoldrick, M. (1980). The family life cycle and family therapy: An overview. In E. A. Carter & M. McGoldrick (Eds.), *The family life cycle.* New York: Gardner.

Combrinck-Graham, L. (1985). A developmental model for family systems. *Family Process, 24*(2), 139-150.

Crockett, S. J. (1987). The family team approach to fitness: A proposal. *Public Health Reports, 102*(5), 546-551.

Curran, D. (1983). *Traits of a healthy family.* Minneapolis, MN: Winston.

Doane, J. A., Falloon, I. R. H., Goldstein, M. J., & Mintz, J. (1985). Parental affective style and treatment of schizophrenia: Predicting course of illness and social functioning. *Archives of General Psychiatry, 42,* 34-42.

Doherty, W. J. (1992). Linkages between family theories and primary health care. In R. J. Sawa (Ed.), *Family health care* (pp. 30-39). Newbury Park, CA: Sage.

Duvall, E. M. (1977). *Marriage and family development.* Philadelphia: Lippincott.

Epright, E., Fox, H., Fryer, B., Lamkin, G., & Vivian, N. (1969). Eating behaviour of pre-school children. *Journal of Nutrition Education, 1,* 16-19.

Epstein, L. H., Wing, R. R., Koeske, R., & Valoski, A. (1987). Long-term effects of family-based treatment of childhood obesity. *Journal of Consulting and Clinical Psychology, 55,* 91-95.

Farris, R. P., Frank, G. C., Webber, L. S., & Berenson, G. S. (1985). A nutrition curriculum for families with high blood pressure. *Journal of School Health, 55,* 110-111.

Fisher, L., Nakell, L., Terry, H. E., & Ransom, D. C. (1992). The California Family Health Project: III. Couple emotion management and adult health. *Family Process, 31,* 269-288.

Fisher, L., & Ransom, D. C. (1995). An empirically derived typology of families: I. Relationships with adult health. *Family Process, 34,* 161-182.

Fisher, L., Ransom, D. C., & Terry, H. L. (1993a). The California Family Health Project: VI. Multidomain analyses. *Family Process, 32,* 49-68.

Fisher, L., Ransom, D. C., & Terry, H. L. (1993b). The California Family Health Project: VII. Summary and integration of findings. *Family Process, 32,* 69-86.

Fisher, L., Ransom, D. C., Terry, H. E., & Burge, S. (1992). The California Family Health Project: VI. Family structure/organization and adult health. *Family Process, 31,* 399-420.

Fisher, L., Ransom, D. C., Terry, H. E., Lipkin, M., & Weiss, R. (1992). The California Family Health Project: I. Introduction and a description of adult health. *Family Process, 31,* 231-250.

Fox, B. J., & Luxton, M. (1993). Conceptualising the family. In B. J. Fox (Ed.), *Family patterns, gender relations* (pp. 19-30). Don Mills, ON: Oxford University Press.

Gochman, D. S. (1992). Health cognitions in families. In T. J. Akamatsu, M. A. P. Stephens, S. E. Hofboll, & J. H. Crowther (Eds.), *Family health psychology* (pp. 23-39). Washington, DC: Hemisphere.

Green, L. W., & Kreuter, M. W. (1999). *Health promotion planning: An educational and environmental approach* (3rd ed.). Mountain View, CA: Mayfield.

Green, L. W., & Raeburn, J. (1990). Contemporary developments in health promotion: Definitions and challenges. In N. Bracht (Ed.), *Health promotion at the community level* (pp. 29-44). Newbury Park, CA: Sage.

Harkness, S., & Super, C. M. (1994). The developmental niche: A theoretical framework for analyzing the household production of health. *Social Science and Medicine, 38,* 217-226.

Hertzler, A. A. (1983). Children's food patterns: A review II, family and group behavior. *Journal of the American Dietetic Association, 83*(5), 555-560.

Hill, R. (1958). Generic features of families under stress. *Social Casework, 39,* 139-159.

Hoffman, M. L. (1975). Moral internalization, parental power and the nature of parent-child interaction. *Developmental Psychology, 11,* 228-239.

Israel, A. C., Stolmaker, L., & Andrian, C. A. G. (1985). The effects of training parents in general child management skills on a behavioral weight loss program for children. *Behavior Therapy, 16,* 169-180.

Katz, D., & Kahn, R. L. (1966). *The social psychology of organization.* New York: John Wiley.

Kickbusch, I. (1986). Health promotion: A global perspective. *Canadian Journal of Public Health, 77,* 321-326.

Kirschenbaum, D. S., Harris, E. S., & Tomarken, A. J. (1984). Effects of parental involvement in behavioral weight loss therapy for preadolescents. *Behavior Therapy, 15,* 485-500.

Klein, J. I. (1991). A theory of partial systems: Implications for organizational effectiveness. *Behavioral Science, 36,* 224-236.

Klesges, R. C., Coates, T. J., Brown, G., Sturgeon-Tillisch, J., Moldenhauer-Klesges, L. M., Holzer, B., Wollfry, J., & Vollmer, J. (1983). Parental influences on children's eating behavior and relative weight. *Journal of Applied Behavior Analysis, 16,* 371-378.

Klesges, R. C., Malott, J. M., Boschee, P. F., & Weber, J. M. (1986). The effects of parental influences on children's food intake, physical activity and relative weight: An extension and replication. *International Journal of Obesity, 5,* 335-346.

Lewis, J. (1979). *How's your family? A guide to identifying your family's strengths and weaknesses.* New York: Brunner/Mazel.

Loveland-Cherry, C. G. (1989). Family health promotion and protection. In P. J. Bomar (Ed.), *Nurses and family health promotion: Concepts, assessments and interventions.* Baltimore, MD: Williams & Wilkins.

Medalie, J. H., & Goldbourt, U. (1976). Psychosocial and other risk factors as evidenced by a multivariate analysis of a five year incidence study. *American Journal of Medicine, 20,* 910-921.

Minuchin, S., Rosman, B. L., & Baker, L. (1978). *Psychosomatic families: Anorexia nervosa in context.* Cambridge, MA: Harvard University Press.

Nader, P. R., Baranowski, T., Vanderpool, N. A., Dunn, K., Dworkin, R., & Ray, L. (1983). The family health project: Cardiovascular risk reduction for children and parents. *Developmental and Behavioural Paediatrics, 4,* 3-10.

Nader, P. R., Sellers, D. E., Johnson, C. C., Perry, C. L., Stone, E. J., Cook, K. C., Bebchuk, J., & Luepker, R. V. (1996). The effect of adult participation in a school-based family intervention to improve children's diet and physical activity: The child and adolescent trial for cardiovascular health. *Preventive Medicine, 25,* 455-464.

Nolte, A. E., Smith, B. J., & O'Rourke, T. (1983). The relative influence on health beliefs, parental and peer behaviors upon youth smoking behavior. *Journal of School Health, 53,* 264-271.

Overman, S. J., & Rao, V. V. (1981). Motivation for an extent of participation in organized sports by high school seniors. *Research Quarterly for Exercise and Sport, 55*(2), 228-237.

Patterson, J. M., & Garwick, A. W. (1994). The impact of chronic illness on families: A family systems perspective. *Annals of Behavioral Medicine, 16*(2), 131-142.

Patterson, T. L., Sallis, J. F., Nader, P. R., Kaplan, R. M., Rupp, J. W., Atkins, C. J., & Senn, K. L. (1989). Familial similarities of changes in cognitive, behavioral, and physiological variables in a cardiovascular health promotion program. *Journal of Pediatric Psychology, 14*(2), 277-292.

Perkins, D. V., Burns, T. F., Perry, J. C., & Nielsen, K. P. (1988). Behavior setting theory and community psychology: An analysis and critique. *Journal of Community Psychology, 16,* 355-372.

Perry, C. L., Luepker, R. V., Murray, D. M., Hearn, M. D., Halper, A., Dudovitz, B., Maile, M. C., & Smyth, M. (1989). Parent involvement with children's health promotion: A one year follow-up of the Minnesota Home Team. *Health Education Quarterly, 16*(2), 171-180.

Pratt, L. (1973). Child rearing methods and children's health behavior. *Journal of Health and Social Behavior, 14,* 61-69.

Pratt, L. (1976). *Family structure and effective health behavior: The energized family.* Boston: Houghton-Mifflin.

Ransom, D. C. (1992). New directions in the methodology of family-centered health-care research. In R. J. Sawa (Ed.), *Family health care.* Newbury Park, CA: Sage.

Ransom, D. C., & Fisher, L. (1995). An empirically derived typology of families: II. Relationships with adolescent health. *Family Process, 34,* 183-197.

Ransom, D. C., Fisher, L., & Terry, H. E. (1992). The California Family Health Project: II. Family world view and adult health. *Family Process, 31,* 251-267.

Ransom, D. C., Locke, E., Terry, H. E., & Fisher, L. (1992). The California Family Health Project: V. Family problem solving and adult health. *Family Process, 31,* 421-432.

Ransom, R. (1991). *Healthy housing: A practical guide.* London: E. & F. N. Spon.

Reiss, D. (1981). *The family's construction of reality.* Cambridge, MA: Harvard University Press.

Reiss, D., & De-Nour, A. K. (1989). The family and medical team in chronic illness: A transactional and developmental perspective. In C. N. Ramsey (Ed.), *Family systems in medicine.* New York: Guilford.

Richard, L., Potvin, L., Kishchuk, N., Prlic, H., & Green, L. W. (1996). Assessment of the integration of the ecological approach in health promotion programs. *American Journal of Health Promotion, 10,* 318-328.

Rissman, R., & Rissman, B. Z. (1987). Compliance: A review. *Family Systems Medicine, 5,* 446-467.

Sallis, J. F., & McKenzie, T. L. (1991). Physical education's role in public health. *Research Quarterly for Exercise and Sport, 62,* 124-137.

Sallis, J. F., & Nader, P. R. (1988). Family determinants of health behaviors. In D. S. Gochman (Ed.). *Health behavior: Emerging research perspectives* (pp. 107-124). New York: Plenum.

Schor, E. L., & Menaghan, E. G. (1995). Family pathways to child health. In B. C. Annick III, S. Levine, A. R. Tarlov, & D. C. Walsh (Eds.), *Society and health* (pp. 18-45). New York: Oxford University Press.

Schor, E. L., Starfield, B., Stidley, C., & Hanks, J. (1987). Family health: Utilization and the effects of family membership. *Medical Care, 25,* 616-626.

Shattuck, A. L., White, E., & Kristal, A. B. (1992). How women's adopted low-fat diets affect their husbands. *American Journal of Public Health, 82,* 1244-1250.

Smith, S. J. (1991). Housing opportunities for people with health needs: An overview. In S. J. Smith, R. Knill-Jones, & A. McGuckin (Eds.), *Housing for health* (pp. 61-72). Harlow, Essex: Longman.

Snyder, E. E., & Purdy, D. A. (1982). Socialization in sport: Parent and child reverse and reciprocal effects. *Research Quarterly for Exercise and Sport, 52*, 263-266.

Steen, S., & Schwartz, P. (1995). Communication, gender, and power: Homosexual couples as a case study. In M. A. Fitzpatrick & A. L. Vangelisti (Eds.), *Explaining family interactions* (pp. 310-343). Newbury Park, CA: Sage.

Steinglass, P. (1992). Family systems theory and medical illness. In R. J. Sawa (Ed.), *Family health care* (pp. 18-29). Newbury Park, CA: Sage.

Syme, S. L. (1986). Strategies for health promotion. *Preventive Medicine, 15*, 492-507.

Tietjen, A. M. (1989). The ecology of children's social support networks. In D. Belle (Ed.), *Children's social networks and social supports* (pp. 37-69). New York: John Wiley.

Ward, S., & Wackman, D. (1972). Television advertising and intra-family influences on children's purchase, influence attempts and parental yielding. *Journal of Marketing Research, 9*, 316-319.

Waxman, M., & Stunkard, A. J. (1980). Calorie intake and expenditure of obese boys. *Journal of Pediatrics, 96*, 187-193.

Wolin, S. J., & Bennett, L. A. (1984). Family rituals. *Family Process, 23*, 401-420.

World Health Organization, WHO Regional Bureau for Europe. (1984). *Health promotion: A discussion document on the concepts and principles.* Copenhagen: Author.

World Health Organization. (1986). Ottawa charter for health promotion. *Health Promotion, 1*(4), iii-v.

Zimmerman, S. L. (1992). *Family policies and family well-being: The role of political culture.* Newbury Park, CA: Sage.

COMMENTARY

Lawrence Fisher

Soubhi and Potvin present a cogent argument for considering the family as a central focus for health promotion. Buttressed by well-constructed research, their point of view is based on four primary propositions. First, they understand that the family serves an integrating function, processing the input from other socioenvironmental settings into a form that is personally meaningful and coherent for family members. Second, they describe the family as a system, with its own mechanisms for responding to environmental input and its own structures for managing its past, present, and future. Third, they emphasize the need to study the interface between the family as a group and community-based programs of health promotion. Fourth, they suggest that strategies of health promotion that employ several components simultaneously, such as the family, are more likely to succeed than strategies that employ only one at a time.

These propositions are appealing in several ways, especially because they tie a consideration of the family in health promotion to similar considerations that have been undertaken in primary care (Doherty & Baird, 1983), chronic disease (Cole & Reiss, 1993), and general health (Fisher, Ransom, Terry, Lipkin, & Weiss, 1992; Fisher, Terry, & Ransom, 1990). That is, they bring to the literature on health promotion, and to the designers of programs of health promotion, a perspective that is gaining acceptance in other segments of the health care arena.

I would like to expand on Soubhi and Potvin's arguments both conceptually and practically. I do this because I believe that although these authors provide an articulate presentation of the principles of a family-centered perspective on health, there are sufficient data now available to suggest that we may go even further than they suggest in considering the role of the family in programs of health promotion. In other words, I would like to suggest that we take Soubhi and Potvin's position as a major point of reference and then build on it to construct a view of the family that can be used to direct a strategy for intervention. Following, I address issues of definition and application in separate sections and end with a brief concluding statement.

DEFINING THE FAMILY AS CONTEXT

Let me begin by defining what I mean by *family,* as this word has so many meanings and is so easily misused and confused. At its simplest, I have adopted Ransom and Vandervoort's (1973) phrase that the "family is a group of intimates with a history and a future." This simply phrased definition need not submerge us into an endless sociological and political morass charged with biased stereotypes because it does not assume a preconceived family configuration or form. It simply assumes three characteristics of relationships: they persist over time, they are emotionally intense, and they involve high levels of personal intimacy. These conditions set the family apart from other forms of social relationships that have traditionally been viewed as vehicles of *social support,* a term that I have found difficult to define and specify and have therefore elected not to use. These three characteristics identify the family as a powerful set of ongoing psychosocial ties that, as Soubhi and Potvin suggest, create a pattern of structured social relationships that go beyond the individuals who maintain them. In doing so, these individuals, these family members, create a shared social reality that defines a way of living and being in the world that has definitive links with health and well-being (Doherty & Campbell, 1988). More than any other social unit, families develop characteristic methods for solving problems, approaching conflicts, responding to emotions, interpreting culture, and staking a claim, overtly or covertly, to a shared sense of the world that evolves over time. It is this shared sense of continuity and meaning that holds the greatest import for health and health care because it suggests that families create, over time, the context for defining, learning about, and responding to issues of health.

If one adopts this description of family as useful, and I suggest that a consideration of one's own family during a health crisis might add personal meaning to this description, then two interrelated points emerge, points that Soubhi and Potvin allude to but do not elaborate.

First, in this context it makes little sense to distinguish between the individual and the family. Ransom (1987) puts the case well, although somewhat formally:

> Although neither can be reduced to the other, in the world of human interaction, an ontological unity exists between the state (or process) of a family and the states (or processes) of its members. That is to say, what the individual is doing, along with any processes that can be identified with or used to describe that individual (psychological or physical), and what the relevant family is doing, along with any processes that can be ascribed to the family, are occurring simultaneously as an unbroken unity of action or process in the world. (p. 383)

In other words, a family-centered approach suggests that the individual, in the context of health, may best be understood within the seamless context of the family. A 50-year-old woman's inability to reduce her obesity and hypertension needs to be viewed alongside her 55-year-old husband's depression and her 30-year-old son's chronic unemployment. All three family members revolve around a common history and reality "that organizes a pattern of finely tuned role relationships" (Ransom, 1992, p. 76). Interventions that affect one affect all, and the shared perceptions and resistances to change that pervade the family system need to be considered carefully as part of a program of health-related interventions that include primary, secondary, and tertiary prevention.

Second, there is little question that the positive, health-related coping strategies of individual family members are often thwarted by the press of opposing family group forces (Fisher & Ransom, 1990). I do not suggest that research on personal health-related behavior is unnecessary; rather, I suggest that a context for observing and understanding behavior must be included both in the research enterprise and in the strategy of intervention. For example, an individual's desire to seek consultation from experts regarding a health-related concern may receive censure from family members who view the world as essentially hostile and adopt the stance that the family alone handles the problems of its members, the so-called fortress family (Reiss, 1981). Furthermore, an individual's actions to seek aid in the community for a health issue can be countered by a family ethic of "pulling oneself up by the bootstraps." These family ethics contradict some forms of personal health behavior. The confluence of these personal and contextual forces must be viewed in perspective and taken as a whole. Deciding where the individual stops and the family begins is fruitless; considering both at the same time is essential.

This elaborated family-centered view adopts a position of social context and meaning that widens the lens for viewing the health-related behaviors of individuals. I do not view the family as one of several social institutions (e.g., work, school, church, community group) that may be selected as starting points for programs of health promotion. Such an approach suggests that, although each is unique, each provides equivalent access to the individual. That is, one can select one setting or another depending on ease, availability, program content, and so on. A family-centered approach, in contrast, suggests that the individual-family dialectic is always the central target but that it can be approached directly or through any one of a number of community institutions. This approach places the family above other community, educational, religious, social, and work settings in terms of framing the process of health promotion as it relates to behavioral change. A family-centered approach begins with the family as the overarching organizational unit that defines and directs the health behavior of its members. This perspective suggests that other settings are only points of intersection with this ongoing, emotionally powerful, and interpersonally intimate social unit.

CREATING A FAMILY-BASED STRATEGY OF INTERVENTION

Soubhi and Potvin list three ways in which a family-centered perspective might be applied to programs of health promotion. They suggest taking account of (a) the family's life stage, (b) the unique interactions that occur between families and the community, and (c) the internal characteristics of families that have been linked to health in previous research. With these as starting points, I again expand on Soubhi and Potvin's point of view by suggesting several additional ways that a family-centered perspective can be applied to programs of health promotion. These suggestions are based on the recent family and health intervention research (Campbell & Patterson, 1995).

One Size Does Not Fit All

Program developers must continue to recognize the enormous variety of family lifestyles in the community. Even within the stereotypic, but increasingly rare, two-adult-and-two-child family setting, the ways families construct themselves vary considerably even within the same cultural and socioeconomic community. Data from the California Family Health Project are noteworthy in this regard (Fisher, Ransom, & Terry, 1993; Fisher et al., 1992). This longitudinal, community-based study documented how patterns of family characteristics were related to the health and well-being of family members. We recruited 225 heterosexual adult couples, each with at least one adolescent offspring, from a Central California community. Each family underwent an intensive, 12-hour family assessment and completed a battery of self-report health and functional status instruments. We followed these families for 6 years and reassessed each member on the same health and well-being instruments over time. Intensive multivariate analyses produced a profile of family variables that were consistently related to adult health and well-being scores. Eleven tables and variable composites were created that summarized these scores, and we ran a series of cluster analyses to identify distinct family types that best described the data (Fisher & Ransom, 1995; Ransom & Fisher, 1995). Analyses revealed four replicated family types that we labeled *Balanced, Traditional, Distant,* and *Emotionally Strained.* The first two included families with relatively healthy family members, whereas the latter two included families with relatively distressed members who reported high numbers of emotional and somatic symptoms. We therefore found two types of relatively healthy families and two types of relatively unhealthy families. Of considerable interest was our finding that these family types not only distinguished the health and well-being of the adult family members, whose family appraisals were included in the original family profile, but also distinguished the health and well-being of the adolescents in these families, who made minimal contributions to the original family profile. The family types were related to the health and well-being of all members of the family.

The Balanced and Traditional families, the two well-functioning family types that made up 65% of this community sample, for example, reflected very different ways of "being in the world." Balanced families were open to new information, were highly flexible, had permeable family boundaries, engaged in life actively, were moderately cohesive, were moderate risk takers, and preferred variety to constancy. Traditional families were inwardly focused, highly cohesive, and practiced traditional gender-based roles; they were well organized, followed a high number of rituals and routines, and were above sample average on religiousness. These are two quite different types of families that suggest very different family patterns of responding to and processing input provided by programs of health promotion. For example, a general community-oriented strategy might work well for Balanced families, who take in and evaluate new materials easily as part of their engagement in the world. A similar strategy for Traditional families probably would not work as well. Entrance to Traditional families might best be established through highly identified community groups such as trusted religious and fraternal organizations. Thus, differences among families need to be rec-

ognized, and programs need to be designed to address the significant variations that occur among families in the targeted communities.

Reframing the Intervention

A visit to a primary care setting provides sobering evidence of the difficulty of changing many health-related behaviors. Changes in diet, exercise,
smoking, and substance use are hard to affect clinically, and immediate results often are not maintained over time. Family routines are often tied to
these behaviors, and changes are frequently met with subtle family resistance, even though most family members recognize the importance of behavior change. Furthermore, values placed on exercise and body weight are
often dictated by prevailing culture and modified by family culture so that
weight reduction, for example, assumes much more than a simple reduction
of food intake; it is configured around a profound construction of meaning
and experience. Indirect approaches to behavior change that account for
the meaning of behavior within the context of the family have been applied
to several clinical problems (Rissman & Rissman, 1987). Once it is recognized that health information and social pressure alone are not guarantees
of successful behavioral change for many family members over time, indirect methods of intervention that redefine the goals and meanings of the behavior within an accepted family context are sometimes useful. For example, a discussion of physical exercise can be taken out of the context of
physical activity and cast in social, relational, or institutional terms that are
relevant to the family and its culture and targeted to specific family groups.
This indirect route acknowledges the rigidity of changing ingrained family
patterns and, by reframing the meaning and goals of the health promotion
intervention, seeks to side-step a direct assault on these well-supported family beliefs and routines.

Address Interventions to Relationships, Not Individuals

Because most health-related behavior occu s within the family setting, a
change in health behavior by one family member has implications for other
family members. For example, an obese patient abruptly stopped following
her diet and exercise program when she realized her husband's dismay at
not being able to adhere to his carefully designed weight program. As she
told it, she simply could not highlight her husband's failure by her own more
successful behavior. A jointly designed weight and exercise program for this
couple, one that accounted for the differences between the spouses and the
differences in the trajectory of change that each could hope to achieve,
might have led to a different outcome. In this light, programs of health-

related behavioral change can be enhanced by considering the setting of behavioral change and how a change in behavior by one family member will affect the behavior of other family members.

Allying With the Power

Change in any partially self-contained system is very difficult, especially when the object of change is usually a set of highly repetitive, routinized behaviors. One family technique that has been used clinically for many years is to link a program of behavior change to an existing, well-supported family routine or, alternatively, to tie the change to a powerful family member or external community figure (Minuchin, Rosman, & Baker, 1978). For example, we might assume that household menus change only if the person who prepares the food is responsive to the new diet. But if that person is very sensitive to a powerful other who is frequently critical and domineering, efforts to alter the cook's behavior may be doomed. Power in families has been the subject of much research and debate (Farrington & Chertok, 1993). Identifying culturally defined, powerful family figures as allies in the change process reduces resistance and spurs progress until the outcomes can be more fully integrated into the family system.

Expand the Definition of Outcome in Family Terms

If a family-centered approach to health promotion is adopted, then a reconsideration of the strategy of outcome assessment also needs to occur. This means that outcomes that are sensitive to gender, developmental level, relationship, and culture for all family members, not just for a targeted individual, may be required. Change affects the system; thus, it needs to be assessed from several perspectives and defined in terms that are meaningful and relevant to each member so that the ripple effect of the intervention across the family system can be assessed (Fisher, Terry, & Ransom, 1990). For example, we recently completed a study of three-generation families in which a member of the first generation had received a diagnosis of Alzheimer's disease or related dementia. Our goal was to define attributes of this multigeneration family system that were linked with the health and well-being of all family members, not just the members who provided direct, hands-on patient care (Lieberman & Fisher, 1995). Several findings are relevant to the present discussion. First, we found that all family members were affected by the presence of an elder with Alzheimer's disease in the family, regardless of the amount of care provided. Second, characteristics of the family predicted how well the family responded to caregiving over time, even after the amount of care required was controlled (Fisher & Lieberman, in press). These effects were gradual but persistent over time, and outcome assessment had to be sufficiently sensitive to record the process of change. Third, qualities of the family either exacerbated or moderated the effects of caregiving from affecting non-disease-related family role functioning, such as adult offspring marital and parental roles, roles that have little to do with caregiving for an ill elder. These findings attest to the pervasive effects of health behaviors in families and argue for the need to (a) assess all members of the family, (b) consider characteristics of the family itself when measuring change, and (c) sample a sufficient range of outcomes to demonstrate the variety and trajectory of change for all family members.

Attempt to Modify the Family Setting

All of these suggestions focus on making use of the family as a setting for promoting behavioral change. Another strategy is to modify the family itself to improve the health and well-being of family members. Two paths through which family change may lead to change in family member health and well-being have been proposed. First, improving the family environment by, for example, increasing family cohesion and reducing family conflict reduces family stress and enhances the emotional climate of the family. In turn, this change in family atmosphere leads to a more healthy and satisfying interpersonal environment. Thus, improving the family setting is health enhancing in and of itself. Second, altering the family environment by, for example, enhancing the stability, predictability, and orderliness of family life may lead to an improvement in the display of personal health-related behaviors among family members, such as exercise and diet. In this case, a change in defined aspects of the family environment encourages the display of specific health promoting behaviors among family members.

Although these are logical alternatives to the suggestions listed above, recent research in this and related areas suggests somewhat unclear findings. For example, Campbell and Patterson (1995) reviewed the literature on family interventions to reduce hypertension, smoking, and adult obesity and concluded that, to date, the results were mixed. They cautioned, however, that in their view the approaches tried were often not systematic or adequately based on family theory. Families are by definition well-circumscribed, well-defended, and self-protective social units with a penchant for maintaining the status quo. Efforts to change family structures and systems of beliefs through family therapy or family psychoeducational interventions have been shown to be effective, but they often require relatively intensive efforts over time and have been applied most frequently to families managing a chronic disease in a family member. Although the outcomes of these interventions seem to be more positive than the outcomes of family-based programs of health promotion, probably because there are more of them and they have been developed more systematically, the cost and complexity of these interventions are considerable. Despite this somewhat pessimistic view, I believe that we have not as yet devoted the kind of energy and resources necessary to capitalize on the potential positive effects that family change can have on altering the health behaviors of individual family members. Promoting family change as a practical route for health promotion represents a promising target for future research.

CONCLUSIONS

Soubhi and Potvin have framed the issues that define a family perspective to studies of health promotion. They have provided both a theoretical and empirical context for including the family as a central focus of study and intervention. Drawing from both the clinical literature and the literature on family and health, I suggest that we can build on their suggestions by defining the family as a point of entry for the study of health behavior instead of as an "assimilated" part of an ecological social system. Family-centered intervention brings with it a framework for defining the target of intervention and a strategy for assessing outcomes. This coherent, yet flexible approach presents a challenge to the developer of programs of health promotion and disease prevention: It introduces new complexities at every level, but at the same time it frames a realistic and sensitive approach that addresses a powerful and meaningful social system.

REFERENCES

Campbell, T. L., & Patterson, J. M. (1995). The effectiveness of family interventions in the treatment of physical illness. *Journal of Marital and Family Therapy, 21,* 545-584.

Cole, R. E., & Reiss, D. (1993). *How do families cope with chronic illness?* Hillsdale, NJ: Lawrence Erlbaum.

Doherty, W. J., & Baird, M. A. (1983). *Family therapy and family medicine: Toward the primary care of families.* New York: Guilford.

Doherty, W. J., & Campbell, T. L. (1988). *Families and health.* Beverly Hills, CA: Sage.

Farrington, K., & Chertok, E. (1993). Social conflict theories of the family. In P. G. Boss, W. J. Doherty, R. LaRossa, W. R. Schumm, & S. K. Steinmetz (Eds.), *Sourcebook of family theories and methods: A contextual approach.* New York: Plenum.

Fisher, L., & Lieberman, M. A. (in press). The effects of family context on adult offspring of patients with Alzheimer's disease: A longitudinal study. *Journal of Family Psychology.*

Fisher, L., & Ransom, D. C. (1990). Person-family transactions: Implications for stress and health. *Family Systems Medicine, 8,* 109-122.

Fisher, L., & Ransom, D. C. (1995). An empirically derived typology of families: I. Relationships with adult health. *Family Process, 34,* 161-182.

Fisher, L., Ransom, D. C., & Terry, H. L. (1993). The California Family Health Project: VII. Summary and integration of findings. *Family Process, 32,* 69-86.

Fisher, L., Ransom, D. C., Terry, H. E., Lipkin, M., & Weiss, R. (1992). The California Family Health
    Project: I. Introduction and a description of adult health. *Family Process, 31,* 231-250.

Fisher, L., Terry, H. E., & Ransom, D. C. (1990). Advancing a family perspective in health research:
    Models and methods. *Family Process, 29,* 177-189.

Lieberman, M. A., & Fisher, L. (1995). The impact of chronic illness on the health and well-being of
    family members. *The Gerontologist, 35,* 94-102.

Minuchin, S., Rosman, B. L., & Baker, L. (1978). *Psychosomatic families.* Cambridge, MA: Harvard
    University Press.

Ransom, D. C. (1987). On light versus electron microscopes in family research. *Family Systems
    Medicine, 5,* 383-390.

Ransom, D. C. (1992). New directions in the methodology of family-centered health-care research.
    In R. I. Sawa (Ed.), *Family in primary care.* Newbury Park, CA: Sage.

Ransom, D. C., & Fisher, L. (1995). An empirically derived typology of families: II. Relationships
    with adolescent health. *Family Process, 34,* 183-197.

Ransom, D. C., & Vandervoort, H. E. (1973). The development of family medicine: Problematic
    trends. *Journal of the American Medical Association, 225,* 1098-1102.

Reiss, D. (1981). *The family's construction of reality.* Cambridge, MA: Harvard University Press.

Rissman, R., & Rissman, B. Z. (1987). Compliance: A review. *Family Systems Medicine, 5,* 446-467.

COMMENTARY

An Environmental Perspective on
Health Promotion in the Home Setting

Ilze Kalnins

Soubhi and Potvin provide an overview and synthesis of literature related to understanding the social processes within the family that must be considered in family health promotion from a settings perspective. Fisher further emphasizes the necessity for a systems perspective that recognizes that the behavior of an individual family member can be influenced by other members in the system and vice versa. In both of these papers, the beginning point for health promotion is individual members of the family or the family as a unit. Implicit in this approach is the idea that the more health promotion practitioners understand about the determinants of family health such as family composition, social interaction patterns, income, or education, the more they will be able to design health promotion interventions that are perceived as relevant and helpful by the family.

The assumption that health promotion should focus on the family unit is not unreasonable because, ultimately, families play a dominant role in the socialization of health behavior of their members. This influence can be seen in the many concordances that have been demonstrated between the health behavior of parents and their children. Familial aggregation, or the greater similarity of the frequency or the pattern of certain behaviors within families than between families, has been demonstrated for a wide range of behaviors such as the utilization of health services, weight and overweight, eating habits and food preferences, smoking, use of alcohol, exercise, symptom reporting, and medicine use (see reviews by Baranowski & Nader, 1985, and Tinsley, 1992). Although some of the relationships are modest, and other explanations for each of the findings are possible, it is the consistency of significant relationships across many health behaviors that argues for the influential role of the family. Thus, it is appropriate for health professionals to be concerned with social processes within the family and to attempt to enlist families as vital partners in health promotion.

I believe that the focus on the family and its psychosocial processes is legitimate. I also believe that for a settings approach to health promotion, it is important to remember that the family lives in a home. The dictionary definition of *home* is that it is a physical dwelling place that houses a social unit, typically a family. This definition implies two separate, although interrelated, "targets" for health promotion: the family as a social unit and the physical dwelling place, that is, the surroundings or the environment in which the family lives. The "social unit" aspects of the definition have been reviewed by Soubhi and Potvin and by Fisher, so I will address my comments more to the physical dwelling place or environmental aspects of the home in terms of the resources available to the family in or surrounding the home setting. I will first discuss in general terms the home as a health promotive environment and then illustrate the challenges and possibilities that an environmental perspective poses for health promotion.

THE HOME AS A HEALTH PROMOTIVE ENVIRONMENT

The concept of health promotive environments is based on the idea that there is a dynamic transaction between individuals or groups and their sociophysical milieu (Lindheim & Syme, 1983; Stokols, 1992). In the context of health promotion, this concept focuses on the interplay between the environmental resources available in an area (in this instance, the home) and the particular health habits and lifestyles of the people who occupy the area (in this case, the family). For example,

> environmental designers, facility managers and urban planners can incorporate a variety of physical features in new or renovated settings to promote healthfulness, such as physical fitness facilities in or adjacent to the setting to

encourage health promotive exercise regimens among occupants of an area; ergonomically sound and injury resistant materials in the design and construction of the settings to reduce occupants' risk of injury; and avoidance of toxic materials and sources of psychosocial stress (e.g., poor lighting and air conditioning systems in buildings and insufficient shielding from noise or other distractions) to minimize environmentally induced illness and discomfort. (Stokols, 1992, p. 9)

Considering the home setting from the perspective of a health promotive environment has important advantages. First, by working through the home environment, health promotion practitioners can gain entry into the home and access to the family. In general, health professionals do not have direct access to the home setting except in instances of illness or when events in the home contravene the law. Families that may most need help may be the most difficult to access. The home is quite unlike hospitals, schools, or other community locales in which close liaisons with health professionals or teachers give health promotion practitioners an entrée to the audience they wish to influence. Environmental approaches, especially when incorporated into policy, provide the means for influencing large numbers of families.

Second, research suggests that environmental interventions are valuable as an adjunct to behaviorally oriented health promotion programs. For example, within the work environment, in addition to health education programs for the workers, environmental measures to improve health have included ventilation systems to improve air quality, improved lighting, ergonomically designed furniture, safe stairways and hallways to reduce injuries, and/or provision of facilities to improve fitness. Such design features are rarely discussed in the health promotion literature on family health promotion, although it is acknowledged that housing is a factor in family health. Substandard housing has been shown to be directly associated with a range of outcome measures, including physical illness, interruptions in adolescent development, and strained patterns of family interaction (Smith, 1990; Smith, Smith, Kearns, & Abbott, 1993; Tognoli, 1991). Despite the recognized links between the home environment and health, the literature in health promotion focuses more on delineating the psychological and social processes such as crowding, stress, and/or lack of social support that occur in substandard housing. Consequently, health promotion interventions are proposed to enhance the functioning of the family within a poor environment rather than to enhance the environment in which the family must function.

An environmental approach to health promotion in the home setting requires familiarity with residential architecture, urban planning, public policy, and regulatory legislation at municipal, national, or international levels. These may not be areas of expertise for health promotion, and at first glance they may appear daunting. However, the environmental perspective cannot be ignored and has the potential for moving health promotion in new directions. In the next two sections, I will illustrate challenges and possibilities raised by an environmental perspective on health promotion in the home by discussing injury prevention and the provision of health information in the home setting.

THE HOME AS A SAFETY ENVIRONMENT

The home is an important health and safety environment. As a physical plant, it provides shelter, and some spaces within it, such as the bathroom, kitchen, laundry area, and bedroom, are particularly central to the health and well-being of the family. Yet, statistics on injuries clearly show that the home is not a particularly safe place for its occupants. Records from pediatric hospitals show that the most common reason for children's visits to the emergency department is injuries sustained in the home, followed by those sustained in playgrounds, roads, schools, and recreational facilities. Within the home, the injuries that cause death, morbidity, permanent disability, or disfigurement among children are primarily caused by falls, poisoning, burns, and suffocation (Canadian Institute of Child Health, 1994). Falls in the home are also a major cause of injury among the elderly (Ontario Medical Association, 1992).

Injury control strategies are frequently categorized as active or passive (see review by Finney et al., 1993). Active strategies require repeated actions by individuals in order to achieve injury protection. For example, parents must close a safety gate at the top of stairs time and again to prevent a toddler from falling down the stairs; nonskid pads must be placed under area rugs to prevent older people from falling when a rug slips. Passive strategies require limited or no individual action. These include, for example, legislatively mandated childproof caps on medicines and poisons, fire-resistant sleepwear for children, product design for cribs to prevent strangulation, and hot-water heating with built-in thermostat settings that prevent the heating of water to scalding temperatures. Passive strategies have been shown to be highly effective. For example, children's falls from high-rise apartments dropped by 50% following mandatory installation of window guards in upper story apartments (Spiegel & Lindman, 1977). Although not mutually exclusive, active strategies are more behavioral in nature; passive strategies are structural or environmental.

To achieve the safest home environment possible, active and passive strategies must be combined, as there are situations in which no passive strategy is possible. Thermostats can be built in that prevent hot water from reaching temperatures that will scald a child in the bathtub, but only adult vigilance will prevent scalding burns from boiling pots on the stove top. Only adult vigilance will prevent small children from drowning in the bathtub. Even mandated childproof caps are ineffective if not replaced properly by parents after use.

The home setting requires equal consideration of the behavior of the family and the development of policies and provision of resources and products that enhance the safety quotient of the home setting. The provision of injury prevention resources and assistance with their installation can be built into health promotion programs. For example, in a community project in Sweden (Schelp, 1987), parental awareness of child safety was raised through media and the involvement of professionals. At the same time, the project ensured that child-protective products such as cupboard safety locks, outlet caps, and nontoppling stools were available. Over a period of 4 years, child and youth injuries decreased from 48.6% to 32.2%, with the greatest decreases recorded for preschool children. In a similar vein, health promotion programs to prevent falls in the home among the elderly could include environmental measures such as the installation of simple safety devices (e.g., timers that automatically turn on a light at dusk at the entrance of the house or a motion detector that turns on lights when a person gets out of bed). Color strips can be placed on steps to highlight the edge, and nonskid backing can be attached to area rugs (recommended in Ontario Medical Association, 1992).

An obvious issue associated with environmental interventions is their potential inaccessibility to all families because of cost or lack of installation skills. However, such deterrents can be overcome by broadening the base of stakeholders who are invited to participate in community-based projects. For example, in addition to public health agencies and the traditional safety services of the fire and police departments, participation could be sought from local businesses and civic government.

THE HOME AS AN INFORMATION ENVIRONMENT

Health promotion in the home setting is seriously challenged by the media, which provide families with information and access to resources that are not always health promoting. For health promotion practitioners and advocacy groups, television commercials have long been a major concern. Although estimates vary, the average weekly hours of television watching for Canadian viewers 2 years old and older is approximately 3 hours per day (A. C. Nielsen Co., 1990). Data from a national survey of adolescents 11 to 16 years old show that between 18% and 31% of them watch television at least 4 hours per day (King, Wold, Tudor-Smith, & Harel, 1996). The number of television commercials seen by a typical child each year runs as high as

40,000 (Condry, Bence, & Scheibe, 1987). Children's attention drops when commercials appear, and this drop increases with age (Gaines & Esserman, 1981); nonetheless, market research shows that children try to influence their parents to buy products they have seen on television and that they are successful in getting their parents to purchase these (Moore, 1990).

Commercials aimed at children and adolescents focus on four basic product categories: toys, cereals, candy and snacks, and fast-food restaurants. On adult programs, there is a heavy emphasis on food and alcohol (beer). Although the overall nutritional content of the prime-time TV commercial diet appears to broadly reflect current Canadian nutrition patterns, the foods shown present a diet that underemphasizes proteins, fats, and dietary fibers and overemphasizes sugars and alcohol (Ostbye, Pomerleau, White, Coolich, & McWhinney, 1993).

Commercials are designed to appeal to viewers by stressing fun, friendship, and health. Because of the prohibitive expense of developing new commercials, it is generally accepted that health promotion practitioners with meager budgets cannot compete with the multinational conglomerates. Instead, advocacy groups have sought to influence advertising policy that requires "separators" between children's programs and commercials, forbids the host of shows from pitching products at children, and limits the amount of advertising time in children's programs (Huston, Watkins, & Kunkel, 1989). Attempts have also been made to involve parents in teaching children to understand the commercial nature of advertising (Desmond, Singer, & Singer, 1990; Peterson & Lewis, 1988).

The coming years will see an explosion of information aimed at families through the Internet, the World Wide Web, and interactive television. All of North America and most of the world except for a narrow section of Central Africa and small areas of western South America have access to some sort of Internet capabilities. The number of people linked to the Internet is growing exponentially. Although computers are a long way from being affordable in every household, even that may change if efforts to develop cheap $500 computers that gain access to software through central network stations are successful. Interactive television, although still in the developmental stage, will allow subscribers to feed in information about themselves and to receive, in return, information they request. "Smart homes" that have the capacity for interactive television or computer linkages are already being built as test sites. Because of the enormous cost of developing the technological infrastructure for the new on-line services, development is being funded by the private sector, which ultimately hopes for financial returns through selling information and services to families.

Among advocacy groups such as the Center for Media Education in the United States, there is already considerable concern about on-line advertising directed at children and youth (Center for Media Education, 1996). This segment of the population is seen as an extremely accessible and valuable market. It is estimated that children and youth in the United States influence about $160 billion of their parents' annual spending. In addition, their tendency to be early adopters of high-tech products makes them a disproportionately important market for new interactive media. Thus, advertising agencies have begun to devote major resources to using on-line media for accessing children. Because the Internet is unregulated, on-line advertising can be more invasive and manipulative than television commercials. None of the advertising codes accepted by television advertisers apply. On-line practices solicit detailed personal information through the use of games, prizes, and surveys and track children's on-line activities to design personalized advertising. They also seamlessly integrate advertising and content so that as children are engrossed by the interactive events on screen, they are unaware that they are being manipulated. For example, Frito Lay's web site offers a number of entertaining interactive areas, including a "Dreamsite" where children are asked to design their dream date. Although children are first asked to describe the guy or gal of their dreams, eventually they are asked to choose which Frito Lay snack their virtual date prefers. Upon choosing, the dream date is pictured holding the snack (Center for Media Education, 1996, p. 15). The potential for inserting advertising in hidden ways into content areas is enormous.

> Eventually children will be able to click on various products woven into stories, and be transported to Web sites for those products. The interactive nature of on-line media will foster the development of new forms of product placement. Unlike products placed at fixed points in movies, products could be placed more dynamically on-line. Children engaged in interactive narratives may be able to use the special powers of certain products over and over again. (Center for Media Education, 1996).

To guard children and youth against these invasive and manipulative forms of advertising, advocacy groups are lobbying for implementation that would forbid (a) the collection of personal information from children, (b) the seamless integration of content and advertising, (c) the direct linkage of advertising sites to children's content areas, (d) direct interaction between children and product spokespersons, and (e) direct-response marketing based on personal profiles. In addition, there are efforts to protect children through parental control software that blocks access to particular sites or particular kinds of material (e.g., pornography, alcohol) or that prevents children from disclosing personal information. Again, like other environmental challenges, these technological "fixes" will need considerable support so that parents can afford to install, maintain, and use them.

In addition to advertising, families will be offered a range of health services on-line that provide health assessments, risk appraisal, health information, and access to resources that can include a telephone connection to a health professional, typically a nurse, for personal discussion. Such systems are already in place and available via telephone alone. It is expected that linking these to a computer will make them more powerful and appealing.

The on-line information explosion challenges health promotion professionals to join other advocacy groups in the fight for some regulation. However, so far, attempts at regulation of on-line content as pornography or hate messages have failed (Chidley, 1995). Thus, it seems unlikely that efforts aimed at regulating the advertising of food products, tobacco, or alcohol will be more successful. An alternative may be for health professionals to design their own health information and resource systems for families. In other words, "if you can't beat them, join them." Health promotion is already engaged in the creation of public health information systems in settings such as libraries, community health centers, or wellness centers. It remains to be seen how these will fare in the home setting when pitted against the on-line commercial offerings.

At the moment, access to technology serves to divide the less affluent from the more affluent segments of the population. In the future, however, once interactive television is developed, on-line information beamed into the home will be a fact of life for most families. The question is, therefore, how health promotion will participate in the development of the content that is transmitted.

CONCLUSION: IMPLICATIONS
FOR HEALTH PROMOTION PRACTICE

In summary, although I agree that health promotion in the home must be based on understanding the family unit and its social interactions, I have proposed that attention must also be paid to the physical environment of the home and the resources within it. Obviously, the two are interrelated. As Stokols (1992) points out, the potential benefits of a well-designed and resource-rich environment may go unrealized if the interpersonal or intergroup relationships in the setting are chronically conflicted or stressful. Conversely, a socially well-organized family interested in finding resources that promote health may feel frustrated when such resources are unavailable.

To meet the challenges posed by an environmental perspective on health promotion in the home will require involvement in advocacy, a willingness to step outside the traditional boundaries of health to work closely with other types of professionals, and a solid understanding of communication strategies using the latest technology.

REFERENCES

A. C. Nielsen Co. (1990). *Media research: TV usage levels. Nielsen television insights 1990.* Northbrook, IL: Author.

Baranowski, T., & Nader, P. R. (1985). Family health behavior. In D. C. Turk & R. D. Kearns (Eds.), *Health, illness and families.* New York: John Wiley.

Canadian Institute of Child Health. (1994). *The health of Canada's children: A CICH profile.* Ottawa: Author.

Center for Media Education. (1996). *Web of deception: Threats to children from online marketing.* Washington, DC: Author.

Chidley, J. (1995, May 22). Cracking the Net. *Maclean's Magazine,* pp. 54-58.

Condry, J., Bence, P., & Scheibe, C. (1987). The non-program content of children's television viewing. *Journal of Broadcasting and Electronic Media, 32,* 255-270.

Desmond, R. J., Singer, J. L., & Singer, D. G. (1990). Family mediation: Parental communication patterns and the influences of television on children. In J. E. Bryant (Ed.), *Television and the American family.* Hillsdale, NJ: Lawrence Erlbaum.

Finney, J. W., Christopherson, E. R., Friman, P. C., Kalnins, I. V., Maddux, J. E., Peterson, L., Roberts, M., & Wolraich, M. (1993). Society of Pediatric Psychology Task Force report: Pediatric psychology and injury control. *Journal of Pediatric Psychology, 18,* 499-526.

Gaines, L., & Esserman, J. (1981). A quantitative study of young children's comprehension of television programs and commercials. In J. F. Esserman (Ed.), *Television advertising and children: Issues, research and findings.* New York: Child Research Service.

Huston, A. C., Watkins, B. A., & Kunkel, D. (1989). Public policy and children's television. *American Psychologist, 44,* 424-433.

King, A., Wold, B., Tudor-Smith, C., & Harel, Y. (1996). *The health of youth: A cross-national survey.* Copenhagen: World Health Organization.

Lindheim, R., & Syme, S. L. (1983). Environments and people. *Annual Review of Public Health, 4,* 335-359.

Moore, R. L. (1990). Effects of television on family consumer behavior. In J. E. Bryant (Ed.), *Television and the American family.* Hillsdale, NJ: Lawrence Erlbaum.

Ontario Medical Association. (1992). *Falls in the elderly* (Report of the Ontario Medical Association Committee on Accidental Injuries). Toronto: Author.

Ostbye, T., Pomerleau, J., White, M., Coolich, M., & McWhinney, J. (1993). Food and nutrition in Canadian "prime time" television commercials. *Canadian Journal of Public Health, 84,* 370-374.

Peterson, L., & Lewis, K. E. (1988). Preventive intervention to improve children's discrimination of the persuasive tactics in televised advertising. *Journal of Pediatric Psychology, 13,* 163-170.

Schelp, L. (1987). Community intervention and changes in accident pattern in a rural Swedish municipality. *Health Promotion, 2,* 109-125.

Smith, C. A., Smith, C. J., Kearns, R. A., & Abbott, M. A. (1993). Housing stressors, social support and psychological distress. *Social Science and Medicine, 37,* 603-612.

Smith, S. (1990). Health status and the housing system. *Social Science and Medicine, 31,* 753-762.

Spiegel, C. N., & Lindman, F. C. (1977). Children can't fly: A program to prevent childhood morbidity and mortality from window falls. *American Journal of Public Health, 67,* 1143-1147.

Stokols, D. (1992). Establishing and maintaining healthy environments. *American Psychologist, 47,* 6-22.

Tinsley, B. J. (1992). Multiple influences on the acquisition and socialization of children's health attitudes and behavior: An integrative review. *Child Development, 63,* 1043-1069.

Tognoli, J. (1991). Residential environments. In D. Stokols & I. Altman (Eds.), *Handbook of environmental psychology* (Vol. 1). Malabar, FL: Krieger.

3

The School as a Setting for Health Promotion

Guy S. Parcel

Steven H. Kelder

Karen Basen-Engquist

School-aged youths are frequently considered to be among the healthiest of all Americans, with nearly the lowest mortality rate of all age groups (Coiro, Zill, & Bloom, 1994). Their morbidity rates for chronic medical and psychiatric disorders are low compared with the adult population (Gans, 1990). A closer look, however, reveals that morbidity and mortality rates do not adequately portray the health status of most children and adolescents. Many American young people are threatened by what have been called "social morbidities," including substance abuse, violence, hazardous environments, unintended pregnancy, sexually transmitted diseases, and poverty. In addition, children and adolescents may develop unhealthy and persistent behavior patterns, such as poor dietary intake, low levels of physical activity, and tobacco use that can affect their risk of chronic disease later in life.

The task of improving the health status of youths is complex and difficult. Great strides in medical treatments have alleviated many acute and chronic conditions. Still, in 1991, it was reported that 46% of black, 40% of Hispanic, and 16% of white children were living in poverty, most with limited access to health care services (U.S. Bureau of Census, 1992). The task is confounded by concurrent problems in educational performance, interrupted family relationships, poor living conditions, and a culture that supports and reinforces many unhealthy behaviors (U.S. Department of Education, 1993). Dramatic improvements in child and adolescent health are unlikely without global changes in health care provision, improvements in economic conditions, and wide-scale health promotion efforts. Health care provision and economic reform are beyond the scope of this chapter, but several innovative health promotion programs have shown promise. This chapter will provide an overview of the rationale for youth health promotion, present conceptual models for school health promotion, review examples of school health promotion programs, and offer suggestions for preparing schools for the adoption and implementation of school health promotion programs.

RATIONALE FOR YOUTH HEALTH PROMOTION

For school-aged youths, health promotion interventions are most often concerned with the modifiable risk factors closely related to current or future health outcomes. The Centers for Disease Control and Prevention (CDC) have identified six behaviors that place adolescents at higher risk for chronic and acute conditions: (a) intentional and unintentional injuries, (b) substance use, (c) early and unprotected sexual activity, (d) tobacco use, (e) poor nutrition, and (f) low levels of physical activity (Kolbe, 1990). Table 3.1 provides data from the 1993 Youth Risk Behavior Survey, a national representative sample of high school students, conducted by CDC. These data indicate that many youths are engaging in behaviors that place them at risk for health problems.

Although acute risk due to unhealthy behaviors clearly warrants immediate intervention, a great deal of research has been conducted to alter future chronic disease risk. Efforts directed toward the early prevention of adult chronic diseases have typically focused on the modification of health behaviors such as physical activity, dietary intake, and cigarette smoking. The rationale behind chronic disease youth health promotion is based on the following assumptions:

1. A certain proportion of children and adolescents are at excess physiologic and behavioral risk.

2. The development of physiologic risk factors begins early in life and tracks from childhood into adulthood.

3. The development of physiologic risk depends largely on the initiation of health-compromising behaviors that also track into adulthood.

4. Primary prevention can be achieved through the modification of behaviors related to physiologic risk factors before behavior patterns are more fully established and resistant to change (Perry, Kelder, & Klepp, 1994).

Table 3.1 Percentage of High School Students Who Reported Each Risk Behavior,
by Gender—U.S. Youth Risk Behavior Survey, 1993

Risk Behavior	Females (%)	Males (%)
Rarely or never use safety belts	14.3	23.8
Rarely or never used motorcycle helmets[a]	39.0	40.4
Rarely or never used bicycle helmets[b]	93.6	92.2
Rode with a driver who had been drinking alcohol[c]	34.5	36.3
Carried a weapon[c]	9.2	34.3
In a physical fight[d]	31.7	51.2
Made a suicide plan[d]	22.9	15.3
Attempted suicide[d]	12.5	5.0
Current cigarette use[c]	31.2	29.8
Smokeless tobacco use[c]	2.0	20.4
Current alcohol use[c]	45.9	50.1
Five or more drinks of alcohol on one occasion[c]	26.0	33.7
Current marijuana use[c]	14.6	20.6
Current cocaine use[c]	1.4	2.3
Ever had sexual intercourse	50.2	55.6
Four or more sex partners during lifetime	15.0	22.3
Currently sexually active (sex in past 3 months)	37.5	37.5
Condom use during last sexual intercourse[e]	46.0	59.2
Birth control pill use during last sexual intercourse[e]	22.3	14.7
Ate two or more fruits and vegetables[f]	13.0	17.6
Ate two or fewer servings of high fat food[f]	75.6	57.6
Engaged in vigorous physical activity on 3 or more of past 7 days	56.2	74.7

SOURCE: Kann et al. (1995).
a. Among students who rode a motorcycle at least once during the 12 months preceding the survey
b. Among students who rode a bicycle at least once during the 12 months preceding the survey
c. One or more times during the 30 days preceding the survey
d. One or more times during the 12 months preceding the survey
e. Among students who have had sex during the 3 months preceding the survey
f. During the day preceding the survey

SCHOOLS AS A SETTING

A number of settings can be considered for delivery of youth health promotion
programs. Appropriate settings reflect both the places where youths spend most
of their time and the people who may have influence over them; these most commonly include schools and teachers, home and parents, churches or community
centers and their leaders, as well as health care facilities and physicians.

The school as a setting for youth health promotion is particularly attractive for
a variety of reasons. The majority of the nation's children (approximately 50 million) attend school regularly, and while in school they constitute a "captive audience." The amount of time children spend in school, both in a single day and on a

weekly basis, provides a large window of access to this population. The breadth of activities that students engage in during this time, including learning, playing, eating, and socializing, provides a diverse array of controlled environments in which children can learn, practice, and be reinforced in making healthful decisions.

Another advantage of this setting for health promotion is that the school is an important social and physical environment for children. They will spend a large proportion of their waking hours in school, and relationships formed in school are frequently central in children's social networks (Feiring & Lewis, 1989). In many communities, the school is a central focus for community activities as well. Thus, changes in either the physical environment of the school (e.g., decreasing the fat content of food served in the cafeteria, display of health-related messages through wall posters or bulletin boards) or the social environment (e.g., forming student organizations to work on health issues, encouraging students to make a public commitment to health behavior) can have an impact on student health.

The organization of schools into classrooms that address special interests, skill levels, and individual student needs further facilitates tailoring of programs into meaningful lessons for each child. In this setting, teachers can provide opinion leadership, role modeling, reinforcement, and feedback for each student, as well as monitor students' progress and select appropriate classroom activities. In addition to the classroom teacher, the availability of other adult role models in the school setting can provide constant reinforcement and support for children in the development of healthy behaviors. This continuous availability of multiple, adult supervisors who share common goals for health and education is difficult to replicate in a family, doctor's office, or community center.

Aside from the resources offered by the school setting, promoting the health of children and adolescents is consistent with improved academic achievement, because poor health can disrupt learning. State and federal mandates that guide school health education reinforce the consistency of health priorities with academic achievement and ensure that students who attend school will be provided with the essential knowledge and skills to function as healthy adults (Institute of Medicine, 1997).

There are also disadvantages to working in the school setting, however, and these must be considered in the course and context of program development. Competing school resources, academic priorities, and public opinion are among a number of barriers that affect health promotion program implementation and success in the school setting.

The broad-ranging host of demands placed on teachers is perhaps the most critical barrier to integrating health education into the classroom. A sharp decline over the past three decades in academic achievement among the nation's youths, as measured by both internal and external comparison criteria, has brought about a recommitment to student competency in core academic courses. As a result, teachers and administrators strongly emphasize advancement in math, science, English, and social studies, at the cost of de-emphasizing instruction in health, physical education, and the arts. Moreover, as the information technology industry advances, computer skills have even further displaced health education as an essential skill for competitive job placement and financial success postgraduation. An overburdened teaching staff poses a significant barrier to school health promotion.

A second major problem is that schools are expected to address a multitude of social problems, yet they often lack the resources to do so. They are held responsible for educating youths, but to do so, they must deal with barriers to the educational process, such as poverty, child abuse, substance abuse, and diversity in languages and ability levels. The task of providing a basic education has sufficient challenges so that many school personnel feel unable to take on responsibility for health education. In addition, teachers may lack the training needed to teach health education content effectively (Gingiss & Basen-Engquist, 1994).

Finally, controversy among public opinion leaders as to the importance or appropriateness of educating children about certain health issues, particularly sexuality and drug education, has potential to greatly affect the prioritization of health education in the school setting. As the search for improving the effectiveness of youth health promotion continues, there is an increasing awareness that success must involve a cooperative effort between the schools and other sectors of the community.

Models for School Health Promotion

Knowledge-Based Models

Many traditional school health promotion programs are based on the assumption that if students clearly understand the negative consequences of certain health compromising or risk-taking behaviors, they will make the rational decision not to engage in them. Early approaches to health education in the schools primarily focused on specific types of health problems, particularly those associated with risky or illicit behavior. In the 1950s, it was recognized that the abuse of alcohol had become a serious health and social problem. In an attempt to solve this problem, school personnel were called on to provide instruction, pointing out the dangers and health hazards associated with consuming alcohol. The assumption was that if students knew about these dangers and were told about the health hazards, they would avoid alcohol abuse. Some states went so far as to enact laws requiring public schools to provide instruction in the prevention of alcohol abuse.

It has been demonstrated, however, that even when information is effectively taught, it does not necessarily lead to changes in behavior. Many drug education programs were developed that effectively taught the pharmacological aspects of drug abuse, legal penalties, and the physical risks of taking certain drugs. Program evaluations revealed that these programs had a limited effect on alcohol or other drug use behavior (Bangert-Drowns, 1988). Similar results from nutrition and tobacco education programs in the late 1960s, 1970s, and early 1980s further demonstrated the weaknesses of health education programs primarily based on a knowledge or informational approach (Contento, Manning, & Shannon, 1992; Hansen, 1992).

Affective Education Models

The failure of knowledge-based models reinforced what many educators had been suggesting for years: that health behavior is related not only to knowledge but also to factors such as expectations and values associated with the behavior. It also became apparent that health-related problems could not be effectively dealt with on a crisis basis. If health problems were to be prevented through education, a means of dealing with these problems had to be developed long before they reach a state of crisis.

Teaching methods that focus on the learners' values, attitudes, and feelings fall into the realm of affective education. Teaching in this area is related more to personal development than to the learning of facts and concepts. Affective education programs hypothesized that children who feel good about themselves, who can develop effective relationships with others, and who have a clear understanding of what is important to them are going to be less likely to have problems related to drug and alcohol abuse, sexual behavior, tobacco use, and so on. Teaching methods included building self-esteem, developing interpersonal skills, and work on decision-making and problem-solving skills.

As an outgrowth of the increased interest in affective education, many school health education programs in the 1970s were expanded or redirected to focus more on attitudes, feelings, and values. Some programs de-emphasized the importance of information, whereas other approaches integrated cognitive and affective learning. However, a review of affective approaches to preventing substance abuse concluded that, in general, they made no significant impact on substance use behavior (Schaps, Churgin, Palley, Takata, & Cohen, 1981).

Behavioral Models

In the 1980s, school-based intervention research was more likely to be based on social psychology theories. Typically included were training students to resist social pressures to engage in negative health behaviors (e.g., smoking) and

Table 3.2 Social Cognitive Theory: Determinants of Behavior

Social-environmental factors are aspects of the environment that support, permit, or discourage engagement in a particular behavior. They include influential role models (including peers), situational contexts, social norms for behavior, social support from family and friends, and specific opportunities.

Behavioral factors affect behavior directly, such as existing behavior repertoire, behavioral intentions, capabilities, or coping skills.

Personal factors are particular personal dispositions and cognitive processes that increase or decrease the likelihood of a person's engaging in a given behavior. They include level of knowledge, personal values, attitudes, beliefs, and self-efficacy.

SOURCE: From Perry et al. (1990), p. 410.

the creation of a social environment that encouraged positive health behaviors (Evans, 1984; Flay, 1985). Social Cognitive Theory (SCT) is often cited in the youth health promotion literature as the predominant theoretical model used in the design of successful health promotion programs (Bandura, 1986; Perry, Baranowski, & Parcel, 1990). SCT addresses both the psychosocial dynamics underlying health behavior and the methods of promoting behavior change, while emphasizing cognitive processes and their effect on behavior. Human behavior is explained by SCT in terms of a triadic, dynamic, and reciprocal model in which behavior, social-environmental influences, and personal factors (such as personality, perceptions, expectations, and affect) all interact. An individual's behavior is uniquely determined by these factors.

The determinants of behavior have been further elucidated by Perry and colleagues (Perry, Stone, et al., 1990) in Table 3.2.

Several human capabilities are crucial to SCT, including the individual's capabilities to symbolize the meanings of behavior, to foresee the outcomes of given behaviors, to learn by observing others, to self-determine or self-regulate behavior, and to reflect and analyze experience. These ideas have been particularly valuable in designing effective health education programs.

An expansion of applied SCT methods in the design of health education curricula led to the development of the "social influences approach." This approach emphasized the importance of preparing students to resist the pressures of an environment that may encourage risk-taking behavior. Teaching strategies used in this approach include (a) increasing students' knowledge of short-term consequences of the health risk-taking behavior, (b) peer pressure resistance training, (c) education about manipulative mass media messages, (d) establishment of normative expectations for healthful behavior, (e) use of peer leaders as role models, and (f) encouraging students to make a personal commitment to avoid risk-taking behavior or to engage in healthful behavior. These methods have been successfully applied to smoking prevention and to drug abuse prevention, with evaluations indicating a significant impact on reducing risk-taking behavior (Perry, Kelder, Murray, & Klepp, 1992).

Another extension of SCT that has been demonstrated to be effective in school health promotion interventions is the use of skill development methods for preventing health-risk behavior. The skills approach assumes that a set of social and behavioral skills (such as decision making, problem solving, communication, and stress management or relaxation) is essential for making effective decisions about health behavior. If students are able to develop these skills to complement knowledge of the consequences of health risk behavior and are given opportunities to practice these skills, they will be more likely to avoid risk-taking behavior and develop more healthful patterns of behavior. The skills approach has been shown to be effective when applied to smoking and substance abuse prevention (Botvin, 1990; Botvin, Baker, Dusenbury, Botvin, & Diaz, 1995).

Youth Empowerment Models

An emerging model in school health education is youth empowerment. The underlying tenet of programs using this model is that students must be responsible for identifying and defining the problem to be addressed and determining what action should be taken. Because many of the issues addressed by youth health education have roots in community and social problems, the health education process should enable students to recognize these roots and determine appropriate social or community change actions. The youth empowerment model has its roots in educational and social change approaches such as critical pedagogy (McLaren, 1989), empowerment education (Freire, 1983), and community organization (Minkler, 1990; Rothman & Tropman, 1987).

Implementation of the youth empowerment model requires a departure from traditional health education methods. Although aspects of health education such as skills training or information transfer may be part of a youth empowerment program, this type of program differs from traditional programs in several ways. First, youths themselves must be involved in the process of defining the problem and its meaning for their lives, and the program should include social action and emotion-based objectives (Wallerstein & Bernstein, 1988). Examples of social action objectives could include changing a school smoking policy, working to improve relationships between teachers and students, or making information about contraceptives available at school. Emotion-based objectives refer to explicitly addressing participants' fears, attitudes, and anger about a problem. Without addressing these issues, learning may be blocked.

Little research or description exists in the literature about youth programs operating in schools. A notable exception is the Alcohol Substance Abuse Prevention (ASAP) program (Wallerstein & Bernstein, 1988; Wallerstein & Sanchez-Merki, 1994). Based on the work of Paolo Freire, ASAP uses a listening-dialogue-action methodology to educate adolescents about alcohol use in a student centered participatory mode. Students interview individuals in hospitals and jails who are experiencing negative consequences of alcohol use (listening). They meet in small groups to discuss and critically analyze the interviews and other relevant experiences (dialogue). Finally, students are trained as peer educators to conduct education in their home school and feeder schools. They also work on other social actions, such as developing recommendations to change the alcohol environment in their community.

To facilitate the listening, dialogue, and action cycle, Wallerstein and colleagues have developed a series of steps for analyzing situations or interviews that are summarized by the acronym SHOWED. In Steps 1 and 2, participants are asked questions about what they *see* in the situation and what's really *happening,* to describe the concrete events and feelings they elicit. In Step 3, the situation is personalized by asking students how this situation relates to *our* lives. In the fourth step, the facilitator helps participants analyze the underlying causes of the situation by asking *why* there is a problem. The goal of the final two steps is action. Questions are oriented toward how participants can feel *empowered,* and what they can *do* about the problem.

The youth empowerment model has promise as a health education approach for school. However, more qualitative research is needed to determine the effectiveness of this approach and the best methods for undertaking such an effort. Qualitative studies of the implementation of such programs are especially needed, because of the significant difficulties that schools often face when programs require relinquishing control to students.

MULTIPLE COMPONENT APPROACH
TO SCHOOL HEALTH PROMOTION

The Division of Adolescent and School Health of the CDC has developed and promoted an eight component approach for school health promotion (Allensworth & Kolbe, 1987). As shown in Table 3.3, the eight components are intended to provide programs that influence the health promotion and risk reduction behavior of the students as well as the faculty and staff of the school. This approach for school health promotion provides several important elements for organizing school health programs. The approach views student health and learning as intrinsically interdependent. Therefore, programs that improve health will contribute to improved school performance, and improved school performance will

Table 3.3 The CDC Multicomponent Approach for School Health Promotion

Health education consists of a planned, sequential, K-12 curriculum that addresses behaviors that promote health or reduce the risk for disease or injury.

Physical education is a planned, sequential, K-12 curriculum promoting physical fitness and enjoyable lifelong physical activity.

Health services focus on prevention and early intervention, including the provision of emergency care, primary care, access and referral to community health services, and management of chronic health conditions.

Nutrition services provide access to a variety of nutritious and appealing meals, an environment that promotes healthful food choices, and support for nutrition instruction in the classroom and cafeteria.

Health promotion for staff provides health assessments, education, and fitness activities for faculty and staff, and encourages their commitment to promoting students' health by becoming role models.

Counseling, psychological, and social services include school-based mental health interventions, case management, and referrals to community providers.

A healthy school environment addresses both the physical and psychosocial climate of the school.

Parents and community members engage in a wide range of activities to encourage parent and social support for student healthful behavior and to link school programs to community programs.

contribute to improved health of the students. This conceptualization has the advantage of presenting health promotion programs and activities as integral to the school's educational program and not as extracurricular or outside of the main goals for the school's educational mission.

The CDC approach for school health promotion is not limited to classroom instruction but is viewed as cutting across all school components that have the potential to affect student health. Therefore, it is possible to coordinate efforts across components to influence priority health behaviors. This multicomponent approach offers the opportunity to change the environment of the student while addressing students' individual changes, such as knowledge, skills, and self-efficacy. For example, a program addressing nutrition behavior by providing instruction in the classroom can also reinforce and support the targeted nutrition behavior by modifying the school lunch program, thus providing children access to the healthful food choices emphasized in the classroom.

Several state departments of education have adopted the eight-component approach and are attempting to operationalize it in planning and developing school health promotion programs at the local level. Application of this approach is not easy because administrative and funding sources for the eight components are often diffuse and not coordinated within schools or at the school district level. Therefore, the effectiveness and practicality of this multicomponent approach have not been fully tested. Several major research and demonstration projects have taken a multicomponent approach to the design of school-based health promotion programs, but these have been primarily categorical and not comprehensive in addressing all of the priority health risk behaviors (the programs discussed later in the chapter are examples of multicomponent programs).

Criticism of the multicomponent approach is that it is too vague and too general to provide specific guidance on how programs conducted within each of the components can be linked to each other to modify both environmental and behavioral risks. Others might criticize the approach as being too focused on behavior and not enough on the underlying conditions that might cause or exacerbate the behavior, such as poverty, school size and structure, teacher-student relationships, school and classroom climate, quality of the neighborhood environment, and family involvement in and support for the students' education. In addition, this model requires program planners to design interventions based on a specified model of how school-based programs can prevent or modify the potential causes or determinants of health problems.

Multicomponent Interventions

In the development of innovative school health promotion programs, great emphasis is currently placed on multiple component and theory-based interventions. Approaches include interventions that address not only behavioral change at the individual level but also changes within the environment designed to support behavioral change (Parcel, Simons-Morton, & Kolbe, 1988; Parcel, Simons-Morton, O'Hara, Baranowski, & Wilson, 1989). In the translation from theory to programmatic components, several intervention components for youth health promotion are being developed and studied. In addition to the curriculum approaches discussed in preceding sections, interventions are expanded to the school environment, parental education, and community reinforcement.

School Environment. Changes in the school organization offer powerful means of modifying the school environment and culture to support health promotion goals. Research has identified organizational factors such as policy and practices, organizational mission, and human resource development as important instruments for institutional change (Parcel et al., 1988). Examples of policy actions include banning smoking schoolwide, improving nutritional content standards of school food service (both in purchasing and food preparation), establishing parental fines for student fighting, or defining athletic eligibility criteria. The strategy of relating environmental interventions to classroom interventions is theoretically consistent with the social cognitive theory construct of reciprocal determinism (Bandura, 1986) in which the school environment reinforces the norms, skills, and behaviors emphasized by the health education curriculum.

Policy level intervention calls for the creation of local coalitions and planning councils to define, coordinate, and implement health promotion programs. Ideally, teachers, administrators, parents and other interested citizens would participate in discussions to increase their awareness of the importance of school health promotion and be given guidance on how to establish a policy in their schools. This process includes (a) obtaining commitment, (b) forming an advisory committee, (c) gathering information, (d) developing the policy, (e) planning the implementation strategy, (f) communicating the policy, (g) implementing the new policy, and (h) evaluating policy effectiveness (Kelder, Parcel, & Perry, 1995).

Parental Components. Parents are perhaps the most potent and significant health role models for their children (Coleman, 1991; Nader et al., 1989). They also provide specific opportunities or barriers to child and adolescent health behaviors, such as determining the foods that are purchased, access to physical activity, selection of school and neighborhood, and alcohol use at home. Research in youth health promotion supports the inclusion of parents through home learning to increase program efficacy (Perry, Kelder, & Komro, 1992). In these programs, parents are given activities to complete with their child that typically include parenting tip sheets, games, or parent interviews. These activities are designed to increase communication between the parent and child and to reinforce at home the messages learned at school.

In addition, several studies have demonstrated the importance of parents in adolescent life. Children's involvement in or attitudes about risk behaviors such as sexual initiation (Treboux & Busch-Rossnagel, 1990), condom use (Schaalma, Kok, & Peters, 1993), and drug experimentation (Jurich, Polson, Jurich, & Bates, 1985) have been found to be positively related to their parents' attitudes about these behaviors. Parents are important role models prior to substance use onset and can be useful allies in drug prevention programs. Parents maintain their influence in the determination of their child's peer group where group norms often dominate health choices (Brown, Mounts, Lamborn, & Steinberg, 1993). In this sense, parents can directly and indirectly influence their child's health behaviors. However, after students begin to use alcohol and drugs, peers appear to exert greater influence (Kandel & Andrews, 1987).

Community Reinforcement. Although schools are efficient and appropriate organizations for implementing prevention programs, community support and reinforcement for these programs also appear to be necessary for sustained change. There are several reasons for considering health promotion efforts that involve the community (Perry, Kelder, & Komro, 1992). First, high-risk students, those most likely to use substances or engage in early sexual activity, are also most likely to drop out of school prior to graduation and therefore might be missed with a school-based program. These same high-risk students may also be more alienated from messages delivered at school. Second, the social influences that affect risk behaviors frequently occur outside schools. The direct modeling of healthy or unhealthy behaviors and norms supporting or opposing these behaviors come from family members, other peers, adults in the community, and mass media images. A consistent preventive message from these various sources would be optimal. Third, community policies that regulate the opportunities and barriers for health behaviors, as well as the normative climate of a community, affect children and adolescents. Finally, in some communities, the school is the safest place that children have to go, and many do not want to leave school and go home. For these children, an expansion of heath promotion efforts into the local housing project, community center, or parks and recreation is warranted.

Over the last two decades, formative and empirical evaluations have led to several large-scale projects that incorporate one or more of the above-mentioned components. In the next section, we will illustrate the application of the multi-component approach by reviewing several school health promotion projects that have recently concluded or are currently in progress.

YOUTH HEALTH PROMOTION PROJECTS

The following projects embrace the multiple-component intervention principles and strategies described above and provide illustrations of interventions designed for both acute and chronic disease prevention. Most of the research is ongoing; thus, effects have yet to be determined for all of the projects. However, each of the projects is unique and builds on the existing literature where previous studies have indicated promise. Selected for this chapter are projects with which the authors have had direct involvement, including the translation of theoretical methods into practical program strategies. Clearly, the presented programs do not represent the only way to intervene or all of the options for intervention but are examples of well-documented studies that can assist in improving our knowledge of how to intervene in schools to promote health and reduce the risk for health problems. The four studies are the Child and Adolescent Trial for Cardiovascular Health, Project Northland, Safer Choices, and Students for Peace.

The Child and Adolescent Trial for Cardiovascular Health (CATCH)

CATCH is a randomized, multicentered trial funded by the National Heart Lung and Blood Institute designed to assess the effects of a school- and family-based intervention to reduce the risk of cardiovascular disease among third- to fifth-grade elementary school students (1987–1994). The interventions components include classroom curricula and school environmental modifications related to food consumption, physical activity, and tobacco use, as well as family- and home-based programs to complement the school-based activities (Perry, Stone, et al., 1990). It is hypothesized that the interventions will result in a lower level of total fat and sodium consumption, increased physical activity, and non-use of tobacco. These behavioral changes are expected to influence favorable blood concentrations of lipids, blood pressure, body fat, and physical fitness. The major comparison will juxtapose schools that take part in the CATCH intervention (14 schools per site) with schools in the control group (10 per site).

The CATCH Intervention Programs. There are four school-based program components: (a) classroom curricula, (b) food service, (c) physical education, and (d) tobacco control policies, and two family-based programs—(a) home team programs and (b) family fun nights. Two versions of the intervention program are implemented: One version, the "school-based intervention," consists of the classroom curricula and school environmental modifications in physical education classes, smoking policies, and school food service; the other version adds a family- and home-based component to the school-based program.

Classroom Curricula. The Adventures of Hearty Heart and Friends program is the classroom curriculum used for the third grade (Perry, Luepker, Murray, & Hearn, 1988). The program consists of 15 classroom sessions of approximately 40 minutes each. Five of the lessons involve actual preparation of heart-healthy snack foods by the children. These lessons also involve menu analysis and evaluation of the healthfulness of the prepared food. Ten of the lessons improve behavioral capacity and skills. The students receive basic eating patterns information from the adventure stories, see new role models for healthy food and exercise choices, and become involved in a story in which characters exhibit a lifestyle that places a high value on health.

The Go for Health curricula are organized into six modules each for Grades 4 and 5, consisting of a total of 12 weeks of instructions per grade (Parcel et al., 1989). The modules focus on eating behaviors and physical activity changes relevant to each grade level. A variety of learning activities are used in each module, including modeling, monitoring, goal setting, contracting, skill training, practice, and reinforcement. These activities focus on healthful lunches, snacks, and eating out as well as on increasing moderate to vigorous exercise at school and at home. The curriculum focuses on differentiating between GO, SLOW, and WHOA foods and physical activities and on increasing the selection of GO foods and activities.

Facts and Activities about Chewing Tobacco & Smoking is a four-session classroom program for fifth-grade elementary school students that incorporates a variety of educational methods, including large-group discussions, peer-led cooperative learning groups, demonstrations, and role-play presentations (Parcel et al., 1989). The activities are designed to build protection against tobacco use by emphasizing the dangerous, costly, and aversive aspects of smoking and chewing tobacco, the benefits of not using tobacco, and that to be tobacco-free is now the acceptable way of life. Skills training to resist influences to use tobacco are also included.

School Food Service. The Eat Smart School Nutrition Program is designed to provide children with tasty lower-fat and lower-sodium meals at school while maintaining recommended levels of essential nutrients (Nicklas et al., 1989). The specific nutritional objectives are to reduce the amount of total fat in school lunch to no more than 30% of calories served, with saturated fat making up no more than 10% of calories served, and to reduce sodium intake at lunch by at least 25% (to between 600 and 1000 mg). The program addresses six major areas within quantity food production to implement the above-mentioned dietary guidelines: menu planning, food purchasing (commodities and vendor-prepared food items), recipe modification, food preparation, food production, and food presentation and promotion.

Physical Education. The CATCH physical education (PE) program is designed to increase the amount of moderate to vigorous physical activity (MVPA) that children obtain during physical education classes at school. The goal is to provide students with the opportunity to experience and practice physical activity that may be carried over into other times of the day and maintained later in life (Parcel et al., 1989). The CATCH PE program provides a collection of health-related, physical fitness activities on cards packaged in a convenient and easy-to-use activity box and guidebook. The activity box includes a variety of activities on index cards for specific units, such as walk/run/jog, aerobic game, aerobic sports, jump rope, and dance. Each class session includes (a) introductory/warm-up activities, (b) lesson focus, (c) fitness development, and (d) cool-down activities.

Tobacco Control Policies. Smart Choices is an environmental approach to tobacco use prevention in school that involves the establishment of a school policy of nontobacco use (Parcel et al., 1989). Teachers and administrators participate in discussions to increase their awareness of the importance of a school nonto-bacco use policy and are provided with guidelines on how to establish a policy in their schools.

Family Home Team. The Home Team Programs are introduced to families through a weekly packet distributed at school in which the child encourages parental involvement (Perry et al., 1988). Weekly scorecards recording points for completing home activities are used to tally family participation on a classroom chart. The Home Team concept is used in Grades 3 through 5, but the format and content differs slightly, depending on the grade level. The three years of Home Team Programs include health-enhancing activities that complement the classroom curricula; goal-setting activities designed to improve eating, physical activity, and nonsmoking behavior at home and away from home; and weekly goal-setting activities to monitor progress.

Family Fun Night. Family Fun Nights are provided to third and fourth graders and their parents (Perry et al., 1988). The general content consists of aerobic dance performances by students, health booths featuring heart-healthy snacks and recipes, tips regarding heart health themes (such as reduced salt, reduced fat, increased complex carbohydrates, increased physical activity, healthy dining, and label-reading information), games and contests rewarding knowledge of heart health, and prizes.

Main Intervention Findings From CATCH. Results showed that students in the CATCH intervention schools had a lower daily caloric intake from total fat and saturated fat than students in the control schools (Luepker et al., 1996). The CATCH interventions successfully improved school lunches to meet federal guidelines, which recommend no more than 30% of each day's calories come from fat and 10% from saturated fat. Moreover, the changes were seen in the intervention students' home eating patterns too. Blood cholesterol measures, however, did not differ significantly between children in the control and intervention schools. The self-reported dietary and physical activity behaviors initiated during elementary years persisted to early adolescence at 3 years follow-up (Nader et al., 1996).

The CATCH interventions also exceeded the Federal Year 2000 goal of having students spend at least 50% of time in physical education classes being moderately to vigorously active. And the improvement extended beyond the classroom: Students in the intervention school reported significantly higher levels of vigorous activity throughout the day than did those in the control schools.

Finally, extensive process evaluations were collected from students, teachers, school food service personnel, and PE specialists throughout the 3 years of the CATCH intervention. High levels of participation, dose, completeness, fidelity, and compatibility were observed for the four programs over the 3 years (Perry et al., 1997). All of the data support CATCH as a model of a feasible multilevel health promotion program.

Project Northland

Project Northland is a 5-year (1990–1995) communitywide research program funded by the National Institute on Alcohol Abuse (Perry et al., 1993). An educational research project, Project Northland is designed to test the effectiveness of a communitywide effort to prevent or delay the onset of alcohol use among young adolescents. Twenty combined school districts and adjacent communities in northeastern Minnesota were recruited and then randomly assigned to either *education* or *delayed* program conditions. The 10 education school districts agreed to participate in 3 years of intervention programs in schools, with parents, and in the community at large.

Project Northland Intervention Programs. The 3-year intervention program includes (a) parental involvement, (b) peer-led school-based programs, and (c) communitywide policy changes in the education communities. Adolescents are exposed to the intervention during their sixth to eighth grades (1991–1994). Project Northland is unique because it targets alcohol-related environmental variables (such as opportunities, barriers, social support, and modeling) more comprehensively than in previous prevention research.

Parental Involvement. The sixth-grade intervention focuses on parents to provide skills for parents prior to alcohol use onset and to establish policies around alcohol at home. The Slick Tracy Home Team consists of four activity books and a family night at school. Each book includes introductory materials on a given theme presented in a comic strip. The comic strip includes two to three short activities for sixth graders and their parents, as well as a section for parents that provides information and tips on how to communicate with their children about alcohol use. The major themes include facts and myths about adolescent alcohol use, alcohol advertising and adult role models, friends and peer pressure, the consequences of drinking, and setting up family guidelines. A family fun night at school (Slick Tracy Night) follows the 4 weeks of activities, with a display of posters created by the sixth graders around the Slick Tracy themes.

Classroom Curricula. Two programs have been designed for the seventh and eighth graders. Each program consists of eight 45-minute classroom sessions taught by teachers and elected classroom peer leaders. Classroom teachers are trained to organize these sessions and to facilitate productive peer group discussions and role plays.

The seventh-grade program, Amazing Alternatives!, focuses on skills training to remain a nondrinker. First, students begin by identifying the short-term consequences of use, such as smelling bad, having an accident, getting in trouble with their parents, or doing things they later regret. Second, the students discover that substance use is not a normative behavior for young adolescents. Discussions of how few students use alcohol instills a conservative norm. Third, the reasons why adolescents use alcohol are explored (e.g., making friends or as a sign of maturity), and positive alternatives to achieve these same goals are provided. Fourth, the students learn how these meanings are established in our culture through advertising and through peer and adult role models. Fifth, and most important, the students learn and practice skills to resist these influences. They create anti-alcohol advertisements and skits (role-playing) around possible social encounters. Finally, at the end of the program, the students make a public commitment to abstain. This commitment acts as a psychological anchor and explicitly creates the intention not to experiment with substances.

The eighth-grade program, PowerLines, is designed to reinforce the messages and behaviors learned in sixth and seventh grades. PowerLines introduces eighth graders to groups within communities that influence adolescents' alcohol use, including peers, parents, local government agencies, or liquor store owners. Through work on small-group projects, students learn about these groups and the influences they have within their own communities. The students conduct a mock "town meeting" based on a star high school athlete's DWI arrest. In addition, students work on small community projects such as interviewing community leaders on alcohol issues, investigating school alcohol policies, or teaching younger students alcohol refusal skills. In the final session, small groups present their projects and findings to the class.

Communitywide Policy Changes. The Project Northland communitywide approaches are intended to empower citizens in these communities to build their own capacity for prevention, based on building networks of support and encouraging broad-based participation. Practically, this means engaging networks of public and private organizations in coordinated activity around adolescent alcohol use prevention and forming communitywide task forces. These task forces, working with university investigators and staff, identify major community problems around adolescent alcohol use, develop and implement a policy action plan, evaluate this plan after 1 year, and then refocus as necessary.

Strategies that task forces are asked to consider fall into four categories: (a) communitywide education efforts, such as educating merchants about the legal consequences and ways of avoiding under-age sales; (b) enforcement of existing laws; (c) development of local ordinances and administration of policies, such as restricting the location of alcohol advertising and outlets; and (d) the development and enforcement of school policies. These policies are designed to reduce the burden of personal decision making for the adolescent; place major responsibility for behavior change on adult merchants, law enforcement officials, and policymakers; and project community-level norms around adolescent alcohol use consistent with the parent involvement and school-based programs.

Main Intervention Findings From Project Northland. The outcomes of Project Northland, after 3 years of interventions during early adolescence, provide additional evidence supporting communitywide, multiple-component approaches to alcohol use prevention (Perry et al., 1996). At the end of eighth grade, students in the intervention communities reported significantly less past-month and past-week alcohol use compared with the control communities. Perry and colleagues (1996) summarize the main outcomes and other effects of Project Northland:

> For the intervention students as a group, Project Northland appears to have been successful in: 1) reducing alcohol use; 2) reducing the tendency to use alcohol; 3) the combination of cigarette and alcohol use; 4) in changing the functional meanings of alcohol use; 5) reducing peer norms and peer influence to use; 6) introducing skills to resist peer influences; and 7) in increasing parent-child communication around the consequences of drinking. The larger social environment, including access to alcohol in the community, perceptions of social groups that influence teen alcohol use, and consequences of driving after drinking, was less likely to be affected. (p. 963)

Safer Choices

Safer Choices is a 5-year research project funded by the CDC (Coyle et al., 1996; Basen-Engquist et al., 1997). The primary purpose of the Safer Choices Project is to develop and evaluate the effectiveness of a multiple-component, school-based intervention to reduce risk behaviors or increase protective behaviors to prevent pregnancy, HIV, and STD infections in adolescents 14 to 18 years of age. The interventions include classroom curricula, activities to support school organizational change, program elements to create a supportive school environment, peer resource programs, parent programs, and links to community services. It is hypothesized that the program will result in lower levels of adolescent sexual risk-taking behavior. The effects of the program are assessed through a randomized trial carried out at two sites—large urban areas in Southeast Texas and Northern California. Ten schools participated at each site (20 in all), divided into 10 treatment and 10 control schools.

Safer Choices Intervention Components. The intervention is implemented as a single, integrated program consisting of multiple components. Furthermore, the program is designed to exist within the school's major administrative and decision-making structures to ensure that the elements are sustained, cumulative, and interconnected. The components are designed to influence student behaviors and the school environment through classroom instruction, schoolwide efforts, and community-linked efforts. Educational and support activities for parents, administrators, and school faculty and staff also play a role in the intervention. In operation, the various program elements are structurally and substantively interrelated through the coordination of a School Health Promotion Council.

School Organization. Research on school improvement has demonstrated that changes in a school's organizational and social climate are necessary for meaningful educational change to occur. In the Safer Choices Project, the school organization component targets three methods for changing school climate to enhance the prevention effort: (a) creating a School Health Promotion Council, (b) establishing a school mission and policies supportive of the prevention efforts, and (c) providing schoolwide staff development for faculty and staff. The School Health Promotion Council consists of parent, teacher, administrator, staff, student, and community representatives. Broadly speaking, the function of the council is to work with project staff to establish health promotion goals for the school; to develop, implement, and monitor plans for achieving those goals; and to assess their achievement. A part-time site coordinator appointed from the school faculty leads the council, providing leadership and coordination for its activities. In addition to meeting regularly as a group, the council is organized into working committees corresponding to the key program elements (e.g., curriculum, peer involvement, parent involvement). The councils have evolved differently depending on the needs of their schools. Some councils remain actively involved in project decision making and activity implementation, whereas others serve more of an advisory and support function.

Classroom Curriculum. The curriculum is based on Reducing the Risk: Building Skills to Prevent Pregnancy (RTR), which has been evaluated and demonstrated to reduce unprotected intercourse, especially among those who have not yet initiated intercourse (Kirby, Barth, Leland, & Fetro, 1991). The RTR curriculum has been lengthened and restructured so that a 10-session component is implemented in the 9th grade and a second, 10-lesson component is implemented in the 10th grade. The curriculum is taught by schoolteachers, who have attended training and receive ongoing coaching as needed from project staff. Student peer leaders help facilitate some of the activities, especially those designed to affect peer norms.

The curriculum emphasizes the costs of unprotected intercourse and uses peers to model socially desirable ways of successfully avoiding unprotected intercourse. Consistent with SCT, the curriculum employs a series of discussions and role-play exercises to help students recognize both social pressure to engage in unprotected intercourse and social situations that might lead to such pressure; it helps students to recognize "lines" used to exert social pressure; and gives them practice in developing and vocalizing different ways of resisting. Students practice talking to other students about choosing not to have sex and the use of birth control in situations that, over the course of the curriculum, increase in difficulty. This controlled practice is intended to increase students' perceived self-efficacy to resist pressure.

Peer Resources and School Environment. According to SCT and other theories that form the basis of the Safer Choices program, the school environment should reinforce the norms, expectancies, skills, and behaviors emphasized in the curriculum. Thus, the goal of the peer resources and school environment component is to saturate the school environment with messages supportive of HIV, STD, and pregnancy prevention to alter the social environment and normative culture. To achieve environmental change, the program employs key instruments of the school culture and social fabric, such as social network structures (e.g., tapping into student clubs in the school), the physical environment, media, and school policy.

The environmental change activities are planned and conducted by a representative group of students trained to be peer educators. These students are organized and recognized on campuses as Safer Choices Peer Teams. Using a peer education approach provides positive role models for students on campus, reinforces norms against unprotected sex, provides youths with opportunities to help one another, and empowers youths through meaningful program involvement.

The peer teams are trained at the beginning of each school year and meet regularly with an adult peer coordinator to plan and implement activities. The activities conducted by the peer teams include (a) use of the school newspaper or other schoolwide media for promotional and HIV/STD prevention messages, (b) school opinion polls, (c) public forums (e.g., public speakers and special assemblies), (d) small media (e.g., posters, buttons, T-shirts, calendars), (e) small-group discussions, and (f) drama productions.

Parent Programs and Involvement. Past research has demonstrated that parent-child sex education programs do increase both the frequency of communication about sexual issues and the comfort with those conversations (Kirby, 1984). However, there remain three major impediments to effective parent-child sex education programs:

1. Most parents—especially parents of youths most in need—are not willing to attend separate programs.

2. Parent-child programs are labor intensive and costly on a per-pupil basis.

3. Greater parent-child communication about sexual issues may reduce risk-taking behavior only if the proper messages are conveyed and reinforced (Moore, Peterson, & Furstenberg, 1986).

Thus, the challenge for program developers is to create programs that effectively serve a large percentage of parents, do so cost-effectively, and ensure that the proper messages are conveyed and reinforced.

To meet this challenge, the Safer Choices program integrates parents primarily through "at-home" teaching assignments connected to the school-based curriculum, through newsletters sent to parents, and through other activities developed and organized by individual School Health Promotion Councils.

The classroom curriculum includes four homework assignments to be done with parents (two in 9th grade and two in 10th grade). The activities in the homework assignment foster child-adult communication ab   t HIV, STD, and pregnancy prevention. The topics covered by the homework assignments include why it is difficult to talk about sensitive issues such as relationships and sexuality, steps that can be taken to improve communication between parent and child, and beliefs about sexuality and prevention of pregnancy and STD.

Parent newsletters are sent home with students three times each school year. The topics in the newsletter vary each time. The first newsletter focuses on project activities, the second provides functional information about HIV, STD, and pregnancy, and the third covers how to discuss sexuality and preventing HIV, STD, and pregnancy with adolescents. In addition to the information provided, each newsletter includes interviews with other parents related to the topics in the newsletter. The parents interviewed serve as role models for the other parents, modeling support for the program, recognition of the risks of unprotected sexual activity for adolescents, and discussion of these risks with their children.

In addition to the homework assignments and newsletters, some schools' Health Promotion Councils also developed additional activities for parents. Examples included back-to-school-night activities to introduce parents to the project, a mother-daughter lunch with a presentation by a local gynecologist on STD prevention and women's health, an AIDS quilt display for parents and students, and a theatrical production about AIDS.

School-Community Links. Community links are critical to ensure that students have access to the health services they need. This component of the program attempts to establish and/or strengthen community links for on-site resources (e.g., materials and speakers) as well as for referral and treatment services off-campus. The specific activities included in this component are (a) development and distribution of a resource guide, which provided information about community services related to HIV, STD, and pregnancy prevention to students and faculty; (b) development of a list of community agency personnel willing to lead small-group discussion sessions or speak at public forums; and (c) homework assignments in the curriculum that require students to gather information about local resources.

The final results for Safer Choices are not yet available. However, preliminary analysis of qualitative and quantitative data on the implementation indicate that most components have been favorably accepted by school personnel and students. For example, 82% of students receiving the curriculum rated it as good or excellent, and 50% strongly agreed that the information presented would be helpful to them in the future. After teaching the curriculum once, 95% of the teachers agreed or strongly agreed that the curriculum seemed relevant to the students, and 66% reported no problems implementing the curriculum. Nearly three quarters of School Health Promotion Council members reported being satisfied or very satisfied with the overall progress of the program in their school at the end of the first year of program implementation. Given information such as this as well as information obtained in interviews with school personnel, we feel that the multicomponent approach used in the Safer Choices program is both feasible and useful as an approach to school health education.

Students for Peace

Students for Peace (SFP) is a 3-year, school-based intervention that seeks to prevent violence among sixth-, seventh-, and eighth-grade students in a large urban school district in Texas (Kelder et al., 1996). The study examines the hypothesis that students exposed to a 2-year multiple component intervention will reduce aggressive behavior compared with students who receive the district's "usual care" of violence prevention activities. Eight schools are involved in the study: four intervention and four control.

The intervention component includes four main elements:

1. A School Health Promotion Council to organize and coordinate schoolwide intervention activities and to influence organizational change at the school level

2. A violence prevention curriculum that provides conflict resolution knowledge and skills

3. Peer mediation and leadership training to modify social norms about violence and to provide alternatives to violence

4. Parent education through newsletters presenting role models that parents can emulate at home to reduce conflict and aggression

School Health Promotion Council. The School Health Promotion Council formed at each SFP intervention school includes a site coordinator, teachers, a school administrator, and a school nurse or counselor. The council meets monthly to coordinate the intervention components and to influence school organizational change. Council members and site coordinators at all four intervention schools participated in a 1-day team-building workshop.

Site coordinators from each school are paid a $200 stipend per month during the school year to coordinate the intervention and to act as a liaison between the school and the SFP project staff. The School Health Promotion Councils also have organized special peace-related activities such as a "Peace Day" for Christmas, in which students made "peace ornaments" for the school Christmas tree. Such activities help to promote the project and change the school environment. Each council receives $1,000 annually to use for violence prevention strategies of their own choice.

Curriculum. In 1992, the school district selected *Second Step: A Violence Prevention Curriculum* (Committee for Children, 1990) as its classroom-based, violence prevention curriculum aimed at reducing impulsive and aggressive behaviors and increasing social competence. The curriculum includes information about violence and trains students in empathy, conflict resolution, and anger management. The teacher-taught curriculum is skills based and composed of 15 lessons, each approximately 80 minutes long. At the district level, implementation of the curriculum by any school was voluntary. Before SFP, no school had implemented Second Step schoolwide (at all grade levels).

In the first year of intervention (1994–1995), SFP's task was to expand the implementation of Second Step to ensure that students at all grades were exposed to the curriculum. In two intervention schools, the entire teaching staff was trained to teach Second Step. In the other two schools, 10% to 25% of the teaching staff were trained to teach Second Step, but all teachers received at least a 2-hour training in conflict resolution.

In the second year of intervention (1995–1996), schools could choose to teach Second Step again or they could choose an alternative curriculum. Regardless of the choice, the intervention schools are expected to provide a violence prevention intervention curriculum to all students during the school year before the final measurement period.

Peer Training. To promote nonviolent norms and provide students with an alternative method to solve conflicts, two programs were implemented schoolwide in the intervention schools—Peer Mediation and Peers Helping Peers. These programs were part of the school district's menu of violence prevention programs; however, they had not been fully implemented in any of the SFP participating schools. The Peer Mediation program trains students to mediate conflicts, both formally and informally, among other students. Peer mediators usually address behaviors such as name-calling, rumors, and threats. The Peers Helping Peers program trains students to meet one-to-one with students who request their help because of personal problems, such as alcohol and drug use, school attendance, conflicts with other students or within their family, and academic problems.

Before implementing the peer-related programs, we conducted a 1-hour in-service training for teachers and a 2-day training for students. Fifty to 60 students per school were trained to be both peer mediators and peer helpers. Two teachers per school serve as sponsors, meet regularly with students, and keep a log of the activities. Students keep a log of each mediation or interview and are required to report life-threatening situations.

Students are also involved in schoolwide activities such as special-topic discussion groups, production of antiviolence printed material, and special presentations. The trained students emphasize the impact of violence on their lives and attempt to communicate norms and expectations regarding nonviolence. These messages are conveyed through posters, morning announcements, school television, school newspaper, art activities, and parent newsletters.

Parent Education. McAlister (1995) has developed a theory-based communication strategy using "small" media displays of positive peer models to reinforce and encourage health behavior change. Efforts to reach parents and educate them about these concepts depend mainly on the in-class distribution of newsletters for students to take home to their parents. The newsletters encourage parents to use positive conflict resolution tactics with their children, increase parental monitoring, and reduce their own modeling and praise of aggressive behavior. Each story explicitly models an interpretation-reaction-response process. Modeling of interpretations includes attributions that reduce enmity—for example, attributing minor aggressive behavior to common personal problems of the aggressive student rather than to racism or personal disrespect. Modeling of reactions includes disapproval of loss of temper and reinforcement of anger management skills. Diffusion of verbal or physical aggression and reliance on school resources and on-campus police to settle disputes, punish aggressors, or provide protection from threats are among the several responses modeled in the newsletters. Student role models for the newsletter are recruited and asked if they are willing to recount an event when they behaved nonviolently. Students who have appropriate stories give their names and phone number so their parents may be contacted. Project staff screen parental role models by telephone and arrange for an interview and photography session. When possible, photographs of student and parent role models are posed to reproduce target behaviors.

Parental involvement is elicited through parents' (a) review of the story content, (b) approval of the modeled course of action, and (c) recommendation that their child imitate the model. The newsletters are distributed monthly in the classroom at which time the story is reviewed, student approval is elicited, and students are encouraged to take the newsletters home to read with their parents.

The final results for Students for Peace are not yet available, although several lessons learned in the field can be reported (Kelder et al., 1996; Orpinas et al., 1996). Building support and developing relationships are essential to working successfully in the school environment. It has been important to work closely with and to assist the district with their current efforts so that, if found effective, the necessary documentation, personnel, and skills would exist for broader dissemination within the district. We also learned several valuable lessons on improving intervention delivery. The most important of these is a realization on our part that multiple-component programs such as SFP are difficult to implement and require patience and recognition of the pressures on inner-city schools. Academic and other competing interests often receive a higher priority, even over pressing health needs. A phased-in approach, in which one program is added every year, might be more realistic than trying to implement several new programs at once. A paid site-based coordinator and liaison has been essential in identifying environmental barriers to program implementation and in suggesting effective strategies to overcome those barriers.

Finally, both qualitative and quantitative data indicate a population in need of violence prevention interventions even greater than anticipated. Fighting (30-day prevalence, 23%), injuries due to fighting (12-month prevalence, 14%), weapon carrying (30-day handgun carrying prevalence, 11%), taunts and threats at school (30-day prevalence, 27%), and going to and from school (30-day prevalence, 26%) are more commonplace than is acceptable for middle school students.

EFFECTIVE SCHOOL HEALTH PROMOTION PROGRAMS

Over the last 20 years, an ever-expanding literature has been published covering the findings of numerous youth intervention studies across many risk and protective behaviors. Because funding for research and development is typically categorical (i.e., by risk factor or disease), there have been few empirical evaluations of the multicomponent interventions that address more than one or two risk behaviors. Thus, evidence for the effectiveness of the multicomponent intervention strategy recommended in Table 3.3 is based on theory and the cumulative evidence from small single-component studies to a handful of well-designed larger studies covering greater channels of influence, some of which have been described in this chapter.

It is beyond the scope of this chapter to review the empirical evidence in support of the multicomponent intervention model of intervention; therefore, this brief review will cover several of the larger multiple-component projects conducted during the 1980s and early 1990s. For the interested reader, several recent review articles cover the numerous categories of adolescent health promotion research (Bruvold, 1993; Hansen, 1992; Kelder, Edmundson, & Lytle, in press; Kirby et al., 1994; Lytle & Achterberg, 1995; Pentz et al., 1989; Sallis & McKenzie, 1992; Tobler, 1992; Tolan & Guerra, 1994).

Community-Level Substance Use Prevention

Several comprehensive reviews of the smoking prevention literature, including several meta-analyses, have reported positive intervention group findings in smoking onset when compared with an equivalent or randomly assigned control group (Bruvold, 1993; Pentz et al., 1989; Tobler, 1992). In these studies, the impact on regular (i.e., weekly) smoking ranged from reductions of 43% to 60%, with maintenance of these effects generally 1 to 3 years postintervention. Unfortunately, the effects of the social influences programs appear to diminish over time, suggesting that additional booster education programs are needed during middle adolescence (Botvin, 1990; Flay et al., 1989; Ellickson, Bell, & McGuigan, 1993; Ennett, Tobler, Ringwalt, & Flewelling, 1994).

Because of the diminished effect over time, several smoking and drug use prevention programs have gone beyond the classroom into the larger school and community environments. The Minnesota Heart Health Program, Finland North Karelia Project, and Vermont School and Mass Media Project provide support for the importance of community-level interventions (Flynn et al., 1994; Perry, Kelder, Murray, & Klepp, 1992; Vartiainen, Pallonen, McAlister, & Puska, 1990). The former two studies included smoking prevention programs embedded within a larger heart health program that emphasized smoking cessation, healthy eating, and physical fitness for all community members. The Vermont study compared school plus mass media programs to school programs alone. Long-term results for these studies indicated that smoking rates throughout the follow-up period were substantially lower in the intervention communities.

Project Northland (Perry et al., 1993) and the Midwestern Prevention Project (Pentz et al., 1989) are two communitywide substance use prevention programs that include (a) school-based education (using a peer-led social influences model), (b) parental education and organization, (c) mass media, (d) organized community efforts, and (e) changes in school and local government policy. By involving the community, both programs attempt to create environmental support for the changes made within the school-based component, thus changing the social norm of drug use. Results from both of these studies indicate that onset rates for alcohol and marijuana are significantly lower in the intervention communities (Johnson et al., 1990; Komro et al., in press).

Community-Level Cardiovascular Disease Prevention

Several community-level youth cardiovascular disease health promotion projects have reported modest but encouraging results. In the Oslo Youth Study, significantly lower blood cholesterol levels were observed among both genders (Tell & Vellar, 1988). In the North Karelia Youth Study, fat consumption was reduced for both genders, and total cholesterol was reduced for females (Puska et al., 1982). Finally, results from the Class of 1989 study of the Minnesota Heart Health Program suggest that multiple intervention components, such as behavioral-oriented health education in schools coupled with communitywide health promotion strategies, can produce modest but lasting improvement in adolescent knowledge and choices of heart-healthy foods and less frequent food-salting practices (Kelder, Perry, Lytle, & Klepp, 1995). It should be noted that the culmination of the research investigations of the 1980s on nutrition and physical activity is the CATCH program (Perry, Stone, et al., 1990), described earlier in this chapter.

Multicomponent Pregnancy and STD Prevention

Although many programs, have emphasized skill building in areas such as communications and assertiveness, Kirby's extensive review of the effects of such programs revealed such a diverse range in the quality and type of programs being implemented that the results measuring the impact on sexual behavior are mixed (Kirby et al., 1994).

Two notable studies, however, with controlled research designs and sound evaluation methods have demonstrated favorable program effects. A study conducted in New York City high schools evaluated an AIDS prevention curriculum based on the health belief model, SCT, and a model of social influence. Evaluation results indicated modest but significant effects for knowledge, beliefs, self-efficacy, and sexual risk-taking behaviors (Walter & Vaughan, 1993). The authors of the New York study do comment that such curricula may need supplementation by broader-based prevention efforts to achieve substantial risk behavior change. Second, a Dutch study tested the effectiveness of an AIDS/STD prevention curriculum for middle school students that addressed knowledge about transmission, prevention, and risk perception; attitudes toward safe sex and condom use; values, social influences, and communication skills; and self-efficacy, negotiating skills, and practicing condom use. The educational program had a favorable impact on students' knowledge, beliefs, intentions for using condoms, and sexual risk-taking behavior (Schaalma et al., 1996). The unique feature and strength of both of these programs is that the development of the interventions was guided by a theoretically based assessment of the determinants of sexual risk and protective behavior in the target population (Schaalma et al., 1993; Walter et al., 1992).

Youth Violence Prevention

Although many efforts have been made to address violent injury, relatively few careful evaluations have been conducted, and of these, few have demonstrated effectiveness. Tolan and Guerra (1994) have conducted an exhaustive review of the literature and have concluded:

> There has been relatively limited sound empirical program evaluation that permits judgment of effects. There is also a considerable gap between the most commonly used programs and the most frequently evaluated ones. . . . most approaches have not been well evaluated and the effects shown must be qualified and enthusiasm for given approaches tempered. (p. 46)

In many cases, informal records of teacher or student enthusiasm about a program, individual success stories, or program longevity have been the only basis to judge program effects. Thus, although many empirical evaluations are underway, the field of violence prevention is relatively young compared with chronic disease and HIV/STD prevention.

Summary

Although the majority of what is known about youth health promotion takes place at school, it must be recognized that given the pressing academic responsibilities of schools, it is neither realistic nor optimal for schools alone to carry the responsibility for youth health promotion. Schools should have a central role, but effective programs appear to require multiple components, including the support and cooperation of parents, community agencies, and actively enforced communitywide policies. Thus, a major conclusion is that early, repeated, and strong intervention strategies will have a higher probability of success than single-component approaches or those of short duration.

IMPLEMENTING SCHOOL
HEALTH PROMOTION PROGRAMS

The process of change in school systems tends to occur slowly, frequently due to the lack of a systematic approach to effect change. This phenomenon is especially relevant to the introduction of innovative school health promotion programs, an area in which change often needs to occur within several components of the total school program. Parcel et al. (1988) offer a model for implementing change in schools that includes four phases: (a) organizational commitment, (b) alterations in policies and practices, (c) alterations of roles and actions of staff, and (d) implementation of learning activities and other interventions. The intent of this model is to provide a systematic approach to change that includes school components that support behaviors addressed by health education programs in the classroom. Health education is viewed as a core component, but not the only component so that change can occur at several levels, including organizational and environmental change as well as individual change.

In the first phase, commitment is obtained from key decision makers in the school system to proceed with the planning of a new or modified health promotion program. A top-down approach would involve school board members, superintendents, and program directors arriving at a decision to commit to the proposed program. The proposal for the new program may come from an agency outside the district, such as the health department or voluntary health agency, or from inside groups, such as curriculum-planning committees or task force groups appointed to address specified problems. Usually, commitment is obtained through a series of meetings with key decision makers. Typically, these meetings involve written or verbal presentation on the importance, rationale, and need for the proposed program.

Commitment also needs to be obtained from a bottom-up, or grassroots approach, in which the persons who implement the program (teachers and staff members) and potential participants (students and parents) are actively involved in making decisions about planning new or modified programs. One method for obtaining this type of commitment that has been implemented in several states is the "seaside" model (named for a seaside retreat in Oregon). The seaside model involves the participation of teams from school districts coming together in a conference to explore their own personal health promotion needs as well as those of the students. The process involves planning a health promotion program or activity for their district. Recently, the seaside model has been expanded to include community representatives, parents, and students. Out of this type of experience often comes a strong commitment on a personal and professional level for health promotion programs. A second way that bottom-up commitment is accomplished is through the involvement of existing committees in the schools, such as site-based planning committees, or creating special structures for health promotion, such as a health promotion council. As a result of the spread of site-based management, many schools have decision-making committees composed of teachers, administrators, parents, and community members.

Once commitment is demonstrated, the second step is to establish a policy-planning group composed of the program directors and key administrators to develop and define policies that support the program's high priority in terms of importance and value. The policies then are given to a second planning group to address the changes that will need to be made in current practices to follow through on the intent of the policies and to implement the new program. This planning group usually consists of program directors and representatives of teachers and staff members who will be implementing the program.

The third phase focuses on preparing the teachers and staff members to implement the program. For the most part, teachers are trained in the knowledge-based model of health education. Changing their teaching practices to incorporate methods such as role play, use of peer leaders, modeling, and skill training requires specialized preparation. In-service training, technical assistance, and monitoring and feedback are methods that can be used to alter roles and actions of personnel to implement new programs. Such staff development needs to pay particular attention to the need for ongoing, rather than one-time, training. In addition, training programs must be able to address the needs of teachers with differing levels of comfort and facility with the new practices (Hall, Loucks, Newlove, & Rutherford, 1975; Hall, Newlove, George, & Rutherford, 1986; Hord & Huling-Austin, 1985). Finally, with these changes in place, the school health promotion program is ready to be implemented.

REFERENCES

Allensworth, D. D., & Kolbe, L. J. (1987). The comprehensive school health program: Exploring an expanded concept. *Journal of School Health, 57*(10), 409-411.

Bandura, A. (1986). *Social foundations of thought and action.* Englewood Cliffs, NJ: Prentice Hall.

Bangert-Drowns, R. L. (1988). The effects of school-based substance abuse education: A meta-analysis. *Journal of Drug Education, 18*(3), 243-264.

Basen-Engquist, K., Parcel, G. S., Harrist, R., Kirby, D., Coyle, K., Banspach, S., & Rugg, D. (1997). The Safer Choices project: Methodological issues in school-based health promotion intervention research. *Journal of School Health, 67*(9), 365-371.

Botvin, G. J. (1990). Substance abuse prevention: Theory, practice, and effectiveness. *Crime and Justice, 13,* 461-519.

Botvin, G. J., Baker, E., Dusenbury, L., Botvin, E. M., & Diaz, T. (1995). Long-term follow-up results of a randomized drug abuse prevention trial in a white middle-class population. *Journal of the American Medical Association, 273*(14), 1106-1112.

Brown, B. B., Mounts, N., Lamborn, S. D., & Steinberg, L. (1993). Parenting practices and peer group affiliation in adolescence. *Child Development, 64,* 467-482.

Bruvold, W. H. (1993). A meta-analysis of adolescent smoking prevention programs. *American Journal of Public Health, 83*(6), 872-880.

Coiro, M. J., Zill, N., & Bloom, B. (1994). *Health of our nation's children* (Vital Health Statistics, Series 10, No. 191; PHS 95-1519). Hyattsville, MD: National Center for Health Statistics.

Coleman, J. (1991). *Parental involvement in education* (Office of Educational Research and Improvement, U.S. Department of Education; PIP 91-983). Washington, DC: Government Printing Office.

Committee for Children. (1990). *Second Step: A violence prevention curriculum. Grades 6-8.* Seattle, WA: Author.

Contento, I. R., Manning, A. D., & Shannon, B. (1992). Research perspective on school-based nutrition education. *Journal of Nutrition Education, 24,* 247-260.

Coyle, K., Kirby, D., Parcel, G., Basen-Engquist, K., Banspach, S., Rugg, D., & Weil, M. (1996). Safer Choices: A multiple component school-based HIV/STD and pregnancy prevention program for adolescents. *Journal of School Health, 66*(3), 89-94.

Ellickson, P. L., Bell, R. M., & McGuigan, K. (1993). Preventing adolescent drug use: Long-term results of a junior high program. *American Journal of Public Health, 83*(6), 856-861.

Ennett, S. T., Tobler, N. S., Ringwalt, C. L., & Flewelling, R. L. (1994). How effective is drug abuse resistance education? A meta-analysis of Project DARE outcome evaluations. *American Journal of Public Health, 84*(9), 1394-1401.

Evans, R. I. (1984). A social inoculation strategy to deter smoking in adolescents. In J. D. Matarazzo, S. M. Weiss, J. A. Herd, N. E. Miller, & S. M. Weiss (Eds.), *Behavioral health: A handbook for health enhancement and disease prevention* (pp. 765-777). New York: John Wiley.

Feiring, C., & Lewis, M. (1989). The social networks of girls and boys from early through middle childhood. In D. Belle (Ed.), *Children's social networks and social supports.* New York: John Wiley.

Flay, B. R. (1985). Psychosocial approaches to smoking prevention: A review of the findings. *Health Psychology, 4,* 449-488.

Flay, B. R., Koepke, D., Thompson, S. J., Santi, S., Best, J. A., & Brown, K. S. (1989). Six-year follow-up of the first Waterloo School Smoking Prevention Trial. *American Journal of Public Health, 79,* 1371-1375.

Flynn, B. S., Wordon, J. K., Sacker-Walker, R. H., Pirie, P. L., Badger, B. M., Carpenter, J. H., & Geller, B. M. (1994). Mass media and school interventions: Effects two years after completion. *American Journal of Public Health, 84,* 1148-1150.

Freire, P. (1983). *Education for critical consciousness.* New York: Continuum.

Gans, J. E. (1990). *America's adolescents: How healthy are they? Profiles of adolescents health series* (Vol. 1). Chicago: American Medical Association.

Gingiss, P. L., & Basen-Engquist, K. (1994). HIV education practices and training needs of middle school and high school teachers. *Journal of School Health, 64,* 290-295.

Hall, G. E., Loucks, S. F., Newlove, B. W., & Rutherford, W. L. (1975). Levels of use of the innovation: A framework for analyzing innovation adoption. *Journal of Teacher Education, 29*(1), 26-52.

Hall, G. E., Newlove, B. W., George, A. A., & Rutherford, W. L. (1986). *Measuring stages of concern about facilitating use of an innovation: A manual for use of the CFSOC questionnaire.* Austin: University of Texas, Research and Development Center for Teacher Education.

Hansen, W. B. (1992). School-based substance abuse prevention: A review of the state of the art in curriculum, 1980–1990. *Health Education Research, 7,* 403-430.

Hord, S. M., & Huling-Austin, L. L. (1985). Acquiring expertise. *The Diabetes Educator, 11,* 13-20.

Institute of Medicine. (1997). *Schools & health: Our nation's investment.* Washington, DC: National Academy Press.

Johnson, C. A., Pentz, M. A., Weber, M. D., Dwyer, J. H., Baer, N., MacKinnon, D. P., & Hansen, W. B. (1990). Relative effectiveness of comprehensive community programming for drug abuse prevention with high-risk and low-risk adolescents. *Journal of Consulting and Clinical Psychology, 58*(4), 447-456.

Jurich, A. P., Polson, C. J., Jurich, J. A., & Bates, R. A. (1985). Family factors in the lives of drug users and abusers. *Adolescence, 20,* 143-159.

Kandel, D. B., & Andrews, K. (1987). Processes of adolescent socialization by parents and peers. *International Journal of the Addictions, 22*(4), 319-342.

Kann, L., Warren, C. W., Harris, W. A., Collins, J. L., Douglas, K. A., Collins, M. E., Williams, B. I., Ross, J. G., & Kolbe, L. J. (1995). State and local YRBSS coordinators. Youth risk behavior surveillance—United States, 1993. *Morbidity and Mortality Weekly Report, 44*(No. SS-1), 1-56.

Kelder, S. H., Edmundson, E. W., & Lytle, L. A. (in press). Youth health promotion. In D. Gochman (Ed.), *Handbook of health behavior research.* New York: Plenum.

Kelder, S. H., Orpinas, P., Parcel, G. S., McAlister, A., Frankowski, R., & Friday, J. (1996). The Students for Peace Project: A comprehensive violence-prevention program for middle school students. *American Journal of Preventive Medicine, 12*(5, Suppl.), 22-30.

Kelder, S. H., Parcel, G. S., & Perry, C. L. (1995). Health promotion. In L. Siegel (Ed.), *Advances in pediatric psychology: Behavioral perspectives on adolescent health.* New York: Guilford.

Kelder, S. H., Perry, C. L., Lytle, L. L., & Klepp, K. I. (1995). Community-wide youth nutrition education: Long-term outcomes of the Minnesota Heart Health Program. *Health Education Research: Theory and Practice, 10*(2), 119-131.

Kirby, D. (1984). *Sexuality education: Programs and their effects.* Santa Cruz, CA: Network Publications.

Kirby, D., Barth, R. B., Leland, N., & Fetro, J. V. (1991). Reducing the risk: Impact of a new curriculum on sexual risk taking. *Family Planning Perspectives, 23,* 253-263.

Kirby, D., Short, L., Collins, J., Rugg, D., Kolbe, L., Howard, M., Brent, M., Sonenstein, F., & Zabin, L. S. (1994). School-based programs to reduce sexual risk behaviors: A review of effectiveness. *Public Health Reports, 109,* 339-360.

Kolbe, L. J. (1990). An epidemiological surveillance system to monitor the prevalence of youth behaviors that most affect health. *Health Education, 6,* 44-48.

Komro, K. A., Perry, C. L., Williams, C. L., Veblen-Mortenson, S., Forster, J., Munson, K., Farbakhsh, K., Lachter, R. B., & Pratt, L. (in press). Research and evaluation design of a community-wide program to reduce adolescent alcohol use: Project Northland Phase II. In *Community action research and the prevention of alcohol and other drug problems.* Wellington, New Zealand: Alcoholic Advisory Council.

Luepker, R. V., Perry, C. L., McKinlay, S. M., Nader, P. R., Parcel, G. S., Stone, E. J., Webber, L. S., Elder, J. P., Feldman, H. A., Johnson, C. C., Kelder, S. H., & Wu, M., for the CATCH Collaborative Group. (1996). Outcomes of a field trial to improve children's dietary patterns and physical activity: The Child and Adolescent Trial for Cardiovascular Health (CATCH). *Journal of the American Medical Association, 275*(10), 768-776.

Lytle, L., & Achterberg, C. (1995). Changing the diet of America's children: What works and why? *Journal of Nutrition Education, 27*(5), 250-260.

McAlister, A. (1995). Behavioral journalism: Beyond the marketing model for health communication. *American Journal of Health Promotion, 9*(6), 417-420.

McLaren, P. (1989). *Life in schools: An introduction to critical pedagogy in the foundations of education.* White Plains, NY: Longman.

Minkler, M. (1990). Improving health through community organization. In K. Glanz, F. M. Lewis, & B. K. Rimer (Eds.), *Health behavior and health education: Theory, research and practice.* San Francisco, CA: Jossey-Bass.

Moore, K., Peterson, J., & Furstenberg, F. (1986). Parental attitudes and the occurrence of early sexual activity. *Journal of Marriage and the Family, 48,* 777-782.

Nader, P. R., Sallis, J. F., Patterson, T. L., Abramson, I. S., Rupp, J. W., Senn, K. L., Atkins, C. J., Roppe, B. E., Morris, J. A., Wallace, J. P., & Vega, W. A. (1989). A family approach to cardiovascular risk reduction: Results from the San Diego Family Heart Project. *Health Education Quarterly, 16,* 229-244.

Nader, P. R., Stone, E. J., Lytle, L. A., Perry, C. L., Osganian, S. K., Webber, L. S., Elder, J. P., Montgomery, D., Feldman, H. A., Wu, M., Johnson, C., Parcel, G. S., & Luepker, R. V. (1999). Three-year maintenance of improved diet and physical activity: The CATCH study. *Archives of Pediatrics and Adolescent Medicine, 153,* 695-704.

Nicklas, T. A., Forcier, J. E., Farris, R. P., Hunter, S. M., Webber, L. S., & Berenson, G. S. (1989). Heart Smart School Lunch Program: A vehicle for cardiovascular health promotion. *Health Promotion, 4,* 91-100.

Orpinas, P. M., Kelder, S. H., Murray, N. G., Fourney, A., Conroy, J., McReynolds, L., & Peters, R. (1996). Critical issues in implementation of a comprehensive violence prevention program for middle schools: Translating theory to practice. *Education and Urban Society, 28*(4), 456-472.

Parcel, G. S., Simons-Morton, B. G., & Kolbe, L. J. (1988). Health promotion: Integrating organizational change and student learning strategies. *Health Education Quarterly, 15,* 435-450.

Parcel, G. S., Simons-Morton, B. G., O'Hara, N. M., Baranowski, T., & Wilson, B. (1989). School promotion of healthful diet and physical activity: Impact on learning outcomes and self-reported behavior. *Health Education Quarterly, 16,* 181-199.

Pentz, M. A., MacKinnon, D. P., Flay, B. R., Hansen, W. B., Johnson, C. A., & Dwyer, J. H. (1989). Primary prevention of chronic diseases in adolescence: Effects of the Midwestern Prevention Project on tobacco use. *American Journal of Epidemiology, 130,* 713-724.

Perry, C. L., Baranowski, T., & Parcel, G. S. (1990). How individuals, environments, and health behavior interact: Social learning theory. In K. Glanz, F. M. Lewis, & B. Rimer (Eds.), *Health behavior and health education.* San Francisco, CA: Jossey-Bass.

Perry, C. L., Kelder, S. H., & Klepp, K. I. (1994). The rationale behind early prevention of cardiovascular disease with young people. *European Journal of Public Health, 4*(3), 156-163.

Perry, C. L., Kelder, S. H., & Komro, K. (1992). The social world of adolescents: Family, peers, schools, and community. In *Carnegie Council on Adolescent Development, Volume on Adolescent Health Promotion.* New York: Oxford University Press.

Perry, C. L., Kelder, S. H., Murray, D. M., & Klepp, K. I. (1992). Community-wide smoking prevention: Long-term outcomes of the Minnesota Heart Health Program. *American Journal of Public Health, 82,* 1210-1216.

Perry, C. L., Luepker, R. L., Murray, D. M., & Hearn, M. D. (1988). Parent involvement in children's health promotion: A one year follow-up of the Minnesota Home Team. *Health Education Quarterly, 16,* 171-180.

Perry, C. L., Sellers, D. E., Johnson, C., Pedersen, S., Bachman, K. J., Parcel, G. S., Stone, E. J., Luepker, R. V., Wu, M., Nader, P. R., & Cook, K. (1997). The Child and Adolescent Trial for Cardiovascular Health (CATCH): Intervention, implementation, and feasibility for elementary schools in the United States. *Health Education and Behavior, 24*(6), 716-735.

Perry, C. L., Stone, E. J., Parcel, G. S., Ellison, R. C., Nader, P. R., Webber, L. S., & Luepker, R. V. (1990). School-based cardiovascular health promotion: The Child and Adolescent Trial for Cardiovascular Health (CATCH). *Journal of School Health, 60,* 406-413.

Perry, C. L., Williams, C. L., Forster, J. L., Wolfson, M., Wagenaar, A. C., Finnegan, J. R., McGovern, P. G., Veblen-Mortenson, S., Komro, K. A., & Anstine, P. (1993). Background, conceptualization, and design of a community-wide research program on adolescent alcohol use: Project Northland. *Health Education Research Theory and Practice, 8,* 1126-1136.

Perry, C. L., Williams, C. L., Veblen-Mortenson, S., Toomey, T. L., Komro, K. A., Anstine, P. S., McGovern, P. G., Finnegan, J. R., Forster, J. L., Wagenaar, A. C., & Wolfson, M. (1996). Project Northland: Outcomes of a communitywide alcohol use prevention program during early adolescence. *American Journal of Public Health, 86*(7), 956-965.

Puska, P., Vartiainen, E., Pallonen, U., Salonen, J. T., Poyhis, P., Koskela, K., & McAlister, A. (1982). The North Karelia Youth Project: Evaluation of two years of intervention on health behavior and cardiovascular disease risk factors among 13- to 15-year old children. *Preventive Medicine, 11,* 550-570.

Rothman, J., & Tropman, J. E. (1987). Models of community organization and macro practice: Their mixing and phasing. In F. M. Cox, J. L. Erlich, J. Rothman, & J. E. Tropman (Eds.), *Strategies of community organization* (4th ed.). Itasca, IL: Peacock.

Sallis, J. F., & McKenzie, T. L. (1992). Physical education's role in public health. *Research Quarterly for Exercise and Sport, 62*(2), 124-137.

Schaalma, H. P., Kok, G., Bosker, R. J., Parcel, G. S., Peters, L., Poelman, J., & Reinders, J. (1996). Planned development and evaluation of AIDS/STD education for secondary school students in the Netherlands: Short-term effects. *Health Education Quarterly, 23*(4), 469-487.

Schaalma, H., Kok, G., & Peters, L. (1993). Determinants of consistent condom use by adolescents: The impact of experience of sexual intercourse. *Health Education Research: Theory and Practice, 8*(2), 255-269.

Schaps, E., Churgin, S., Palley, C. S., Takata, B., & Cohen, A. Y. (1981). Primary prevention research: A preliminary review of program outcome studies. *International Journal of the Addictions, 15*(5), 657-676.

Tell, G. S., & Vellar, O. D. (1988). Physical fitness, physical activity, and cardiovascular disease risk factors in adolescents: The Oslo Youth Study. *Preventive Medicine, 17,* 12-24.

Tobler, N. S. (1992). Drug prevention programs can work: Research findings. *Journal of Addictive Diseases, 11*(3), 1-28.

Tolan, P., & Guerra, N. (1994). *What works in reducing adolescent violence: An empirical review of the literature.* Boulder, CO: Center for the Study and Prevention of Violence.

Treboux, D., & Busch-Rossnagel, N. (1990). Social network influences on adolescent sexual attitudes and behaviors. *Journal of Adolescent Research, 5,* 175-189.

U.S. Bureau of the Census. (1992). Poverty in the United States: 1991. *Current Population Reports* (Series P-60, No. 181). Washington, DC: Government Printing Office.

U.S. Department of Education, Office of Educational Research and Improvement, National Center for Educational Statistics. (1993). *Youth Indicators 1993* (NCES 93-242). Washington, DC: Government Printing Office.

Vartiainen, E., Pallonen, U., McAlister, A., & Puska, P. (1990). Eight-year follow-up results of an adolescent smoking prevention program: The North Karelia Youth Project. *American Journal of Public Health, 80,* 78-79.

Wallerstein, N., & Bernstein, E. (1988). Empowerment education: Freire's ideas adapted to health education. *Health Education Quarterly, 15*(4), 379-394.

Wallerstein, N., & Sanchez-Merki, V. (1994). Freirian praxis in health education: Research results from an adolescent prevention program. *Health Education Research, 9*(1), 1105-1118.

Walter, H. J., & Vaughan, R. D. (1993). AIDS risk reduction among a multiethnic sample of urban high school students. *Journal of the American Medical Association, 270*(6), 725-730.

Walter, J. H., Vaughan, R. D., Gladis, M. M., Ragin, D. F., Kasen, S., & Cohall, A. T. (1992). Factors associated with AIDS risk behaviors among high school students in an AIDS epicenter. *American Journal of Public Health, 82,* 528-532.

COMMENTARY

Cheryl L. Perry

Chapter 3, "The School as a Setting for Health Promotion" by Parcel, Kelder, and Basen-Engquist, provides an excellent summary of empirically validated approaches to health promotion in schools. Health promotion and school-based educational research efforts have a history of being perceived as nonscientific, nonquantitative, and "soft." Unfortunately, this continues to be a dominant perception, with recent requests for budget cuts at the National Science Foundation and the Department of Education targeting the social sciences. Therefore, it is particularly important that a body of research in school-based health promotion has evolved over the past 20 years that is theory driven, is based on etiological data, has advanced progressively and systematically, and has repeatedly demonstrated "harder" outcomes.

The authors of this chapter conclude that multicomponent interventions using strong behavioral intervention strategies and sustained multiyear efforts can be successful in changing health outcomes for young people. This has been documented for smoking prevention (Perry, Kelder, Murray, & Klepp, 1992), dietary changes (Luepker et al., 1996), physical activity (Kelder, Perry, & Klepp, 1993), unprotected sexual behavior (Kirby, 1992), and alcohol and drug use prevention (Botvin, Baker, Dusenbury, Tortu, & Botvin, 1990; Perry et al., 1996). Effectiveness of these interventions appears to be related to several factors.

First, the programs change significant and potent psychosocial factors, as suggested by Social Learning Theory and etiological data (Bandura, 1977, 1986). Etiological data are particularly useful, because they reveal, in quantitative terms, which factors are predictive of a given behavior and which factors change as a result of an intervention. In Project Northland, for example, significant changes were observed in alcohol use onset and prevalence after 3 years of intervention (Perry et al., 1996). Significant changes were also noted in peer influence, self-efficacy, and parent-child communication around alcohol use. Therefore, we can conclude that Project Northland was able to successfully create changes in role models and self-efficacy, key components of social cognitive theory, and that these resulted in behavior changes.

Second, the successful multicomponent programs "fit" within the given structure, policies, and practices of schools and therefore are likely to be implemented with fidelity. Although the policies and practices of schools may independently contribute to health outcomes (Pentz et al., 1989) and model programs have demonstrated that these policies and practices can be modified (Comer, 1988), comprehensive changes in school structure are generally beyond the scope of school health promotion programs. The successful implementation of CATCH in 96 schools in four states, among middle- and lower-middle-class students, is therefore encouraging and noteworthy, because outcomes were noted across all sites (Luepker et al., 1996). None of the schools dropped out of the study or failed to implement the intervention in its entirety. Rates of attendance at trainings and observations of the teachers, PE specialists, and food service staff all revealed very high levels of implementation fidelity as well as high levels of support for CATCH (Perry et al., 1997).

Third, the intervention components are developed to be both complementary and supplementary to each other. This increases the power of an intervention to change targeted psychosocial factors, because the most potent factors are those that come from multiple sources in a young person's social environment, such as normative expectations or role models (Jessor & Jessor, 1977). For example, in Project Northland, peer leaders were elected and trained to conduct classroom discussions on why kids their age (in seventh grade) use alcohol, therefore eliciting the reasons or functional meanings of alcohol use (Jessor & Jessor, 1977; Perry et al., 1993). One of the most cited reasons was that alcohol use was a way "to have fun with friends." At the same time, a peer participation program was initiated in which seventh graders planned and implemented activities in their schools and communities for young adolescents, with the provision that these would be alcohol-free activities (Komro, Perry, Veblen-Mortenson, & Williams, 1994). The results included significant differences between intervention and reference communities in the number of students who attended parties where alcohol was present and perceptions of the functionality of alcohol use (Perry et al., 1996). The multicomponent intervention, then, can simultaneously change environmental factors (such as "ways to have fun") and personal factors (such as the perception that alcohol use is a "way to have fun").

Fourth, the greater the breadth and coordination of the intervention, in terms of intervention components, the more likely there will be sustained changes in health outcomes. This is consistent with the point that multiple levels of the social environment of youths need to be changed to reinforce changes made at the individual level. The involvement of peer leaders created changes in alcohol use among adolescents, even when compared with a program in which teachers presented the same activities (Perry & Grant, 1991). High levels of parental involvement have contributed to lower fat consumption among children when compared with the same material being taught at school (Perry, Luepker, et al., 1989). Smoking onset has been reduced by 30% to 40% through 12th grade when a peer-led smoking prevention curriculum was embedded in a community in which adults were being encouraged in multiple ways to quit smoking (Perry et al., 1992). This same peer-led program had diminished effects without community support (Murray, Pirie, Luepker, & Pallonen, 1989). The careful links of behavioral curricula, parental involvement, community support, and peer participation and leadership, with messages that are consistent and coordinated, have demonstrated efficacy beyond the implementation of a single strategy.

Several questions emerge from this review that might be useful to address. First, should school health promotion programs be implemented, delivered, and provided, or should they be encouraged, supported, and enabled? In other words, who should be responsible for program design and development? Several points can be made relative to multicomponent interventions. Demonstrable outcomes have overwhelmingly been achieved when the interventions were designed by those external to schools (Bruvold, 1993; Lytle & Achterberg, 1995). The application of social-psychological theories to program development was a key to successful intervention programs, and this is not a theoretical orientation that has been traditionally taught in graduate educational curricula. The design of attractive, compelling, and powerful programs is both time-consuming and costly, requiring staff members from multiple disciplines, and therefore may not be feasible at the local school or even district level. The programs implemented in Project Northland, for example, required a year of development time for each year of intervention. Still, as health promotion programs progress, the challenge of realizing changes in some factors has required a shift in "who develops" the intervention. For example, efforts to change community norms and access to alcohol by minors have required active participation on the part of many sectors of the community (Wagenaar & Perry, 1994). A top-down model, similar to that used by corporations with advisory boards, was not as effective as a bottom-up model of community organization through direct-action strategies (Blaine et al., 1997; Boyte, 1989). Within schools, community organizing models also have been used so that proposed changes come from the students, staff, parents, and community members. Sometimes these school teams decide that a classroom curriculum is needed, but then they don't have the resources to develop a program and either quickly create an ineffective program or find a program that has already been developed and evaluated. On the other hand, changes in school policies—for example, to ban cigarette smoking from school premises—have been far more successful when a bottom-up approach has been applied. Some components of school health promotion, then, such as the design and development of behavioral curricula or parental involvement programs appear to be more effective when they come from outside. However, issues concerning the policies and practices of a given school seem best served by the people who are involved in that setting.

The second question concerns theory. How is theory useful for school health promotion programs? The selection of a theory depends, in part, on the selection of outcomes. As the chapter points out, due to categorical research funding and a physical health orientation in this society, the outcomes most sought in the past few decades have been changes in behavior. Regardless of the type of outcome, a theory should specify the predictors of those outcomes. That is, the theory should be a plausible explanation of what causes the outcomes to occur (Glanz, Lewis, & Rimer, 1990). Theory, then, can guide intervention development, by specifying the most potent predictors of outcomes. This is critical, because these predictors are the targets (for change) of a health promotion program. It is also important because "potency" can be measured using etiological data, which means some theories are "better" than others, because they are better able to explain the outcomes (statistically). In addition, the targeting of the most potent predictors should be cost-effective. For example, the factors identified in Problem Behavior Theory (Jessor & Jessor, 1977), derived from Social Learning Theory, can account for about half the variance in adolescent problem behaviors. The most potent of these factors has been very useful in guiding the development of successful health promotion efforts with adolescents (Perry & Jessor, 1985). Recent data from Project Northland suggest that two factors—school and community norms and role models around alcohol use—accounted for over half the variance in eighth-grade alcohol use and therefore reinforces how critical these two social-environmental factors should be in intervention design (Roski, 1995; Roski et al., 1997).

Even if a factor identified by theory is predictive and potent, the factor must also be amenable to intervention to be useful in program development. For example, self-esteem has been shown to be predictive of obesity in adolescent populations but proves resistant to intervention (French, Story, & Perry, 1995). Low socioeconomic status and poverty are clearly associated with health outcomes (Syme, 1986) yet are generally beyond the scope of an individual health promotion program. These factors, however, may be critical in understanding the population being served, in deciding on which schools are at highest risk and should be given higher priority, and in recognizing potential barriers to program implementation. For example, in a recent intervention program in St. Paul, Minnesota, schools to encourage consumption of five or more fruits and vegetables each day, fruits and vegetables were provided to families, as "snack packs," because formative data suggested limited fruit and vegetable options in the poorer homes. These snack packs were well received; further action at the close of the research study has resulted in a managed-care organization interested in sponsoring the continuance of "snack packs" as part of the organization's interest in promoting community health.

Theories to guide health promotion efforts should also be robust so that they are applicable across settings and so that the programs derived from them are also robust. The Child and Adolescent Trial for Cardiovascular Health (CATCH) program was equally effective in schools in four states, with multiple ethnic groups, both genders, and varying levels of socioeconomic status (Luepker et al., 1996). There were no significant differences in the main outcomes by site, ethnic group, or gender. This suggests that the model used to develop CATCH was robust and generalizable. Similarly, in a study of alcohol education among eighth graders in Australia, Chile, Norway, and Swaziland, peer-led education was more effective in reducing alcohol use than was teacher-led education across all four countries and within each of the four countries, suggesting that peer role models and peer influence are strong factors in adolescent alcohol use independent of culture and are therefore powerful targets for intervention (Perry, Grant, et al., 1989). Clearly, how the theoretical factors manifest in different settings may differ, but the usefulness of a robust theoretical model is that it can provide guidance across settings as to which factors to consider.

There should be much optimism in the field of school-based health promotion. Schools provide perhaps the most successful site for promoting health, because a range of programs from intensive to impersonal have been possible and have proven effective. The successes in this field should not be ignored, and this chapter provides ample documentation and direction for future efforts.

Our advances in multicomponent interventions can serve as a basis for future development in this field. Still, when compared with the potential that schools have for promoting health, the interventions to date have been limited. They have focused almost exclusively on physical health concerns, such as smoking, eating behaviors, or alcohol use. Social health, or role fulfillment, has been partially addressed with violence prevention programs, life skills training, and social competency promotion (Botvin et al., 1990; Dodge et al., 1990; Kelder et al., 1996). Some other social roles have not been addressed very comprehensively—such as becoming active citizens, responsible parents, or employees in changing work environments. Moreover, school health promotion programs have not addressed the psychological and spiritual health of young people, where issues of loneliness, sense of purpose, and meaning are paramount (Perry & Jessor, 1985). To become a truly health-promoting school, the multiple domains of health need to be recognized and advanced. Schools have the potential to become "enclaves" in our society, devoted to the optimal development of young people, as well as settings that are safe, respectful, energized, and challenging and where there are abundant healthful role models and opportunities. This goal may require new partnerships, theories, and structures to achieve, but these may be necessary and salutary challenges for school health promotion as we approach the next century.

REFERENCES

Bandura, A. (1977). *Social learning theory*. Englewood Cliffs, NJ: Prentice Hall.

Bandura, A. (1986). *Social foundations of thought and action: A social cognitive theory*. Englewood Cliffs, NJ: Prentice Hall.

Blaine, T. M., Forster, J. L., Hennrikus, D., O'Neil, S., Wolfson, M., & Pham, H. (1997). Creating tobacco policy control at the local level: Implementation of a direct action organizing approach. *Health Education and Behavior, 24,* 640-651.

Botvin, G. J., Baker, E., Dusenbury, L., Tortu, S., & Botvin, E. M. (1990). Preventing adolescent drug abuse through a multimodal cognitive-behavioral approach: Results of a 3-year study. *Journal of Consulting and Clinical Psychology, 58,* 437-446.

Boyte, H. (1989). *Commonwealth: A return to citizen politics*. New York: Free Press.

Bruvold, W. H. (1993). A meta-analysis of adolescent smoking-prevention programs. *American Journal of Public Health, 83*(6), 872-880.

Comer, J. P. (1988). Educating poor minority children. *Scientific American, 259*(5), 42-48.

Dodge, K. A., Elias, M. J., Hawkins, J. D., Jason, L. A., Kendall, P. C., Perry, C. L., Rotheram-Borus, M. J., Weissberg, R. P., & Zins, J. E. (1990). Support for school-based social competence promotion. *American Psychologist, 45*(8), 986-988.

French, S. A., Story, M., & Perry, C. L. (1995). Self-esteem and obesity in children and adolescents: A literature review. *Obesity Research, 3,* 479-790.

Glanz, K., Lewis, F. M., & Rimer, B. K. (1990). *Health behavior and health education: Theory research and practice*. San Francisco, CA: Jossey-Bass.

Jessor, R., & Jessor, S. L. (1977). *Problem behavior and psychosocial development: A longitudinal study of youth*. Orlando, FL: Academic Press.

Kelder, S. H., Orpinas, P., Parcel, G. S., McAlister, A., Frankowski, R., & Friday, J. (1996). The Students for Peace Project: A comprehensive violence-prevention program for middle school students. *American Journal of Preventive Medicine, 12*(5, Suppl.), 22-30.

Kelder, S. H., Perry, C. L., & Klepp, K-I. (1993). Communitywide youth exercise education: Long-term outcomes of the Minnesota Heart Health Program. *Journal of School Health, 63*(5), 218-223.

Kirby, D. (1992). School-based programs to reduce sexual risk-taking behavior. *Journal of School Health, 62,* 280-287.

Komro, K. A., Perry, C. L., Veblen-Mortenson, S., & Williams, C. L. (1994). Peer participation in Project Northland: A community-wide alcohol use prevention project. *Journal of School Health, 164*(8), 318-322.

Luepker, R. V., Perry, C. L., McKinlay, S. M., Nader, P. R., Parcel, G. S., Stone, E. J., Webber, L. S., Elder, J. P., Feldman, H. A., Johnson, C. C., Kelder, S. H., & Wu, M. (1996). Outcomes of a field trial to improve children's dietary patterns and physical activity: The Child and Adolescent Trial for Cardiovascular Health (CATCH). *Journal of the American Medical Association, 275*(10), 768-776.

Lytle, L. A., & Achterberg, C. (1995). Changing the diet of America's children: What works and why? *Journal of Nutrition Education, 27*(5), 250-260.

Murray, D. M., Pirie, P., Luepker, R. V., & Pallonen, U. (1989). Five- six-year follow-up results from four seventh-grade smoking prevention strategies. *Journal of Behavioral Medicine, 12*(2), 207-218.

Pentz, M. A., Dwyer, J. H., MacKinnon, D. P., Flay, B. R., Hansen, W. B., Wang, E. Y. I., & Johnson, C. A. (1989). A multicommunity trial for primary prevention of adolescent drug abuse. *Journal of the American Medical Association, 261*(22), 3259-3266.

Perry, C. L., & Grant, M. (1991). A cross-cultural pilot study on alcohol education and young people. *World Health Statistics Quarterly, 44*(2), 70-73.

Perry, C. L., Grant, M., Ernberg, G., Florenzano, R. U., Langdon, M. D., Blaze-Temple, D., Cross, D., Jacobs, D. R., Myeni, A. D., Waahlberg, R. B., Berg, S., Andersson, D., Fisher, K. J., Saunders, B., & Schmid, T. (1989). W.H.O. collaborative study on alcohol education and young people: Outcomes of a four country pilot study. *International Journal of Addictions, 24*(12), 1145-1171.

Perry, C. L., & Jessor, R. (1985). The concept of health promotion and the prevention of adolescent drug abuse. *Health Education Quarterly, 12*(2), 169-184.

Perry, C. L., Kelder, S. H., Murray, D. M., & Klepp, K-I. (1992). Community-wide smoking prevention: Long-term outcomes of the Minnesota Heart Health Program and the Class of 1989 Study. *American Journal of Public Health, 82*(9), 1210-1216.

Perry, C. L., Luepker, R. V., Murray, D. M., Hearn, M. D., Halper, A., Dudovitz, B., Maile, M. C., & Smyth, M. (1989). Parent involvement with children's health promotion: A one-year follow-up of the Minnesota Home Team. *Health Education Quarterly, 16*(2), 1156-1160.

Perry, C. L., Sellers, D., Johnson, C., Pedersen, S., Bachman, K., Parcel, G., Stone, E., Luepker, R. V., Wu, M., Nader, P., & Cook, K. W. (1997). The Child and Adolescent Trial for Cardiovascular Health (CATCH): Intervention, implementation and feasibility for elementary schools in the U.S. *Health Education and Behavior, 24,* 716-735.

Perry, C. L., Williams, C. L., Forster, J. L., Wolfson, M., Wagenaar, A. C., Finnegan, J. R., McGovern, P. G., Veblen-Mortenson, S., Komro, K. A., & Anstine, P. S. (1993). Background conceptualization, and design of a communitywide research program on adolescent alcohol use: Project Northland. *Health Education Research: Theory & Practice, 8*(1), 125-136.

Perry, C. L., Williams, C. L., Veblen-Mortenson, S., Toomey, T., Komro, K. A., Anstine, P. S., McGovern, P. G., Finnegan, J. R., Forster, J. L., Wagenaar, A. C., & Wolfson, M. (1996). Outcomes of a community-wide alcohol use prevention program during early adolescence: Project Northland. *American Journal of Public Health, 86*(7), 956-965.

Roski, J. (1995). *The influence of the social environments of schools and communities on adolescent alcohol and drug use.* Doctoral dissertation, University of Trier, Germany.

Roski, J., Perry, C. L., McGovern, P. G., Williams, C. L., Farbakhsh, K., & Veblen Mortenson, S. (1997). School and community influences on adolescent alcohol and drug use. *Health Education Research: Theory and Practice, 12,* 255-266.

Syme, S. L. (1986). Social determinants of health and disease. In J. Last (Ed.), *Public health and preventive medicine* (pp. 953-970). Norwalk, CT: Appleton-Century-Crofts.

Wagenaar, A., & Perry, C. L. (1994). Community strategies for the reduction of youth drinking: Theory and application. *Journal of Research on Adolescence, 14*(2), 319-345.

COMMENTARY

Peter McLaren
Zeus Leonardo
Xóchitl Pérez

In the United States, there have been some attempts to develop health promotion programs in a few urban schools. However, many of them are based on behavioral models and in such manner exclude the possibility of using the students' communities as partners in health promotion. The logic behind using behavioral models is partly based on the fact that the schools piloted are located in urban areas, thereby fulfilling the goal of surveying a large sample. We know of at least two programs, both of which were presented at the 1995 American Public Health Association (APHA) Conference in San Diego that fall within the broad category of behavioral modeling:

- *The Brightwood School Health Project:* A comprehensive elementary school-based health center in an urban Hispanic community and led by E. Senghas, M.D. and A. Warren, F.N.P.

- *Obtaining Active Parental Informed Consent for Student Surveys to Evaluate School Health Programs in Urban Settings: Successful Strategies and Resource Requirements:* Three schools in Brooklyn, New York: cooperative work between the Education Development Center and the Department of Human Development and Family Studies, University of Illinois—Urbana-Champaign.

Other models of school health promotion that involve the community and attempt to create the conditions for students to acquire ownership of their own health promotion have failed for several reasons—primarily because they require a great amount of community resources for classroom instruction. Although the intent of using community resources is well-founded, it is difficult collectively to mobilize resources when the majority of the students in the piloted schools are dispersed among several communities or, worse, when the communities have limited resources. An example of this kind of program was presented at the 1995 APHA conference in San Diego:

- *Health Promotion in Multicultural Community: An Organizational Perspective:* Led by Kazue Shibata—an Asian Pacific Health Venture, in cooperation with UCLA, ongoing study; midterm report presented at the 1995 APHA conference in San Diego.

In response to using the school as a setting for health promotion that Parcel, Kelder, and Basen-Engquist present, three issues are worth considering: first, the value-laden approach to health promotion in the classroom; second, the "prescriptive" approach to curricula covered by the authors; and third, implementation approaches that are theoretically based rather than community driven.

IDEOLOGICAL TECTONICS:
SHIFTING HEALTH EPISTEMOLOGY

Health promotion discourses in the United States can be grouped into three areas: religious (dogma) justification, psychosocial explanations, and psychocognitive explorations. *Religious* justification in the schools attempts to identify an origin of species, either through the theory of evolution or through the theory of creationism. This discourse justifies authority, either god or science, through the venue of biology, but it does not empower the student to "manage" his or her own health and well-being. This model also involves issues of confidentiality, communication and transfer of information, and determination of appropriate timing for intervention. The following program is an example:

- *Ethical Dilemmas and Decision Making Policies in School Based Health Centers:* Led by Ferdinand Fuentes, M. Div., Karen Hacker, M.D., and Linda Corrine, F.N.P.

The *psychosocial* discourse traces health to social behavior; its roots are found in human behavioral patterning and modification. It is often manifested in discussion over reward and punishment for student behavior or in recommendations, for instance, to combat violent behavior in schools. The following programs are examples of this approach:

- *Development of Risk Behavior by Inner City Adolescents: When to Intervene:* Hannelore Vanderschmidt, Ph.D., Janet Lang, Sc.D., and Fred Vanderschmidt, Ph.D.

- *Public Perceptions of Risk: Using Opinion Poll Data to Shape CDC Prevention Policies:* Led by Diana Cassady, Dr.P.H., and Jeannie Gazzaniga, Ph.D.

Like the religious approach, this also fails to engage the students' sense of self-direction.

Finally, the *psychocognitive* argument attempts to explore the relationship between the logical and antilogical human behaviors. The following program is an example:

- *Identification and Tracking of Program Components in Evaluation of an Individualized Social-Support Program:* Led by Evelyn Knight, Ph.D., Lann Forrest, Ph.D., Kristin Candell, and Judith Hammond, Ph.D.

Often, this approach focuses on traumatic experiences in families so that a deficiency in parenting or trauma in the home is associated with problems with performance in schools. In education, this runs the risk of returning to a simplistic moral code that blames the victim rather than ameliorating unhealthful social conditions.

These approaches have ignored the paradigmatic shift in educational epistemology, or philosophy of knowledge, that questions the power of the subject to act on health choices in a completely free way: for example, critical theory, historical materialism, and poststructuralism. The previous models have explored only a consensual demand for public health action; consequently, they have neglected the distortions to consensus caused by factors such as ideology and capital. U.S. public health approaches have ignored this substantive shift in theoretical paradigms, which has affected both our understanding of what it means to be human and our systematic reflection on what critical theorists might term the "emancipated self." Therefore, it is important to examine this change in our understanding of health and consider its implications for a more democratic health program that considers as well as problematizes human agency.

A CRITICAL PERSPECTIVE ON EDUCATION, HEALTH, AND SCHOOL HEALTH PROMOTION

As social beings, we experience "reality" from our particular social locations: for example, our race, class, gender, and sexual orientation. Our discovery of the universe and universal values is ideological; it is neither innocent nor neutral. Consequently, it is not a "discovery" but rather a "construction." We often invest political interests into our actions and behave in ways that we take for granted. However, we cannot antiseptically remove our actions from other people's decisions to act in certain ways concerning their own health. Social movements centered on AIDS prevention and treatment are a perfect example of how politics enters a nation's policy on what is a worthwhile health issue and what is not. We often define the healthy self in opposition to the unhealthy Other. Thus, it becomes too convenient to dissociate oneself from the diseased Other (Triechler, 1991, p. 79). By remaining complicitous with existing medical ideologies, our actions become politically irresponsible in relation to the suffering Other by hermetically sealing ourselves off from those who are in need of medical attention. In short, AIDS is seen to only *happen* to those who "behave" like the Other. But an ethical health program requires something beyond an abstract unspecified Other. As Seyla Benhabib suggests, a just health promotion necessitates a concrete Other (cited by McLaren, 1995; also see Burbules, 1993) in order to deal with the "realness" of health issues, especially those that disable people in their everyday lives.

Learning about health is an act of self-empowerment, and within the context of learning personal health and hygiene, the knowledge gained can be emancipatory, depending on how educators construct their notion of humanity. Health and well-being are dialectically lived engagements; health is constructed out of self and social interaction: the world acting on people as well as people acting on the environment. We are created by our surroundings, but in acting, we create our environment as well. Incorporating health education that takes seriously students' everyday lived experiences in the classroom—what we could call "embodied perspectives"—would provide individuals with the access to health codes that are self-contained rather than contaminated. In essence, we confirm and legitimate self-direction and reject a dependency on the medical system, but at the same time, we contribute to students' need for empathy and affirmation. Hence, health promotion in schools cannot simply be guided by the problematic maxim, "Pull up your health by your own bootstraps." It is also necessary to argue for the rediscovery of the "self" that is emancipated from common biomedical conceptions of pathology. In other words, we must expose as problematic our "common sense" notions of what constitutes health and disease and invoke a broader critical examination of what constitutes the "good society," human well-being, and "community" than is implied in state-sanctioned moral imperatives of health-promoting (disease-avoiding) bodily practices that otherwise impose taken-for-granted limitations on the self. As such, we are arguing that common sense is never neutral or "obvious" but partisan and complex. And it must be understood within the totality of the larger society, one that is shaped by capitalist social relations of production and circuits of capitalist exchange.

From another perspective, health consciousness involves our process of understanding and what meaning and status our statements about reality carry—in other words, our primary epistemology. It profoundly affects (and liberates) how students conceive their view of social reality when they embody the space (are empowered) to choose their own health codes. In turn, this transformative possibility alters how they perceive the consequences of their behaviors when they own their health and body. Revolutionary changes in understanding how we comprehend (i.e., metacognition) and construct notions of truth have *reformed* the way we think about the human body and therefore have reformed the human body itself. That is, depending on the nature of discourses that refract rather than reflect social life, the body actually looks different. To reform health codes, we must also attend to how the effects of knowledge claims have formed and reformed the body. We argue for a similar restructuring of health programs.

From a historical perspective, health scholars have perceived manifestations of sickness and disease as partially the products of our environmental circumstances. Indeed, concrete environmental circumstances determine what is worth noticing as illness in the first place (e.g., AIDS, breast cancer). Health scholars then classified these abnormalities in a particular intellectual language (allopathic, homeopathic, or polemic as well as some literary forms—e.g., mythic or metaphysical). These scholars argued that the illnesses could properly be understood only if placed in their original environment. The understanding of the text could be found only in context. Like-wise, we argue that illnesses be examined within their context. However, we propose that in addition to the medical context, illnesses should be studied in their sociohistorical juncture: economic, political, and ideological.

Although our Western notions of truth have been largely absolute, static, monolithic, and theocentric up to the past century, it has since become cor-porate, massive, and business centered. In newly emerging discourses that problematize the body and intellect as nondistinct entities (anti-Cartesian)—perhaps best exemplified by Michel Foucault's (1977) disciplin-ary society, where health norms are encoded into the body, its posture, its musculature (see Shumway, 1994)—we conclude that this emerging view of well-being has already come about in at least three different, but closely re-lated, ways:

1. *Biological* or *genetic*—where well-being is reduced to the perception that our health is described in terms of genetic determinism, where DNA has coded our well-being (or lack thereof)

2. *Developmental*—where health is controlled by our immediate geography, cul-ture, and social standing, a position that we would argue is all too relative to is-sues of power and privilege (with respect to race, gender, class, and sexuality, which simultaneously interact and inscribe relations between people in a given context)

3. *Hermeneutically*—where all health, all well-being is seen as interpreted truth and hence is demystified by the "self" who is also the interpreter.

A fourth possible, but marginalized, discourse is the corporeal philoso-phy of health. It is a philosophy involving the mutable meanings we derive from life and death. In *Symbolic Exchange and Death,* Jean Baudrillard (1993) suggests that a change in our social construction of death necessi-tates a change in the way we look at life. As such, life-and-death is a form of exchange, not in economic terms, but in symbolic terms, like a gift. Cur-rently, we ostracize unhealthy bodies from social interaction and sequester dead bodies in cemeteries to dissociate ourselves from illness—or more pre-cisely, from the sick Other. Our separation of the living from the dead, and the sick from the healthy, is not only physical. It is also social. We stigmatize the *ideas* associated with illness and death. In our society, to be sick or dead is not normal. As a result, we divorce ourselves from our own bodies and live out disembodied experiences. Baudrillard argues for the asymptotic inter-mingling between the spheres of the living and the dead, the sick and the healthy. A critical health program reinserts the body into our search for well-being, not as a site for improvement—for this treats the body as an instrument—but as a site for material emancipation, a site for practical and trans-formative knowledge (embodiment of equity and justice).

To reemphasize, our (postmodern) understanding of self, truth, and real-ity has undergone a radical shift. This new paradigm declares that all state-ments about reality, especially about the *meaning* of events, are historical, intentional, relational, partial, interpretive, and dialectic. What is common to all of these qualities is the notion of *difference*. That is, all statements or understandings of reality are relationships between the knower and the known. The autonomous knowing self has been fractured. We have inaugu-rated the heteronomous self, a self that is historically produced. The new self is *heteroglossic* in the sense that Mikhail Bakhtin (1981) refers to it—an effect of the multiplicity of discourses and languages available at any one time (see also Stam, 1993). To avoid recolonization of the "student body," health edu-cation and promotion should not just recodify the knowledge to be im-parted to students. For self-emancipation requires that we unsettle, if not rupture, the existing rules for knowledge claims and truth statements as we have known them.

Critical theorists have acknowledged that any statement about well-being can be at most only a partial description of the reality the public is trying to describe. As Tunji Braithwaite (1987), summarizing St. Thomas Aquinas, so eloquently reminds us, "Things known are in the knower according to the mode of the knower." In other words, our reality is relative to our experi-ence. Moreover, our experiences are asymmetrical in the sense that they do not carry the same political weight. When we share a collective or common experience, reality often takes on the appearance of truth. However, a criti-cal pedagogy of health, as Antonio Gramsci might suggest, illustrates how political ideology marries common sense (see Giroux, 1992, p. 186). It is at the level of common sense that ideas and experiences are naturalized and therefore remain generally unquestioned. Truth statements are just that: statements. A critique of health programs requires what Paulo Freire (1993) calls a "deep structural analysis" of the language of health that is being pro-moted and how it enables and disables certain groups of people. Health programs must be interrogated from the context of how they have been pro-duced with the logic of capital and how they are functionally advantageous for the reproduction of capitalist social relations. The multiple approach to school health promotion that Parcel et al. propose must bear this in mind.

A self-reflexive theoretical approach to health must also be wary itself of the pitfalls of relativism. When we are able to interrogate the positivistic ar-ticulation of meaning and truth (i.e., that objective truth is waiting to be dis-covered), we are able to face the specter of relativism, the opposing Other of absolutism. Unlike the term *difference*, a term that suggests the quality of being in relationship, *relativism*, like so many "isms," is a basically negative term. If it can no longer be claimed that any statement about the truth of the meaning of things is absolute, or totally objective, because the claim does not square with our experience of reality, it is equally impossible to claim that every statement about truth is completely relative, totally subjective, for that also does not square with our experience of reality. Of course, this would logically lead to an atomizing isolation that would bring all dialogue to a resounding halt, all statements being as equally valid as others. Instead, we prefer to say that none of our perceptions and descriptions of reality is total, complete, absolute, or objective in the sense of being independent of a subject or viewer. Public health, as a social issue, is always an *interview*. At the same time, however, it is also obvious that there is a soft objectivism, doubtless a "true" aspect to each perception and description even though each is relational to what Maurice Merleau-Ponty (1963) theorized as the body-subject.

Where does this leave public health promotion? Public health programs will arrest their own democratic potential if they do not consider the changing epistemology in education. A critical pedagogy of health does not endorse a traditional, centralized governing body, and we discourage public health promoters from employing a technocratic management of schools. The medical profession, like the traditional school of education, must recognize that an enslaved individual dependent on the system for knowledge of "self-control" will not self-actualize into a critical citizen. Instead, public health promoters should promote a collaborative engagement between communities and individuals that will produce knowledge of healthy self-maintenance and emancipate students by increasing their participation in decision making. As we liberate the individual from dependency, we might also liberate the medical and educational profession from what Howard Blum (1985) calls the "anxiety of influence," which might transform these professions from disabling to enabling ones.

TRANSFORMING THE SCHOOL CURRICULA

We suggest that schools and public health promoters reflect on their historical, public nature by acting as mediating, not mitigating, institutions. Here, the role of these sectors as advocates of public health is to meet the associated needs of participants in schools. The role that schools can equally embrace is one that establishes links between individual and general societal needs. In this sense, the school becomes the mediating institution for society. At the same time that educators recognize that capitalism is the driving force in curriculum development, health trends, and behaviors, they can recognize that schools can serve as mediating institutions that can participate in an active critique of these trends and attitudes and eventually can participate in an active critique of and resistance to larger capitalist social relations.

However, the project toward this reconciliation is not simple. Like the religious indulgences of the past, there is potential for abuse when the battle is limited—that is, when it is waged between traditional beliefs and science. Current approaches to school health promotion constitute a prerogative determined more by efficiency than social justice. Although fairness and equity may be on the platter of school health promotion programs, justice should not take the form of a descriptive notion. As Jean-François Lyotard (Lyotard & Thébaud, 1985) argues, justice cannot be described. It is a prescription, a linguistic proposition that guides our actions as they pertain, for example, to health. It is not in the realm of the knowable, and we will surely fail if we ground "the ought" in the "what is." Justice should always be out of reach and enigmatic: "pagan," as Lyotard refers to it. We can only anticipate justice while never really experiencing it. We are not suggesting that justice is only a social construction. Surely we advocate that suffering is real and needless suffering must be eliminated. We are arguing that social justice is never really achieved, that it must always be struggled for. This is as much a Marxist challenge as it is a postmodern one.

For justice to become the priority of health reforms, community solidarity must describe theologically, philosophically, historically, sociologically, and psychologically the tensions that make solidarity a necessary ethic in all parts of life. This does not mean that we need to fix curricula into standardized multicultural or diversity-driven modules but, rather, that we should recognize the interconnectedness of the different areas in an individual's life. Second, for those who acknowledge these tensions, solidarity building in the form of social movements must then work to expose social needs, or "generative themes" as Freire (1993) refers to them, that become the content of any discussion. Meeting these needs of others and of oneself makes the project of solidarity not just a therapeutic benefit but also an ethical obligation toward the establishment of a socialist praxis. Third, within the context of public health institutions, we encourage health educators to recognize that these institutions are morally coded. Cracking the opaque window of political ideology in health takes collective work.

CONCLUSIONS

We take the position that international, national, and local health promotion initiatives—even initiatives that are multidimensional approaches such as the one presented by Parcel et al.—are problematic and, worse, reproductive because they lack a heuristic for agency, or how people act *collectively* to produce liberatory health conditions. Within our perspective, the body can no longer be seen as a physical machine but, rather, must be seen as a fluid, contextual assemblage anticipating liberation from state control and the larger relations of production and consumption within late capitalism. The discussion presented here shows that there exist spaces of possibility and resistance to regimes of capitalist discipline and state control over the body.

The ethical center of this discussion is the idea that human existence ought to be motivated and judged by a recognition of the inherent connectedness of all people. Politically, it is underwritten by a commitment to fighting capitalist relations of exploitation. Philosophically, we endorse the critical/historical dialectical method, and ethically we encourage solidarity building because democratizing health promotion cannot be accomplished by reaffirming the "rugged individual." Such a conception requires political, legal, and economic structures in which difference is recognized and nurtured. Developing these structures is a task of ethics and justice and a struggle for a socialist society. Thus, the task is not to reject current normative theory but to reinvent such theory with respect to the current challenges facing public health policy and practice. Even a proposal as limited as this covers a great deal of political, economic, sociological, historical, theological, managerial, and philosophical territory. Health education must be seen as a societal commitment to the lifelong provision of welfare and well-being. It is a commitment to the society of which Emile Durkheim spoke, a society composed not only of a group of individuals but especially "of ideas, beliefs, and sentiments of all sorts which realize themselves through individuals" (Bellah, 1973, p. 4). It is also a commitment grounded in Gramsci's (1971) call for the recovery of agency (also see McLaren, Fischman, Serra, & Antelo, 1998). But more important, it is a society that works toward the imperatives of Marx: From each according to her ability, to each according to her need.

Our perspective bears some similarity in content to Parcel et al.'s suggestions but maintains some radical difference in terms of its overall project. It not only asks social actors (e.g., teachers and community members) to become organic intellectuals but also asks individual students and teachers to assume control of the decisions and consequences of their actions with respect to their bodies. Because students' responses are not determined exclusively by structural forces beyond their control, the community (which includes these students) can become a partially autonomous site of agency where both resistance and transformation can occur. With the influence of teachers, the cooperation of the community, and collective resistance to the normalizing practices of state intervention, students can act as informed agents. In other words, they can embody or enflesh (McLaren, 1995) narratives of health that promote well-being.

REFERENCES

Bakhtin, M. (1981). *The dialogic imagination* (M. Holquist, Ed.; C. Emerson & M. Holquist, Trans.). Austin: University of Texas Press.

Baudrillard, J. (1993). *Symbolic exchange and death* (I. H. Grant, Trans.). Thousand Oaks, CA: Sage.

Bellah, R. (1973). *Emile Durkheim on morality and society*. Chicago: University of Chicago Press.

Blum, H. (1985). *Wishful thinking*. New York: Atheneum.

Braithwaite, T. (1987). The oracles, natural law, and positivism. In *The jurisprudence of the living oracles*. Benin, Nigeria: Ethiope Publishing.

Burbules, N. (1993). Reasonable doubt: Toward a postmodern defense of reason as an educational aim. In W. Kohli (Ed.), *Critical conversations in philosophy of education*. New York: Routledge.

Foucault, M. (1977). *Discipline and punish*. New York: Vintage.

Freire, P. (1993). *Pedagogy of the oppressed*. New York: Continuum.

Giroux, H. (1992). *Border crossings*. London: Routledge.

Gramsci, A. (1971). *Selections from the prison notebooks*. New York: International Publishers.

Lyotard, J.-F., & Thébaud, J.-L. (1985). *Just gaming* (W. Godzich, Trans.). Minneapolis: University of Minnesota Press.

McLaren, P. (1995). *Critical pedagogy and predatory culture*. New York: Routledge.

McLaren, P., Fischman, G., Serra, S., & Antelo, E. (1998). The specters of Gramsci: Revolutionary praxis and the committed intellectual. *Journal of Thought, 33*(3), 9-41.

Merleau-Ponty, M. (1963). *The structure of behavior*. Pittsburgh, PA: Duquesne University Press.

Shumway, D. (1994). Reading rock 'n' roll in the classroom: A critical pedagogy. In H. Giroux & P. McLaren (Eds.), *Critical pedagogy, the state, and cultural struggle*. New York: State University of New York Press.

Stam, R. (1993). Bakhtin and the Left cultural critique. In E. A. Kaplan (Ed.), *Postmodernism and its discontents*. New York: Verso.

Triechler, P. (1991). How to have theory in an epidemic: The evolution of AIDS treatment activism. In C. Penley & A. Ross (Eds.), *Technoculture*. Minneapolis: University of Minnesota Press.

4

Promoting the Determinants of Good Health in the Workplace

Michael F. D. Polanyi

John W. Frank

Harry S. Shannon

Terrence J. Sullivan

John N. Lavis

New technology, rising levels of global trade and investment, and increasingly intense economic competition are among the forces bringing about fundamental changes in the workplaces of developed countries. The physical demands of heavy manual labor and the toxicity of work environments appear to be decreasing as mechanization spreads and the bulk of work is shifting from the manufacturing to service sectors. Nevertheless, the overall human and economic burden of work-related illness and disability remains high.[1]

A number of factors are related to workplace injuries and illness (see Figure 4.1). The physical work environment (e.g., lighting, noise level, toxic exposures, and air quality) and the physical demands and hazards of jobs (e.g., lifting, turning, repetitive movements, etc.) remain relevant. However, social and psychological demands of work are becoming increasingly important. These social, psychological, and physical demands typically stem from company-level decisions that are in turn constrained by the social, economic, and policy environment. Therefore, strategies to reduce these demands need to address determinants of health both inside and outside workplaces.

To improve the health of individuals, we must change the social and economic conditions in which people live. This was the central message of the Ottawa Charter for Health Promotion (World Health Organization, 1986). Both
health promotion and population health frameworks call for attention to the underlying determinants of health (such as income distribution, employment, and
social support; Frank, 1995).[2] Hence, the promotion of health in the new workplace must go beyond traditional occupational health and health promotion
strategies. Neither the achievement of safe physical environments nor the promotion of healthy lifestyles is sufficient. Efforts to improve workplace health
must identify and address fundamental social and psychological, as well as
physical, factors at play.

In this chapter, we describe and assess the impact of three strategies to improve health in the workplace: occupational health and safety (OHS), workplace
health promotion (WHP), and a newer approach that we call "promoting workplace determinants" (PWD), which places a greater emphasis on organizational
and societal determinants of worker health (see Table 4.1). We then outline a
framework for PWD that includes issue identification, issue analysis, and action. In conclusion, we suggest both opportunities for, and barriers to, the successful implementation of PWD.

THREE APPROACHES TO IMPROVING
WORKPLACE HEALTH

Occupational Health and Safety (OHS)

Goals and Strategies

OHS is primarily concerned with "health protection": the reduction of the
physical and chemical hazards of the work environment and the reduction of
work-related injury and disability due to hazardous job demands. OHS involves
a variety of preventive measures (such as improved personal protection and the
modification of machinery, equipment, and work practices) as well as curative
and rehabilitation services (Rantanen, 1995).

Relevance and Effectiveness

OHS developed out of a recognition of the serious hazards of industrial exposure to toxic chemicals (such as lead, silica, asbestos, and coal) and dangerous
worksites in many industries. The combination of an increase in industrial accident rates of almost 30% in the 1960s, a 1968 coal mine explosion in West Vir-
ginia, and an emerging environmental movement helped bring about occupational health legislation in the United States (Baker & Green, 1991).

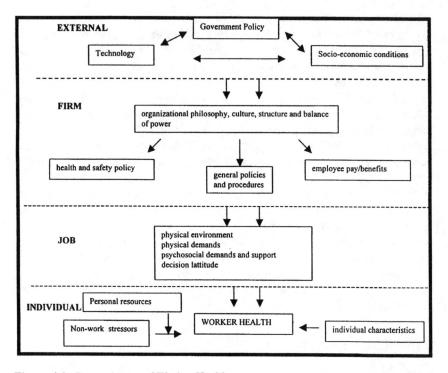

Figure 4.1. Determinants of Worker Health

Over the past 25 years, OHS has achieved a number of things. Work-related fatalities have been significantly reduced in Canada (Workplace Health and Safety Agency, 1994), and exposure to toxic substances has been reduced through improved occupational hygiene and knowledge of hazardous materials and legislation giving workers increased ability to control their work environment. The more flagrant occupational health hazards associated with heavy manufacturing, although not disappearing, are affecting smaller numbers of people.

Evidence of OHS health benefits is often hard to obtain because of the latency of occupational disease (e.g., a reduction in exposure to carcinogens may not affect cancer prevalence rates for many years). Improvements in health through ergonomic redesign are similarly difficult to demonstrate: Despite laboratory evidence that ergonomic interventions should reduce the risk of, for example, low back pain, few controlled interventions have shown a clear reduction in incidence (Frank et al., 1995).

Table 4.1 Strategies to Improve Workplace Health

Strategy	Stimulus	Goals	Examples
Traditional occupational health and safety (OHS)	Physical hazards of heavy industrial labor	Reduce toxicity of environment Reduce physical demands of work	Industrial hygiene Modification of equipment and practices Protection
Traditional workplace health promotion (WHP)	High absenteeism and benefits costs	Reduce individual risk of illness through education, skills development, and support programs	Fitness programs Smoking cessation courses Counseling Weight reduction programs
Promoting workplace determinants (PWD)	Recognition of relationship between "job strain" and ill health	Reduce workplace psychosocial demands Increased social support Increased worker participation in decision making	Flexible hours and holidays Job redesign Job rotation Worker decision making Supervisor training

Strengths and Limitations

Although the definition of OHS is expanding to include psychological and social well-being (Rantanen, 1995), attempts by occupational health activists in North America to act on this broader definition seem to have been set back by the conservative political climate of the 1980s (Sass, 1989) and the steady decline in unionization levels in the United States (to 16% of the workforce; Walker, 1993).[3] Unions have had to be concerned with opposing layoffs and increases in the pace of work, leaving little time to address broader psychosocial issues related to work organization (Walker, August 1995, personal communication).

Traditional occupational health hazards are not disappearing; however, they are affecting smaller numbers of people. At the same time, psychological and psychosocial problems are playing a larger role as demands for worker productivity increase (Rantanen, 1995). Even musculoskeletal disorders, which make up an increasing proportion of injuries in many industrialized countries, have both physical and psychosocial origins (Hagberg et al., 1995).

Workplace Health Promotion (WHP)

Goals and Strategies

WHP programs developed in the 1970s out of a growing emphasis on healthy lifestyles and a belief that such programs would reduce employee health costs, which were rising by up to 20% to 30% a year in the United States (Conrad, 1988). In the United States, health benefits now cost 9% of corporate payrolls, up from about 3% in the early 1980s (Northwestern National Life Insurance, 1994, p. 4). Health care expenditures have also increased sharply in Canada since the 1970s, and an increasing proportion is being paid through the private sector (*Public and Private Financing,* 1995).

The majority of WHP programs seek to encourage healthier individual behaviors through the provision of support and information and the development of skills. Programs commonly focus on fitness, cardiopulmonary resuscitation, nutrition, stress reduction, weight control, alcohol and drug abuse counseling, and smoking cessation. Organizational interventions tend to be limited to the establishment of nonsmoking policies, improving nutrition in cafeteria food, and setting up fitness facilities.

WHP programs are offered at over 80% of U.S. worksites, although this includes low-intensity activities such as the distribution of nutritional pamphlets (Biener, DePue, Emmons, Linnan, & Abrams, 1994). Health promotion in the workplace appears to be a predominantly North American phenomenon: There are comparatively few programs in Europe.

Although recent wellness programs are said to go "beyond corporate fitness centres and anti-smoking seminars" (Tully, 1995), the programs winning the 1994 Everett Koop health promotion awards in the United States still focus on urging individuals to renounce their high-risk behaviors:

> To the extent we encourage people of all ages to adopt healthier habits, we address health care and the attendant costs at their roots . . . [people] are being invited to check their own health risk levels under health risk assessment programs. The point is that awareness of the consequences of high risk health behavior . . . smoking, substance abuse, cholesterol . . . are the road signs pointing to their solution. (Health Project, 1994, pp. 1, 5-6)

Despite perhaps a decade of repeated calls to address organizational effects on workplace health, WHP in small (Eakin & Weir, 1995) and large (Hollander & Lengermann, 1988) workplaces remain primarily focused on changing individual worker lifestyles with little consideration of the conditions that shape such behaviors.

Relevance and Effectiveness

Measuring the impact of WHP is difficult. Most health indicators (absenteeism, sick leave, benefits usage) are not pure indicators of worker health because they also reflect nonworksite factors (such as outside life stresses on employees or secular disease trends in the community). On-the-job accident rates and workers' compensation claim rates are more directly related to worksite conditions, although they may ignore less acute health problems, as well as more positive indicators of health, such as sense of well-being.

A number of studies show the effectiveness of WHP programs in blood pressure control and smoking cessation, although other lifestyle effects are more tentative (Baker & Green, 1991; Bertera, 1990; Fielding, 1990). Many corporate evaluations are anecdotal, short-term, and cross-sectional, making it difficult to determine causality (Warner, Wickizer, Wolfe, Schildroth, & Samuelson, 1988). Bly, Jones, and Richardson's (1986) often-cited 5-year controlled study of Johnson and Johnson's Live for Life lifestyle and environment program found a $30 per year savings on inpatient costs per employee—a small portion of total health costs. Even this small impact is uncertain, because of the difficulty of fully controlling for differences between groups and the need for longer-term and clinically based data (Bly et al., 1986). Shephard (1992) found that "in the short term, work-site fitness and health programs appear to yield corporate benefits [i.e., savings] that more than match program costs, although this view would be strengthened by more controlled experiments" (p. 366). He also points out that the proportion of employees who participate in fitness programs is small, that few evaluations continue for as long as 10 years, and that long-term increases in pension costs are likely to offset some of the short-term economic gains. Benefits also may be limited by the fact that up to two thirds of employer health costs in the United States are for spouses and children who are not directly involved in programs (Conrad, 1988).

Other studies have found reductions in health care costs, numbers of sick days, outpatient costs, and hospitalization costs; however, the cost-effectiveness of the majority of WHP programs has not been rigorously evaluated (Fries et al., 1993). One study found that only 11% of employers tried to measure the economic impact of their programs (Warner, 1990).

Finally, there is some evidence of improved worker morale and labor-management relations and increased productivity as a result of WHP programs, although productivity is difficult to measure (Biener et al., 1994) and the case is not made convincingly by the literature as a whole (Warner et al., 1988). A review of more recent interventions concluded, somewhat more favorably, that the weight of the evidence indicates positive, if inconsistent, health effects of WHP programs but that "even the 'better' outcome studies have significant limitations that preclude conclusive statements about whether the health promotion program caused the observed changes" (Rush, 1995, p. 39).

Strengths and Limitations

The attractions of the workplace as a site for lifestyle-oriented programs are apparent. Workplace programs tend to have higher participation rates than off-site programs (Dooner, 1990) and employees' behavior is significantly influenced by workplace peer pressure. Large workplaces often have health staff and facilities to support programs, as well as established communication mechanisms through which to reach their relatively stable employee populations (Warner, 1990).

Yet although there is some evidence of short-term individual behavioral changes and even improvements in economic performance from WHP, there are a number of serious limitations to behavioral WHP approaches.

First, this approach hardly deals with the "roots" of human motivation and behavior: the social and economic determinants of health emphasized in the Ottawa Charter and elsewhere (e.g., Gerstein, Labelle, Mustard, Spasoff, & Watson, 1991). Even the Workplace Health System model (Health and Welfare Canada, 1991), one of the few programs that explicitly addresses environmental factors, has mostly been limited to individually targeted interventions. Such interventions fail to stem the development of new cases "because [they] do nothing about those forces in society that cause our problems in the first place, and that will continue to provide a fresh supply of at-risk people, forever" (Syme, 1994, p. 59).

Second, even if individual lifestyles could be successfully changed, health outcomes may not necessarily improve, because health status has to do with more than lifestyle. Even after controlling for lifestyle differences, there is still a significant gradient in health outcomes across occupational hierarchy (Marmot et al., 1991). Moreover, behavioral "lifestyle" risk factors tend to influence the incidence of specific diseases, such as cardiovascular outcomes, whereas socio-economic status (SES) extends to a wide array of health problems, including heart disease, cancer, stroke, diabetes, hypertension, infant mortality, arthritis, back ailments, mental illness, kidney disease, and many others (Anderson & Armstead, 1995).

Third, behavioral changes tend to be short-term in nature without concurrent changes to the social and cultural context that shapes individual behavior. For example, 90% of smokers who quit resume smoking within a year (Benowitz & Henningfield, 1994); only 10% of people continue to use stress management skills over the long term (Aaron, 1995); and weight loss and fat reduction success rates are low (Syme, 1988). One of the most rigorous of behavioral change programs, the Multiple Risk Factor Intervention Trial (MRFIT) in the United States, achieved no significant improvement in cardiovascular outcomes despite highly motivated participants, a well-designed behavioral intervention plan, very generous resources, and excellent staffing (MRFIT Research Group, 1982). Clearly, "cultural inertia" and difficult social and economic circumstances seriously hinder behavioral changes:

> One's capacity to modify potentially pathogenic behaviors and to "stick with it" is directly related to one's wealth, power and education—in short the degree of control one has over one's future . . . one's "will to change" is largely predetermined by one's social environment. (Renaud, 1994, p. 321)

Fourth, WHP programs may be reaching a limited and unrepresentative group of workers. WHP programs have tended to focus on large, profitable, white-collar workplaces (Hollander & Lengermann, 1988), largely ignoring small workplaces (about one third of the total workforce), which have higher rates of injury and ill health (Eakin & Weir, 1995). As well, health promotion programs are often provided as benefits for full-time employees, meaning that contract, low-wage, and nonunionized employees have less access to them. Healthier employees also may be more likely to participate in health promotion programs (Conrad, 1987), although there is conflicting evidence about this (Zavela, Davis, Cotrell, & Smith, 1988). In sum, the cost-effectiveness of programs is not synonymous with public health impact if only a small number of those at risk participate in programs (Fielding, 1990).

Fifth, and finally, there is the danger that a focus on individual lifestyles is simply a self-serving effort by competitive companies to reduce health care benefits costs as much as possible, without addressing deeper, job-related and organizational factors influencing health. The philosophy behind the Everett Koop awards, for example, is clear: "What we are really talking about here is a sense of responsibility for one's own health" (Health Project, 1994, p. 6). Steelcase North America (n.d.), a Koop award winner, seeks to "help . . . people work more effectively . . . no matter when, where or how they work," apparently ignoring the importance of work conditions. Steelcase materials state that lifestyle factors are the main cause of mortality, ignoring the social environmental factors that often underlie determinants of lifestyle behaviors (Hertzman, Frank, & Evans, 1994). Indeed, we know relatively little about social environmental factors because it is often felt that nothing can be done about them (Syme, 1994), whereas it may indeed be possible to reduce social and economic inequities (Vagero, 1995).

Some see the focus on lifestyle as an invasive form of social control being used to shore up an eroding work ethic (Conrad & Walsh, 1992). Indeed, the Everett Koop award-winning companies are reported to "systematically pursue," "prod," "advise," and "motivate" "stubborn," "secretive," and "crotchety" workers to change their habits (Tully, 1995). This sounds more than a little coercive. It is only a small step from emphasizing personal responsibility to blaming workers for their health problems and withholding support because an employee may not have taken all possible actions to prevent the problem from occurring. To quote from Steelcase North America (n.d.) again: "Employees are responsible for their own health. If they become injured or ill, either at work or at home, they are responsible for their own recovery" (p. 4).

Although laws forbid the discrimination of workers on the basis of their health, some employer actions (job applicant screening on health status, switching employees to less appealing jobs, passing over certain employees for advancement) are difficult to prevent by legal measures. Moreover, the frequent lack of clear-cut "objective" clinical evidence of conditions such as low back and repetitive strain injuries has led to a questioning of their legitimacy by managers and other workers (Reid, Ewan, & Lowy, 1991). This can deter employees from taking steps to report or prevent the worsening of such conditions (Tarasuk & Eakin, 1995).

In summary, properly developed health promotion programs can have an impact on health behaviors and individual health status. However, benefits will be limited until there is greater consideration of the social and psychological demands of work conditions. There is a need for a more comprehensive approach to health promotion and occupational health that integrates lifestyle and organizational change strategies to address job-, firm-, and societal-level factors affecting the health status of working people.

Promoting Workplace Determinants (PWD)

Objectives and Strategies

Occupational health and workplace health promotion have only peripherally addressed the psychosocial impacts of job-, organizational-, and societal-level conditions. A model for practice that deals more directly with these factors is needed. The framework for such a model can be developed by integrating aspects of organizational change, participatory or action research, and health promotion approaches.

All these approaches involve a structured yet democratic process of issue identification, analysis, and action. In the workplace, the successful implementation of such a process would ideally include, to the greatest extent possible, (a) broad-based commitment and participation of both workers and management in all stages of the project, (b) an openness of worksite participants to deal with the full range of internal and external determinants of health, (c) targeting health issues that are a priority of workers (and likely significant epidemiologically), (d) researchers acting as technical resources and process facilitators, (e) both quantitative and qualitative research methods, (f) a long-term commitment, and (g) ongoing evaluation of both process and outcomes to feed back into project planning and implementation. PWD focuses on organizational level interventions to reduce stress and improve employee wellness. Examples of such interventions, already implemented by some companies, include more flexible work hours, worksite redesign, improved supervisor attitudes and practices (e.g., by training), enhanced office communications, the provision of child care facilities, leaves of absence, and educational advancement opportunities (Aaron, 1995; Canadian Mental Health Association, 1988; Ontario Women's Directorate, 1991).

Relevance and Effectiveness

There have been few controlled evaluations of job and organizational change on health outcomes. Still, numerous observational studies show a correlation between various job- and firm-level factors and worker health. Although the mechanism through which stress functions is unclear, the study of the effects of high amounts of stress on the body's immune and endocrine systems (psychoneuroimmunology and -endocrinology) is starting to show that "the past and present social environments of individuals, and their perceptions of these environments [are] . . . key links . . . [in] the chain that runs from the behavior of cells and molecules, to the health of populations" (Evans, Hodge, & Pless, 1994, p. 184).

Job Factors. Studies in the 1950s concluded that genetic and demographic characteristics (gender and age) largely determined who contracted coronary heart disease (CHD). In the 1960s and 1970s, the importance of lifestyle factors (e.g., smoking, exercise, and diet) was recognized. A plethora of smoking cessation, fitness, and nutrition education programs arose. Then a study of British civil servants in the 1980s (the Whitehall study) uncovered an anomaly. As expected, people in higher-level positions in the civil service had fewer heart disease cases and better health than those in lower positions. But the differences in individuals' lifestyle-related behavior and even their measured blood pressures and serum lipids accounted for only a small part of the difference. Something else appeared to be important to health, a portion of which now appears to be related to psychological job strain (low control and high demand) and inability to relax after work, perhaps exacerbated by social isolation. Recently, a number of studies have shown consistent association between CHD risk on one hand and mental strain/decision latitude, degree of social isolation, and ability to relax at the end of the day on the other (Davey Smith, Shipley, & Rose, 1990; Gyntelberg, Suadicani, & Hein 1993; Hammar, Alfredsson, & Theorell, 1994; Marmot, 1989; Orth-Gomér, Rosengren, & Wilhelmsen, 1993; Welin, 1995). Occupational stressors are likely a key link between working conditions and overall health status, although at present only a modest link has been established, perhaps because of the difficulty of measuring the stress construct, particularly in women. For example, a recent analysis from Framingham suggests that women who work outside the home have substantially elevated coronary risks if they are concerned about financial problems, unlike women in the unpaid labor force (Eaker, Pinsky, & Castelli, 1992).

The nature of work itself is important, but its effect is mediated by the conditions of one's personal and home life. Daytime blood pressure levels appear to be less important than whether one's blood pressure comes down at the end of the work day, which depends on whether one is stressed by and can relax after work (Gyntelberg et al., 1993; Marmot, 1989). In short, the perceptions one has about work may be more important links in the causal chain than "objective" characteristics of the workplace. Thus, to better understand how work influences health, we need to use more qualitative methods to assess, in depth, personal interpretations of work experiences. Such perceptions also vary from culture to culture. This specificity of context may be one reason for the inconsistent relationship between job satisfaction and heart disease (Netterstrom & Suadicani, 1993).

Karasek and Theorell (1990) summarize a number of studies showing that "the most adverse reactions of psychological strain (fatigue, anxiety, depression, and physical illness) occur when psychological demands are high and the worker's decision latitude in the task is low" (pp. 32-33). In this way, the pace and volume of work, the repetitiveness of tasks, and the range of skills used are all related to health outcomes. According to one review of 36 studies of the relationship between job strain and cardiovascular disease (CVD) or symptoms, "a body of literature has accumulated that strongly suggests a causal association between job strain and CVD" (Schnall, Landsbergis, & Baker, 1994, p. 405). The relationship between job characteristics and health, however, is complex, as illustrated by the evolution of understanding of the causes of CHD over recent decades.

Finally, PWD may even be appropriate in reducing work-related musculoskeletal disorders (such as low-back pain and upper-limb strains), which seem to be more prevalent in psychosocially demanding environments. Musculoskeletal disorders now make up about half of all workers' compensation claims in Canada (Statistics Canada, 1989, 1991, 1994). Indirect costs and lost earnings in the United States associated with musculoskeletal disorders have been estimated at $65 billion (Holbrook, Grazier, Kelsey, & Stauffer, 1984).

Organizational Factors at Unit or Firm Level. Organizational factors such as level and method of remuneration and quality of benefits, level of worker participation in decision making, approach to OHS, and overall management philosophy toward workers and their well-being all have an impact on health in the workplace.

The recognition that poor people have poorer health has been documented since the early days of Western medical tradition, in particular by the 19th-century European public health movements and in modern epidemiological and social science research (Krieger, Rowley, Herman, Byllye, & Phillips, 1993). In fact, in every society, past or present, for which data have been analyzed, health status has been positively related to wealth, income, or social status (Hertzman et al., 1994).

The level of pay, therefore, that employees receive is a key to health status. Companies that pay "by the piece" or organize work in shifts are likely to have higher accident rates (Karasek & Theorell, 1990; Sloan, 1987). From the detailed studies of British civil servants noted earlier, it is also clear that being higher on the organization hierarchy relates to better health. Stress levels also appear to increase with fears of income (or job) loss (Karasek & Theorell, 1990).

Employee participation in the workplace is increasingly seen as contributing to good health. There is evidence that worker participation both generally and in health and safety decision making is correlated with reduced workers' compensation lost-time frequency rates (Shannon et al., 1996), with less alienation and superior mental health (Rothschild & Russell, 1986), with job satisfaction and morale, and perhaps level of performance (Rubenowitz, Flemming, & Tannenbaum, 1983). Miller and Monge's (1986) review of 47 studies found that participation has a positive effect on job satisfaction and, to a lesser extent, on productivity.

An organization's approach to occupational health and safety programs is also important. Senior management involvement in health and safety matters and the ability of health and safety committees to solve their occupational health conflicts internally, without threatening to obtain outside party involvement, have been related to lower lost-time injury rates (Shannon et al., 1996). Companies that tie manager appraisals and incentives to health and safety performance have better safety records (Shannon et al., 1992).

Firms with older workers, longer seniority, and lower turnover have also been found to have lower accident rates (Shannon et al., 1992, p. 15). Modified work provision and some physical environment variables—good housekeeping and safety controls on machinery—are also significant factors (Shannon, Mayr, & Haines, 1995).

Strengths and Limitations

There are barriers to establishing links between job and organizational conditions and health of workers. Most studies testing these relationships are cross-sectional, making it hard to infer causality. Longitudinal studies on psychosocial factors are largely observational, failing to control for all the factors at play and not usually able to hold enough factors constant to assess the relative weights of various psychosocial variables. As well, most research is on men, for whom perceived control may be a more important contributor to well-being than for women (Heaney, 1993). Finally, the mechanisms through which psychological strain function also remain obscure.

Still, given our significant knowledge about how organizational factors affect health and safety, we may ask why such factors have not been addressed from a health perspective. Here it becomes important to look at the relationship (and possible tensions) between the goal of productivity and profitability on one hand and the creation of a healthy workforce on the other.

Over the past two decades, there has been a freeing up of the international movement in capital and goods. Firms have been faced with increased competition and the need for greater productivity, flexibility, and innovation. Has this encouraged the development of healthier workforces? There seem to be two very different responses to this question.

Some management theorists argue that worker satisfaction and autonomy are increasingly crucial to the success of companies in industrialized countries (Levering, 1988). Competitiveness is seen to be based on the creation of a flexible, skilled, and motivated workforce (Premier's Council on Economic Renewal, 1993; Verma & Irvine, 1992). A recent review found that employee participation, training, and progressive management and organizational structure increase productivity and profits (Mavrinac, Jones, & Meyer, 1995). Mainstream health promoters agree, suggesting that "good health practices will lead to individual and organizational self-fulfillment and productivity" (Dooner, 1990, p. 2). These writers argue that worker well-being and productivity go hand in hand: Workers are more productive when they are supported and involved in decision making, and a healthy and empowering work environment leads to a profitable company.

Unfortunately, the health implications of new more participative organizational approaches have not been evaluated. Indeed, there are examples of companies that have ostensibly sought to increase worker control and recognition but have if anything increased demands and further alienated workers (Robertson et al., 1995). One recent U.S. survey found that one third of workers believe their employers "never" value their ideas (Smith, 1995).

Critics of free trade and globalization argue that the drive for competitiveness is undermining worker rights and worsening work conditions. Firms seek to reduce costs and increase flexibility by cutting wages and laying off full-time staff, who tend to be unionized and have better pay and benefit packages, and by contracting out work to workers who have less job security and less control over their work conditions and remuneration. Two of three new private sector jobs are temporary, and 25% of U.S. jobs are temporary, part-time, or contract, at pay levels 20% to 40% less than full-time workers doing comparable work (Rifkin, 1995). The emerging service sector has low union participation, shifting the balance of power in favor of employers. Increased government debts have resulted in cuts to income support and social programs, exacerbating worker fears of job loss (and reducing their bargaining power). Almost half of all American workers feel insecure in their jobs (Carey, 1995).

Although free trade proponents argue that these changes encourage worker flexibility and support innovation, others hold that they only support competitiveness based on cheap labor (Myles, 1988).

Technological and economic change do seem to be encouraging the development of a "dual economy," with a small stratum of well-paid professionals and a large group of unskilled workers with little job security. In the 1980s, the top 5% of U.S. wage earners saw their salary increase by 23% to $148,400, while the bottom 20% experienced a slight decline to $9,400 (Rifkin, 1995).

If healthy organizations can become more competitive within a reasonable time frame, then there is much common ground to be forged, and health promoters can build on that common ground with workers and management. Employers will be more likely to voluntarily undertake the longer-term efforts and greater expenses of reorganizing the work environment to improve workforce health, rather than simply implementing comparatively inexpensive but insufficient educational programs.

If, however, unregulated global production is undermining worker health and work conditions in many firms, then health promoters need to recognize and grapple with the fundamental conflicts of interest that may exist between workers and management. In this case, health promotion approaches will likely require advocacy and sometimes confrontation. Health promoters will also need to support the development of social and economic policies that at least dampen the health effects of such trends and create more opportunities and incentives for firms to improve health in the workplace (see examples below). Working for firm-level change without addressing the economic and social context within which firms function may do little to bring about significant change.

FURTHER NOTES ON PROMOTING WORKPLACE DETERMINANTS (PWD)

Health promoters need structured yet flexible approaches to the practice of initiating action on workplace determinants of health. Organizational development, comprehensive health promotion models, and action research methods all offer elements of such an approach. Organizational change methods seek to enhance creativity and innovation through the development of an empowered and flexible workplace (Premier's Council on Economic Renewal, 1993). Action research supports participant-led processes of research and action. And health promotion models, such as the Workplace Health System (Health and Welfare Canada, 1991), PRECEDE-PROCEED (Green & Kreuter, 1999), and the Path to Community Action (Ontario Ministry of Health, 1993) integrate, with different emphases, both research and action. An effective approach needs to integrate research, education, mobilization, action, and policy advocacy. One matrix of such an approach is outlined below.

Issue Identification

Through a planning process, health promoters need to (a) build key stakeholder ownership over, and commitment to, the process of change and (b) start to identify perceived issues of concern through a needs assessment. Workplace commitment is needed for change to take place. There is a need to decide whether to engage in a joint management-labor approach or not, depending on levels of commitment to change. Health promoter access to the worksite may require involvement of both parties, whereas supporting change through union advocacy and action may not.

Issue Analysis

Both research and action are needed. We need to better understand the interaction between factors that influence both physiological and self-reported health. Qualitative and quantitative methods are needed to understand the mechanisms through which such factors affect health status. But research will have a limited impact on practice unless it is tailored to the values and needs of employees and their organization (Israel, Schurman, & House, 1989). Indeed, experienced researchers in occupational health point to the failure of most traditional research projects to change workplaces at all (Israel et al., 1989). Therefore the process by which research is carried out is important: Workplace parties must have a strong say in research decision making.

Action research and participatory research offer two ways to link workplace research and organizational change. Both involve collective processes of problem identification, analysis, and action by workplace parties facilitated by researchers. Action research assumes a commonality of interests and the potential for mutually beneficial joint action by all workplace parties (Brown & Tandon, 1983). Participatory research emphasizes power imbalances and the need for less powerful groups to work independently from dominant groups and to eventually confront those in positions of authority to change the balance of power (Brown & Tandon, 1983). Increasingly, there are examples of participatory and action research projects aimed at progressive workplace organizational change (Elden & Taylor, 1983; Hugentobler, Israel, & Schurman, 1992; Israel et al., 1989; Pasmore & Friedlander, 1982). The approaches emphasize the building of democratic control over work and the development of social support, both of which are important to health (Israel et al., 1989).

Action

Actions will involve both job and organizational change, as well as advocacy for external policy changes to facilitate organizational changes. PWD should study the relationship between organizational competitiveness and working conditions to delineate policy options that encourage healthy work and to determine the best approach to workplace-based health promotion. PWD should be at the forefront of pushing for a new approach to work-related policy that considers health implications. To do this, indicators of overall work-related health costs are needed. The full burden—economic and noneconomic—of sickness absence, unemployment, and work-related injuries to companies and society, not to speak of individuals, needs to be spelled out clearly. PWD needs to be concerned also with high unemployment rates and job insecurity, both of which have significant health implications (Evans, 1994). The maldistribution of work is an example of a health-related economic problem that needs to be tackled by health promoters. Although one third of Canadians feel they are "constantly under stress" and one in four consider themselves "workaholics," more than 25% of Canadians want to work less with less income (Swift, 1995). PWD should work for a redistribution of work to those currently debilitated by unemployment, reducing government unemployment spending and freeing up money for training and education (Reid, 1995).

There are two main ways to integrate health concerns into trade and economic policy-making. First, one can develop and broaden international standards for working conditions, such as in the European Community. The social charter of the Maastricht Treaty, which aims to improve working conditions for those with the least protection in the Community, offers the potential for the development of coordinated policies to tackle inequalities in health (Whitehead, 1995). A second approach is to use market incentives. Indeed, an impressive confluence of opinion is shaping up around the need for "full-cost accounting," a system of pricing that incorporates the full human and environmental costs of production, an idea well established in environmental thought for some years but that has been recently echoed in social policy, health, and workplace writings. For example, Karasek and Theorell (1990), in calling for a "New Value" system of measuring production, argue that "standard accounting practices fail to measure long-term success, human capital development and worker well-being. . . . The goal of reducing short-term costs is probably the single most widely used justification for actions—increased demands, personnel cuts, and threats of layoffs —that increase worker's stress" (p. 238).

Similarly, in their proposal for a "genuine progress indicator" (GPI), Cobb, Halstead, and Rowe (1995) state that the "social-conservatives and environmentalist camps" are converging to express "the feeling, widespread among the public, . . . that economics must be about more than just the production and consumption of stuff; and that we need larger goals and better ways to measure our achievements as a nation" (p. 78).

Change is starting to take place in the mainstream: The World Bank recently expanded its definitions of a country's wealth beyond income to include natural resources and social capital (strength of families and communities).

Toward Promoting Workplace Determinants

There are barriers to addressing the full scope of work-related determinants of health. Individual choices, not environments, are still seen as the key cause of ill health. The potential growth of disability entitlement when workplace determinants are acknowledged will bring opposition from employers. Indeed, the whole PWD effort, without the involvement of employers and workers, may be resisted as "blaming the employer."

Social epidemiological research will take us only so far in building the broad-based support needed for increased emphasis on the determinants of health. It may provide some evidence of links between various socioeconomic conditions and health, but it will not necessarily reveal the mechanisms through which these conditions function, the subjective perceptions of underlying issues at stake, nor will it bring about the fundamental reordering of priorities that is needed. Regardless of epidemiological findings, political power continues to determine how the competing priorities of society are balanced. Proponents of workplace health promotion must advocate a social and economic policy framework based on the determinants of health and develop broad-based support for such an agenda in collaboration with other groups and individuals concerned with securing access to the determinants of health for all individuals and groups in society.

If organizational change is important to improving health in the workplace, then health promoters need new analytical and intervention skills. They need to be able to critically assess the social and economic constraints to change in often politically polarized workplaces and develop their strategies for action accordingly. Some health promoters have become comfortable with lifestyle education programs. Shifting attention to action on organizational-level factors requires knowledge and skills enhancement.

CONCLUSIONS

Over the past decades, health in the workplace has been significantly improved. Important steps have been made to monitor and control the physical and toxic hazards associated with work. Actions have also been taken to understand and reduce the physical demands of modern workstations. And workplace health promotion has to some extent encouraged healthier behaviors by individual workers. Yet it is possible that these approaches have now fulfilled their potential for change and that new directions need to be pursued.

After 20 years of partial success, it is time for workplace health promoters to start to tackle the bigger, more controversial task of creating healthier workplaces by supporting actions that can create the working conditions necessary for good health. This will require the difficult task of striving to balance economic strength, social equity, and for survival over the longer term, environmental sustainability.

NOTES

1. Lost time injury claim rates in Canada remained relatively constant between 1979 and 1987, while direct costs associated with injuries have tripled, accounting for inflation (Labour Canada, 1990, p. 38). In Canada, there was one compensation claim for every thirteen workers, amounting to direct medical costs of over $250 per person (Association of Workers' Compensation Boards of Canada, 1995), and perhaps twice as much again in indirect costs to society associated with replacement, training, lost productivity and indemnity benefits. The prevalence of work-related disabilities in the United States is 10%

(Northwestern National Life Insurance Company, 1994). U.S. employer Workers' Compensation costs as a percentage of payroll have more than doubled since 1960, totaling over $57 billion in 1993 (Burton, 1995).

2. See Labonte (1995) for a call for a critical integration of health promotion and population health approaches.

3. Although unionization rates stayed relatively steady in Canada, they may decrease in the future as the size of public sectors decrease and work in the private sector shifts from manufacturing to the service sector.

REFERENCES

Aaron, T. (1995). *Stress management approaches for small businesses: A comprehensive review from a health promotion perspective.* Toronto: University of Toronto.

Anderson, N. B., & Armstead, C. A. (1995). Towards understanding the association of socio-economic status and health: A new challenge for the biopsychosocial approach. *Psychosomatic Medicine, 57,* 213-225.

Association of Workers' Compensation Boards of Canada. (1995). *Canadian workers' compensation basic statistical and financial information, 1990–1993.* Edmonton, Alberta: Author.

Baker, F., & Green, G. M. (1991). Work, health and productivity: An overview. In G. M. Green & F. Baker (Eds.), *Work, health, and productivity.* New York: Oxford University Press.

Benowitz, N. L., & Henningfield, J. E. (1994). Establishing a nicotine threshold for addiction: The implications for tobacco regulation. *New England Journal of Medicine, 331,* 123-125.

Bertera, R. L. (1990). Planning and implementing health promotion in the workplace: A case study of the DuPont Company experience. *Health Education Quarterly, 17,* 307-327.

Biener, L., DePue, J. D., Emmons, K. M., Linnan, L., & Abrams, D. B. (1994). Recruitment of work sites to a health promotion research trial: Implications for generalizability. *Journal of Occupational Medicine, 36,* 631-636.

Bly, J. L., Jones, R. C., & Richardson, J. E. (1986). Impact of worksite health promotion on health care costs and utilization: Evaluation of Johnson & Johnson's Live for Life program. *Journal of the American Medical Association, 256,* 3235-3240.

Brown, L. D., & Tandon, R. (1983). Ideology and political economy in inquiry: Action research and participatory research. *Journal of Applied Behavioral Science, 19,* 277-294.

Burton, J. (1995). *John Burton's Workers' Compensation Monitor, 8*(3), 1-15.

Canadian Mental Health Association. (1988). *The Canadian guide to innovative health promotion practice in the workplace.* Toronto: Author.

Carey, E. (1995, August 20). No raises? Just relax. *Toronto Star,* pp. D1-D2.

Cobb, C., Halstead, T., & Rowe, J. (1995, October). If the GDP is up, why is America down? *Atlantic Monthly,* pp. 59-78.

Conrad, P. (1987). Who comes to work-site wellness programs: A preliminary review. *Journal of Occupational Medicine, 29*(4), 317-320.

Conrad, P. (1988). Worksite health promotion: The social context. *Social Science and Medicine, 26*(5), 485-489.

Conrad, P., & Walsh, D. C. (1992). The new corporate health ethic: Lifestyle and the social control of work. *International Journal of Health Services, 22,* 89-111.

Davey Smith, G., Shipley, M., & Rose, G. (1990). Magnitude and causes of socio-economic differentials in mortality: Further evidence from the Whitehall Study. *Journal of Epidemiology and Community Health, 44,* 265-270.

Dooner, B. (1990). Achieving a healthier workplace: Organizational and individual health. *Health Promotion, 29*(3), 2-6.

Eaker, E. D., Pinsky, J. J., & Castelli, W. P. (1992). Myocardial infarction and coronary death among women: Psychosocial predictors from a 20-year follow-up of women in the Framingham Study. *American Journal of Epidemiology, 135*(8), 854-864.

Eakin, J. M., & Weir, N. (1995). Canadian approaches to the promotion of health in small workplaces. *Canadian Journal of Public Health, 86,* 109-113.

Elden, M., & Taylor, J. C. (1983). Participatory research at work: An introduction. *Journal of Occupational Behavior, 4,* 1-8.

Evans, M. F. (1994). *Unemployment and health: Information and intervention for the primary care physician.* Manuscript submitted for publication.

Evans, R. G., Hodge, M., & Pless, I. B. (1994). If not genetics, then what? Biological pathways and population health. In R. G. Evans, M. L. Barer, & T. R. Marmor (Eds.), *Why are some people healthy and others not? The determinants of health of populations* (pp. 161-188). New York: Aldine de Gruyter.

Fielding, J. E. (1990). Worksite health promotion programs in the United States: Progress, lessons and challenges. *Health Promotion International, 5,* 75-84.

Frank, J. W. (1995). Why "population health"? *Canadian Journal of Public Health, 86,* 162-164.

Frank, J. W., Brooker, A., DeMaio, S., Kerr, M. S., Maetzel, A., Shannon, H. S., Sullivan, T. S., Norman, R. W., & Wells, R. (1995). *Disability due to occupational low back pain: What do we know about its prevention?* Toronto: Liberty International Canada.

Fries, J. F., Koop, C. E., Beadle, C. E., Cooper, P. P., England, M. J., Greaves, R. F., Sokolov, J. J., Wright, D. D., & Health Project Consortium. (1993). Reducing health care costs by reducing the need and demand for medical services. *New England Journal of Medicine, 329,* 321-325.

Gerstein, R., Labelle, J., Mustard, F., Spasoff, R., & Watson, J. (1991). Nurturing health: A framework for the determinants of health. In *Premier's Council on Health Strategies.* Toronto: Queen's Printer.

Green, L. W., & Kreuter, M. W. (1999). *Health promotion planning: An educational and ecological approach* (3rd ed.). Mountain View, CA: Mayfield.

Gyntelberg, F., Suadicani, P., & Hein, H. O. (1993). Psychosocial work loads, social inequalities and risk of isachaemic heart disease: A prospective study in the Copenhagen Male Study. In *International Conference on Work and Health: Abstracts* (p. 120). Copenhagen.

Hagberg, M., Silverstein, B., Wells, R., Smith, M. J., Hendrick, H. W., Carayon, P., & Perusse, M. (1995). *Work related musculoskeletal disorders (WMSDs): A reference book for prevention.* London: Taylor & Francis.

Hammar, N., Alfredsson, L., & Theorell, T. (1994). Job characteristics and the incidence of myocardial infarction. *International Journal of Epidemiology, 23*(2), 277-284.

Health and Welfare Canada. (1991). *Corporate health model* (Catalog No. H39-225/1991E). Ottawa, Ontario: Supply and Services Canada.

Health Project. (1994, October 17). *1994 Everett Koop Awards programs highlight the rising tide of demand reduction to cut health costs.* Press release.

Heaney, C. (1993). Perceived control and employed men and women. In B. C. Long & S. E. Kahn (Eds.), *Women, work and coping: A multidisciplinary approach to workplace studies.* Montreal: McGill-Queen's University Press.

Hertzman, C., Frank, J. W., & Evans, R. G. (1994). Heterogeneities in health status and the determinants of population health. In R. G. Evans, M. L. Barer, & T. R. Marmor (Eds.), *Why are some people healthy and others not? The determinants of health of populations* (pp. 67-92). New York: Aldine de Gruyter.

158 SETTINGS FOR HEALTH PROMOTION

Holbrook, T. L., Grazier, K., Kelsey, J. L., & Stauffer, R. N. (1984). *The frequency of occurrence, impact and cost of selected musculoskeletal conditions in the US*. Chicago: American Academy of Orthopedic Surgeons.

Hollander, R. B., & Lengermann, J. J. (1988). Corporate characteristics and worksite health promotion programs: Survey findings from Fortune 500 companies. *Social Science and Medicine, 26*, 491-501.

Hugentobler, M. K., Israel, B. A., & Schurman, S. J. (1992). An action research approach to workplace health. *Health Education Quarterly, 19*, 55-76.

Israel, B. A., Schurman, S. A., & House, J. S. (1989). Action research on occupational stress: Involving workers as researchers. *International Journal of Health Services, 19*(1), 135-155.

Karasek, R., & Theorell, T. (1990). *Healthy work: Stress, productivity and the reconstruction of working life*. New York: Basic Books.

Krieger, N., Rowley, D. L., Herman, A. A., Byllye, A., & Phillips, M. T. (1993). Racism, sexism, and social class: Implications for studies of health, disease and well-being. *American Journal of Preventive Medicine, 9*(Suppl), 6.

Labonte, R. (1995). Population health and health promotion: What do they have to say to each other? *Canadian Journal of Public Health, 86*, 165-168.

Labour Canada. (1990). *Employment injuries and occupational illnesses 1985-87*. Ottawa, Ontario: Ministry of Supply and Services.

Levering, R. (1988). *A great place to work: What makes some employers so good (and most so bad)*. New York: Avon.

Marmot, M. (1989). Socio-economic determinants of child mortality. *International Journal of Epidemiology, 18*(3, Supp. 1), S196-S202.

Marmot, M., Davey Smith, G., Stansfield, S., Patel, C., North, F., Head, J., White, I., Brunner, E., & Feeney, A. (1991). Health inequalities among British civil servants: The Whitehall II study. *The Lancet, 337*, 1387-1393.

Mavrinac, S. C., Jones, N. R., & Meyer, M. W. (1995). *The financial and non-financial returns to innovative workplace practices: A critical review*. Washington, DC: U.S. Department of Labor.

Miller, K. I., & Monge, P. R. (1986). Participation, satisfaction, and productivity: A meta-analytic review. *Academy of Management Journal, 29*, 727-753.

MRFIT Research Group. (1982). Multiple risk factor intervention trial: Risk factor changes and mortality results. *Journal of the American Medical Association, 248*(12), 1465-1477.

Myles, J. (1988). Decline or impasse? The current state of the welfare state. *Studies in Political Economy, 26*, 73-107.

Netterstrom, B., & Suadicani, P. (1993). Self-assessed job satisfaction and ischaemic heart disease mortality: A 10-year follow-up of urban bus drivers. *International Journal of Epidemiology, 22*(1), 51-56.

Northwestern National Life Insurance Company. (1994, April). *Back to work: Managing disability, recovery and re-employment*. Employee Benefits Division. Minneapolis, MN: Author.

Ontario Ministry of Health. (1993). *Community health promotion in action: Healthy lifestyles program*. Toronto: Queen's Printer for Ontario.

Ontario Women's Directorate. (1991). *Work and family: The crucial balance*. Toronto: Ontario Ministry of Community and Social Services.

Orth-Gomér, K., Rosengren, A., & Wilhelmsen, L. (1993). Lack of social support and incidence of coronary heart disease in middle-aged Swedish men. *Psychosomatic Medicine, 55*, 37-43.

Pasmore, W., & Friedlander, F. (1982). An action-research program for increasing employee involvement in problem solving. *Administrative Science Quarterly, 27*(3), 343-362.

Premier's Council on Economic Renewal. (1993, May 21). *Meeting materials prepared by the Task Force on the Organisation of Work.* Toronto: Government of Ontario.

The public and private financing of Canada's health system: A discussion paper. (1995, September). Ottawa: National Forum on Health.

Rantanen, J. (1995). Division of health promotion, education and communication. In *Workers' health working document.* Geneva: World Health Organization, Unit of Occupational Health.

Reid, F. (1995). *Working less and enjoying it more.* Manuscript submitted for publication.

Reid, J., Ewan, C., & Lowy, E. (1991). Pilgrimage of pain: The illness experiences of women with repetition strain injury and the search for credibility. *Social Science and Medicine, 32*(5), 601-612.

Renaud, M. (1994). The future: Hygeia versus Panakeil? In R. G. Evans, M. L. Barer, & T. R. Marmor (Eds.), *Why are some people healthy and others not? The determinants of health of populations* (pp. 317-334). New York: Aldine de Gruyter.

Rifkin, J. (1995). *The end of work: The decline of the global labor force and the dawn of the post-market era* (pp. 165-197). New York: Putnam.

Robertson, D., Rinehart, J., Huxley, C., Wareham, J., Rosenfeld, H., McGough, A., & Benedict, S. (1995). *The CAMI report: Lean production in a unionised auto plant.* Willowdale, Ontario: Canadian Autoworkers–Canada Research Department.

Rothschild, J., & Russell, R. (1986). Alternatives to bureaucracy: Democratic participation in the economy. *Annual Review of Sociology, 12,* 307-328.

Rubenowitz, S., Flemming, N., & Tannenbaum, A. (1983). Some social psychological effects of direct and indirect participation in ten Swedish companies. *Organization Studies, 4*(3), 243-259.

Rush, B. (1995, August). *Program evaluation and the Workplace Health System: What do comprehensive evaluations of health promotion programs in the workplace tell us about program effectiveness and cost-efficiency?* Report prepared for Workplace Health System, Work and Education Health Promotion Unit, Health Promotion Directorate, Health Canada.

Sass, R. (1989). The implications of work organization for occupational health policy: The case of Canada. *International Journal of Health Services, 19*(1), 157-173

Schnall, P. L., Landsbergis, P. A., & Baker, D. (1994). Job strain and cardiovascular disease. *Annual Review of Public Health, 15,* 381-411.

Shannon, H. S., Mayr, J., & Haines, T. (1995). *Overview of the relationship between organisational and workplace factors and injury rates* (Working Paper No. 36). Toronto: Institute for Work and Health.

Shannon, H. S., Walters, V., Lewchuk, W., Richardson, J., Moran, L. A., Haines, T., & Verma, D. (1996). Workplace organizational correlates of lost time accident rates in manufacturing. *American Journal of Industrial Medicine, 29,* 258.

Shannon, H. S., Walters, V., Lewchuk, W., Richardson, R. J., Verma, D. K., Haines, A. T., & Moran, L. (1992). *Health and safety approaches in the workplace* (Report for the IAPA). Hamilton, Ontario: McMaster University.

Shephard, R. J. (1992). A critical analysis of worksite fitness programs and their postulated economic benefits. *Medicine and Science in Sports and Exercise, 24,* 354-370.

Sloan, R. P. (1987). Workplace health promotion: A commentary on the evolution of a paradigm. *Health Education Quarterly, 14,* 181-194.

Smith, K. (1995, November 25). Empowerment a joke, employees say. *Globe and Mail,* p. B5.

Statistics Canada. (1989). *Work injuries 1986–1988.* Ottawa, Ontario: Ministry of Regional Industrial Expansion.

Statistics Canada. (1991). *Work injuries 1988–1990.* Ottawa, Ontario: Ministry of Industry, Science and Technology.

Statistics Canada. (1994). *Work injuries: 1991–1993.* Ottawa, Ontario: Statistics Canada.

Steelcase North America. (n.d). *Well, well, well . . .* Mimeo from Pam Witting, Manager, Wellness & Medical Services, Grand Rapids, MI.

Swift, J. (1995). Time and work. *Canadian Forum, 74*(841), 9-12.

Syme, S. L. (1988). Social epidemiology and the work environment. *International Journal of Health Services, 18*(4), 635-645.

Syme, S. L. (1994). The social environment and health. In *Proceedings of the 11th annual Honda Foundation Discoveries Symposium* (pp. 59-64). Toronto: Canadian Institute for Advanced Research.

Tarasuk, V., & Eakin, J. M. (1995). The problem of legitimacy in the experience of work-related back injury. *Qualitative Health Research, 5,* 204-221.

Tully, S. (1995, June 12). Fortune: America's healthiest companies. *Fortune Magazine,* pp. 98-100.

Vagero, D. (1995). Health inequalities as policy issues: Reflections on ethics, policy and public health. *Sociology of Health and Illness, 1*(1), 1-19.

Verma, A., & Irvine, D. (1992). *Investing in people: The key to Canada's prosperity and growth.* Willowdale, Ontario: Information Technology Association of Canada.

Walker, C. (1993). *Workplace stress.* Willowdale, Ontario: Canadian Autoworkers Union.

Warner, K. E. (1990, Summer). Wellness at the worksite. *Health Affairs,* 64-79.

Warner, K. E., Wickizer, T. M., Wolfe, R. A., Schildroth, J. E., & Samuelson, M. H. (1988). Economic implications of workplace health promotion programs: Review of the literature. *Journal of Occupational Medicine, 30,* 106-112.

Welin, C. (1995). *Psychosocial factors in myocardial infarction patients: A case-control study.* Göteborg, Sweden: Göteborg University, Ostra Hospital, Department of Medicine, Institute of Heart and Lung Diseases.

Whitehead, M. (1995). Tackling inequalities: A review of policy initiatives. In M. Benzeval, K. Judge, & M. Whitehead (Eds.), *Tackling inequalities in health: An agenda for action* (pp. 22-52). London: King's Fund.

Workplace Health and Safety Agency. (1994, March). *The impact of joint health and safety committees on health and safety trends in Ontario.* Ottawa: Author.

World Health Organization, Regional Office for Europe. (1984). *Health promotion: A discussion document on the concept and principles* (ICP/HSP 602 [mo1]). Copenhagen: Author.

World Health Organization. (1986). Ottawa charter for health promotion. *Health Promotion, 1*(4), i-v.

Zavela, K. J., Davis, L. G., Cotrell, R. R., & Smith, W. E. (1988). Do only the healthy intend to participate in worksite health promotion? *Health Education Quarterly, 15,* 259-267.

COMMENTARY

Robert L. Bertera

The authors take on the important challenge of identifying and interpreting the role of health determinants in the context of changing workplaces, health care systems, and international competition. The authors point out the limitations of occupational health and safety and health promotion programs that lack intensity and fail to address the job-, organizational-, and societal-level factors that help to determine health status of the workforce.

One organizational trend that tries to address these factors is increased participation in day-to-day decisions about the organization and flow of work and work assignments, which gives employees greater control through empowerment. Increased employee participation has been achieved through flatter organizations, team building, and greater individual responsibility. However, other influences at the societal and international level increase demands on companies and their employees. These include relentless efforts to reduce costs, increase productivity, increase stockholder value, and compete globally, in many cases with countries where the workforce does not have the benefits of health and safety protections, let alone other opportunities such as health promotion or employee participation opportunities.

The changing social contract between employers and employees on job security can outweigh the other changes that attempt to improve health. Free trade and global competition are market forces that, by their very nature, are difficult to control and channel. The authors observe that company-level changes will have little impact without addressing these forces; however, there are relatively few areas in which health promotion practitioners have influence enough to implement meaningful change without a great deal more collaboration and consent from business and government than is typical in the current climate.

Another area requiring research and action is better integration of categorical and programmatic efforts to deliver health services to the workforce. This integration is designed to reduce waste and duplication, while improving continuity of care for acute, chronic, and lifestyle-related factors. The following case study demonstrates how the DuPont company undertook a series of changes designed to integrate a variety of employee health services, including occupational health and safety, employee assistance, prevention and wellness (health promotion), and managed care.

At the same time that integration of health services was undertaken, other human resources initiatives such as work and family programs were offered to provide flexible work hours, leaves of absence for personal or family reasons, and to assist employees in locating affordable child care and elder care. These human resources initiatives, although not considered a part of company health promotion initiatives, tend to favorably address some of the same outcomes: stress management, employee absenteeism, productivity, and morale. Although these initiatives are well understood and accepted within company research, administrative, and sales organizations, they are not as fully available in manufacturing organizations where 24-hour operations that include shift work are the norm. This does not reflect a lower level of need for work/family programs but rather the large logistical and administrative barriers to implementing them in manufacturing environments.

THE DUPONT COMPANY EXPERIENCE WITH INTEGRATING PREVENTION AND WELLNESS INTO A COMPREHENSIVE HEALTH CARE STRATEGY

Company Profile

Better things for better living. This is a commitment that unites DuPont people around the world: discovering, improving, manufacturing, and marketing products that touch every aspect of people's lives. DuPont is among the top 50 industrial companies worldwide with annual sales of about $40 billion. A research and technology-based global chemical and energy company, DuPont operates 200 manufacturing and processing facilities in more than 40 countries worldwide.

DuPont is a diverse, global community of about 110,000 people, more than 30% of whom work outside the United States. The company serves worldwide markets in the aerospace, apparel, automotive, agricultural, construction, energy, health care, packaging, and printing and publishing industries, among others. DuPont's current wellness program is a key part of an integrated health services organization that also includes employee assistance and occupational medicine. The new organization was part of an effort to implement a DuPont Health Care Strategy, announced in December 1992 by Chairman and CEO, Edgar Woolard (1992). The strategy had five components:

1. Emphasize prevention and wellness.

2. Eliminate waste and unnecessary cost through managed health care.

3. Increase health care cost sharing so that the employee pays 20% of health care expenses.

4. Continue health care benefits for retirees and provide them with the same health care coverage as employees.

5. Become involved in the national debate on health care.

Prevention and Wellness Priorities

The emphasis on prevention and wellness applies across the board to all integrated health services, including employee assistance and occupational medicine. For example, routine employee physicals were moved off-site into the benefit plan and revised to reflect current medical consensus regarding exam intervals, lab tests, and screenings. The reorganization and integration of health care functions at DuPont that occurred during a 3-year period was preceded by a 2-year period of internal review and external benchmarking. Key learnings included the need to (a) integrate health care benefits with employee health services, (b) create a preventive health orientation in all programs, (c) improve communication to members and among health disciplines, and (d) develop systems and metrics to make informed decisions on program design and resource allocation.

The priority areas for the wellness competency, staffed by approximately 25 site and regional health education and wellness specialists, include the following:

1. Employees, pensioners, and spouses are encouraged to complete a lifestyle assessment every 3 years to identify areas to improve lifestyle and health behaviors that control cancer and cardiovascular risk factors. Invitations, questionnaires, and personalized lifestyle assessment results are mailed to the homes of eligible persons. Interested participants are also offered telephone follow-up, counseling, referrals, and health education materials, such as booklets, videos, or articles on various health topics.

In addition, employees are offered a second chance to complete a lifestyle assessment during a wellness appraisal, offered every 3 years. The appraisal includes blood pressure, cholesterol, and weight measurement, and interpretation, facilitation, and follow-up of the areas for health improvement, identified in the lifestyle assessment.

2. Clinical preventive services based on U.S. Preventive Services Guidelines are available to 400,000 persons covered by DuPont health care plans. Well baby, well child, and adult preventive visits are covered by all health care plan options. Preventive screenings, lab tests, and immunizations are covered at 100% to encourage use (DuPont Human Resources, 1995).

3. Self-care and health consumerism education to improve self-management of acute and chronic conditions, communication with primary physicians, and appropriate use of health services. Interventions include introductory meetings on self-care and health consumerism, the distribution of the *Healthwise Handbook,* and continuous message reinforcement through corporate communications and local education programs.

4. Wellness education in the areas of nutrition, fitness, smoking cessation, and stress management is offered on-site. Many of DuPont's wellness interventions have links with community resources such as nonprofit health associations, hospitals, or fitness facilities. Because of staffing reductions and cost cutting, most educational sessions, for example, are provided by outside contract instructors. This provides flexibility in programming by drawing on a variety of skills to deliver on- and off-site programs. However,

these efforts often focus on support for individual self-improvement, while avoiding controversial areas, including organizational dynamics and management behavior that may unwittingly have a negative impact on outcomes related to health, safety, diversity, competition (internal and external), or family.

5. Partnerships with other program areas such as employee assistance, work and family, and occupational medicine have been developed. However, other attempts to improve links to community health care organizations, such as managed-care networks, have met with mixed results. Many managed-care providers that serve the workforce are skilled at providing clinical services; their use of health promotion, however, is often limited to special events such as annual health care plan enrollment campaigns. Most other educational activities emphasize individual rather than population approaches. Their impact on the health of the workforce as well as the community would be enhanced by greater attention to organizational- and community-level interventions designed to address the full range of public health, nutrition, safety, fitness, social actions, and family support issues.

Integrated Health Care Information System

Program planning, administration, and evaluation are guided by information from an integrated data system that brings together elements from health care claims, finance, benefits eligibility, and lifestyle assessments. Studies are under way to measure participation, impact, and outcome using the Health Plan Employer Data and Information Set (HEDIS), modifiable claims audits, and other measurement tools.

The current prevention and wellness components of DuPont's integrated health services have their roots in a health promotion and disease prevention initiative announced in 1984. One hallmark of these earlier efforts that continues today was a commitment to use a systematic approach in the planning and implementation process and to measure impact and outcomes (Green & Kreuter, 1999). Four studies have been completed to evaluate the program's impact on absenteeism, behavioral risks, and illness costs. All are available on request and are summarized as follows:

• Two pilot programs were launched in 1981 and 1982 to refine program design and demonstrate impact on key health indicators. Declines in manufacturing absenteeism averaged 6.8% per year over 4 years at one location and 7.9% per year over 6 years at the other. This compared with a 2.1% decline per year at nonprogram sites (Bertera, 1990b).

• Another study showed that 29,315 manufacturing employees at 41 intervention sites experienced a 14% decline in absenteeism over 2 years compared with a 5.8% decline among 14,573 employees at control sites (Bertera 1990a). This resulted in a net difference of 11,726 fewer disability days over 2 years at program sites compared with nonprogram sites. Savings due to lower disability costs at intervention sites offset program costs in the first year ($.11 to $1) and provided a return of $2.05 for every dollar invested in the program by the end of the second year.

• A third study followed up 7,178 program participants for 2 years to determine changes in behavioral risks (Bertera, 1993). The number of employees with three or more behavioral risks declined by 14% over 2 years. This group also experienced a 12% decrease in the mean number of self-reported days absent due to illness over the same period. Individual risk factor changes ranged from a 78.9% increase in reported percentage of time seat belts were worn to no change in the mean percentage overweight. These results were consistent with other published studies for most variables despite some differences in methodology and study population.

• A fourth study examined the impact of behavioral risk factors on absenteeism and estimated health care costs among 45,976 employees (Bertera, 1991). Employees with any of six behavioral risks had absenteeism that was 10% to 32% higher than those without risks. Annual excess illness costs per person at risk were smoking, $960; overweight, $401; excess alcohol, $389; elevated cholesterol, $370; high blood pressure, $343; inadequate seat belt use, $272; and lack of exercise, $130. The total cost to the company of excess illness costs for employees was conservatively estimated at $70.8 million annually.

CONCLUSION

DuPont has steadily increased its investment in preventive care and wellness education. It is a cost-effective way of meeting the health needs of employees, pensioners, and family members. This investment is also an appropriate way to remain competitive in global markets where a healthy, committed workforce is essential to business success. Finally, company health promotion interventions that emphasize individual behavior change without consideration of organizational and societal forces are destined to have limited health impact. Multinational companies such as DuPont need to recognize the influence that global competition and organizational dynamics have on the psychological climate at work, readiness to change, and management-employee relations. Companies should use and support community resources available outside the workplace to address societal and organizational factors. These resources include public, private, and nonprofit educational, health care, safety, religious, and recreational organizations. They provide opportunities to address forces beyond the control of the individual or the company by identifying needs, finding innovative solutions, and organizing collective actions. Like other public health undertakings of the past, these community approaches hold promise for improving health by addressing root causes through prevention and leveraging of scarce resources.

REFERENCES

Bertera, R. L. (1990a). The effects of workplace health promotion on absenteeism and employment costs in a large, industrial population. *American Journal of Public Health, 80,* 1101-1105.

Bertera, R. L. (1990b). Planning and implementing health promotion in the workplace: A case study of the DuPont Company experience. *Health Education Quarterly, 17*(3), 307-327.

Bertera, R. L. (1991). The effects of behavioral risks on absenteeism and health care costs in the workplace. *Journal of Occupational Medicine, 33*(11), 1119-1124.

Bertera, R. L. (1993). Behavioral risk factor and illness day changes with workplace health promotion: Two-year results. *American Journal of Health Promotion, 7*(5), 365-373.

DuPont Human Resources. (1995, February). *A guide to using your DuPont preventive care benefit* (Rev.). Wilmington, DE: DuPont.

Green, L. W., & Kreuter, M. W. (1999). *Health promotion planning: An educational and ecological approach* (3rd ed.). Mountain View, CA: Mayfield.

Woolard, E. S., Jr. (1992, December). *DuPont integrated health care plan.* Letter to all employees, DuPont Company, Wilmington, DE.

COMMENTARY

Joan M. Eakin

Polanyi et al. make three main points:

1. Psychosocial, organizational, and societal determinants of workplace health are important and in need of attention.

2. These determinants are not adequately addressed within the two primary approaches to promoting health in the workplace—workplace health promotion (WHP) and occupational health and safety (OHS).

3. Their proposed approach—promoting workplace determinants (PWD)—is better positioned to promote health in the workplace.

I would like to comment on each of these arguments and discuss why the setting is a critical determinant of health promotion practice.

THE DETERMINANTS OF WORKPLACE HEALTH

The authors identify a broad range of health determinants in the workplace but emphasize the psychosocial and organizational aspects of work and

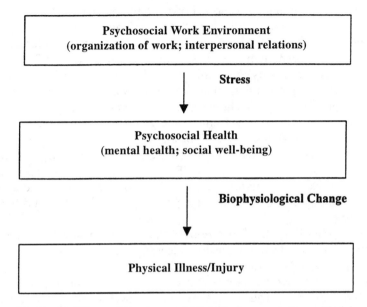

Figure 4.2. Health Effects of Psychosocial Work Environment: Stress Model

draw our attention to the significance of broader, societal-level factors for workplace health and intervention. An elaboration of the concepts associated with the psychosocial dimension of workplace health may contribute to their discussion. First, one can distinguish psychosocial determinants (causes) from psychosocial consequences (effects). As revealed in the authors' review of the literature, there are many psychosocial/organizational sources of ill health and injury among workers, including, for example, role conflict, autocratic supervisory practices, lack of control over work, and lack of social support. Underlying much of the literature they cite, and indeed their own model, is an etiological conceptualization that portrays the health effects of the psychosocial work environment as a psychologically mediated process (Figure 4.2).

This model proposes that features of the psychosocial environment can be stressful for employees, which can diminish their psychosocial health, which in turn can induce biophysiological changes and, ultimately, illness and injury. The work of Karasek and colleagues (Karasek & Theorell, 1990), and the burgeoning "demand-control" research tradition it has since spawned, exemplifies this conceptualization. Psychosocial dimensions of work (particularly job discretion, psychological demands, and social support) are linked to cardiovascular disease through the notion of job strain (stress).

This basic conceptual framework, however, seems incomplete in several ways. First, in the attempt to highlight the role of the psychosocial environment, the role of the physical environment is downplayed. Consideration of the physical environment, however, is essential to full understanding of the psychosocial determinants of workplace health. Although the impact of the physical environment on physical health is readily acknowledged (e.g., the physiological effects of toxic chemicals), its consequences for psychosocial health are also important. For example, dangerous working conditions can induce psychological distress and promote health-damaging behavior, such as drinking or smoking (Mullen, 1992), and "dysfunctional" occupational adaptations, such as risk taking (Barnes, 1997). The physical characteristics of work (e.g., isolation, noise) may also affect social interaction between workers or the structure of supervision, which in turn has health implications.

Another limitation of this basic model is that it does not allow for routes to ill health other than through psychological processes (i.e., stress). Health and the psychosocial environment may be linked in physical, or material, ways. For example, working alone at night in a gas station may endanger a worker's health both because social isolation is psychologically harmful and because he or she may be physically assaulted on the job. Piecework may be harmful to health both because it is a stressful, alienating form of work and because it is an organizational structure that may act as an incentive to take health risks (e.g., by working beyond points of fatigue or bypassing safety precautions in the interests of short-term production efficiency).

A final limitation of the Figure 4.2 model is that it implies a linear process, with psychosocial determinants leading to the health outcomes. The relationship, however, might be better conceived as reciprocal. For example, in a study of workers' experience of work-related back injury (Tarasuk & Eakin, 1994), the injury appeared to have considerable consequence for the psychosocial work environment. Back injury (and ensuing time off work and compensation) raised issues of legitimacy and mistrust (e.g., suspicion of malingering or secondary gain), which damaged relations with supervisors and coworkers (the psychosocial work environment), which in turn appeared to delay recovery and return to work. A similar reciprocal relationship between the psychosocial environment and health is also evident in my current research on the health of small-business employees. Ill health and injury both affect and are affected by the perceived quality of labor relations in the workplace (Eakin & MacEachen, 1998).

In Figure 4.3, the basic model is elaborated to reflect these issues. This model distinguishes between psychosocial determinants and psychosocial outcomes, includes a link between the psychosocial work environment and physical health that is not mediated by psychological health, adds a link be-

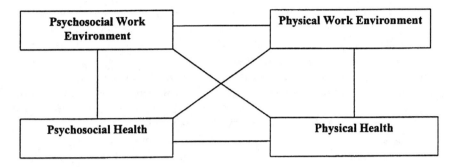

Figure 4.3. Health Effects of Psychosocial Work Environment: Expanded Model

tween both kinds of health and the physical/material environment, and recognizes that the relationship between the work environment and health is reciprocal.

This conceptual elaboration broadens our understanding of the relationship between health and the workplace environment, primarily by introducing the possibility of pathways other than social-psychological ones and by countering a tendency to equate the notion of "psychosocial environment" with stress.

THE LIMITATIONS OF WHP AND OHS

Polanyi et al.'s second point is that OHS and WHP are limited in what they can bring to promoting a healthful psychosocial and organizational work environment. In their analysis, however, the deck seems stacked against WHP. The purpose of WHP is generally not to promote workplace health but to enhance the lifestyle-related well-being of those who happen to be working there (Eakin & Weir, 1995). That is, to WHP, the workplace represents the location of health promotion intervention, not its target. The workplace is a convenient, efficient site for health promotion programming, an access point for reaching and mobilizing an elusive at-risk population—adults. Evaluated as an approach to addressing workplace health and the psychosocial determinants of health, WHP necessarily comes up wanting. Most important, such an assessment misses the features of WHP that do have potential for contributing to the psychosocial workplace health agenda. I return to this point in the concluding section.

Polanyi et al. also assert, as does an increasingly critical literature on workplace health promotion (e.g., Conrad & Walsh, 1992; Levenstein & Moret, 1985; Roman, 1987), that the WHP approach is limited by its focus on lifestyle and its lack of recognition of other determinants of health, particularly those in the workplace itself. OHS, however, has a parallel limitation: its exclusive focus on the workplace determinants of health. Neglect of the nonwork dimensions of health reflects the institutional and ideological environment in which OHS is situated, including a compensation system based on ability to demonstrate work-relatedness of harm and the embedding of health issues in negotiated employment contracts. Thus, the OHS approach may be as hobbled by its lack of a holistic perspective as is WHP.

Polanyi et al. also caution that the WHP approach may serve the interests of the most powerful workplace parties (management) and that a lifestyle focus may constitute an "invasive" form of social control. It could be noted, however, that OHS can also be appropriated by the most powerful and also become a vehicle for social control both in and beyond the workplace, such as in the case of drug screening (Draper, 1991) or worker participation schemes that some propose have been appropriated for managerial ends (Holloway, 1991).

Thus, an addendum to Polanyi et al.'s analysis of the "limitations" of WHP and OHS might be that the sins of the former are often paralleled in the latter and that, in both cases, the limitations need to be put into context. As I will argue further, the workplace setting is a key determinant not just of health but also of the possibilities for intervention and change.

POTENTIAL OF THE PWD APPROACH

Polanyi et al.'s third point is that health is affected in significant ways by job and organizational factors and that a PWD approach would promote health by addressing such factors. They point out, however, that the effectiveness of the organizational change approach is not currently known, primarily because there are "few controlled evaluations." They make the important point that a PWD approach is limited by the contradiction between worker health and broader societal goals of productivity, profitability, and global competitiveness.

Other limitations may also lurk in the "ideal-type" PWD approach laid out in their chapter. For example, how much can the participation of workers achieve given the inherently unequal distribution of power between workers and management? Given their particular standpoints and objectives, what incentive is there for management or workers to take responsibility for "the full range of internal and external determinants of health" as required in the approach? What happens when perspectives collide, such as, for example, when the priorities of workers differ from those indicated by epidemiological evidence? If it turns out, despite wishful thinking, that not all that is good for worker health is also profitable, what indications are there that regulatory (or voluntary) approaches can be effective in bringing about health-enhancing organizational change? Because PWD is still primarily a theory as opposed to a practice that can be observed and assessed, it does not offer the same opportunity for critique as do OHS and WHP. If and when approaches to workplace health do assume a PWD posture, we can begin to answer some of these questions.

The limitations of all three approaches are, in many respects strikingly similar. Each can be accused of being restricted—restricted conception of the determinants of health, restricted availability or application, restricted possibilities for worker participation. Each also confronts contradictions—contradictions between theory and practice, between demands to be comprehensive while not being socially invasive, and between the needs of workers and the needs of organizations. The reason that the three approaches turn out to have common types of limitations is that they all are practiced in the same setting—the workplace.

THE SETTING AS A KEY DETERMINANT
OF HEALTH PROMOTION

The setting of health promotion is critical to the form, content, and outcome of practice. Perhaps in no field of health promotion is this more true than in the workplace. The setting refers to the immediate physical and built environment (e.g., the building, the work process) and the psychosocial environment (e.g., the organizational, economic, legal, and political environments referred by Polanyi et al.). Importantly, the setting also includes the ideological context of work and industrial organization, the assumptions and beliefs embodied in laws and social practices, such as the employment relationship, the rights of private enterprise, and labor-management customs. The notion of setting thus includes both material and sociopolitical context.

The setting—including all these aspects—influences workplace health promotion in two different ways. It influences the target of health promotion (the health of workers), and the practice of health promotion (what health promoters can or cannot actually do).

In terms of the target of health promotion, the setting has evident consequences for health of workers. It may expose workers to both noxious physical environments (e.g., toxic chemicals) and noxious psychosocial environments (e.g., organizational stress). Health promoters need to know about these wide-ranging determinants of health in the workplace—no simple requirement given the multidisciplinary nature, limitations in scientific knowledge, and differing political constructions of reality in this field.

The workplace as a setting is of consequence to health promoters not just in terms of the determinants of health but also insofar as it profoundly influences the way in which health promotion can be practiced. Health promoters cannot begin to address the workplace determinants of health without acute sensitivity to the social and political environment in which their intervention is situated. Promoting the use of safer equipment or the elimination of toxic substances in the workplace are enormously challenging tasks—to which the history of occupational health and safety bears witness—but they may prove easy compared with the challenges posed by trying to change noxious organizational arrangements, management styles, or interpersonal relationships. Addressing these determinants of health will ultimately entail confronting legal and economic structures and strongly held norms of management practice and corporate prerogative. Typically, workplace health promoters depend on management in one form or another (they may be employees of the organization themselves or be external public health professionals who depend on management for entry into the worksite and for their continued support for subsequent programming). In such circumstances, health promoters may find themselves unwilling or unable to take on tasks that will engender conflict or incur the disapproval of management, particularly if there is any risk for the health agency they represent. An example of this comes from my current research (unpublished), a study of a public health department health promotion program for small workplaces. Despite the health promoters' (public health nurses) ideological commitment to addressing the workplace determinants of health, programming gravitated toward "safer" lifestyle-related topics (e.g., nutrition rather than occupational stress). This outcome was prompted, at least in part, by structural sociopolitical constraints on the social determinants approach to workplace health promotion, such as the nurse's own conditions of employment (e.g., accountability to a pro-business local elected board of health) and power differences and conflicting interests and agenda between nurses and corporate management (e.g., human service orientation vs. corporate profitability).

The setting, then, is of critical consequence to workplace health promotion both because it is itself a key determinant of health and because it constrains and shapes the content and strategy of health promotion practice. At the same time, despite a seeming preponderance of constraints over opportunities, health promoters have the potential to play a key role in improving the health of working people. One inviting opportunity for health promotion may emerge from the observation that traditional approaches to workplace health adopt definitions of health "determinants" that are too partial—too focused on lifestyle or too closed to nonwork dimensions of health. Health promotion may be ideally situated to take a holistic approach to health by identifying the relationship between the work and nonwork determinants of health and by mediating and integrating them in their practice.

Thus, for example, one strategy for workplace health promoters might be to take on health issues that have relatively clear work and nonwork components. For example, stress can stem from work (e.g., conflictful supervisory relationships) and from home (e.g., child care or elder caregiving responsibilities); reproductive health is affected by work (e.g., chemical harm to fetus and reproductive organs) and by health-related behaviors outside of work (e.g., diet); substance abuse is associated with work environments (e.g., drinking "cultures" in certain industries) and with problematic nonwork factors (e.g., marital strain). Health issues such as these may enable health promoters to take a more comprehensive approach to health, one that bridges the traditional concerns of occupational health and safety and of lifestyle health promotion. Furthermore, by "splitting" responsibility for health between individuals and their work and nonwork environments, health promoters may be able to navigate more effectively the political waters of workplace health. For example, such a strategy may facilitate the challenging task of defining and responding to employee- rather than employer-defined needs. The nonwork aspects of these health issues can be taken up first, with the workplace determinants being addressed incrementally as trusting relationships are established.

Ultimately, however, the workplace as a setting for health promotion is inherently limited by the fact that health interests of workers will seldom prevail if they conflict with corporate profitability, particularly in the current economic context of globalization and "bottom-line" competition. However, work-related determinants of health can be addressed in other ways besides direct intervention in the workplace. Change can be initiated from the bottom-up as well as from the top-down. As the owner of a small flooring company once explained when asked about what he had done with respect to health and safety at work, "We took up our own [shop] floor. They ere asbestos tiles . . . the guys [workers] wanted it; they had read about the problems, you know, with the cancer and all, I guess in the newspaper."

Health promoters could, for example, incorporate work and health issues into their other health promotion programming. They could introduce occupational health and safety topics into schools and colleges or use community television to raise public awareness and understanding of workplace health hazards and legal rights and responsibilities.

In conclusion, perhaps the major distinguishing feature between approaches to workplace health promotion is between approaches that focus on the workplace determinants of health and those that are more concerned with the workplaces as a location for the promotion of the health of adults more generally. Key to both approaches, however, is knowledge and understanding of the workplace as a social organizational context—that is, as a setting.

REFERENCES

Barnes, P. (1997). *Life as a "coiled spring."* Doctoral dissertation, Griffith University, Australia.

Conrad, P., & Walsh, D. (1992). The new corporate health ethic: Lifestyle and the social control of work. *International Journal of Health Services, 22*(1), 89-111.

Draper, E. (1991). *Risky business: Genetic testing and exclusionary practices in the hazardous workplace.* New York: Cambridge University Press.

Eakin, J. E., & MacEachen, E. (1998). Health and the social relations of work: A study of the health-related experiences of employees in small workplaces. *Sociology of Health and Illness, 20*(6), 896-914.

Eakin, J., & Weir, N. (1995). Canadian approaches to the promotion of health in small workplaces. *Canadian Journal of Public Health, 86,* 109-113.

Holloway, W. (1991). *Work psychology and organisational behavior: Managing the individual at work.* London: Sage.

Karasek, R., & Theorell, T. (1990). *Healthy work: Stress, productivity and the reconstruction of working life.* New York: Basic Books.

Levenstein, C., & Moret, M. (1985). Health promotion in the workplace. *Journal of Public Health Policy, 6*(2), 149-151.

Mullen, P. (1992). A question of balance: Health behavior and work context among male Glaswegians. *Sociology of Health and Illness, 14*(1), 73-97.

Roman, P. (1987). Ethics in workplace health programming: Who is served? *Health Education Quarterly, 14*(1), 57-70.

Tarasuk, V., & Eakin, J. (1994). The problem of legitimacy in the experience of work-related back injury. *Qualitative Health Research, 5*(2), 204-221.

5

The Health Care Institution as a Setting for Health Promotion

Joy L. Johnson

Health promotion is directed toward helping individuals, families, and communities increase control over and improve their health. This chapter addresses the potential for health promotion in health care institutions, particularly hospitals, which for the most part are illness or disease oriented and seemingly unresponsive to other family and community needs. Our notions of health care institutions seem to be antithetical to the philosophy that underlies health promotion. Rather than assisting individuals to increase control over their lives, the structures, policies, and procedures of health care institutions seem systematically to strip power and control from individuals, families, and communities. Health care institutions usually are located in enclosed buildings. Their activities are largely curative, performed for those individuals who find their way to them. They have developed as institutions diverging from the lives and comprehension of the majority of people. This divergence has been magnified in the past several decades by the march of technical medicine. Indeed, the more technically sophisticated the institution, the wider the gap between its special capacities and the population's overall health needs and demands (Paine & Tjam, 1988). The

AUTHOR'S NOTE: I wish to gratefully acknowledge the thoughtful suggestions and contributions made by the editors of this text. I would also like to thank Dr. Pamela Ratner for her helpful comments concerning this chapter.

gulf that has developed between these scientific temples of healing and the basic health requirements of the population is, in many countries, vast.

Despite an apparent mismatch between health care institutions and health promotion, many individuals have argued that health care institutions are potentially ideal locations for health promotion activities. For example, Dr. Halfden Mahler, past Director-General of the World Health Organization (WHO), in recognizing the chasm between health care institutions and communities, called for these institutions to be "converted into agents for the service of society instead of precincts for individual medical transactions between doctors and patients" (cited in Paine & Tjam, 1988, p. 104).

In this chapter, I explore the fit and misfit between health promotion and health care institutions. In particular, I consider the factors within the setting that impede or enhance health promotion initiatives, beginning with an examination of the historical development of health care institutions. Prior to proceeding, some working definitions are offered to frame the discussion. Health promotion is broadly defined as "any planned combination of educational, political, regulatory, and organizational supports for actions and conditions of living conducive to the health of individuals, groups, or communities" (Green & Kreuter, 1999, p. 432). Health care institutions, in this chapter, are defined as large, established organizations primarily directed toward the provision of medical care, including acute care, long-term care, rehabilitation, and psychiatric care. In that the hospital is viewed by many to be the institutional center of Western health care delivery systems and the majority of literature concerning health promotion within institutional settings focuses on the hospital setting, much of the discussion that follows centers on the hospital setting in particular. In addition, although physicians' offices and public health units are health care institutions, their characteristics are sufficiently different to warrant separate consideration in other chapters in this book (see Chapter 6 for a discussion of clinical general practice and Chapter 7 on the community, as settings for health promotion).

THE NATURE OF HEALTH CARE INSTITUTIONS: A SOCIOHISTORICAL PERSPECTIVE

To understand the nature of health care institutions, a historic perspective will be employed to highlight some of the social and political factors that have influenced the evolution of these institutions. The societal role and purpose of health care institutions have changed over the course of the last 150 years; these changes are strongly linked to developments in biomedical science and technology. For example, the 19th-century hospital bears little resemblance to its modern equivalent. Prior to the 1900s, hospitals were marginal institutions primarily of service for society's most neglected and shunned people: the sick, poor, or dispossessed members of the lower working class. The more fortunate, those with resources such as caring relatives and money, received their care at home. Most 19th-century persons lived and died never entering, and perhaps never seeing, a hospital. The historical terms provided to hospitals, hospices (homes for the destitute or sick), and spitals (foul and loathsome places), seem to capture the essence of the hospital of the 19th century (Reverby, 1987).

The shift in the locus of sick care from the home to the hospital took place around the beginning of this century. The germ theory of disease and advances in science created what has been termed the "bioengineering approach" to illness care and the movement of sick care from the home to the institutional setting. The basis for this change lay in the development of aseptic techniques, which necessitated personnel and resources that could not readily be taken to the patient's home (Blumhagen, 1979). With this development, the societal mission of the hospital was transformed from an institution that cared for social outcasts to a place where the sick could be healed. Within the emerging bioengineering perspective, the patient was viewed as a set of biological subsystems, with one or more of those damaged during illness. Accordingly, the role of health workers was designed to repair that damage using a variety of interventions.

Shifting patterns of morbidity also shaped health care institutions. As advances were made in the prevention of communicable diseases, such as malaria, rubella, poliomyelitis, measles, and mumps, the number of patients requiring institutional care for these conditions diminished. Modern medicine consequently turned its attention toward the leading causes of death, which increasingly included cancer, heart disease, and cerebrovascular disease. The orientation toward the care of patients suffering from these conditions has been, and remains today, focused on offering a complex armamentarium of technologic interventions, including surgery, chemotherapy and pharmaceutical interventions, radiography, and machine assistance.

As the technologies became increasingly complex and long-term, it became necessary to provide patients with instruction so that they could maintain their regimens once they left the health care institution. This need spurred the development of many early patient education programs; the management of diabetes, ostomy care, and cardiac rehabilitation are examples of the kinds of educational programs that began to emerge in the late 1960s. In addition, it was recognized that patients fared better within the institutional setting if they were properly prepared for their procedures and understood the nature of their treatments. The outgrowths of this insight were additional educational programs that helped prepare patients for procedures such as surgery and diagnostic tests. These educational programs can be considered precursors to health promotion in that they focused on providing individuals with the skills to manage their health care regimens and to maintain control over their health (illness).

By the early 1970s, all developed nations had in place extensive and expensive systems of health care, the focal point of which were health care institutions. Yet the resulting health gains from these systems seemed more modest than some had anticipated (Roos & Roos, 1994). There was an increasing skepticism about the role that health care institutions could play in furthering social welfare. Many "sound" health care practices were revealed to be more loosely connected with empirical evidence than the official rhetoric suggested. As a result, the public experienced disappointment and disillusionment with these institutions. Health care systems centered on the institutional setting were criticized because they focused almost exclusively on disease and illness care, which was viewed as protecting the interests of existing health care institutions rather than advancing population health (Evans & Stoddart, 1990).

Health care institutions were not the only institutions to draw criticism in the past two decades. Society at large became suspicious of most large institutions, including political, educational, and religious institutions. In the academic world, authors such as Foucault (1975) offered penetrating criticisms of public institutions, which he depicted as places whose central purpose is to discipline and punish rather than to further the welfare of society. Foucault (1991) contended that disciplines, knowledge, technologies, and institutions were involved in the process of "normalization" in which authority is intent on maximizing power and constraining the liberty of citizens.

Albeit harsh, Foucault's view of public institutions was not off the target. Health care institutions had become a network of expert advice in which wisdom was dispensed and the lives of others often controlled. This circumstance is described by Dr. David E. Rogers in a presidential address to the Association of American Physicians:

> As our interventions have become more searching, they have also become more costly and more hazardous. Thus, today it is not unusual to find a fragile elder who walked into the hospital, [and became] slightly confused, dehydrated, and somewhat the worse for wear on the third hospital day because his first 48 hours in the hospital were spent undergoing a staggering series of exhausting diagnostic studies. (Reiser, 1978, p. 161)

Although not their intent, a case could be made that health care institutions have often inadvertently harmed rather than helped. Foucault (1991) equates knowledge with power, and this thesis is perhaps no more obvious than in the case of health care institutions. Given the degree of specialization and expert knowledge that characterizes health care institutions, one might legitimately ask if it is possible for these institutions to overcome their predilection to exert power and instead to heed and respond to individual and community needs.

In the past two decades, the role of hospitals and other health care institutions has once again begun to shift. As the alienation between hospitals and communities began to take form, disillusionment with these institutions took root and many individuals in the health policy arena began to turn to health promotion as a strategy for increasing the health of populations (Evans & Stoddart, 1990). Sensing the potential of the health promotion movement, health care institutions, once exclusively dedicated to the care and treatment of disease states, began to consider the incorporation of health promotion strategies. As a result, the health care institution's focus on disease treatment and illness care was expanded to include some of the concepts of health promotion and illness prevention.

Many forces prompted health care institutions to expand their focus. One of the driving forces has been shifting patterns of morbidity and mortality and growing recognition that the bioengineering approach to illness is limited. It is now recognized that most illness in the developed and underdeveloped world has its origins in social conditions. In light of this recognition, policymakers around the world have called for an expanded vision of health care that addresses factors beyond the biologic, including lifestyle, environmental, social, and economic factors. This appeal for an expansionist view of the determinants of health is perhaps clearest in the *Ottawa Charter for Health Promotion*: "The role of the health sector must move increasingly in a health promotion direction, beyond its responsibility for providing clinical and curative services" (World Health Organization, 1986, p. 427). Although many have interpreted the Ottawa Charter as a call to redistribute services from the institutional setting to the community, individuals working within health care institutions have tended to view the charter as a call to expand and reorient existing services. Indeed, over the past decade, the hospital sector has taken up the challenge of the Ottawa Charter and has begun to explore ways to expand the services it provides.

The movement to expand the legitimate mandate of health care institutions has received support from organizations such as the WHO-sponsored International Network of Health Promoting Hospitals. The network, founded in 1990, has as its aim the development of hospitals that are health-promoting organizations. Currently, there are more than 1,000 participants in the network representing 32 countries. Rather than viewing health promotion simply as a matter of offering some lifestyle or patient education programs, the members of the network have recognized that hospitals must undergo profound organizational change to orient themselves toward the promotion of health. Accordingly, a health-promoting hospital "incorporates the concepts of health promotion into its organizational structure and culture by means of organizational development" (World Health Organization, Regional Office for Europe, 1995, p. 1).

Other important trends have had an impact on the shape of modern health care institutions. For example, spiraling health care costs have forced many health care institutions to assess carefully the kinds of programs they offer. In an attempt to cut costs, alternative approaches to health care delivery are under consideration. Whereas the majority of patients were once seen and treated on an inpatient basis, many health care institutions now offer alternative approaches to institutionalization, such as respite care, home support services, and ambulatory services, and more patients are now seen on an outpatient basis. This trend provides an important link between health care institutions and the community. Ambulatory patients are more likely to offer opportunities and pressures for hospital staff members to attend to the real world of patients' living conditions.

Without a doubt, market forces are among the major factors spurring the interest of health care institutions in health promotion programming. One market force is consumer demand. There is a growing interest in disease prevention and health promotion. With this awareness, there has been a concomitant growing awareness of the limitations of acute medicine. Health care institutions are also recognizing that these consumers represent a lucrative market. In Canada, as well as in the United States, most hospitals are actively considering the expansion of programs to "tap into these markets." There is evidence that similar trends are apparent in countries such as the Netherlands (Fahrenfort, 1990) and Australia (Degeling, Salkeld, Dowsett, & Fahey, 1990). In addition to the possible revenue these programs can generate, hospital administrators increasingly view health promotion programs in terms of their "reputation revenue." Administrators want to revive the image of their hospitals as places associated with good health and not just emergency treatment. A review of the administrative literature makes these trends readily apparent; health promotion programs are described using terms such as "strategic extensions" and "revenue generators" (Baragon, 1989; Boscarino, 1989; Speros & Sol, 1991). The irony is that rather than viewing health promotion as a means of empowering individuals and communities, many institutions are using the banner of health promotion to extend and expand their own empires. In a study that focused on health promotion and managed care in California, Schauffler and Chapman (1998) found that the majority of managed-care programs offered health promotion programs as a marketing vehicle.

Currently, many health care institutions, once exclusively directed toward the provision of health services, are expanding their mandates. In North America, Europe, Australia, and New Zealand, hospitals are expanding their wellness and health promotion services. A survey conducted in 1984 by the American Hospital Association revealed that 80% of the responding hospitals provided health promotion programs to inpatients and 70% provided them to outpatients (Lee, Giloth, Longe, & Jones, 1985; Ross et al., 1985). Similar results were obtained in a survey of Canadian hospitals in 1986 (Baskerville & LeTouzé, 1990; Canadian Hospital Association, 1987). Those who conducted the Canadian study concluded that, although Canadian hospitals are involved in promoting health, there were very few well-organized programs and that most of the activities offered could be classified as ad hoc. This survey also revealed that the majority of health promotion activities offered by Canadian health care institutions focus on education related to managing or preventing disease states. In countries with highly developed health care systems, the "health promotion" activities undertaken by health care institutions have tended to remain focused on individual responsibility and lifestyle rather than on the structural conditions that contribute to the health of individuals. This approach has been subject to a sustained and penetrating criticism by those who view health promotion as a social movement. According to this perspective, activities that are disease based, directed toward individuals, and largely controlled by health professionals are correctly classified as health education or disease prevention activities rather than health promotion activities (Hancock, 1994; Labonte 1994).

In developing countries, there is some evidence that a broader view of health promotion is being embraced by health care institutions. In countries such as Nepal, Costa Rica, and China, a policy of active liaison between particular hospitals and primary health care services has been implemented. These hospitals are attempting to fulfill a new role—namely that of a community health-oriented institution. According to WHO (1987), the designation community health-oriented hospital means that the hospital is not only disease oriented but has responsibilities in the fields of preventive medicine and health promotion. Such an institution can be used as a base for continuing education and training of community personnel. Frontline hospitals, according to this view, are part of an integrated primary health care system, serve as focal points for referral, and provide resources for planning and developing the health system.

It is clear that social and political forces have conspired over the past century to shape health care institutions. It is apparent that these institutions are attempting to shape their missions and mandates so that they may be more responsive to community needs. Perhaps now, more than at any other time, health care institutions are ready to embrace the principles of health promotion. In the following section, I consider the kinds of health promotion services that have been typically offered within health care institutions.

THE NATURE AND EFFECTS OF HEALTH PROMOTION SERVICES OFFERED WITHIN HEALTH CARE INSTITUTIONS

Within health care institutions, health promotion has tended to be associated with particular programs and services. This is noteworthy in that it has generally been assumed that health promotion is something that can be added to an institution's menu of programs and that a reorientation of the values and structures of the system is not necessary. The health promotion programs offered in health care institutions have typically included patient education and counseling services, clinical rehabilitation, and community and corporate wellness services. These programs support individual efforts to achieve a state of optimal health and physical, mental, and emotional well-being. Each of these forms of health promotion programming is considered separately in the following sections.

Patient Education

One of the earliest health promotion initiatives within an institutional setting was the establishment of formal programs for patient education, including spousal or parental education. Patient education services include a variety of activities designed to (a) inform patients about their illnesses and the effect of those illnesses on their daily lives, (b) prepare patients for diagnostic and treatment procedures and the experience of being in the hospital,(c) assist patients in managing their diseases after discharge, and (d) modify their behavior to promote optimal health and prevent further illness. Institutions offer patient education programs as part of inpatient care, outpatient care, or outreach care.

Patient education is more than the transfer of information because it seeks to change human behavior to optimize health outcomes. In addition, patient education can help to foster an active partnership between patients, their families, and health care providers. By sharing information and skills, patients and families can be empowered to act on their own behalves and to take a more active role in decision making.

There have been numerous reviews of studies that have measured the impact of health education and counseling on the behavior change of patients with acute and chronic conditions. Positive effects have been demonstrated for chronic conditions, including asthma (Newhouse, 1994), arthritis (Hirano, Laurent, & Lorig, 1994), coronary heart disease (Mullen, Mains, & Velez, 1992), diabetes mellitus (Brown, 1990), and hypertension (Linden & Chambers, 1994). Other reviews have examined the effects of counseling and education on women prior to the birth of a child (Jones, 1986) and on patients prior to surgical procedures (Devine, 1992) and have concluded that these programs can lead to significant positive effects.

Many studies have demonstrated the benefits that patients realize from a planned and coordinated approach to patient education. Numbered among the benefits most widely documented in the literature are reductions in duration of hospital stays, reductions in complications, and reductions in admissions and readmissions to hospitals (Alogna, 1985; Devine & Cook, 1983). Principles of good patient education such as individualizing the approach, providing explicit feedback on learning or clinical progress, and providing reinforcement are more likely to result in behavior change. Relying exclusively on information-sharing approaches is less effective than using information tailored to individual psychosocial variables that effect readiness for change in combination with behavioral and skills training (Mullen et al., 1995).

Clinical Rehabilitation

Clinical rehabilitation programs that incorporate exercise therapy, health education, and behavior change counseling enhance the continuity of care and treatment of people moving from an inpatient unit to an outpatient unit or home treatment. Following treatment and stabilization of an illness, a rehabilitation program is designed to return the person to a level of health equal to or greater than the level before the illness. The goal of clinical rehabilitation programs is to improve stamina and strength, return people to their homes and activities of daily living, and to prevent the recurrence of the illness or injury. Examples of rehabilitation programs provided by institutions include cardiac rehabilitation, stroke recovery, and exercise therapy. Clinical rehabilitation programs begin with inpatients and continue when they become outpatients. These programs provide a continuum of supervised care and treatment until the patient is trained in self-care skills and ready for discharge from the program.

Community and Corporate Wellness

A wellness program can be defined as a positive lifestyle approach to realizing a person's best potentials. Wellness programs are designed to educate and motivate individuals to reduce their risk of preventable diseases and to help individuals maximize their potential for health and well-being. Wellness programs based in health care institutions typically are directed at one of three audiences: well individuals within the community, employees of local businesses, and the employees of the health care institution itself. The emphasis of these programs tends to be on self-awareness and self-responsibility. Topics included in such wellness programs typically include nutrition, stress management, physical fitness, and interpersonal skills development, as well as more clinical problems such as smoking cessation and weight management (Liang, 1980).

To plan programs, many health care institutions have segmented their markets as they focus on specific groups such as the elderly, women, or new parents. The interventions used in wellness programs are designed to help inform, motivate, and support health behaviors. To support wellness initiatives, many health care institutions have sponsored self-help groups and programs. By working in cooperation with established groups, health care institutions have been able to expand the menu of services provided. It is interesting to note that employees of these institutions are often an audience not included in hospital wellness programs. Although difficult to develop, many argue that the development of wellness programs for employees are essential if an institution is to be viewed as a credible force in the field of health promotion. Best, Lovato, Learmonth, and Williams (1995) suggest that hospital employee programs can serve as living laboratories, and that the findings of these programs can be used to refine and later to market effective approaches.

DOES HEALTH PROMOTION BELONG IN HEALTH CARE INSTITUTIONS?

It can be argued that health care institutions should maintain their long-established role as centers for the care of the sick and injured, relegating the responsibility for health promotion to the public health sector and other community agencies. Those who hold this position maintain that health care institutions are currently using health promotion to serve their own ends rather than those of the community. In contrast, it can be argued that hospitals are an important part of communities and that all institutions, particularly those involved with public services, must be actively involved in health promotion planning. Suffice it to say that arguments can be levied both for and against including health promotion in health care institutions. The principles of intersectoral health promotion planning would suggest that both communities and the institutions that serve those communities must be engaged in health promotion if it is to be effective. The practicalities of health promotion resources require that the responsibility be shared by individuals, families, communities, institutions, and governmental organizations. As yet, there has been little evidence to suggest that health care institutions are willing to engage in a meaningful way with the communities in which they are located. The barriers to such engagement are significant. On the side of the public, these barriers include the continued belief that health professionals "know best" and that biomedicine constitutes a "magic bullet." On the side of health care institutions these barriers include the need to protect current interests and maintain control of programs. As Labonte (1994) points out, there is "a tension between the linear, bureaucratic need to manage programs . . . and the spiral flow of community development processes" (p. 82).

Although health care institutions may remain unwilling and unable to engage with communities in a full process of health promotion planning, health care institutions can logically claim to be suitable for offering particular kinds of health promotion programming. Mullen et al. (1995) maintain that there are two characteristics unique to health care institutions that account for the efficacy of the specific kinds of health promotion programs reviewed in the previous section. First, unlike school or workplace settings, improved health is a primary objective of health care institutions. Second, they claim that health care providers are generally considered credible sources of health information, and individuals are more likely to be receptive and attentive to health information when it is offered by a health professional. In addition, health care institutions offer an existing infrastructure for health promotion and are established points of access for many individuals (Best et al., 1995). Finally, for those programs directed at patients, one could add that the period of their hospital stay may constitute a teachable moment, in that patients are easily reached and may be highly motivated to change their behavior.

It would seem that the correct mix of institutional, individual, and community responsibility for health promotion is best considered on a case-by-case basis (Green & Kreuter, 1990). The structures of health care institutions provide channels and mechanisms for influencing and reaching defined populations. These settings, however, are usually organized for purposes other than health promotion. In the following section, I consider the organizational culture of health care institutions.

THE CULTURE OF HEALTH CARE INSTITUTIONS

Many of the challenges to the delivery of health promotion programs in other settings are also present in the institutional setting. The cultural complexity and elaborate bureaucracies of health care institutions, however, make working within these settings particularly challenging. Culture is to the institution what personality is to the individual—a hidden, yet unifying theme that provides meaning and direction (Schulz & Johnson, 1990). To develop health promotion programs effectively within health care institutions, one needs to understand the culture of these settings. I next explore some of the dimensions that typify the culture of health care institutions.

Bureaucratization of Health Care

One significant factor that defines the nature of health care institutions is the bureaucracy. In 1967, Friedson applied the term "health factories" to large hospitals and expressed concern about what the rationalization of services did to patients who became the objects of depersonalized care. This concern remains equally germane today. An important dimension of health care bureaucracies as a setting for health promotion is their size. Many health care institutions are behemoths that employ thousands of workers and offer hundreds of services. Size and complexity imply a large administrative cadre attempting to coordinate activities. Size and bureaucratization also make it more difficult to implement change in these settings than in smaller organizations. Indeed, it might be easier to add new programs than to change existing programs or to achieve integrated services in a large bureaucracy. Health care institutions, for these reasons, often have a difficult time responding to current needs and demands. These institutions are so caught up in fulfilling their individual mandates that they have remained largely unresponsive to the communities in which they are situated.

The Prevailing Values and Interests

The greatest challenges to developing health promotion programs within institutional settings are the prevailing values and interests that typify these settings. Health care institutions, particularly those in a for-profit system, are concerned with keeping beds filled or raising revenue by other means rather than with promoting the health of individuals and communities (Best et al., 1995). For example, a 1993 Canadian survey revealed that only 5 out 523 hospitals qualified for "Baby Friendly" designation by meeting the requirement for promoting breast feeding as set out by the WHO. One thousand hospitals around the world have been certified as "baby friendly" by UNICEF; Sweden with 28 hospitals leads developed countries (Dunlop, 1995). Companies that make baby formula have been very effective in promoting bottle feeding as an acceptable routine feeding approach, and many hospitals have lucrative long-term contracts for dispensing infant formula during the postpartum hospital stay. This situation exemplifies the shift in interests that must take place if health is to be promoted within health care institutions.

The necessary value shift is particularly difficult because many health professionals working within these settings have been educated to think exclusively about health care in relation to illness care, particularly acute illness care. Health professionals are often not educated about health promotion strategies and consequently direct their interests and attention toward the treatment and management of acute illness and disease. For example, Belcher (1990) points out that physicians are so intensely trained within the biomedical model that they have lost their perspective about patients' larger experiences.

If the ideals of health promotion are to be initiated within health care institutions, the professional-client relationship needs to be reconsidered. Health care professionals working within health care institutions have paid minimal attention to the needs of the individuals and communities that they serve. For example, Eakin (1987) studied the experiences of chronically ill patents within the acute care system and concluded that a profound change in the commitments and goals of health care personnel is required. She pointed out that professionals need to redefine what constitutes professional "help" so that it corresponds to the needs of patients rather than to those of the professionals serving them. Rather than focusing on the services that they want to provide, professionals need to listen to the needs and requirements of the individuals whom their institutions serve.

The values shift that is necessary becomes particularly pressing when one considers how inherently unhealthful many health care institutions are for their own employees. For example, health care institutions have been slow to address the health of their employees. Baskerville and LeTouzé (1990) point out that Canadian hospitals are more likely to provide health promotion programs for the employees of other organizations than for their own employees. The need for health promotion programs within these settings is clear. Hospitals were among the last of the public institutions in many American communities to restrict smoking in waiting rooms, and nurses have continued to have one of the highest smoking rates among female professionals (Green, 1990). The working conditions within health care institutions do not facilitate the health of the workers or the patients. Often, hospital staff members are required to work long hours with little professional discretion or control (Green, 1990; Torrance, 1987). Green (1990) points out that

> until health care institutions change their own cultures, until they engage their employees actively in maintaining their own health, until they provide child care and exercise facilities for their employees, they are unlikely to provide health leadership in their communities or credible role models for their patients. (p. 170)

Personnel, Role Definition, and Responsibilities

Health care institutions, particularly hospitals, foster a status hierarchy in which physicians form the pinnacle (Goodman & Steckler, 1990). This hierarchy works against most attempts to engage a wide variety of staff members actively in health promotion planning. The staffing mix and pattern of health care institutions also create several challenges to the development of health promotion programs. First, health care institutions often experience rapid staff turnover. This, in turn, can limit the continuity necessary for planning and implementing a program. In part, this explains why health promotion programs have tended to be developed by one or two "experts" and then added to the "menu" of programs and services offered within health care institutions.

The second way in which the hierarchy of health care institutions may challenge attempts to develop health promotion programs is that the key professionals in the hierarchy are often skeptical about health promotion programs. The culture of the institution revolves around immediate solutions to problems and focuses on "cures" rather than on the prevention or management of problems. Orlandi (1987) and others (Battista, 1983; Sobal, Valente, Muncie, Levine, & Deforge, 1986) have concluded that beliefs regarding the effectiveness of health promotion interventions can act as a major barrier to the implementation of health promotion programs in institutional settings. If key hospital staff members do not believe in the effectiveness of health promotion, or if they do not see it as part of their role, there will be difficulty in implementing health promotion programs. For some staff members, it is not a lack of belief regarding the effectiveness of health promotion interventions that causes the problem but, rather, a perceived lack of self-efficacy or their own skill and training. Surveys have consistently revealed that health care personnel, including physicians and nurses, believe that they do not have adequate training to engage in health promotion activities (McBride, 1994; Valente, Sobal, Muncie, Levine, & Antiltz, 1986; White & Berland, 1993).

A role refers to the set of activities or expected behavior of an individual within an organization. Within the health care setting, the roles of the various workers are often defined narrowly. For example, roles define where an employee works as well as the breadth and scope of the jobs to be performed. Furthermore, another bureaucratic consequence of the size of health care institutions is that standardization of routines has been viewed as essential. As a result of rather rigid roles, there are often disputes about the legitimate scope of practice of each professional group. Inherently, interdisciplinary and multidisciplinary activities, such as health promotion, can be the source of territorial fighting or can fall through the cracks because no department is willing or has a clear mandate to assume responsibility. In addition, health care institutions have traditionally viewed their employees' work only within the scope of the institution's walls. Nurses, for example, are discouraged from making contact with patients who have been discharged into the community because these patients are no longer considered the responsibility of the institution (McBride, 1994).

Another important role within health care institutions is that of the patient. Orlandi (1987) reminds us that patients usually come into contact with the health care system because they want to solve existing problems and are not necessarily interested in receiving information or advice regarding nonexisting or potential problems. Any initiative an individual may take in relation to health is often stifled within the culture of the health care institution. When they are admitted to health care institutions, patients are often stripped of their personal belongings, and they are told when they should eat and sleep and what tests they will have done. In light of this, it is not surprising that when patients adopt the sick role, which includes a relief from obligations other than cooperating with their treatment, they are unable or unprepared to discuss broader issues regarding their responsibility for health and preventive actions. Individuals who do assert themselves and try to retain control of their care and treatment are often labeled as "problem patients" or as "noncompliant."

Another noteworthy aspect of the patient role, particularly within acute care settings, is how busy patients are with treatments and procedures. The acuteness of the average patient's medical condition within the hospital setting has soared over the past decades. Patients are being sent home earlier; whereas they once remained in hospital for 2 to 3 weeks following open heart surgery, they are now discharged after 5 days. With shortened hospital stays, many patients are exhausted during their postoperative or brief convalescent period and may be unable to assume an active and full partnership with the hospital staff (Waterworth & Luker, 1990). Indeed, studies have demonstrated that patients who are hospitalized for relatively shorter periods of time are less likely to be exposed to health promotion activities (Pineault, Champagne, Maheux, Legault, & Paré, 1989).

WORKING EFFECTIVELY WITHIN HEALTH CARE INSTITUTIONS

Many of the health promotion principles relevant to the community setting require some qualification to apply to the institutional setting. Although it is essential that health promotion programs be developed with a sound understanding of the community or population's needs, wants, and desires, it must be remembered that some patient needs are beyond their consciousness or control. The promotion of health demands collaboration with community-based health agencies and an awareness of the collective needs of the community, but the urgency of a patient's needs takes precedence in the health care setting. With this in mind, let us turn next to a consideration of the ways in which we can effectively develop health promotion programs within an institutional setting.

The foregoing discussion has explicated cultural and organizational aspects of health care institutions. Empirical and theoretical evidence suggests that the best approach for developing and instituting health promotion within institutional settings is one that is systematic; is directed toward the needs of the individuals, workers, and community currently served by the institution; and takes, as its starting point, the culture and values of the institution (Goodman & Steckler, 1990). This latter point cannot be stressed enough. Organizational development (OD) strategies found to be useful in other settings have failed within health care institutions because they have not been based on sound understanding of institutional culture. Cohen (1982), for example, describes a process in which OD was used by a group of medical residents to develop a team approach to health care in which the patient was an active participant. The experiment failed miserably. Cohen maintains that the approach failed because the culture of the hospital works against OD approaches. In particular, he cites the factors of time constraints, staff turnover, and the inherent hierarchy as barriers to the achievement of OD goals.

The Canadian Advisory Committee on Institutional and Health Services developed guidelines for implementing health promotion programs within health facilities (Health and Welfare Canada, 1990). These guidelines outline a multiphased implementation procpss that includes the phases of preparation and commitment, assessment, organization, action, and evaluation. Because each health care institution has its own unique traditions and attitudes, implementation of this process must be tailored to the institution. Notwithstanding this caveat, these phases create a helpful framework for discussing the implementation of health promotion programs in health care institutions.

Preparation and Commitment

Prior to commencing health promotion programming, it is essential that the key players be identified. Although community involvement is essential, the first question to consider is what constitutes community. Depending on the scope and nature of the program being considered, the community may be defined as a particular group of patients and their families, those who reside in the hospital community, or it may include other organizations as well as members of the public.

Once the essential stakeholders are defined, the preparation stage can begin. During the stage of preparation, the groundwork is laid for a health promotion program. In particular, one attempts to ensure that a common understanding of health promotion and the institution's potential role is developed among members of the staff and the community. The goal of this phase is to establish understanding and cooperation from the public and from the staff members working within the institution. Before beginning this phase, it is important to consider the timing of a program and the organization's climate. Massive restructuring within an institution is often accompanied by the deletion of staff positions and reallocation of duties. Programs introduced that do not have the support of the staff members and the public are destined for failure. For example, the public may be reticent to support health promotion activities within a hospital when they are concerned about bed closures and waiting lists for surgery. Similarly, staff members may be reluctant to commit to any additional programs when their work roles are in states of flux and their morale is low.

Realistically, there are few optimal occasions for the introduction of new programs within institutions. The pace of change is so rapid that it is difficult to follow the edict that the organization should be in a period of stability prior to the introduction of any change. Rather than concerning oneself with the timing of a change, it is perhaps more important to realize that change takes time. Radical departures from traditional practice require time. Such a perspective is embedded in behavioral and organizational stage theory, which accounts for the cultivation of appreciation and acceptance of a change prior to the adoption and implementation of a change (Goodman & Steckler, 1990).

A major limitation within the health care institution setting is that staff members often have difficulty finding time to engage in the groundwork necessary for effective program planning. Staff members are rarely given the release time necessary to engage in work that is perceived to be beyond their defined roles. In addition, the regular patient and organizational crises that occur within these busy institutions can create barriers to participation. Members of the community also may feel diffident about becoming involved in a program planning process within an institutional setting.

The preparation phase can be facilitated by ensuring that credible and knowledgeable individuals serve as the spokespeople for health promotion projects. Activities such as workshops and study groups that involve the public, as well as staff members, can help to ensure "buy-in" and can assist the program planners in acquiring accurate assessments of the needs and concerns of relevant stakeholders. Some individuals recommend moving these planning activities from the actual setting so that participants are free from distractions and can be encouraged to think beyond the existing circumstances (Schulz & Johnson, 1990). The preparation phase can also be facilitated by establishing contact with other health care facilities and community services and groups. These contacts can broaden one's understanding of the kinds of programs available and can arouse the interest of staff members and the public in the potential of innovative action.

Commitment is the most important result of the preparation phase. When key individuals involved in the institution are committed to the concept and benefits of health promotion, successful implementation becomes possible. With this support developed, it is possible to begin program development and to build on successes. It is particularly important that support for health promotion programming is evident at the senior management level. Only in this way can one ensure that resources will be in place to act effectively on initiatives (Goodman & Steckler, 1990).

Assessment

Once knowledge about, interest in, and commitment to health promotion are generated, those involved can begin to engage in the assessment process. An assessment helps to recognize what is currently being done and to evaluate its effectiveness in light of community needs. In addition, assessment involves determining the strengths, resources, and experiences that can serve the process of developing a health promotion program. Ultimately, an understanding of opportunities and barriers will help to shape efforts in health promotion programming. The assessment should include an organizational assessment, an assessment of the service providers, and a community assessment or the evaluation of existing data concerning community needs.

Care needs to be taken to not undermine existing programs and efforts in the area of health promotion. The most effective programs build on existing activities or focus on areas of mutual cooperation. Ideally, the goal is to have health promotion become part of all activities, not something new added to the workload.

Health promotion is not something that a health care institution can do for a community or an individual. To be effective, it must be a joint collaborative effort in which the institution and the community pool their resources to work for their mutual advantage toward a common goal. Often, community interests may differ from those of the staff, administration, or board. Working with the community in the needs assessment process, and in the design and development of health promotion activities, can help to generate a sense of commitment and ensure that the programs developed meet real community needs.

Organization

Once needs have been identified, the organization and implementation of health promotion programs begins. The organizational process involves a process of setting priorities, selecting strategies, and developing a plan of action. In the document, *A Guide for Health Promotion by Health Care Facilities* (Health and Welfare Canada, 1990), it is recommended that the organizational process be guided by four questions. First, what is the health goal? It is helpful to clearly identify the goal that is to be addressed. This will facilitate subsequent program evaluation. Second, what health factors are being targeted? The answer to this question will help to determine which staff members should be involved and will give direction for strategy development. Third, whose health is it? Before any action is taken, those whose health is likely to be affected should be identified and involved in the process. This is a vital question that has been too easily discounted within more traditional health care institutions largely because of a curative perspective in which the care provider is in control as well as bureaucratic circumstances. The final question to be considered is, What is the most appropriate action? Once the first three questions have been answered, and all affected parties involved, the most appropriate action can be determined.

Action and Evaluation

Having agreed on a health promotion strategy, plans for the implementation of the program can be developed and the program can be implemented. An essential component of the action phase is evaluation. The purpose of evaluation is to collect information that will facilitate informed decision making. It can be used to improve programs and to direct future efforts. Among those who should be involved in the evaluation process are service providers, administrators, target groups, and funding agencies.

MEASURING THE SUCCESS OF HEALTH PROMOTION INTERVENTIONS: IS PATIENT COMPLIANCE THE APPROPRIATE OUTCOME?

Traditionally, patient compliance has been viewed as the appropriate outcome of health promotion activities within health care institutions. This putative outcome is based on the premise that the role of health professionals is to encourage clients to comply with prescribed regimens known from previous research to produce health benefits. The problem with this measure is that it is rooted in the professional's view of what constitutes "appropriate behavior." Patients and health professionals may differ in their understanding of what is relevant in a situation and what represents an appropriate course of action. Practitioners, in turn, tend to view noncompliance as a frustrating response that represents an insult to their professional authority (Heszen-Klemens, 1987) or as a sign that the patient simply cannot understand or cooperate. As a result, the patient's behavior is often the source of conflict and confrontation.

An important premise of health promotion is that it is directed toward helping individuals increase control over their health. Accordingly, approaches that are collaborative and that do not assume that patients must comply with predetermined regimens are more in keeping with the principles of health promotion. Outcomes that may be more appropriate include situational control, self-efficacy, enhanced self-care, enhanced self-concept, improved pain control, enhanced social support, improved functioning with activities of daily living, and improved health status (Berkman, 1995; Jenny, 1993; Kemper, Lorig, & Mettler, 1993; Lincoln & Gladman, 1992).

CHALLENGES AND FUTURE OPPORTUNITIES

The majority of literature concerning health promotion within health care institutions has been directed toward the acute care hospital sector. Conspicuously less developed in this literature is consideration of health promotion within psychiatric facilities, extended-care facilities, nursing homes, and veterans' homes. A notable exception to this is some of the earliest case studies and research on patient education in tuberculosis hospitals and outpatient clinics. This is unfortunate in that many of the residents of residential facilities are long-term or permanent occupants who can benefit from health promotion programming. In many ways, the residents of these facilities constitute whole communities and consequently are an appropriate focus for health promotion approaches that consider empowerment and mutual aid. A future challenge will be to develop and test health promotion programs within health care institutional settings other than acute care hospitals.

The majority of health promotion activities that have been conducted within health care institutions can be classified as ad hoc activities. There are relatively few examples of organized institutional programs of health promotion. A challenge for the future is to develop more systematic approaches to health promotion that include a reorientation of the value systems of institutions.

Many anticipate that, in the future, health care institutions will assume a larger role in the field of health promotion. Although the enthusiasm is encouraging, it will be important to ensure that health promotion does not abrogate the whole field to this new and powerful partner. It has been argued elsewhere that the community is the appropriate center of gravity for health promotion (Green & Kreuter, 1999). To ensure that the community remains central—and hence health promotion activities integrated, comprehensive, and balanced—health care institutions will have to tread lightly as they begin to engage in partnerships with members of the community. The challenge for those working in these settings will be to ensure that an attempt is not made to dominate and control health promotion activities and to ensure that the voices of others are heard. Hancock (1986) prudently reminds us that improving health within a community has little to do with health care services, per se, and a great deal to do with community action. In relation to community programming and health promotion, the role of health care institutions must be that of one of many community institutions, although a shift from "little to do with" to "greater partnership with" should be welcomed.

Although health care institutions, most notably hospitals, have been implementing health promotion programs with increasing frequency, there is relatively little evaluative research completed in the area (Thompson, Davidson, & LeTouzé, 1986). Research is required to determine the optimal time and place to intervene, to determine ways in which we can support the motivation of health care providers to become more involved in health promotion activities, to explore the use of technologies such as computers in health promotion, and to determine the effectiveness of alternative patient education and teaching strategies (Mullen et al., 1995). There are many promising signs that this work is under way. The International Network of Health Promoting Hospitals has sponsored a number of projects in which hospitals are documenting their efforts to change and adjust their structures to become more healthful institutions for patients, staff members, and the community. We can anticipate that the findings of this work will provide new insights into the process of changing institutions to become oriented to health promotion.

The nature of health care institutions will continue to develop and change. With these changes, new opportunities and challenges for health promotion will present themselves. Currently, three emerging trends hold particular promise for the development of meaningful and integrated health promotion programs within health care institutions. These trends have the potential to provide avenues of extension for the fledgling efforts in health promotion that currently characterize health care institutions.

The first trend is the movement toward the decentralization and regionalization of health care services. Those involved in health planning have recognized that health systems must be responsive to local needs and that increased citizen participation in shaping and directing health care institutions is required. In many countries, health care planning is being brought "closer to home," and citizens are being asked to participate in the decisions about their health care system. In the Canadian province of British Columbia, as in many other provinces in the country, regional health boards are being formed because citizens "want to be involved in the decisions about health services that affect their community" (British Columbia Ministry of Health, 1993, p. 8). Where once health care institutions were isolated from the lives of community members, members of the community are being given the power to make decisions about the nature of their health care institutions. With this new arrangement comes the potential for meaningful partnerships between the community and health care institutions.

A second noteworthy trend is the greater emphasis on preventive practices by clinical practitioners. Preventive practices once were viewed as being outside the realm of routine practice; now there is growing expectation and acceptance that all primary care practitioners will be involved in preventive practices. To a large degree, this trend mirrors the increased interest in prevention and health promotion that exists among members of the general public (Green, Eriksen, & Schor, 1988). This alteration in role perception signals a shift from an exclusive focus on care and cure to a broader concern for health that, in turn, necessitates the consideration of the contextual factors that affect health.

A third noteworthy trend is a change in the formulas applied in the funding of health care institutions. For-profit health care institutions, and those funded on global budgets, are provided rather perverse economic incentives, such as keeping beds occupied in the former case and spending all funds provided in the latter (Rachlis & Kushner, 1994). Currently, we are witnessing greater use of capitation funding in health care in which fixed funds are paid to an institution to service a population of clients. Using this funding model, health care institutions and group practices are now being asked to accept responsibility for the care of a population rather than the individuals who happen to enter their institutions. Rather than motivating high occupancy rates, incentives are being created to keep entire populations healthy. Not only does capitation create new incentives, it enables institutions to respond to community needs and to work with communities to facilitate their health. As Rachlis and Kushner point out, "Capitation has the added advantage of giving centres enormous flexibility to innovate and make changes to accommodate patients' needs" (p. 284). Unfortunately few organizations that use capitation funding, such as health maintenance organizations, have offered health promotion programming to achieve the goals of health improvement and cost control (Schauffler & Chapman, 1998).

The three trends described here may provide opportunities for health care institutions to more fully respond to the needs of individuals, families, and communities to develop greater control over and improve their health. Health care institutions have frequently been criticized for their isolation, paternalism, and unresponsiveness. If truly desired, opportunities can be seized so that health care institutions, at the beginning of the next millennium, will be one component of a well-integrated, intersectoral, approach to health promotion.

REFERENCES

Alogna, M. (1985). CDC diabetes control programs: Overview of diabetes patient education. *Diabetes Educator, 10*(4), 32-36, 57.

Baragon, E. (1989). Wellness programs flourish in B.C. hospitals. *Health Care, 31*(4), 10-12.

Baskerville, B., & LeTouzé, D. (1990). Facilitating the involvement of Canadian health care facilities in health promotion. *Patient Education and Counseling, 15,* 113-125.

Battista, R. N. (1983). Adult cancer prevention in primary care: Patterns of practice in Quebec. *American Journal of Public Health, 73,* 1036-1039.

Belcher, D. W. (1990). Are physicians obligated to provide preventive services? *Journal of General Internal Medicine, 5,* S104-S111.

Berkman, L. F. (1995). The role of social relations in health promotion. *Psychosomatic Medicine, 57,* 245-254.

Best, J. A., Lovato, C., Learmonth, C., & Williams, R. M. (1995). The future of wellness care. *Journal of Healthcare Resource Management, 13*(9), 7-14.

Blumhagen, D. W. (1979). The doctor's white coat: The image of the physician in modern America. *Annals of Internal Medicine, 91,* 111-116.

Boscarino, J. A. (1989). Hospital wellness centers: Strategic implementation, marketing, and management. *Health Care Management Review, 14*(2), 25-29.

British Columbia Ministry of Health. (1993). *Forming community health councils and regional health boards.* Victoria, BC: Author.

Brown, S. A. (1990). Studies of educational interventions and outcomes in diabetic adults: A meta-analysis revisited. *Patient Education and Counseling, 16,* 189-215.

Canadian Hospital Association. (1987). *Health promotion in Canadian hospitals: A study.* Ottawa, Ontario: Author.

Cohen, A. R. (1982). Organizational development as radical surgery: An experiment in delivering better patient care. In N. Margulies & J. D. Adams (Eds.), *Organizational development in health care institutions* (pp. 137-167). Reading, MA: Addison-Wesley.

Degeling, D., Salkeld, G., Dowsett, J., & Fahey, P. (1990). Patient education policy and practice in Australian hospitals. *Patient Education and Counseling, 15,* 127-138.

Devine, E. C. (1992). Effects of psychoeducational care for adult surgical patients: A meta-analysis of 191 studies. *Patient Education and Counseling, 19,* 129-142.

Devine, E. C., & Cook, T. D. (1983). A meta-analytic analysis of effects of psychoeducational interventions on length of postsurgical hospital stay. *Nursing Research, 32,* 267-274.

Dunlop, M. (1995). Few Canadian hospitals qualify for "baby friendly" designation by promoting breast-feeding: Survey. *Canadian Medical Association Journal, 152,* 87-89.

Eakin, J. M. (1987). Care of the unwanted: Stroke patients in a Canadian hospital. In D. Coburn, C. D'Arcy, G. M. Torrance, & P. New (Eds.), *Health and Canadian society: Sociological perspectives* (2nd ed., pp. 533-544). Markham, Ontario: Fitzhenry & Whiteside.

Evans, R. G., & Stoddart, G. L. (1990). *Producing health, consuming health care* (CIAR Population Health Working Paper No. 6). Toronto: Canadian Institute for Advanced Research, Population Health Program.

Fahrenfort, M. (1990). Patient education in Dutch hospitals: The fruits of a decade of endeavors. *Patient Education and Counseling, 15,* 139-150.

Foucault, M. (1975). *The birth of the clinic: An archeology of medical perception.* New York: Vintage.

Foucault, M. (1991). Governmentality. In G. Burchell, C. Gordon, & P. Miller (Eds.), *The Foucault effect: Studies in governmentality* (pp. 87-104). Hemel Hampstead, UK: Harvester Wheatsheaf.

Friedson, E. (1967). Health factories: The new industrial sociology. *Social Problems, 14,* 493-500.

Goodman, R. M., & Steckler, A. B. (1990). Mobilizing organizations for health enhancement: Theories of organizational change. In K. Glanz, F. M. Lewis, & B. K. Rimer (Eds.), *Health behavior and health education* (pp. 314-341). San Francisco: Jossey-Bass.

Green, L. W. (1990). Hospitals and health care providers as agents of patient education. *Patient and Education Counseling, 15,* 169-170.

Green, L. W., Eriksen, M. P., & Schor, E. L. (1988). Preventive practices by physicians: Behavioral determinants and potential interventions. In R. N. Battista & R. S. Lawrence (Eds.), *Implementing preventive services* (pp. 101-107). New York: Oxford University Press.

Green, L. W., & Kreuter, M. W. (1990). Health promotion as a public health strategy for the 1990s. *Annual Review of Public Health, 11,* 319-334.

Green, L. W., & Kreuter, M. W. (1999). *Health promotion planning: An educational and ecological approach* (3rd ed.). Mountain View, CA: Mayfield.

Hancock, T. (1986). Creating a healthy community: The preferred role for hospitals. *Dimensions, 63*(6), 22-23.

Hancock, T. (1994). Health promotion in Canada: Did we win the battle but lose the war? In A. Pederson, M. O'Neill, & I. Rootman (Eds.), *Health promotion in Canada: Provincial, national, and international perspectives* (pp. 350-373). Toronto: W. B. Saunders.

Health and Welfare Canada. (1990). *A guide for health promotion by health care facilities* (Cat. No. H39-184/1990/E). Ottawa, Ontario: Health Services and Promotion Branch, Health and Welfare Canada.

Heszen-Klemens, I. (1987). Patients' non-compliance and how doctors manage this. *Social Science and Medicine, 24,* 409-416.

Hirano, P. C., Laurent, D. D., & Lorig, K. (1994). Arthritis patient education studies, 1987–1991: A review of the literature. *Patient Education and Counseling, 24,* 3-7.

Jenny, J. (1993). A future perspective on patient/health education in Canada. *Journal of Advanced Nursing, 18,* 1408-1414.

Jones, L. C. (1986). A meta-analytic study of the effects of childbirth education on the parent-infant relationship. *Health Care for Women International, 7,* 357-370.

Kemper, D. W., Lorig, K., & Mettler, M. (1993). The effectiveness of medical self-care interventions: A focus on self-initiated responses to symptoms. *Patient Education and Counseling, 21,* 29-39.

Labonte, R. (1994). Death of a program, birth of a metaphor: The development of a health promotion in Canada. In A. Pederson, M. O'Neill, & I. Rootman (Eds.), *Health promotion in Canada: Provincial, national, and international perspectives* (pp. 72-90). Toronto: W. B. Saunders.

Lee, E., Giloth, B., Longe, M. E., & Jones, L. (1985). *Hospital-based health promotion programs: Report and analyses of the 1984 survey.* Chicago: American Hospital Association.

Liang, F. Z. (1980). Health promotion options. In M. M. Melum (Ed.), *The changing role of the hospital: Options for the future* (pp. 125-134). Chicago: American Hospital Association.

Lincoln, N. B., & Gladman, J. R. (1992). The extended activities of daily living scale: A further validation. *Disability and Rehabilitation, 14,* 41-43.

Linden, W., & Chambers, L. (1994). Clinical effectiveness of non-drug treatment for hypertension: A meta-analysis. *Annals of Behavioral Medicine, 16,* 35-45.

McBride, A. (1994). Health promotion in hospitals: The attitudes, beliefs and practices of hospital nurses. *Journal of Advanced Nursing, 20,* 92-100.

Mullen, P. D., Evans, D., Forster, J., Gottlieb, N. H., Kreuter, M., Moon, R., O'Rourke, T., & Strecher, V. J. (1995). Settings as an important dimension in health education/promotion policy, programs, and research. *Health Education Quarterly, 22,* 329-345.

Mullen, P. D., Mains, D. A., & Velez, R. (1992). A meta-analysis of controlled trials of cardiac patient education. *Patient Education and Counseling, 19,* 143-162.

Newhouse, M. T. (1994). Hospital-based asthma education: Achieving goals and evaluating the outcome. *Chest, 106*(4), 237S-241S.

Orlandi, M. A. (1987). Promoting health and preventing disease in health care settings: An analysis of barriers. *Preventive Medicine, 16,* 119-130.

Paine, L. H. W., & Tjam, F. S. (1988). *Hospitals and the health care revolution.* Geneva: World Health Organization.

Pineault, R., Champagne, F., Maheux, B., Legault, C., & Paré, M. (1989). Determinants of health counseling practices in hospitals: The patient's perspective. *American Journal of Preventive Medicine, 5,* 257-265.

Rachlis, M., & Kushner, C. (1994). *Strong medicine: How to save Canada's health care system.* Toronto: Harper Perennial.

Reiser, S. J. (1978). *Medicine and the reign of technology.* Cambridge, UK: Cambridge University Press.

Reverby, S. (1987). *Ordered to care: The dilemma of modern nursing, 1850–1945.* Cambridge, UK: Cambridge University Press.

Roos, N. P., & Roos, L. L. (1994). Small area variations, practice style, and quality of care. In R. G. Evans, M. L. Baer, & T. R. Marmor (Eds.), *Why are some people healthy and others not? The determinants of health of populations* (pp. 231-252). New York: Aldine De Gruyter.

Ross, C. K., Sherman, S. L., Berg, K. L., Radbill, L., Lee, E., Giloth, B., Jones, L., & Longe, M. (1985). Health promotion programs flourishing: Survey. *Hospitals, 59*(16), 128, 132-135.

Schauffler, H. H., & Chapman, S. A. (1998). Health promotion and managed care: Surveys of California's health plans and population. *American Journal of Preventive Medicine, 14*(3), 161-167.

Schulz, R., & Johnson, A. C. (1990). *Management of hospitals and health services: Strategic issues and performance* (3rd ed.). St. Louis: C. V. Mosby.

Sobal, J., Valente, C. M., Muncie, H. L. Jr., Levine, D. M., & Deforge, B. R. (1986). Physicians' beliefs about the importance of 25 health promoting behaviors. *American Journal of Public Health, 73,* 1427-1428.

Speros, C. I., & Sol, N. (1991). Health promotion in hospitals. *WHO Regional Publications: European Series, 37,* 267-281.

Thompson, C., Davidson, S., & LeTouzé, D. (1986). Survey reveals how hospitals promote health. *Hospital Trustee, 10*(5), 11-14.

Torrance, G. M. (1987). Hospitals as health factories. In D. Coburn, C. D'Arcy, G. M. Torrance, & P. New (Eds.), *Health and Canadian society: Sociological perspectives* (2nd ed., pp. 479-500). Markham, Ontario: Fitzhenry & Whiteside.

Valente, C. M., Sobal, J., Muncie, H. L., Levine, D. M., & Antiltz, A. M. (1986). Health promotion: Physician's beliefs, attitudes, and practices. *American Journal of Preventive Medicine, 2,* 82-88.

Waterworth, S., & Luker, K. A. (1990). Reluctant collaborators: Do patients want to be involved in decisions concerning care? *Journal of Advanced Nursing, 15,* 971-976.

White, N., & Berland, A. (1993). *The role of hospital nurses in health promotion: A collaborative study of British Columbia Hospital Nurses.* Vancouver, BC: Registered Nurses Association of British Columbia.

World Health Organization. (1984). *Health promotion: A discussion on the concepts and principles.* Copenhagen: Author.

World Health Organization. (1986). Ottawa charter for health promotion. *Canadian Journal of Public Health, 77*, 425-430.

World Health Organization. (1987). *Hospitals and health for all: Report of a WHO expert committee on the role of the hospitals at the first referral level* (WHO Technical Report Series, No. 744). Geneva: Author.

World Health Organization, Regional Office for Europe & Ludwig Boltzmann-Institute. (1995, July). *What is the International Network of Health Promoting Hospitals?* Copenhagen: Author.

COMMENTARY

Jane Lethbridge

Addressing the health care institution as a setting for health promotion in the late 1990s is particularly challenging because of the rapid rate of reform of health care systems in many countries. The health care institution is not static and is undergoing extensive change partly thrust on it for cost containment reasons but also because of technological advances in diagnosis and treatment of illness. During periods of change, new innovations and ways of thinking can be introduced to traditionally resistant institutions. It is with this understanding of the opportunities for change that health promotion within the health care institution must be considered.

There is an accurate awareness of some of the barriers that health care institutions present for any form of health promotion activity. Joy L. Johnson sets these out clearly as well as outlining the successes of health promotion and some of the issues that have to be addressed. I would like to take a different perspective by focusing on the future of the health care institution and the role of health promotion within it.

I will approach the future by trying to imagine the role that health promotion will play in the health care setting in the year 2006. Less than a decade away, it is important for health promoters to consider where health promotion should be located in strategic terms. The first problem for health promotion is its marginality within the health care setting. The need for health care will not disappear, but how could health promotion become a major player in the health care setting?

FUTURE PUBLIC HEALTH/HEALTH PROMOTION ISSUES

Rather than try to adjust to the existing institutional structures, a positive starting point is to consider the public health issues and subsequent health promotion and health care needs that will shape our views in 2006. Within Europe and North America, there are several trends to consider. The reemergence of some infectious diseases that were thought to have disappeared—for instance tuberculosis—will require a system of education, treatment, and care that will make new demands on the health care system. The interface between the community and the hospital will have to become more flexible with information and education as an essential part of health care delivery. Continuation of treatment for people who are homeless, poor or in low-quality housing requires a health care system that can actively reach out to its patients (Parsons, 1991; Richman, Roderick, Victor, & Lissauer, 1991).

The impact of HIV/AIDS on questioning patterns and standards of care has been widespread in many countries. The boundaries between the hospital and the community have been redefined in many cases with patients, their friends, and relatives demanding changes in how health care is delivered and in the information made available to them. For instance, the experience of a district health authority in central London found that the needs of AIDS patients meant that the way services were delivered had to be rethought with the boundaries between hospital and home becoming less rigid. A Home Support Team was set up that coordinated services delivered to people's homes with acute services. It aimed to give practical care, coordinate others, and teach by example, to (a) deliver care to people's homes during periods of disability, (b) deliver terminal care, and (c) maintain contact with well patients (Pye, Kapila, Buckley, & Cunningham, 1989). The changes brought about by patient and consumer demands for accessible and acceptable forms of health care need to be built on in the future (Dworkin, 1992; Froner & Rowniak, 1989).

A second dimension that the future hospital in 2006 will have to consider, is the increase in older people and the need to coordinate health and social care provision. Once again, this provides an opportunity for redrawing the boundaries of health care and integrating health promotion into a wide range of activities. Links with local primary health care teams, local communities, and the concept of the "hospital at home" will need to be central to the successful delivery of seamless packages of care (World Health Organization, 1995a). Hospital outreach teams are already established in many cities and rural areas.

The size of the health care institution necessary to deliver care is currently being questioned (King's Fund Commission, 1992; Smith, 1993). After decades of centralization and the development of large institutions in the United Kingdom, demands are surfacing for small-scale treatment centers, controlled by general practitioners, to deliver health care. This is also becoming part of UK government policy (NHS Executive, 1996). Establishing and maintaining links with local communities will be easier with smaller-scale institutions. The implications of small-scale delivery of care will increase the potential for health promotion activities and advice with older people. The effectiveness of health promotion for older people will also support the development of this.

RETHINKING HEALTH AND DISEASE

New thinking on disease and the relationship between physical disease and mental well-being suggests that in the future, this may be incorporated in health care delivery, leading to new opportunities for health promotion. The implications for self-therapy and medical treatments in treating cancers, allergies, and other infections are considerable (Bezold, 1995; Hancock & Garrett, 1995). It is predicted that psychoneuroimmunology will have a lasting impact on the design of hospital environments, the way that health care is delivered and other aspects of health care. The challenge of rethinking traditional ways of treating diseases should provide health promotion with the opportunity to influence the promotion of health in a broad sense. Recognizing the importance of the psyche in maintaining health helps to support the argument that there has to be an understanding of the environment where patients come from. This in turn supports the need for health care institutions to maintain links with local communities.

The relationship between hospitals and local communities will become increasingly important in addressing some of the major determinants of health in 2006. Global economic changes are affecting the resources available for the survival of communities. Increasing unemployment and job insecurity is leading to social instability with an impact on the health of whole communities. This will lead to an increased demand for health care at primary and secondary levels. It will also become more essential for the health care institution to consider partnerships with other sectors as a way of working toward the alleviation of ill health. The importance of the health care institution as a focal point of attachment within a community will strengthen any joint action it might take with other sectors. Health promoters working within these institutions will be able to use their skills of working in alliances as well as organizational development to enable the most effective partnerships to be built up with the community.

It is worthwhile considering how people perceive hospitals, health care, and health promotion. People are often very perceptive about the causes of ill health and their need for health care (Laughlo, 1984). Over the past 15 years of change in the United Kingdom, I have been struck by the attachment that local communities feel toward some hospitals. Historically, many hospitals in the United Kingdom were built through charitable donations from local people. The attachment expressed to hospitals built originally by charitable funds has often continued through two or more generations, well after a national health service took over the management of these hospitals. In some countries, the role of the church in establishing and running hospitals has led to hospitals' maintaining stronger links with local communities. Campaigns against closures have often led to a wider consideration of health and health promotion for local communities. This in turn has led local authorities and other urban authorities to consider their role in improving health.

These attachments to health care institutions need to be built on to facilitate interest in health and health promotion within the health care setting. The debates about the separation of health promotion from disease prevention, particularly secondary and tertiary prevention have often blocked an appreciation of the opportunities that still exist for health promotion (Roberts et al., 1995). The debate about a population versus a clinical approach has had a significant impact on the development of health promotion. A consideration of health promotion within the future health care system poses the question again, and we need to build on what has been learned. The Canadian experience has shown that a population-based approach to disease prevention can be effective. Activities on lifestyle issues as well as action on psychosocial and environmental determinants of health have been combined in many partnership initiatives working with local, provincial, and federal health departments and with the private sector and Health Canada (Stachenko, 1996). The importance of training health care professionals in health promotion techniques, involving public education, and strengthening community capability and skills for health promotion has become clear. The success of the Canadian Heart Health Initiative has shown the potential for collaboration between "prevention" and "health promotion" (Stachenko, 1996). A pragmatic approach to developing partnerships, strategies, and resources has been a key to success.

CONSUMERS AND HEALTH INFORMATION

Within the past decade, there has been an increased emphasis on patients as consumers of health care. In countries where the link between payment and delivery of health care is clear, it is easier to perceive the patient as a consumer. Where health care is still free at the point of delivery, the concept of consumers rather than users of a service has been slow to develop. However, the growth of user groups and self-help groups in the United Kingdom has focused attention on the provision of information on health care services and increasingly on disease and treatment.

Some hospitals have responded by setting up health information centers that are often funded initially by charitable funding. They use information gathered from academic sources and from self-help and voluntary groups.

The provision of information on the nature and treatment of specific diseases to patients and individuals within the community is an important development in starting to empower users of health care services. The centers are often used by both patients and their families within the local community. Health information centers often run groups for patients with specific conditions to support each other and share information. The health promoter has an important role to play in developing these activities so that patients can use information in an empowering way. In part, this will involve challenging professional assumptions and practices about restricting access to information. For health care professionals involved in health-promoting practice, this may be difficult, initially.

There will be an increasing need for new information about new treatments and approaches to health and disease to be given to patients and their families. This may involve using new technology that has the potential to provide more information to a greater number of people. However, fundamental issues of access will still have to be addressed. Health promoters should be taking a lead role in both developing information and facilitating its provision in empowering ways. They may start by facilitating alliances of nongovernmental organizations (NGOs), health care institutions, and professional bodies to provide information. This process is already beginning in the United Kingdom with links to private sector funding. The role of NGOs in this process is important if the needs of different communities are to be articulated. Health promoters may work closely with NGOs to ensure that the process remains controlled by people using the service.

MANAGEMENT AND HEALTH PROMOTION

Current trends in the United Kingdom show that hospitals are beginning to adopt health promotion activities as a way of improving their "added value" and image as part of the process of becoming more competitive. This is influenced as much by the attempts of hospitals to develop the "unique selling points" that will lead to more business as through any public demand for health-promoting activities. Although not necessarily motivated by public health concerns, the move to open the hospital to community needs may lead to improved standards of health care and opportunities to promote health. The interdependence of hospitals and local communities will have to be strengthened if accessible and acceptable health care is to be delivered. Members of the local community may be invited to be members of a hospital board.

Health care institutions have been shaped organizationally by their need to deliver health care in particular ways. Systems of management and control evolved to support them in this task. If the relationship between hospi-

tals and communities is to undergo extensive change, the way that these organizations run will also have to change. The WHO Health Promoting
Hospitals project has started to use organizational development as a way of
making hospitals more health promoting. Effective influencing and negotiating skills coupled with an acute organizational awareness and ability to work
across an organization could be seen as essential to get health promotion on
the agenda. For too long increased health promotion activities within the
health care setting have been seen as dependent on health care practitioners having appropriate health promotion skills. The ability to influence
organizations is probably much more important. There is now an awareness
that this is the case (Caraher, 1994).

Recognizing that the successful integration of health promotion within
the health care setting depends on organizational and management skills
has an important influence on thinking about the future. Returning to our
hospital in 2006, it will have strong and effective links with the local community, it will provide access to health information from across the world for the
local community, and it will reflect its understanding of the link between
state of mind and physical illness through the design of its buildings and the
delivery of care. But how will this organization be managed. I suggest that if
health promotion is to play a key role, then health promoters will have to engage proactively in the management process.

Current thinking about new ways of managing changing organizations
should be considered in the context of health promotion skills. Many health
promotion practitioners have recognized that the skills that they bring, especially the ability to develop and manage the health promotion process and
collaborative working, are highly transferable to organizations going
through change. The perception of health promoters as change agents will
become increasingly important in the future.

Responding effectively to the needs of the external environment will be
key to the success of any future health care institution. Health promoters are
in a good position to inform and interpret the external environment for
health care providers because they understand how factors within the external environment affect the health of local communities. Yet knowledge of
the external environment will not be enough to ensure the survival of the
health care institution. The ability to play an active role within this changing
environment will also be critical. Once again, health promotion has a lot to
offer in terms of future health strategies and intersectoral collaboration.

Management approaches that try to integrate activities that have traditionally been separate will be key to the successful management of a health
care institution effectively working in partnership with local communities.
The ability to encourage innovation and risk taking at all levels of the organi-

zation will require leadership and commitment (Kiser, Boario, & Hilton, 1995). Organizational learning has been identified as one of the keys to success for organizations (Argyris, 1994). The process of learning and ways of enabling people to learn from their experience will be familiar to many health promoters. They will have to translate these skills for use in an institutional environment.

The hospital of 2009 will bear little resemblance to the health care institutions that we are currently trying to turn toward addressing health as well as treating illness. If health promotion is to become a central focus of health care institutions, it will require a change in thinking for all health promoters. Rather than being overwhelmed by the marginality of health promotion within the health care setting, health promoters need to develop the strategic and managerial skills to influence and shape the agenda of the future health care institutions. This will mean that promoting health within a health care setting will be increasingly about developing policies, influencing organizational systems, and challenging professional power. In many ways, the door is already open, the impact of health care reforms on hospitals is pushing them to rethink the ways in which care is delivered and the relationship between the hospital and its patients in local communities. Health promoters can build on this but must also begin to engage more actively in management processes that will shape the functions of the health care institution of 2006.

REFERENCES

Argyris, C. (1994). *On organizational learning.* Oxford, UK: Blackwell.

Bezold, C. (1995). The future of health futures. *Futures, 27*(9-10), 921-925.

Caraher, M. (1994). A sociological approach to health promotion for nurses in an institutional setting. *Journal of Advanced Nursing, 20,* 544-551.

Dworkin, J. (1992). AIDS education for health care professionals in an organizational or systems context. *Public Health Reports, 107*(6), 668-674.

Froner, G., & Rowniak, S. (1989). The health outreach team: Taking AIDS education and health care to the streets. *AIDS Education and Prevention, 1*(2), 105-118.

Hancock, T., & Garrett, M. (1995). Health challenges and strategies in the 21st century. *Futures, 27*(9-10), 935-951.

King's Fund Commission. (1992). *London health care.* London: King's Fund.

Kiser, M., Boario, M., & Hilton, D. (1995). Transformation for health: A participatory empowerment education training model in the faith community. *Journal of Health Education, 26*(6), 361-365.

Lauglo, M. (1984). *The Spitalfield health survey.* London: Tower Hamlets Department of Community Medicine.

NHS Executive. (1996). *Primary care: The future.* London: Department of Health.

Nicholson, D., Hadridge, P., & Royston, G. (1995). Some practical hints for newcomers to health futures. *Futures, 27*(9-10), 1059-1065.

Parsons, L. (1991). Homeless families in Hackney. *Public Health, 105,* 287-296.

Pye, M., Kapila, M., Buckley, G., & Cunningham, D. (1989). *Responding to the AIDS Challenge: A comparative study of local AIDS programmes in the UK.* London: Health Education Authority.

Richman, S., Roderick, P., Victor, C. R., & Lissauer, T. (1991). Use of acute hospital services by homeless children. *Public Health, 105,* 297-302.

Roberts, J., Browne, G. B., Streiner, D., Gafni, A., Pallister, R., Hoxby, H., Jamieson, E., & Meichenbaum, D. (1995). The effectiveness and efficiency of health promotion in speciality clinic care. *Medical Care, 33*(9), 892-905.

Smith, J. (1993). *London after Tomlinson: Re-organising big city medicine.* London: BMJ Publishing.

Stachenko, S. (1996, October). *Health promotion and disease prevention in Canada: Approaches and complementarities.* Paper presented at the Second Meeting of the European Committee for Health Promotion Development, Ormoz, Slovenia.

World Health Organization. (1995a). *From hospitals to home health care: An alternative requiring careful planning.* Geneva: Author.

World Health Organization. (1995b). *Health promoting hospitals working for health.* Copenhagen: Author.

COMMENTARY

Patricia Dolan Mullen
L. Kay Bartholomew

   Dr. Johnson's chapter has presented a broad menu of roles that health care settings, primarily hospitals, can play in health promotion, emphasizing the World Health Organization philosophy of taking a community health perspective and an intersectoral approach (Speros & Sol, 1991; World Health Organization, 1986, 1987, 1995). Two of her specific criticisms of the gap between ideal and actual practice are that health care institutions are focused on illness or disease rather than other family and community needs and that they strip power and control from patients and families as the price of treatment and cure.

   In this commentary, we will argue that in the North American context at least, Johnson's first criticism has the effect of excusing too many health care institutions from failure to perform their basic business. We take the position that they should make illness and disease their primary focus. We do, however, endorse the second criticism and call for care that supports control and decision making by health care clients, and families. Thus, we recommend a health promotion and self-management model instead of the narrow biomedical and compliance model. We will present evidence on the perfor-

AUTHORS' NOTE: We are grateful to Ms. Karen Hobbs for her help with library research and Ms. Donna White for assistance with the references.

mance of health care institutions that justifies the need for improved health promotion among health care clients and discuss health care trends that are facilitators and barriers for health promotion.

NEEDS-BASED HEALTH PROMOTION
IN HEALTH CARE SETTINGS

Health care institutions in North America have several close-to-home challenges for health promotion that they should address fully before venturing further afield from their historic missions. The first is to ensure that effective health promotion is delivered to their own patients as the standard of care. This implies that patient choice and decision making are encouraged (e.g., elective surgery patients learn coping and recovery skills in advance of the surgery and are able to exercise control over pain medications afterward). The second challenge is to provide self-management training to patients and family members for a disease or problem as they move across the sites of care—inpatient, outpatient, and home or rehabilitation settings. Challenge number three is for health care institutions to move more fully into population-based disease management and make available self-management training for chronic disease populations through affiliated medical groups and also directly to affected individuals. The last challenge is to include prevention activities such as smoking cessation for patients in an acute phase of a chronic illness (e.g., asthma or chronic obstructive pulmonary disease) as well as for scheduled patients (e.g., smokers before elective surgery when a general anesthetic will be given) and potential patients (e.g., pregnant women).

AVAILABLE, EVALUATED, AND NEGLECTED:
SURGERY PREPARATION AND PAIN MANAGEMENT

Johnson notes that numerous reviews have concluded that education and counseling for individuals with acute and chronic conditions have a positive and clinically significant effect (Brown, 1990; Devine, 1992; Hirano, Laurent, & Lorig, 1994; Jones, 1986; Linden & Chambers, 1994; Mullen, Mains, & Velez, 1992; Newhouse, 1994). Presentation of such evidence, however, has not resulted in prompt and widespread adoption by health care institutions.

This problem is illustrated by the early set of randomized trials testing the impact of programs to prepare patients for surgery and for pain management and recovery. Despite their various labels indicating a passive role for the patient, "patient teaching," "counseling," and "psychoeducation," these programs do generally arm patients with information, skills, and support that gives them more autonomy and control over the hospitalization experience.

In 1982, 49 studies were available (Devine & Cook, 1983) and by 1985, 102 studies evaluating "psychoeducational" care for adult surgery patients were located (Devine & Cook, 1986). Nevertheless, despite ample evidence for their effectiveness, such programs were far from being usual care (Lee, Giloth, Longe, & Jones, 1985). In fact, by 1989, the management of acute pain after operative procedures in the United States was recognized as a target for a guideline by the Agency for Health Care Policy and Research because of the potential impact on health outcomes and because of the wide variation observed in healthcare practice. In that year alone, of the estimated 23.3 million operations only an estimated 50% received the benefit of standard pain relief techniques (Acute Pain Management Guideline Panel, 1992a, 1992b).

Some improvement in use of pain relief techniques has taken place in the United States and the United Kingdom since publication of the guideline (Davies, 1996; Rousseau, 1994; Warfield & Kahn, 1995; Windsor, Glynn, & Mason, 1996), but many surgery patients are not receiving the acknowledged benefit. In particular, the use of patient-controlled pain medication and the assessment of the patient's preference for pain control are important contributions to patient health promotion.

DISEASE MANAGEMENT FOR THE CHRONICALLY ILL: ASTHMA AND DIABETES

Self-management education programs for chronic illness have been shown to improve patient outcomes. A few examples are programs for diabetes (Kaplan, Chadwick, & Schimmel, 1985), heart disease (Clark, Janz, Dodge, & Sharpe, 1992), osteo and rheumatoid arthritis and other rheumatic diseases (Lorig & Holman, 1993), asthma (Clark et al., 1986; Hindi-Alexander, & Cropp, 1984), and cystic fibrosis (Bartholomew et al., 1997). However, despite the documented effectiveness of patient health promotion for such chronic diseases, many of those who have these conditions have little access to knowledge, skills, and support from health care institutions and personnel to perform self-management behaviors during their hospital stays or afterward. The evidence for both patient outcomes and hospital and health care provider process makes a strong case for further attention to health promotion efforts with disease populations across the sites of care. And when a hospital episode indicates that a particular individual has not acquired the requisite knowledge, skills, and confidence, then hospital staff members need to ensure their acquisition.

Asthma provides a striking illustration of an increasingly prevalent disease for which patient outcomes are in need of improvement, yet available and effective programs are not widely applied. Asthma is one of the most common chronic diseases in the United States and Canada, affecting more than 10 million people in the United States. In recent decades, both prevalence and mortality have increased rapidly among children, adolescents, and young adults, and asthma is now the leading cause of hospitalizations and school absences. The key to preventing acute exacerbations of asthma and the related morbidity, mortality, and medical care use is appropriate treatment for the underlying inflammatory disorder and performance of patient self-management strategies (Ernst, Fitzgerald, & Spier, 1996; U.S. Department of Health and Human Services, 1991b). Effective treatment, consensus guidelines, and patient health promotion programs that include specific instructions for health care provider communication are available.

Nevertheless, unnecessary emergency room visits, hospitalizations, and deaths from asthma continue to increase, especially among urban, minority populations (Carr, Zeitel, & Weiss, 1992; Gerstman, Bosco, & Tomita, 1993; Gottlieb, Beiser, & O'Connor, 1995; LeSon & Gershwin, 1996; Targonski, Persky, Kelleher, & Addington, 1995). In one study of hospitalized young adults, 17% had mild and 51% had moderate disease. In other words, they had *controllable* asthma (LeSon & Gershwin, 1996). Other indications of the scarcity of appropriate patient health promotion (i.e., intervention focused on both health care provider and patient behavior) include the inverse correlation of inhaled anti-inflammatory (long-term preventive) to bronchodilator (rescue) medication (Gottlieb et al., 1995) and lack of use of written asthma action plans for patients and critical elements of practice guidelines (Hartert, Windom, Peebles, Freidhoff, & Togias, 1996).

Diabetes has been diagnosed in over 7 million people in the United States, with approximately 700,000 new cases identified each year. Diabetes in the United States is the most important cause of lower-extremity amputation and end-stage renal disease, the major cause of blindness among working-age adults, and an important risk factor for the development of many other conditions, including heart disease and stroke. Diabetes also is a major cause of disability and premature mortality. Between 1980 and 1987, hospitalization rates for major coronary vascular disease and stroke with diabetes as a secondary diagnosis increased 34% and 38%, respectively, and rates increased 21% for diabetic ketoacidosis and 29% for lower-extremity amputations. And from 1982 to 1986, treatment for end-stage renal disease related to diabetes increased more than 10% each year (Wetterhall et al., 1992).

Like asthma, diabetes is a public health problem with a strong role for hospitals and health care providers in prevention—a role that is largely unfilled. Providers who care for people with diabetes have suspected for decades what has now been strongly confirmed by the Diabetes Control and Complications Trial (Diabetes Control and Complications Trial Research Group, 1993; Lasker, 1993): There is a strong and direct correlation between early and "tight" control of glycemia and reduction of complications. Therefore, to decrease complications and related hospitalizations, patients need to work toward normal blood sugar levels by balancing insulin, food intake, and excretion. There is evidence that this balancing act is significantly facilitated by checking blood sugar levels at least daily—optimally, at various times during the day—and that regular practice of this complex self-management regimen is related to having participated in a diabetes education program (Gonder-Frederick, Julian, Cox, Clarke, & Carter, 1988; Harris, Cowie, & Howie, 1993; Peyrot & Rubin, 1988). This link is so well accepted that the need for diabetes education was incorporated into the Healthy People 2000 Objectives (U.S. Department of Health and Human Services, 1991a), the Standards of Care of the American Diabetes Association (1997) and the National Diabetes Advisory Board established by Congress as a part of Public Health Law 96-538 (1980).

Although no other chronic disease has such a clearly defined path toward patient health promotion as an integral part of in- and outpatient care, the rates of appropriate self-management of diabetes are startlingly low. Of individuals with insulin dependent diabetes (IDDM), 40% monitored their blood glucose at least once per day, and 20% had never tested blood glucose; of noninsulin dependent diabetics (NIDDM), only 26% of those treated with insulin and 5% of those not treated with insulin monitored one time per day. Forty-seven percent of insulin-treated NIDDM and 76.4% of non-insulin-treated NIDDM had never tested blood glucose. These rates did not appear to be related to level of income or health insurance (Harris, 1996; Harris et al., 1993). Rates of other important diabetes care behaviors such as insulin injections, visits with diabetes care specialists, preventive visits to specialists (e.g., ophthalmologists), and participation in diabetes self-management education were also low (Harris, 1996). And only about 35% of people in the United States with diabetes report having received diabetes education (Harris, 1996).

PRIMARY PREVENTION CLOSE TO HOME:
SMOKING CESSATION FOR HIGH-RISK GROUPS

Historically, when U.S. hospitals have extended into classic public health promotion arenas such as smoking cessation, many of them have conducted classes for "the community" as a marketing technique or separate line of business. They would serve their communities better if they targeted interventions toward their client populations and family members. For example, environmental tobacco smoke (ETS) exposure is a risk factor in new cases of asthma, additional episodes, and increased severity of symptoms in children (Cogswell, Mitchell, & Alexander, 1987; Cunningham, O'Connor, Dockery, & Speizer, 1996; Fergusson, Horwood, Shannon, & Taylor, 1981; Infante-Rivard, 1993; U.S. Environmental Protection Agency, 1992; Weitzman, Gortmaker, & Walker, 1990). Parents of children with asthma can make a major contribution to their health by reducing their children's exposure to ETS (Murray & Morrison, 1993). Smoking cessation or modification among parents of children with asthma and among other patient groups, such as pregnant women prior to the birth and afterward when they are at high risk of resuming smoking (Fingerhut, Kleinman, & Kendrick, 1990; Mullen, Quinn, & Ershoff, 1990), would be a health promotion effort with an impact across the levels of prevention.

FACILITATORS AND BARRIERS FOR PATIENT HEALTH PROMOTION

The aging of the U.S., Canadian, and many European populations and consequential increase in people with one or more chronic conditions is increasing the demand for care (Institute for Health and Aging, 1996) and concern about financing this care. New systems of population-based payment, increasing orientation to patient outcomes, development of "critical pathways," expansion of U.S. Joint Commission for the Accreditation of Health Care Organizations (JCAHO) guidelines, vertical integration of health care institutions (e.g., ownership of physician practices and home health care agencies by hospitals), capitation, and the explosion of information systems technology all can serve to increase the importance of patient health promotion.

Care planning by nurses and multidisciplinary teams of providers that results in "critical pathways" documents or "care maps" can cue patient health promotion over the course of a hospital stay (Blegen, Reiter, Goode, & Murphy, 1995; Montague et al., 1995). Such activities can also enhance the role of patient and family, with the outcome of increased perceived control by the client (Blegen et al., 1995; Hampton, 1993). Some care maps extend to outpatient care, rehabilitation, and home care, thereby presenting a vehicle both to train patients and to enable coordination among caregivers (Corbett & Androwich, 1994). This comes as physicians and hospitals have developed new models for integrating their activities and increasing the potential of providing more comprehensive care (Burns & Thorpe, 1993). Information systems technology can enhance the care mapping procedures by providing real-time data on the progress of patient care, including patient education

(Lee et al., 1995; Ornstein, Garr, & Jenkins, 1993; Ornstein et al., 1995; Norman, Hardin, Lester, Stinton, & Vincent, 1995).

The focus on patient outcomes and on outcomes indicators for entire diagnostic groups within a health care facility, or managed-care population, has the potential to increase recognition of the need for patient health promotion and for the technology to facilitate it. For example, the National Committee on Quality Assurance's Health Plan Employer Data and Information Set (HEDIS) publishes process indicators linked to better outcomes for managed-care patients (Schroeder & Lamb, 1996). Several of these indicators often include an emphasis on the behavioral capability of patients for self-care and motivate patient health promotion from top management of health care organizations. Similarly, publication by JCAHO in 1993 of new, stronger patient education guidelines required health care institutions to ensure organizational infrastructure to support patient teaching, to improve the process, and to focus on outcomes (Camp, 1994; Koska, 1992). This is in contrast to the situation historically, when patient education has been motivated by nurses who saw the needs of patients at the bedside and who had little evidence to persuade managers of effectiveness.

In summary, there are some powerful, new facilitators of systematic patient health promotion that should help health care institutions to focus more attention on their responsibilities for health and well-being of populations within a health care system. Unfortunately, however, these developments do not address all of the barriers to enhancing the behavioral capability of clients and their families to manage disease or hospital stays. We would argue that hospitals and other health care institutions remain bastions of expert power whose workforce fails to provide even the most convenient primary prevention. New barriers arise from the increasing acuity of hospital admissions, decreasing length of stay, downsizing, and a changing skill mix with increased use of unlicensed caregivers (Manuel & Sorensen, 1995).

Many professions have begun to talk about the importance of patient-centered and even family-centered care, but the process of relinquishing the keys to power—patient information and control—may be impossible under current conditions of health care provider training and acculturation. Some researchers argue that medical education in particular, with its emphasis on diagnostic and therapeutic competence, disables the entering students' natural capacity for seeing the whole patient and for caring (Good & Good, 1989). The resulting inability of the workforce of the health care institution to see a whole person rather than a body part or disease entity may explain part of the inadequacy of primary prevention offered in acute care visits.

Even if health care providers were skilled in providing patient health promotion and primary prevention and their training and acculturation supported it, the pressures of inadequate time and resources might be insurmountable. The decreasing length of stay in hospitals means that patient health promotion must be planned and executed in a shorter amount of time, with sicker patients, and with family members who are under acute stress. Even if information can be conveyed in a time-condensed fashion, attitude change, skill acquisition, after-care planning, and anticipatory problem solving involve complex cognitive behavioral processing that requires time. Making these learning and behavior change processes occur also requires advanced skills on the part of the staff members of hospital and outpatient facilities—skills less likely to be present as financial realities push health care institutions to provide services from the least-skilled labor possible.

CONCLUSION

We have agreed with Johnson that health promotion means approaches that help individuals increase control over their health. We differ, however, on our view of the core goals of health promotion in health care institutions, urging that much more attention be paid to the client and family needs for skills to manage chronic disease or hospital procedures. We further suggest that the first priority of health promotion outreach should be target populations and issues that are close to the institution's primary obligations of improving outcomes for clients.

REFERENCES

Acute Pain Management Guideline Panel. (1992a). Acute pain management in adults: Operative procedures. In *Quick reference guide for clinicians* (Report No. 92-0019). Rockville, MD: Agency for Health Care Policy and Research.

Acute Pain Management Guideline Panel. (1992b). Acute pain management in infants, children, and adolescents: Operative and medical procedures. In *Quick reference guide for clinicians* (Report No. 92-0020). Rockville, MD: Agency for Health Care Policy and Research.

American Diabetes Association. (1994). Standards of medical care for patients with diabetes mellitus. *Diabetes Care, 17,* 616-623.

Bartholomew, L. K., Czyzewski, D. I., Parcel, G. S., Swank, P., Sockrider, M. M., Mariotto, M., Schidlow, V., Fink, R., & Seilheimer, D. R. (1997). Self-management of cystic fibrosis: Short-term outcomes of the cystic fibrosis family education program. *Health Education and Behavior, 24*(5), 652-666.

Blegen, M. A., Reiter, R. C., Goode, C. J., & Murphy, R. R. (1995). Outcomes of hospital-based managed care: A multivariate analysis of cost and quality. *Obstetrics and Gynecology, 86*(5), 809-814.

Brown, S. A. (1990). Studies of educational interventions and outcomes in diabetic adults: A meta-analysis revisited. *Patient Education and Counseling, 16,* 189-215.

Burns, L. R., & Thorpe, D. P. (1993). Trends and models in physician-hospital organization. *Health Care Management Review, 18*(4), 7-20.

Camp, P. (1994). Joint Commission for Accreditation of Hospital Organization education standards: Perioperative applications. *Seminars in Perioperative Nursing, 3*(3), 133-144.

Carr, W., Zeitel, L., & Weiss, K. (1992). Variations in asthma hospitalizations and deaths in New York City. *American Journal of Public Health, 82*(1), 59-65.

Clark, N. M., Feldman, C. H., Evans, D., Levison, M. J., Wasilewski, Y., & Mellins, R. B. (1986). The impact of health education on frequency and cost of health care use by low income children with asthma. *Journal of Allergy and Clinical Immunology, 78,* 108-115.

Clark, N. M., Janz, N. K., Dodge, J. A., & Sharpe, P. A. (1992). Self-regulation of health behavior: The "Take PRIDE" program. *Health Education Quarterly, 19,* 341-354.

Cogswell, J., Mitchell, E. B., & Alexander, J. (1987). Parental smoking, breast feeding, and respiratory infection in development of allergic diseases. *Archives of Disease in Childhood, 62,* 338-344.

Corbett, C. F., & Androwich, I. M. (1994). Critical paths: Implications for improving practice. *Home Healthcare Nurse, 12*(6), 27-34.

Cunningham, J., O'Connor, G. T., Dockery, D. W., & Speizer, F. E. (1996). Environmental tobacco smoke, wheezing, and asthma in children in 24 communities. *American Journal of Respiratory and Critical Care Medicine, 153,* 218-224.

Davies, K. (1996). Findings of a national survey of acute pain services. *Nursing Times, 92*(17), 31-33.

Devine, E. C. (1992). Effects of psychoeducational care for adult surgical patients: A meta-analysis of 191 studies. *Patient Education and Counseling, 19,* 129-142.

Devine, E. C., & Cook, T. D. (1983). A meta-analytic analysis of effects of psychoeducational interventions on length of postsurgical hospital stay. *Nursing Research, 32,* 257-274.

Devine, E. C., & Cook, T. D. (1986). Clinical and cost-saving effects of psychoeducational interventions with surgical patients: A meta-analysis. *Research in Nursing and Health, 9,* 89-105.

Diabetes Control and Complications Trial Research Group. (1993). The effect of intensive treatment of diabetes on the development and progression of long-term complications in insulin-dependent diabetes mellitus. *New England Journal of Medicine, 329,* 977-986.

Ernst, P., Fitzgerald, J. M., & Spier, S. (1996). Canadian asthma consensus conference summary of recommendations. *Canadian Respiratory Journal, 3,* 89-100.

Fergusson, D. M., Horwood, L. J., Shannon, F. T., & Taylor, B. (1981). Parental smoking and lower respiratory illness in the first three years of life. *Journal of Epidemiology and Community Health, 35,* 180-184.

Fingerhut, L. A., Kleinman, J. C., & Kendrick, J. S. (1990). Smoking before, during and after pregnancy. *American Journal of Public Health, 80,* 541-544.

Gerstman, B. B., Bosco, L. A., & Tomita, D. K. (1993). Trends in the prevalence of asthma hospitalization in the 5-14 year old Michigan Medicaid population. *Journal of Allergy and Clinical Immunology, 91*(4), 838-843.

Gonder-Frederick, L. A., Julian, D. M., Cox, D. J., Clarke, W. L., & Carter, W. R. (1988). Self-regulation of blood-glucose. Accuracy of self-reported data and adherence to recommended regimen. *Diabetes Care, 11,* 579-585.

Good, M. D., & Good, B. J. (1989). Disabling practitioners: Hazards of learning to be a doctor in American medical education. *American Journal of Orthopsychiatry, 59*(2), 303-309.

Gottlieb, D. J., Beiser, A. S., & O'Connor, G. T. (1995). Poverty, race, and medication use are correlates of asthma hospitalization rates: A small area analysis in Boston. *Chest, 108*(1), 28-35.

Hampton, D. C. (1993). Implementing a managed care framework through care maps. *Journal of Nursing Administration, 23*(5), 21-27.

Harris, M. I. (1996). Medical care for patients with diabetes. *Annals of Internal Medicine, 125*(1), 117-122.

Harris, M. I., Cowie, C. C., & Howie, L. J. (1993). Self-monitoring of blood glucose by adults with diabetes in the United States population. *Diabetes Care, 16*(8), 1116-1123.

Hartert, T. V., Windom, H. H., Peebles, S., Freidhoff, L. R., & Togias, A. (1996). Inadequate outpatient medical therapy for patients with asthma admitted to two urban hospitals. *American Journal of Medicine, 100,* 386-394.

Hindi-Alexander, M. C., & Cropp, G. (1984). Evaluation of a family asthma program. *Journal of Allergy and Clinical Immunology, 74,* 505-510.

Hirano, P. C., Laurent, D. D., & Lorig, K. (1994). Arthritis patient education studies, 1987–1991: A review of the literature. *Patient Education and Counseling, 24,* 3-7.

Infante-Rivard, C. (1993). Childhood asthma and indoor environmental risk factors. *American Journal of Epidemiology, 137*(8): 834-844.

Institute for Health and Aging. (1996). *Chronic care in America: A 21st century challenge.* Princeton, NJ: Robert Wood Johnson Foundation.

Jones, L. C. (1986). A meta-analytic study of the effects of childbirth education on the parent-infant relationship. *Health Care for Women International, 7,* 357-370.

Kaplan, R., Chadwick, M., & Schimmel, L. (1985). Social learning intervention to promote metabolic control in Type I diabetes mellitus: Pilot experimental results. *Diabetes Care, 8,* 152-155.

Koska, M. T. (1992). JCAHO introduces three new areas of survey concentration. *Hospitals, 66*(19), 62-66.

Lasker, R. D. (1993). The diabetes control and complications trial. Implications for policy and practice [Editorial]. *New England Journal of Medicine, 329,* 1035-1036.

Lee, E., Giloth, B., Longe, M. E., & Jones, L. (1985). *Hospital-based health promotion programs: Report and analyses of the 1984 survey.* Chicago: American Hospital Association.

Lee, M., Niemeyer, D., Seilheimer, D., Abramson, S., Lin, Z., Gu, M. (1995). Cat 6 mo ↑ symptoms: online physician charting and more. *Proceedings: The Annual Symposium on Copmputer Applications in Medical Care,* 81-85.

LeSon, S., & Gershwin, M. E. (1996). Risk factors for asthmatic patients requiring intubation. *Journal of Asthma, 33*(1), 27-35.

Linden, W., & Chambers, L. (1994). Clinical effectiveness of non-drug treatment for hypertension: A meta-analysis. *Annals of Behavioral Medicine, 16*(1), 35-45.

Lorig, K., & Holman, H. (1993). Arthritis self-management studies: A twelve-year review. *Health Education Quarterly, 20*(1), 17-28.

Manuel, P., & Sorensen, L. (1995). Changing trends in healthcare: Implications for baccalaureate education, practice and employment. *Journal of Nursing Education, 34*(6), 248-253.

Montague, T., Taylor, L., Martin, S., Barnes, M., Ackman, M., Tuyuki, R., Wensel, R., Williams, R., Catellier, D., & Teo, K. (1995). Can practice patterns and outcomes be successfully altered? Examples from cardiovascular medicine. The Clinical Quality Improvement Network (CQIN) investigators. *Canadian Journal of Cardiology, 11*(6), 487-492.

Mullen, P. D., Mains, D. A., & Velez, R. (1992). A meta-analysis of controlled trials of cardiac patient education. *Patient Education and Counseling, 19,* 143-162.

Mullen, P. D., Quinn, V. P., & Ershoff, D. H. (1990). Maintenance of non-smoking postpartum by women who stopped during pregnancy. *American Journal of Public Health, 80,* 992-994.

Murray, A. B., & Morrison, B. J. (1993). The decrease in severity of asthma in children of parents who smoke since the parents have been exposing them to less cigarette smoke. *Journal of Allergy and Clinical Immunology, 91,* 102-110.

Newhouse, M. T. (1994). Hospital-based asthma education: Achieving goals and evaluating the outcome. *Chest, 106*(4), 237S-241S.

Norman, L. A., Hardin, P. A., Lester, E., Stinton, S., & Vincent, E. C. (1995). Computer-assisted quality improvement in an ambulatory setting: A follow-up report. *Joint Commission Journal on Quality Improvement, 21*(3), 1995.

Ornstein, S. M., Garr, D. R., & Jenkins, R. G. (1993). A comprehensive microcomputer-based medical records system with sophisticated preventive services features for the family physician. *Journal of the American Board of Family Practice, 6*(1), 55-60.

Ornstein, S. M., Garr, D. R., Jenkins, R. G., Musham, C., Hamadeh, G., & Lancaster, C. (1995). Implementation and evaluation of a computer-based preventive services system. *Family Medicine, 27*(4), 260-266.

Peyrot, M., & Rubin, R. R. (1988). Insulin self-regulation predicts better glycemic control [Abstract]. *Diabetes, 37,* 53A.

Rousseau, P. (1994). Pain management: An often-ignored facet of medical care. *Mayo Clinic Proceedings, 69*(8), 811.

Schroeder, J., & Lamb, S. (1996). An introduction to HEDIS. *Hospital Practice (Office Edition), 11*(1), S58-S62.

Speros, C. I., & Sol, N. (1991). Health promotion in hospitals. *WHO Regional Publications: European Series, 37,* 267-281.

Targonski, P. V., Persky, V. W., Kelleher, P., & Addington, W. (1995). Characteristics of hospitalization for asthma among persons less than 35 years of age in Chicago. *Journal of Asthma, 32*(5), 365-372.

U.S. Department of Health and Human Services. (1991a). *Healthy people 2000: National health promotion and disease prevention objectives* (Report No. PHS 91-50212). Washington, DC: Author.

U.S. Department of Health and Human Services. (1991b). *National asthma education program expert panel report. Guidelines for the diagnosis and management of asthma* (Report No. 91-3042). Washington, DC: Author.

U.S. Environmental Protection Agency. (1992). *Respiratory health effects of passive smoking: Lung cancer and other disorders* (Report No. EPA600/6-90-006F). Washington, DC: Government Printing Office.

Warfield, C. A., & Kahn, C. H. (1995). Acute pain management. Programs in U.S. hospitals and experiences and attitudes among U.S. adults. *Anesthesiology, 83*(5), 1090-1094.

Weitzman, M., Gortmaker, S., & Walker, D. K. (1990). Maternal smoking and childhood asthma. *Pediatrics, 85,* 505-511.

Wetterhall, S. F., Olson, D. R., DeStefano, F., Stevenson, J. M., Ford, E. S., German, R. R., Will, J. C., Newman, J. M., Sepe, S. J., & Vincior, F. (1992). Trends in diabetes and diabetic complications. *Diabetes Care, 15*(8), 960-967.

Windsor, A. M., Glynn, C. J., & Mason, D. G. (1996). National provision of acute pain services. *Anaesthesia, 51*(3), 228-231.

World Health Organization. (1986). Ottawa charter for health promotion. *Health Promotion, 1*(4), iii-v.

World Health Organization. (1987). *Hospitals and health for all: Report of a WHO expert committee on the role of the hospitals at the first referral level* (Report No. 744). Geneva: Author.

World Health Organization, Regional Office for Europe & Ludwig Boltzmann-Institute. (1995). *Health promoting hospitals.* Copenhagen: Author.

6

Health Promotion in Clinical Practice

Vivek Goel

Warren McIsaac

Most primary care physicians[1] believe that they include health promotion in their practice. However, on further examination, much of what is described as health promotion in primary care is actually disease prevention. For example, Ornstein (1989) and colleagues labeled as "health promotion" five activities: fecal occult blood testing, pap smears, mammography, cholesterol testing, and tetanus immunizations. Depending on one's perspective, this may or may not be rightly classified as health promotion. Rather, these activities may be seen more as medical interventions for disease prevention that are sometimes quite invasive. Such interventions center control for disease prevention firmly with the physician.

The health promotion movement has been built on concepts that demedicalize health and enhance individual control over one's health. On the other hand, physicians are trained principally to treat disease. A major part of their practice is to do things to their patients—for example, examine them, provide prescriptions, or carry out diagnostic tests. Thus, prevention in clinical practice primarily consists of interventions such as those selected by Ornstein et al. (1989).

Traditional undergraduate medical curricula have paid only minimal attention to the skills required to do health promotion well. These include (a) communication skills, (b) the ability to identify the social context in which patients live, (c) integrating cultural or behavioral factors that influence a patient's response to disease or to recommendations, and (d) recognizing the role of families.

Given this, it may be surprising that we even consider clinical practice as a site for health promotion. Perhaps it makes more sense for physicians to focus on disease prevention and management than it does for them to become involved in health promotion. Some have argued that this should indeed be the case and that physicians should focus on the treatment of disease (Patrick, 1994). We believe that this view is unduly narrow, for health promotion and disease prevention are not two separate entities; rather, there is a significant degree of overlap, particularly when clinical practice is considered as a setting.

It has long been recognized that there are many levels to prevention and that the distinction between health promotion, prevention, and treatment is not black and white (Roemer, 1984). For example, a patient with chest pain may be advised to stop smoking and lose weight. This is a clinical management strategy for the acute illness episode of angina. However, it is also a health promotion activity during a "teachable moment" (Lewis, 1982).

There are, however, some differences between disease prevention and health promotion. Disease prevention starts with a particular target condition and works back through a causal pathway to preventive actions that can reduce the risk of that disease (Rose, 1993). For example, if one looks at coronary heart disease, several risk factors for disease are clearly identified. Most important are smoking, high blood cholesterol, obesity, and lack of physical exercise. Smoking and exercise are amenable to counseling as an intervention. Physicians may also use clinical tools such as nicotine gum to assist with smoking cessation. High blood cholesterol can be detected only through a clinical intervention, screening. Once detected, it can be dealt with through dietary interventions, such as counseling, or through clinical interventions, such as cholesterol-lowering drugs. In this instance, the focus is on preventing disease through a medical model that tends to highlight clinical interventions. This is further influenced by industries based on such clinical interventions—for example, the manufacturers of cholesterol-lowering agents.

A health promotion viewpoint de-emphasizes the disease and focuses instead on enhancing the health of the individual and, in particular, enabling individuals to take control of their own health. Thus, in a heart health model, one looks at improving the environment so that foods that result in lower blood cholesterol are available and appreciated and exercise is a part of everyday routines. Is there a role for clinical practice in such a model?

Physicians' practices are ideal settings for health promotion in several respects. The majority of individuals in most Western countries have a primary care practitioner. In Canada, this is over 90% (Bass & Elford, 1988). Furthermore, most people have one or more contacts with a physician in the period of a year. In the 1990 Ontario Health Survey, about 85% of adults reported at least one contact with a general practitioner in the previous year (Goel, McIsaac, Iron, Brown, & Wu, 1994). Physicians may be the only health professionals who regularly come into contact with certain population groups. Preschool children see physicians at least once a year, if not more often (Palframan, 1995). Within countries of the Organization for Economic Cooperation and Development, the average number of contacts with a physician per year is 5 to 7, with a high of 13 in Japan and 11 in Germany (Sandier, 1989).

Physicians are usually seen as authoritative sources of information, and their advice is often followed. For example, encouragement from a personal physician is a very cost-effective strategy for smoking cessation (Cummings, Rubin, & Oster, 1989; Law & Tang, 1995). Studies have repeatedly shown that the advice of a physician is the single strongest determinant for preventive practices such as mammography (White, Urban, & Taylor, 1993). There are also predisposing factors, such as knowledge and beliefs, that lead to a greater likelihood of mammography use. However, even after controlling for such factors, receiving the advice of a physician to have a mammogram greatly increases the chance that a woman will have one.

Returning to heart health, physicians can be a pivotal component of a heart health promotion program. They can encourage their patients to exercise and eat well and provide them with links to community resources that will facilitate such activities. Where appropriate, they can conduct those screening tests and interventions that have been shown to be effective and are recommended.

OTHER ASPECTS OF HEALTH PROMOTION IN THE CLINICAL SETTING

The role of health promotion in clinical practice is not limited to enhancing disease prevention or merely acting as a referral conduit to community resources. There are other aspects to clinical practice in which health promotion can play a role. In particular, this could involve demedicalizing situations that are dealt with as illnesses with the potential for cure when in fact they are symptoms of another, nonmedical, problem or are problems that cannot easily be dealt with through traditional medical means such as tests and drugs. A health promotion vantage point can help reorient clinicians from automatically reaching for a prescription pad to terminate a consultation, to thinking about why an individual is presenting and considering what they could be doing to foster well-being.

Take, for example, a young single mother who attends her doctor's office with a complaint of difficulty in sleeping at night. With an eye to the next patient in the waiting room, a quick prescription for a mild sedative is written. The treatment given is for the symptom, not the underlying problem.

Consider an alternative scenario. The doctor chats briefly and finds that the patient is nervous about her children's behavior while she is at work. A quick look at a registry of community resources and a referral is made to a self-help group for single mothers. She encounters other mothers in the same situation and they work together to deal with their concerns. As a result, in this case, the use of medications can be reduced or averted altogether. This type of approach is an integral component of modern academic family medicine training. Yet it appears that the former prescription approach remains the standard of practice for many primary care physicians. Many factors drive this behavior, including the way in which the health care system is organized, reimbursement mechanisms, and the expectations of consumers and providers alike.

Examples need not be limited to "psychosocial" issues. The common cold is the most frequent reason for visits to primary care physicians (Weinkauf & Rowland, 1992). Yet in most instances there is little that the physician can do to alleviate the cold that patients cannot do themselves. Yet countless X rays, blood tests, and antibiotic prescriptions are provided for people who have a simple viral infection. This occurs both as a result of expectations from patients that the medical system can provide relief for their symptoms and the fact that health care providers usually do not have the time, skills, or inclination to counsel their patients to discuss self-care strategies for the management of their colds (Vickery et al., 1983). External forces, such as cold remedy advertisements and requirements for doctors' notes from schools and workplace reinforce pressures to visit doctors for a cold. The common cold needs to be viewed simply as a fact of everyday life. Individuals need support to enable them to cope with it rather than treating it as an acute illness requiring remedies.

The power of demedicalizing or refusing to allow conditions to become medicalized is demonstrated with the example of low-back pain. Although low-back pain has become one of the most prevalent chronic conditions in Western society (Frank, Pulcins, Kerr, Shannon, & Stansfeld, 1995), it is virtually unheard of as a clinical syndrome in many parts of Africa and the Middle East. Differences in lifestyle and workplace organization may account for some of this variation, but certainly not all. Some blame the availability of disability insurance and the growth of diagnostic tests, such as X rays, computerized tomography scans, and magnetic resonance imaging, as well as medical and surgical treatments for this growing epidemic. Nearly everyone has back pain at some time in their lives. Many people, with and without back pain, have disk degeneration visible on back X rays. If people with an episode of back pain have X rays, some will be found to have disk degeneration and will be labeled with a diagnosis of a medical back condition. They may have treatment, and in some instances, surgery, for a "normal" condition. Again, in the clinical setting, individuals will have to be taught to understand that disk degeneration is a normal part of aging and be given access to resources and skills to help them cope with their symptoms.

Thus, the principles of health promotion can be applied in the clinical setting in many ways that go beyond disease prevention. However, many of the barriers that limit the application of health promotion principles to more medical or curative types of encounters are similar to the factors that hinder disease prevention. This chapter will draw on literature describing both disease prevention and health promotion in clinical practice. Although there are differences between them, many of the barriers and potential solutions are similar.

DO PHYSICIANS PRACTICE
HEALTH PROMOTION?

The evidence is that physicians are poor practitioners of disease prevention, let alone health promotion. Jaén, Stange, and Nutting (1994) have proposed a model for the competing demands of primary care that facilitates examination of the barriers to effective preventive practices. The model includes three components—the physician, the patient, and the practice environment—that interact to influence these practices. Within the medical encounter, the clinical agenda, patient agenda, and preventive needs agenda all compete for the time available during a particular visit. Although time for preventive practices in clinical settings is to a large part determined by the rewards for such work (i.e., fees), the interaction between the physician and patient and the environment in which they meet also plays a major role.

The Physician

The physician's attitudes toward prevention are critical in determining whether these practices are carried out. If prevention is considered a trivial part of practice compared with curing life-threatening illnesses, it is less likely to be carried out. Physicians tend to be preselected for an interest in curative care and high technology, with their training reinforcing this (Johns, Hovell, Ganiats, Peddecord, & Agras, 1987). Although in one study, physicians reported that the greatest sense of professional satisfaction came from the activities of diagnosis and treatment (Mawardi, 1979), another showed that primary care physicians found health promotion to be a challenging and enjoyable part of their practice (McAlister et al., 1985).

Knowledge of effective preventive activities is an important predisposing factor. Medical schools until recently have not emphasized such areas, and even now, training in the science and skills of preventive practices forms only a small fraction of the total undergraduate curriculum. The medical school philosophy and organization may play a role in the prevention orientation of graduates (Maheux, Pineault, & Beland, 1987). One study failed to demonstrate that the addition of training in epidemiology and community health in the undergraduate curriculum resulted in a change in attitudes (Radovanovic & Djordjevic-Gledovic, 1983). More work is required on how best to get health promotion on to the agenda of undergraduate medical trainees.

Tomorrow's physicians will be influenced by recent changes in medical schools, including (a) new approaches to selecting students, with less focus on students with high grades and training in the biomedical sciences alone; (b) renewal of curricula to emphasize patient-centered approaches (as opposed to disease-based approaches); and (c) the continuing push to de-emphasize medical subspecialization in favor of primary care training. We anticipate that future surveys of physicians will find that they are more likely to have favorable attitudes to prevention and health promotion.

Characteristics such as physician age, speciality training, personal beliefs, and personal exercise habits can all play a role in the likelihood of preventive services being recommended (Attarian, Fleming, Barron, & Strecher, 1987; Orleans, George, Houpt, & Brodie, 1985; Valente, Sobal, Muncie, Levine, & Antlitz, 1982; Wechsler, Levine, Idelson, Rohman, & Taylor, 1983; Wells, Lewis, & Leake, 1984; Wells, Lewis, Leake, Schleiter, & Brook, 1986).

For physicians in practice, it is difficult to remain abreast of the current literature on causes of disease and appropriate preventive activities. This is complicated by the often apparently contradictory studies that appear on issues such as diet and cancer as well as the often contradictory "expert" recommendations that are made (Burack, 1989). In a study of physician's agreement with the recommendations of the U.S. Preventive Services Task Force, it was observed that disagreement was most likely for those items where there were conflicting views from the American Cancer Society (Stange et al., 1992). Physician compliance with such recommendations tends to be poor as well (Bass & Elford, 1988; Lewis, 1988).

These studies date from an era when the underlying philosophy for guideline development and dissemination was simply to convene a panel of "experts" and publish the results in a journal. In fact, this decade has seen major changes in the way in which these activities are conducted. First, it has been recognized that for guidelines to be meaningful, their development must include the people at whom they are targeted. Although in the past, guidelines for prevention tended to be developed by subspecialists in the disease area being considered, now primary care physicians are more likely to be involved. Second, simply publishing guidelines does not change physicians' or consumers' behaviors (Greco & Eisenberg, 1993). Furthermore, traditional lecture-based approaches to continuing medical education have been found to be largely ineffective (Davis, Thomson, Oxman, & Haynes, 1995). More innovative approaches based on principles of adult education are now being tried and evaluated. The development, implementation, and evaluation of guidelines for consumers and practitioners in the area of health promotion/disease prevention should benefit from these advances.

Physicians' expectations of what the outcomes of prevention might be and their own perceived efficacy can influence their practices. The physician obtains immediate gratification when a sick patient gets better whereas the benefits of effective prevention are usually seen much later, if at all. For example, a patient who successfully quits smoking may well be thankful to the physician. However, the physician will never know if that patient would have had lung cancer or not. The majority of smokers do not get lung cancer, even though their risk is higher than that of nonsmokers. Smoking cessation brings the risk of lung cancer down, but it is impossible to say which of these people would have had lung cancer if they had not smoked. Furthermore, if physicians have patients who are unable to immediately make a recommended behavior change, they may see that as a failure on their part. Physicians' own perceptions of their skills at prevention are often poor, resulting in their being less likely to engage in such activities (Wechsler et al., 1983).

Aside from the perception of their own skills, the actual skills necessary for preventive services are often lacking in physicians. In particular, communication skills for effective counseling are not commonly included and reinforced in medical school curricula (Nutting, 1986). Indeed, traditional medical training may actually lead to a deterioration of communication skills (Fletcher, 1980). Physicians often don't have the skills to provide counseling in terms and language that their patients can comprehend. They are often ill equipped to provide counseling that respects the cultures, values, and traditions of different patients.

Also important are technical skills for specific tasks such as performing screening tests. For example, a significant proportion of Pap smears taken are found to be inadequate for interpretation (Canadian Society of Cytology, 1994). Such skills can also include the ability to perform tasks such as assisting patients in selecting appropriate foods for modifying their diets (Elford, Jennett, & Sawa, 1993).

What physicians perceive to be standards of practice in their own communities can often influence what they do. Since physicians in primary care do not usually have good data on how their practice compares with that of their colleagues, perceptions of the standard, rather than the actual standard, are critical. Physicians in primary care often will not know what their colleagues' practices are with respect to prevention and health promotion. They are also often guided to a large extent by key influentials in the community, usually senior specialists. These specialists may well have quite different views of what the important preventive activities are.

Finally, the physicians' view of the clinical encounter often influences their preventive activities. Most physicians' offices are rushed and often running late. A patient attending for a specific complaint is likely to see only that complaint dealt with. Most physicians have been trained to provide preventive services within the context of specific encounters such as the annual health examination. This depends on the patient's being aware that he or she should attend for such an examination and on the physician's having a plan for such an examination. It is now generally accepted that an integrated approach to prevention through periodic health examinations is preferred. With such an approach, an individual's age and sex and previous history are used to create a customized profile of preventive activities that the patient could benefit from. Every clinical encounter, whatever the reason for its initiation, is regarded as an opportunity to reassess which preventive activities are called for.

The Patient

Patients arrive in a physician's office with their own knowledge, attitudes and beliefs about prevention as well as their expectations for the clinical encounter. They may or may not be receptive to advice about prevention or health promotion, depending on their preconceptions about an illness and their desire for specific diagnostic tests or treatment. If a patient does not believe that weight is a problem, then he or she is unlikely to be receptive to counseling about diet and exercise. In particular, patients attending for an acute problem, such as a sore throat, may resent having the physician focus on preventive practices. Patients expect an annual health examination (Romm, 1984), and attempts to remove annual health examinations from provincial fee schedules in Canada have been met with fierce public opposition.

Patients often have expectations for drugs and tests that hinder good preventive practices. For example, it is our experience and those of others (e.g., Poland, 1994) that some patients believe that their doctor can prescribe something that will help them stop smoking (e.g., nicotine replacement aids such as Nicorette gum or the "patch"). They may also believe (or have been led to believe through aggressive marketing) that drugs provide an alternative to lifestyle changes. For example, cholesterol-lowering drugs are often seen as an alternate to dietary changes. Indeed, some patients believe that taking such agents can allow them to indulge in unhealthy foods.

Some surveys suggest that patients would welcome greater involvement from their physicians with respect to health issues (Wallace & Haines, 1984). One study showed that respondents did believe that their physicians wanted them to exercise, regardless of their actual level of exercise (Godin & Shephard, 1990). However, it is still unclear exactly what these patients expect their physicians to do beyond simply offering advice.

Patients appear to need more than just advice that they should change a health behavior and a few words of encouragement. Willms et al. (1991) found that patients evaluate the kind of support that they get from their physicians and separate encouragement and verbal support from sincere understanding. The latter would include being interested in the individual, with mutual respect leading to an understanding that physician and patient are working together. Patients distinguished this type of support from technical expertise and valued both the support and the (more technical) advice.

Demands for unnecessary or unproven tests are often observed. The tremendous growth in the use of the prostate-specific antigen (PSA) test for screening for prostate cancer is in part the result of direct marketing by the medical community and industry to patients (DeAntoni et al., 1992). This has occurred despite cautions from virtually all major health organizations against PSA screening (Woolf, 1995).

The Practice Environment

Reimbursement schemes play a key role in influencing physicians' attitudes and practices. Preventive practices are often not emphasized in fee-for-service schemes (Inui, Belcher, & Carter, 1981; Maheux et al., 1987). In particular, activities such as counseling patients are either paid at very low levels or are not reimbursed at all. Most fee schedules reward interventional procedures (e.g., surgery) and de-emphasize activities such as counseling, which can be time-consuming.

Prepaid and capitated plans and community health center models appear to result in better attention to prevention, although the evidence on this is mixed (Abelson & Lomas, 1990; Battista & Spitzer, 1983). Because physicians are usually reimbursed on either a salary or paid a fixed fee per patient per year under these plans, there is not a fee-for-service "treadmill" where office visits have to be processed to generate an income. Indeed, there is an incentive to keep patients healthy to avoid visits later. Community health centers usually also employ other health professionals, often with expertise in health promotion, who can then be readily involved when needed.

The manner in which a practice is organized can influence preventive practices. The use of reminder systems, whether chart based or electronic, have been shown to improve practices (Geiger, Neuberger, & Bell, 1993; McPhee & Detmer, 1993; Ornstein et al., 1995). Having appropriate materials and educational aids, such as pamphlets, posters, and videotapes, can enhance the quality of prevention. Ready accessibility to services such as those of a nutritionist can facilitate their use. However, such systems and practice organizations are useful in enhancing health promotion activities but are not usually sufficient without commitment to the activities from practice staff.

Models of primary care delivery that emphasize multidisciplinary teams can lead to superior preventive services. When a variety of health professionals work together in a setting such as a community health center under a global or capitated budget, then opportunities for prevention and health promotion are maximized. Physicians can focus on treating illness and preventing disease. They can identify those patients who may be ready for specific prevention and health promotion activities and readily involve other members of the team with the appropriate skills. It is important that the practice organization ensure that there is a ready transition for patients between the different health professionals so that the teachable moment is not lost.

GETTING HEALTH PROMOTION
INTO CLINICAL PRACTICE

Health promotion needs to be incorporated into a primary care physician's daily practice routine so that it is considered in every patient encounter by all members of the office staff. Physicians have to recognize that patients rarely identify health promotion as the reason for their visit. The challenge to the clinician is to incorporate these activities into the routine medical encounter in a sensitive and caring but proactive manner.

The personal relationship between patient and physician is central to health promotion interventions. As Willms et al. (1991) have noted, patients expect physicians to work with them in a context of mutual respect. How physicians treat patients will affect responses. With respect to lifestyle behavior changes in particular, physicians will have to accept a less paternalistic and more shared model of decision making (Emanuel & Emanuel, 1992).

Physicians have to recognize that such interventions do not work overnight and that progress by individual patients will be incremental, idiosyncratic, and will occur over long periods of time. Physicians have to acquire specific skills and techniques for health promotion, including (a) patient assessment, (b) setting realistic objectives, (c) helping patients to integrate behavior change into everyday life and (d) helping the patient to use family and community resources (Nutting, 1986).

Current academic family medicine curricula use a "patient-centered" model of practice. This model focuses on the whole individual within the context of the family and community rather than different body parts or diseases. Furthermore, the model is considered in evaluating the patient. Health promotion, with its de-emphasis on disease, fits firmly into such a model. The challenge is to get this into practice.

The fact that physician advice is such an effective aid to smoking cessation is probably in large part built on the credibility of the physician and the power that he or she wields under this paternalistic model. Physician advice to stop smoking (or any other positive health behavior) is usually rooted in this sort of top-down approach and can be based on implicit or explicit threats. For example, a common line may be "Stop smoking or it will kill you." Such an approach may be effective in some people and could be a component of a broader health promotion strategy.

However, a shared approach that assists the patient in understanding why a behavior needs to be changed and then assists that person in acquiring the skills and capacity to change the behavior and to sustain those changes is to be preferred for several reasons. First, it gives individuals control of their own health. Second, it may lead to better long-term results. Finally, the skills acquired may then be applied to other health issues.

Models to help clinicians in assessing a patient's readiness for change have been proposed by Green (1987) and Prochaska et al. (1994). Such models can assist physicians in working with their patients to improve their health habits. Although the Green model focuses on predisposing, reinforcing, and enabling factors, the Prochaska model assesses the patient's readiness to change.

In the Green model, the first step is to triage the patients according to their motivation. The patient has to believe that a particular behavior will lead to problems and that those problems are severe. The potential benefits of behavior change have to be seen to outweigh the risks, costs, side effects, and hassles involved.

If the patient is not motivated, the physician has to help the patient to assess the reason for the lack of motivation. If it is lack of knowledge, then time and energy should be devoted to assisting the patient to acquire the knowledge necessary to understand why behavior may lead to improved health outcomes. If there are behavioral or attitudinal reasons why motivation does not exist, it may be difficult for the physician to proceed. For example, an individual may not be willing to forgo the pleasure of a second scoop of ice cream to achieve a reduction in cholesterol levels that will lead to lower risk of heart disease. If this is an informed trade-off, it would be inappropriate for the physician to continue.

Once motivation for behavior change is established, the next step is to triage the patient according to enabling factors. In partnership with the patient, skills, resources, and barriers available for invoking the behavior change are assessed. Recommended interventions should take account of these enabling factors.

Once an intervention strategy is recommended, the factors necessary to support maintenance should be assessed. These can be both reinforcing as well as negative factors. The physician can bolster reinforcement by preparing the patient for what is to come, such as potential side effects and with communications to family members. The long-term nature of the patient-physician relationship provides a means for regular reinforcement and education. This could be as simple as an inquiry about the behavior at each subsequent visit. Repetition is a key component of adult education; ensuring that messages are consistent and regularly delivered is essential.

Finally, the physician can assist the patient in designing a self-monitoring program and transferring responsibility for maintaining the behavior change to the patient. The Prochaska model focuses on the individual. An understanding of its stages will facilitate diagnosis by physicians as to where their patients are in terms of readiness to change. This model describes how patients go through the process of behavior change and emphasizes that the actual action, such as smoking cessation, is but a small step in the overall process.

In the precontemplation stage, the patient is not considering change, either by choice or through lack of awareness. The physician can help the patient to identify personal priorities and lifestyle goals. In the contemplation stage, a patient is considering change in the next 6 months but may still require more motivation. Physicians can provide encouragement and information.

In the preparation-for-action stage, patients intend to make changes in the next 30 days. Physicians can be supportive at this stage, review available resources, and assist the patient in setting firm targets, such as a quit date. In the action stage, the patient has initiated the change and the physician can continue to be supportive and ensure that resources continue to be available to the patient. The physician can also help to ensure that the patient is prepared for and has the skills to cope with possible relapses or the situations that may trigger relapse. One of the key features of this model is that it recognizes the possibility of relapse during behavior change and rather than viewing this as failure sees it simply as a step in the process.

Finally, the patients who have successfully made the change are in the maintenance stage. The physician can continue to reinforce the behavior and help the patient in reviewing factors that support the new behavior. The physician should also take note to praise the patient for having been successful.

There is good evidence in the area of physician advice for smoking cessation that properly designed interventions delivered by physicians can result in documented improvements in quit rates (Kottke, Solberg, Brekke, & Maxwell, 1988). The challenge is to get physicians to do so in daily practice and not just in randomized trials. In British Columbia, a provincewide project to recruit physicians to be trained in smoking cessation found that half of those who attended training sessions remained active in smoking cessation activities on follow-up (Bass, 1996). In terms of changing physicians' behaviors, this is a superb achievement, although it comes as a result of an intensive and committed effort.

GETTING CLINICIANS INTO HEALTH PROMOTION

Although the subject of this chapter is health promotion in the clinical setting, we would be remiss to not mention the role that physicians can play in health promotion in the community. Physicians are often called on to assist with health education programs in their communities. For example, physicians may be part of an educational committee for a local cancer society. This can give them an opportunity to work on educational programs that involve local schools, businesses, or media. They can be involved in the organization of health fairs or talks to community groups. Physicians can get involved in community activities in many ways such as through children's aid societies or working with disadvantaged groups. In addition to providing clinical care, physicians are well suited to deliver messages on health promotion and disease prevention. They are often also in a position to assist patients in accessing services. For example, they can work with homeless patients to arrange housing and other support services.

Physicians can play an important role in the political sphere as well (Walters & MacKenzie, 1996). Recently, physicians groups have been instrumental in supporting legislation to restrict smoking in Canada. One component of this campaign was firmly rooted in primary care practice. Canadian physicians sent in a "tombstone" postcard to their Member of Parliament every time one of their patients died of a smoking-related disease. Physicians can make important statements about the health effects of many societal issues such as gun control, child welfare, and even economic policies. One group, Physicians for Social Responsibility, had a major impact on raising awareness of the health effects of nuclear war. The evidence that physicians can bring to such debates is often irrefutable by politicians and highly salient for the general public.

Although physicians can play a political role outside their office, the interface between healthy public policy and their office is a delicate one. For example, encouraging a patient who is concerned about smoking's health effects to stop smoking is clearly an activity that is acceptable in the office. On the other hand, voicing support for workplace smoking restrictions, or asking patients to endorse such a policy, during a clinical encounter, is a violation of the patient-physician relationship. Given the discussion regarding the degree of control that the physician has in the patient encounter, suggestions such as this could be seen as an abuse of authority on the part of the physician.

WORKING TOGETHER WITH HEALTH PROMOTION

Readers may recognize a conflict in our arguments. On the one hand, we suggest that a patient-centered health promotion approach should be adopted by clinicians. Physicians shouldn't tell patients what to do; they should help them to understand what behaviors enhance their health and assist them in developing such behaviors.

On the other hand, we observe that few physicians practice this way and that there are considerable barriers to incorporating medically based disease prevention into clinical practice, let alone health promotion. The evidence is that when physicians do advise disease prevention activities, whether it is to change a behavior such as smoking or to undertake a preventive test such as mammography, the advice of the physician is often a significant indicator of likely uptake.

Much change is coming in clinical settings around the world, with reorganized practice designs, new reimbursement policies, and new curricula in medical schools. The barriers to health promotion in clinical practice in the future may be less formidable.

Even now, we suggest that the health promotion approach and the traditional medical model can work together rather than being seen as mutually exclusive.

Encouragement or advice from physicians can be a motivating factor for some individuals. On the other hand, it may be a turnoff for others. Clinicians have to learn how to best recognize which strategies will work with specific patients. Health promotion advocates also have to be prepared to work with physicians when appropriate. At times, health promotion activities are perceived as being in competition with the medical model of disease prevention, rather than complementary. Health promotion in the clinical setting will work best when it is coupled with community-based health promotion programs (and, of course, the other settings described in this book).

NOTE

1. *Primary care physician* is used to describe all physicians whose practice includes the provision of medical care for well individuals and who act as "gatekeepers" to specialist services. This includes family physicians, general practitioners, and those specialists such as pediatricians, obstetricians, and general internists who take on primary responsibility for the clinical care of individuals.

REFERENCES

Abelson, J., & Lomas, J. (1990). Do health service organisations and community health centres have higher disease prevention and health promotion levels than fee-for-service practices? *Canadian Medical Association Journal, 142,* 575-581.

Attarian, L., Fleming, M., Barron, P., & Strecher, V. (1987). A comparison of health promotion practices of general practitioners and residency trained physicians. *Journal of Community Health, 12,* 31-39.

Bass, F. (1996). Mobilizing physicians to conduct clinical interventions in tobacco use through a medical association program: 5 years' experience in British Columbia. *Canadian Medical Association Journal, 154,* 159-164.

Bass, M. J., & Elford, R. W. (1988). Preventive practices patterns of Canadian primary care physicians. *American Journal of Preventive Medicine, 4*(Suppl.), 17-23.

Battista, R. N., & Spitzer, W. O. (1983). Adult cancer prevention in primary care: Contrasts among primary care settings in Quebec. *American Journal of Public Health, 73,* 1040-1041.

Burack, R. C. (1989). Barriers to clinical preventive medicine. *Primary Care, 16,* 245-250.

Canadian Society of Cytology. (1994). The adequacy of the Papanicolaou smear. *Canadian Medical Association Journal, 150,* 25-26.

Cummings, S. R., Rubin, S. M., & Oster, G. (1989). The cost-effectiveness of counseling smokers to quit. *Journal of the American Medical Association, 261,* 75-79.

Davis, D. A., Thomson, M. A., Oxman, A. D., & Haynes, R. B. (1995). Changing physician performance: A systematic review of the effect of continuing medical education strategies. *Journal of the American Medical Association, 274,* 700-705.

DeAntoni, E., Crawford, E. D., Stone, N. N., Blum, D. S., Berger, E. R., Eisenberger, M. A., Gambert, S. R., & Staggers, F. (1992). Prostate cancer awareness week, 1992: A summary of key findings. *Clinical & Investigative Medicine, 16,* 448-457.

Elford, R. W., Jennett, P., & Sawa, R. (1993). Strategies for implementing coronary artery disease prevention in practice. *Canadian Journal of Cardiology, 9*(Suppl.), 128D-129D.

Emanuel, E. J., & Emanuel, L. L. (1992). Four models of physician-patient relationship. *Journal of the American Medical Association, 267,* 2221-2226.

Fletcher, C. (1980). Listening and talking to patients: I. The problem. *British Medical Journal, 281,* 845-847.

Frank, J. W., Pulcins, I. R., Kerr, M. S., Shannon, H. S., & Stansfeld, S. A. (1995). Occupational back pain: An unhelpful polemic. *Scandinavian Journal of Work, Environment & Health, 21,* 3-14.

Geiger, W. J., Neuberger, M. J., & Bell, G. C. (1993). Implementing the US Preventive Services Guidelines in a family practice residency. *Family Medicine, 25,* 447-451.

Godin, G., & Shephard, R. J. (1990). An evaluation of the potential role of the physician in influencing community exercise behavior. *American Journal of Health Promotion, 4,* 255-259.

Goel, V., McIsaac, W., Iron, K., Brown, E., & Wu, K. (1994). Reported utilisation of health services and health status: Results from the Ontario Health Survey. In C. D. Naylor, G. M. Anderson, & V. Goel (Eds.), *Patterns of health care in Ontario. Institute for Clinical Evaluative Sciences in Ontario* (pp. 47-67). Ottawa: Canadian Medical Association.

Greco, P. J., & Eisenberg, J. M. (1993). Changing physician's practices. *New England Journal of Medicine, 329,* 1271-1274.

Green, L. W. (1987). How physicians can improve patients' participation and maintenance in self-care. *Western Journal of Medicine, 147,* 346-349.

Inui, T. S., Belcher, D. W., & Carter, W. B. (1981). Implementing preventive care in clinical practice: 1. Organizational issues and strategies. *Medical Care Review, 38,* 129-154.

Jaén, C. R., Stange, K. C., & Nutting, P. A. (1994). Competing demands of primary care: A model for the delivery of clinical preventive services. *Journal of Family Practice, 38,* 166-171.

Johns, M. B., Hovell, M. F., Ganiats, T., Peddecord, K. M., & Agras, W. S. (1987). Primary care and health promotion: A model for preventive medicine. *American Journal of Preventive Medicine, 3,* 326-357.

Kottke, T. E., Solberg, L. I., Brekke, M. L., & Maxwell, P. (1988) Smoking cessation strategies and evaluation. *Journal of the American College of Cardiology, 12,* 1105-1110.

Law, M., & Tang, J. L. (1995). An analysis of the effectiveness of interventions intended to help people stop smoking. *Archives of Internal Medicine, 155,* 1933-1941.

Lewis, C. E. (1982). Teaching medical students about disease prevention and health promotion. *Public Health Reports, 97,* 210-215.

Lewis, C. E. (1988). Disease prevention and health promotion practices of primary care physicians in the United States. *American Journal of Preventive Medicine, 4*(Suppl.), 9-16.

Maheux, B., Pineault, R., & Beland, F. (1987). Factors influencing physicians' orientation toward prevention. *American Journal of Preventive Medicine, 3,* 12-18.

Mawardi, B. H. (1979). Satisfactions, dissatisfactions, and causes of stress in medical practice. *Journal of the American Medical Association, 241,* 1483-1486.

McAlister, A., Mullen, P. D., Nixon, S. A., Dickson, C., Gottlieb, N., McCuan, R., & Green, L. (1985). Health promotion among primary care physicians in Texas. *Texas Medicine, 81,* 55-58.

McPhee, S. J., & Detmer, M. (1993). Office-based interventions to improve delivery of cancer prevention services by primary care physicians. *Cancer, 72,* 1100-1112.

Nutting, P. A. (1986). Health promotion in primary medical care: Problems and potential. *Preventive Medicine, 15,* 537-548.

Orleans, C. T., George, L. K., Houpt, J. L., & Brodie, K. H. (1985). Health promotion in primary care: A survey of U.S. family practitioners. *Preventive Medicine, 14,* 636-647.

Ornstein, S. M., Garr, D. R., Jenkins, R. G., Musham, C., Hamadeh, G., & Lancaster, C. (1995). Implementation and evaluation of a computer-based preventive services system. *Family Medicine, 27,* 260-266.

Ornstein, S. M., Garr, D. R., Jenkins, R. G., Rust, P. F., Zemp, L., & Arnon, A. (1989). Compliance with health promotion recommendations in a university-based family practice. *Journal of Family Practice, 29,* 163-168.

Palframan, D. S. (1995, August). Health promotion for preschoolers and families by primary-care physicians. *Ontario Medical Review,* 32-36.

Patrick, J. (1994). Health care and medicine: The case for divorce. *Canadian Medical Association Journal, 150,* 1775-1779.

Poland, B. D. (1994). Concept and practice in community mobilization for health: A qualitative evaluation of the Brantford COMMIT smoking cessation intervention trial. Doctoral dissertation, McMaster University, Canada.

Prochaska, J. O., Velicer, W. F., Rossi, J. S., Goldstein, M. G., Marcus, B. H., Rakowski, W., Fiore, C., Harlow, L. L., Redding, C. A., Rosenbloom, D., & Rossi, S. R. (1994). Stages of change and decisional balance for 12 problem behaviors. *Health Psychology, 13,* 39-46.

Radovanovic, Z., & Djordjevic-Gledovic, Z. (1983). Attitudes of medical students in Belgrade, Yugoslavia, toward preventive medicine and epidemiology. *Social Science and Medicine, 17,* 1873-1875.

Roemer, N. I. (1984). The value of medical care for health promotion. *American Journal of Public Health, 74,* 243-248.

Romm, F. J. (1984). Patients' expectations of periodic health examinations. *Journal of Family Practice, 19,* 191-195.

Rose, G. (1993). *The strategy of preventive medicine.* Oxford, UK: Oxford University Press.

Sandier, S. (1989). Health services utilization and physician income trends. *Health Care Financing Review, 11*(Annual Suppl.), 33-48.

Stange, K. C., Kelly, R., Chao, J., Zyzanski, S. J., Shank, J. C., Jaen, C. R., Melnikow, J., & Flocke, S. (1992). Physician agreement with US preventive services task force recommendations. *Journal of Family Practice, 34,* 409-416.

Valente, C. M., Sobal, J., Muncie, H. L., Levine, D. M., & Antlitz, A. M. (1982). Health promotion: Physicians' beliefs, attitudes and practices. *American Journal of Preventive Medicine, 2*(2), 82-88.

Vickery, D. M., Kalmer, H., Lowry, D., Constantine, M., Wright, E., & Loren, W. (1983). Effect of a self-care education program on medical visits. *Journal of the American Medical Association, 250,* 2952-2956.

Wallace, P. G., & Haines, A. P. (1984). General practitioner and health promotion: What patients think. *British Medical Journal, 289,* 533-536.

Walters, D. J., & MacKenzie, D. (1996). Yes, Minister, Canadians need strong tobacco-control legislation now! *Canadian Medical Association Journal, 154,* 191-192.

Wechsler, H., Levine, S., Idelson, R. K., Rohman, M., & Taylor, K. O. (1983). The physician's role in health promotion: A survey of primary care physicians. *New England Journal of Medicine, 308,* 97-100.

Weinkauf, D. J., & Rowland, G. C. (1992). Patient conditions at the primary care level: A commentary on source allocation. *Ontario Medical Review, 61,* 11-15.

Wells, K. B., Lewis, C. E., & Leake, B. (1984). Do physicians preach what they practice? A study of physicians' health habits and counseling practices. *Journal of the American Medical Association, 252,* 2846-2848.

Wells, K. B., Lewis, C. E., Leake, B., Schleiter, M. K., & Brook, R. H. (1986). The practices of general and subspecialty internist in counseling about smoking and exercise. *American Journal of Public Health, 76,* 1009-1113.

White, E., Urban, N., & Taylor, V. (1993). Mammography utilization, public health impact, and cost-effectiveness in the United States. *Annual Reviews of Public Health, 14,* 605-633.

Willms, D. G., Best, J. A., Wilson, D. M., Gilbert, J. R., Taylor, D. W., Lindsay, E., Singer, J., & Johnson, N. A. (1991). Patients' perspectives of a physician-delivered smoking cessation intervention. *American Journal of Preventive Medicine, 7,* 95-100.

Woolf, S. H. (1995). Screening for prostate-cancer with prostate-specific antigen: An examination of the evidence. *New England Journal of Medicine, 333,* 1401-1405.

COMMENTARY

David Butler-Jones

This commentary is intended to complement the chapter by Goel and McIsaac with examples and commentary on issues faced and potential solutions to the challenges of health promotion in the clinical encounter.

Each encounter is an opportunity for the promotion of health. Whether in the shopping mall, at a party, or in the physician's office, supports or barriers for our behaviors and the environments conducive to better health can be found there. Although the targeting of energy and resources to sites or sectors is an essential and practical strategy, it is most effective when understood and applied in the broader context. It is all too easy to recognize how community-based efforts can be undermined by strategies that do not account for and address the influence of those whom individuals look to for support or expertise in health matters (Morris & Butler-Jones, 1991). These people may be community physicians, nurses, therapists, or the relative who works in the kitchen at the local hospital. When the messages and effects of these players do not work in similar directions, confusion and inaction or misdirected action is more likely to be the result.

Specifically, the goal in the clinical encounter should be to have efforts coordinated with broader community strategies and to see each visit as an opportunity not only for illness diagnosis and treatment but also for the promotion of health (Butler-Jones, 1996). The potential opportunity for health promotion in the clinical setting is well established (Lewis, 1988). The majority of individuals will see a physician in any given year, and their opinions on health matters are generally respected. One illustration is the story of the smoker with claudication, who paid little attention to the advice given about the link of his leg pain to his smoking, until he realized that the other choir member he was talking to was a physician.

The value of physician involvement in this area is not simply to better admonish patients about their behaviors but to be a source of credible information and advice, on matters of health as well as illness, and a link to other resources. This can be true not only in the connection to primary care physicians' offices but also to nurse practitioners, other caregivers, and specialists. (Although this commentary generally will refer to physicians, this is not intended to exclude other practitioners.) These encounters are also often teachable moments, when direct connections can be made between behavior, experience, and outcome. Although the most dramatic time for consideration of the impact of one's diet, physical activity, and smoking may be following a heart attack, it is also an opportune time, when a smoker is feeling ill with sinus infection, pneumonia, or a simple cold, to discuss the link between smoking and these illnesses. It is not necessary (in fact it may be a disadvantage) to wait for a scheduled periodic health exam to talk about other issues of concern or to think about and discuss other potential links between illness and behaviors or conditions (Gilchrist & Alexander, 1994). It can also be educational to talk about how other factors can influence illness experience, when it is connected to a recent occurrence. For example, although asking a teen being seen for a plantar wart about whether he or she is sexually active would be inappropriate at the outset, questions about how things are going at home or school can lead to very important conversations. Visits are also times to avoid missed opportunities, such as catching up on immunization. Computerized or manual chart reminders can assist in this regard.

PRACTICE IN THE CONTEXT OF INFLUENCES ON HEALTH

Increasingly it is being rediscovered that what influences the health of populations, and individuals, goes well beyond the health sector (Evans, Barer, & Marmor, 1994; McKeown, 1979). An understanding of the broader context of influences on health, in which clinical practice takes place, and the roles that practitioners can play in influencing what determines health, is essential.

Physicians and other practitioners have an important role as part of a community in helping to shape that community and its health through their voluntary efforts as well as what they do in their practices (Bass & Elford, 1988). What role clinicians should play in health promotion continues to be debated (Johns, Hovell, Ganiats, Peddecord, & Agras, 1987; Palframan, 1995; Wechsler, Levine, Idelson, Rohman, & Taylor, 1983). The arguments cover a broad spectrum. On one extreme is the position that physicians should focus almost exclusively on good diagnosis, treatment, and medical care, including some proven prevention (screening and immunization) interventions. At the other end of the spectrum are the physicians who devote a significant portion of their time to community and individual education and promotion activities. Unfortunately, efforts to generalize about roles are unlikely to be helpful if the skills and context that health promotion is meant to provide do not have application beyond a few circumscribed strategies. The response needed depends on the circumstances, interest, and understanding of the physicians and their patients/clients. This approach to roles is similar to an analysis of communities for strengths, weaknesses, challenges, and champions. Depending on the situation, the roles that practitioners play may include any or all of what I would characterize as being Partner, Advocate, Cheerleader, or Enabler (PACE).

Partner. There are components of health promotion that can fit into a busy clinical practice as a complement to community efforts. Tools, simple interventions, reinforcing advice: each can support other community-based actions. This may be in the form of information, or advice to patients, or services as an adviser to community groups. For example, physicians, dentists, and others play an import role in addressing concerns by patients about community initiatives such as fluoridation. Providing them with the factual information that assists in debunking the common myths becomes an important tool.

Advocate. Being champions, articulate spokespersons, on issues of concern with respect to health in the community is not a forgotten part of the profession's lexicon, whether in working for improved housing or on environmental health issues. One of many examples is how physicians in Orillia, Ontario, out of concern for the environment and the health of their patients, mounted a campaign to oppose the building of a large incinerator to burn Toronto's garbage, as advocated by some members of the local city council.

Cheerleader. Sometimes what may be most helpful are a few well-placed words, encouragement, and nonobstruction. Keeping physicians informed of activities—for example, through brief notes in a newsletter from the local medical health officer (public health) or in the medical association bulletin—is a simple strategy to improve levels of awareness. It is important that these be brief and clearly identify a link to assisting physicians in benefiting patients.

Enabler. An important role that physicians play is in providing links and supports to self-help, good community agencies, and activities. A simple tool is a current easy-to-use guide to available programs and contacts. For example, the Province of Saskatchewan, for the purposes of public health, developed a binder for physicians that contains indexed sections, including recommended treatment protocols for STDs, immunization, and reporting requirements, as well as information on available programs and services. This can be added to or updated as needed, and provides in one place a range of useful information normally scattered in drawers or elsewhere. Giving permission to pursue actions that promote health or to talk about difficult challenges may be a simple but neglected contribution to well-being. This ranges from, "You may not be thinking about this but . . .," to being supportive in finding constructive ways to resolve issues at home or work or exploring the implications of a change in lifestyle or circumstance. That is, the enabler can pose questions that the individual may not consider but perhaps should. Physicians then can contribute to the matching of needs and abilities that supports the understanding of "health as a resource for living" by assisting individuals and groups to have the tools/resources/information they need to address issues.

Many prevention and health promotion strategies are suited to the clinical setting (Brown, Melinkovich, Gitterman, & Ricketts, 1993; Green, 1987). These include appropriate screening, counseling on health issues, and facilitation of problem solving. Technologies can assist with recall, identification for screening, or counseling at the next scheduled visit. Information sheets can reinforce or help spark questions or discussions. Tools for use in the clinical setting need to be further developed, evaluated, and disseminated.

THE PRACTICE ENVIRONMENT

The practice environment can be supported and facilitated in being more health promoting through the use of a range of tools (Belcher, 1990). This includes items such as reinforcing information sheets, related to the concern or issue being discussed, that the client can read at a point of need or for clarification later. These include both information to assist self-management, such as what to do the next time someone has diarrhea, and general information, such as a pamphlet explaining the different respiratory diseases.

Most offices have racks of pamphlets—usually too many for people to easily find a topic of interest. Simple changes can be made to improve uptake. For example, an unpublished study by this author compared the uptake of pamphlets on the use of infant car restraints from a typical revolving pamphlet rack with a focused display of a poster and actual car restraint with the pamphlets as part of the display. The latter increased dramatically the number of pamphlets read and taken away by parents, grandparents, and others. Although the study did not assess the level of changed behavior, whatever the value or limitations of pamphlets, they are of more benefit if connected with other media, read, and taken away than if left in a rack.

THE PERIODIC HEALTH EXAM

For some, the preventive maneuvers outlined in the Canadian and American Periodic Health or Preventive Services Task Force reports (Canadian Task

Force on the Periodic Health Examination, 1994; U.S. Preventive Services Task Force, 1996) can best be incorporated into a well-person visit, focused on discussions of prevention and health maintenance. For the many who present themselves only at times of trouble or illness, it is necessary to include the recommended actions, of screening or counseling/advice, in a list of things to add to the periodic illness encounter. Easier mechanisms and reminders to physicians or other caregivers that tweak memory (e.g., a checklist in the front of the chart or a manual or computerized reminder system brought forward at each visit) reach the majority who visit a physician only at the time of a problem. Where they are not in place and where licensing bodies do not construe this as advertising, recall systems, computerized or manual, to maintain contact with all patients for preventive screening or periodic health visits can increase participation and improve rates of screening or preventive interventions (Harris & Leininger, 1993). In a comprehensive program of primary health care, consideration could also be given to other forms of contact, such as check-in or supportive phone calls to the elderly, disabled, or new parents. Or one could consider the strategic mailing of information or newsletters that highlight information of a health promotion nature. This requires interest in addressing more than the immediate complaint—by both the patient and the physician—as well as a repertoire of simple techniques and tools to apply.

OTHER ASPECTS OF HEALTH PROMOTION

It would seem that what is advocated for a clinical role in health promotion, is what one might consider as good family-centered primary health care. Asking the right questions to assist the diagnosis and prescription, which includes psychosocial and other factors, then facilitating an appropriate response is part of standard family practice training and evaluation. The demands of busy clinics, in the absence of supportive and enabling structures, challenges the practitioner's ability to carry out model practice (Jaén, Stange, & Nutting, 1994). The expanded notion of the structure and organization of primary health care to include interdisciplinary teams that are able to provide broader services and links can support these patterns of practice but are unlikely of themselves to change patterns of physician or nurse practitioner behavior.

It is not a simple issue of training or attitude alone but a complex mix including environments that reinforce behaviors. Perhaps telling is the story of the anesthetist disillusioned with the physicians' ability to influence patient smoking behavior. She had regularly as part of her preoperative assessment advised smokers to quit but with little success. This experience was then transferred to her view of any preventive or health promotion intervention. The fact that a strange doctor telling a smoker to quit the night before surgery, the concerns of which tend to focus the mind elsewhere, would be unlikely to succeed on it's own, became a dismissive of all efforts. Training and supports need to be clear for practitioners, particularly, that for individual or societal change, it is unlikely they will see the 90% chance of response that antibiotic treatment of bacterial infection enjoys (Valente, Sobal, Muncie, Levine, & Antlitz, 1986). Experiencing a similar fate is the frequent teaching to look beyond the surface in diagnosis; as the admonition goes, "the majority of the diagnosis is in the history." An example is the story of the young Filipino woman with chronic abdominal pain who was referred from GP to specialist and back, and finally to the Tropical Disease Clinic. This last diagnostic request was based on the assumption that being a recent immigrant her pain may be the result of an as yet undiagnosed tropical infection. The unfortunate fact was that she was being sexually abused by her hosts. This critical piece of information was elicited by taking the time to listen to her concerns and going beyond the presenting complaint.

Behaviors, including those of physicians that start well-intentioned, require supports and reinforcement to maintain and enhance them. Tools and techniques, such as those outlined, that allow aspects of health promotion concepts to be easily incorporated into a busy practice are then more likely to be successfully applied.

USING THE TEACHABLE MOMENT

The teachable moment is an opportunity for a connection between action and current experience (Lewis, 1988). A good time to talk about smoking in the home is when it has likely influenced the child's current ear infection or asthma attack. This discussion is not carried out as a means of judgment but in linking how changed behavior (smoking outside) can benefit the health of the child and perhaps even assist the parent in reducing his or her own smoking. This simple intervention can easily be incorporated into the diagnostic interaction—providing a more viable option for many parents than outright quitting, at least initially, and assisting the concerned parent in minimizing the risk to their child. It is striking how many parents act on this intervention, some of whom end up quitting as a result. It is, however, also striking how often the parents remark, despite repeated emergency and clinic visits, that they were not aware of the connection to their child's health or that there could be a practical alternative to improve the risks for their children (i.e., smoking outside) to quitting a difficult addiction altogether.

NORMALIZING HEALTH

Goel and McIsaac make an important point about demedicalizing conditions. Physicians can do much to demedicalize or normalize conditions as part of life's experience. This then can have the ironic benefit of improving health; not minimizing illness or disability but putting it in a more constructive context. It can reflect an underlying philosophy of healing and understanding the scope of influence of mental, spiritual, and social well-being or coherence that can take place. The challenge is finding the balance that allows a skilled clinician to help patients accept "imperfect" physical health while improving their mental well-being and their overall function yet recognizing when another clinical treatment will offer benefit. An illustration is the impact of a physician with a health promotion approach on a person's health, whose chronic illness, symptoms, or disability prompts him or her to continue seeking new doctors or other healers for more tests or treatments to effect a cure. The discussion instead explores what are the theoretical risks to the person given that the cause or cure has not yet been found and recognizing that the pursuit of diagnosis, and the fear of the possibilities, is dominating the person's experience and not allowing them to be well. While not giving up, the focus becomes what the person can value rather than on the difficulties and being consumed by the illness. This transformation in attitude and sense of health can ultimately affect physical health as well, because the concerns or symptoms may (in some cases) diminish or disappear with time.

Having a focus on promotion of health—physical, mental, and spiritual well-being—while not ignoring diagnosis and treatment, may constitute the art of medicine and be characteristic of successful physicians over the centuries. Although difficult to quantify and study, it incorporates a more holistic notion of *healer.*

GETTING HEALTH PROMOTION
INTO CLINICAL PRACTICE

The challenges for adopting new behaviors or preventive strategies are familiar. The immediacy of events often overtake longer-term or system-focused thinking. The issues for a busy practitioner (Kottke, Brekke, & Solberg, 1993) with lineups of patients, rounds to make, families to raise, and bills to pay, although qualitatively and quantitatively different from those facing patients, nevertheless are similar and in the same way dominate day-to-day decision making as to where energy, time, and resources will be focused.

Efforts to improve physicians' and others' commitment to, and abilities in, health promotion will necessarily depend on understanding not only the rightness of the cause but the practical application of it. Part of this depends on a different paradigm of the expert/professional. Most professions now espouse greater emphasis on partnership with clients/patients and greater control for clients over decisions that affect them. This transition has however been neither smooth nor orderly. Thus, generalizations abound that may dishearten those who have moved on, while doing little to encourage change by those who have yet to recognize the need. One example is the use of the term *medical model* as a dismissive rather than a descriptor. Strategies to encourage and reinforce change must recognize the positive underlying motivations of practitioners while "pushing the envelope" further.

Historically, many of our social movements were led or supported by physicians and others who recognized that the well-being of their patients and communities depended on broader social determinants (Bilson, 1980; Bliss, 1991). The reform of medical education and the focus on the popular scientific breakthroughs in treatments, transplantation, and other advances assumed to some extent that progress depended only on newer surgical or technological progress, newer antibiotics, and so on. It seems ironic that most health reform efforts now try to balance the enormous power and influence of hospitals, given that in the last century, hospitals were commonly institutions of last resort for quarantine or charity for those who could not afford adequate care at home. The changes in attitude came about for good reason, as hospitals were increasingly able to provide important diagnostic, treatment, and surgical services. The issue is one of balance.

CONCLUSION

Renewed interest in what truly determines health recognizes the limitations of a strictly clinical or treatment approach. However, with cultural influences conditioned by technical successes, communities have become more dependent on institutional supports. Legal and other requirements, too, emphasize intervention over studious observation. In this context, then, a new understanding and application of the motivations and skills to improve individual and community health that first drew professionals into health care needs to be reaffirmed and strategies applied to assist and reinforce that transition. The link of health promotion efforts to clinical practice is then an opportunity and a challenge worth pursuing.

REFERENCES

Bass, M., & Elford, R. (1988). Preventive practice patterns of Canadian primary care physicians. *American Journal of Preventive Medicine, 4,* 17-23.

Belcher, D. (1990). Implementing preventive services: Success and failure in an outpatient trial. *Archives of Internal Medicine, 150,* 2533-2541.

Bilson, G. (1980). *A darkened house: Cholera in nineteenth-century Canada.* Toronto: University of Toronto Press.

Bliss, M. (1991). *Plague: A story of smallpox in Montreal.* Toronto: Harper Collins.

Brown, J., Melinkovich, P., Gitterman, B., & Ricketts, S. (1993). Missed opportunities in preventive pediatric health care: Immunizations or well-child care visits? *American Journal of Diseases of Children, 147,* 1081-1084.

Butler-Jones, D. (1996). Enhancing prevention in the practice of health professionals. *Canadian Journal of Public Health, 87*(2), S75-S78.

Canadian Task Force on the Periodic Health Examination. (1994). *The Canadian guide to clinical preventive health care.* Ottawa, Ontario: Canadian Communication Group.

Evans, R., Barer, M., & Marmor, T. (1994). *Why are some people healthy and others not? The determinants of health of populations.* Hawthorne, NY: Aldine de Gruyter.

Gilchrist, V., & Alexander, E. (1994). Preventive health care for adolescents. *Well-Child Care: Issues in Prevention, 21*(4), 759-779.

Green, L. (1987). How physicians can improve patients' participation and maintenance in self-care. *Western Journal of Medicine, 147,* 346-349.

Harris, R., & Leininger, L. (1993). Preventive care in rural primary care practice. *Rural Preventive Practice, 72,* 1113-1118.

Jaén, R., Stange, K., & Nutting, P. (1994). Competing demand of primary care: A model for the delivery of clinical preventive services. *Journal of Family Practice, 38*(2), 166-171.

Johns, M., Hovell, M., Ganiats, T., Peddecord, K., & Agras, W. (1987). Primary care and health promotion: A model for preventive medicine. *American Journal of Preventive Medicine, 3*(6), 346-357.

Kottke, T., Brekke, M., & Solberg, L. (1993). Making "time" for preventive services. *Mayo Clinic Proceedings, 68,* 785-791.

Lewis, C. (1988). Disease prevention and health promotion practices of primary care physicians in the United States. *American Journal of Preventive Medicine, 4,* 9-16.

McKeown, T. (1979). *The role of medicine: Dream, mirage, or nemesis?* Princeton, NJ: Princeton University Press.

Morris, B., & Butler-Jones, D. (1991). Community advocacy and the MD: Physicians should stand up and stand out. *Canadian Medical Association Journal, 144*(10), 1316-1317.

Palframan, D. (1995, August). Health promotion for preschoolers and families by primary-care physicians. *Ontario Medical Review,* 32-36.

U.S. Preventive Services Task Force. (1996). *Guide to clinical preventive services: Report of the U.S. Preventive Services Task Force* (2nd ed.). Baltimore, MD: Williams & Wilkins.

Valente, C., Sobal, J., Muncie, H., Levine, D., & Antlitz, A. (1986). Health promotion: Physicians' beliefs, attitudes, and practices. *American Journal of Preventive Medicine, 2*(2), 82-88.

Wechsler, H., Levine, S., Idelson, R., Rohman, M., & Taylor, J. (1983). The physician's role in health promotion: A survey of primary-care practitioners. *New England Journal of Medicine, 308*(2), 97-100.

COMMENTARY

On Finding Common Ground

Jane G. Zapka

Goel and McIsaac undertake the challenge of reviewing the theory and practice of health promotion within the clinical practice setting. This is a particularly daunting task for several reasons:

- The concepts and definition of prevention and health promotion are complex.

- The paradigms of medical care compared with public health, while overlapping, are fundamentally different.

- The focus and emphases of clinical-practice tasks are influenced by multiple factors that frequently compete or conflict.

- Assessing the current practice of health promotion activities in the clinical setting, much less its effectiveness, is extraordinarily difficult.

In this discussion, I highlight these issues. The issues are challenging and complex and require finding common ground to move forward toward difficult goals, as suggested by Goel and McIsaac, in their analyses of physician factors, patient factors, and the practice environment. Further observations for practice in clinical settings are offered.

THE MEANING OF HEALTH PROMOTION

The seemingly simple and generally understood term *health promotion,* as used in common parlance, becomes intricate when trying to scientifically review aspects of practice and application. Health promotion is a unifying concept and a mediating strategy "between people and their environments, synthesising personal choice and social responsibility in health to create a healthier future" (Anonymous, 1986, p. 73). Health promotion requires mobilization of a variety of approaches, including communication, legislation, financial incentives, organizational change, community development, and education. The purpose is "to enable people to gain greater control over the determinants of their own health" (World Health Organization, 1986, p. iii). The combination of approaches recognizes the enormous complexity of addressing issues to promote a healthier future (Green & Kreuter, 1999). Although the concepts and principles of health promotion are philosophically important and distinctive, their translation and application to the tasks of traditional medicine are operationally difficult. To many, they sound diffuse, all encompassing, or even annoyingly esoteric. Broad, unifying concepts are frequently difficult to apply within the context of a brief traditional patient-provider encounter where expectations revolve around symptoms, procedures, medications, and the like.

Within the practice of medical care delivery, reported health promotion activities are actually more correctly termed *secondary prevention,* or early detection of a medical condition, as is pointed out by Goel and McIsaac. In contrast with the variable interpretation of health promotion, clinicians, health educators, and health services researchers appear to share a more common understanding of primary, secondary, and tertiary prevention (Hanlon & Pickett, 1984). Primary prevention activities include those that prevent a hazard altogether by eliminating it; such examples in the clinical setting involve immunizing a child against measles, genetic screening to advise a couple of possible Tay-Sachs in an offspring, or encouraging an adolescent not to use tobacco. Secondary prevention activity focuses on minimizing disability once a process (a risk factor or disease) has started. These activities are perhaps the most common prevention activities undertaken in the clinical process and include various cancer-screening technologies, such as mammograms, Pap smears, and fecal occult blood tests. Other examples include weight-loss programs for obese persons and smoking cessation counseling. Tertiary prevention activities, such as physical therapy for people with arthritis or medication management for diabetics, aim to retard progression of a disease or disability and/or improve quality of life.

Given the difficulty in operationalizing the broad philosophy of health promotion, it may be prudent to focus on the educational and empowering aspects of the delivery of primary, secondary, and tertiary prevention tasks within the clinical setting.

Fundamental Paradigms

The impetus to promote prevention services, and presumably health promotion services, originates from the field of public health and/or academic medicine and to some extent from patient advocacy groups. The benefits of such services are presented largely in public health or community terms (Kottke, Brekke, & Solberg, 1993). Contrast this public health paradigm with that of medical care. Physician training clearly, and appropriately, focuses on individual patients' needs and on presentation of problems; that is, the focus is on the "numerator" patient compared with the "denominator" community. The paradigm carries over into clinical practice (Fulmer, 1974). The current health care system encourages and rewards the clinician's role as responding to symptoms and problems presented by individual patients and views public health improvements as a by-product of the personal health service enterprise (Freidson, 1970).

Although medicine is grounded in basic biological and clinical sciences, public health is grounded in the epidemiological, social, and behavioral sciences. Add to this the fact that the medical care system prioritizes on urgency and currentness rather than on potential severity or importance. Faced with dilemmas of time constraints, physicians focus on their patients with acute problems and on the acute problems of their patients (Kottke et al., 1993). Furthermore, patient demands generally reinforce this tendency. Patients have expectations that favor testing, prescription, and technology rather than counseling, advice, and self-help (Stone & Steward, 1996). Indeed, Oppenheim (1980) dares to opine that expectation for physicians to spend time and energy on "well-patient care" may not be appropriate. The doctor's role is to care for sick people. He asserts that although some physicians and the public protest this view, "laymen give it lip service, but they do not value it much." Oppenheim further notes that he is convinced that people "experience a mystical, atavistic satisfaction in handing over a small amount of their blood to a physician and hearing a few days later the solemn announcement: 'everything was normal' " (Oppenheim, 1980, p. 1119). Yet the patient is less willing to hear about the important need to practice a healthy lifestyle. Thus, public health education and consumer education needs continued support to counteract the expectation and dependence on curative medicine.

In view of these fundamental paradigms and underlying values, it is increasingly necessary to acknowledge each and their respective strengths, while searching for overlap between them (White, 1991). All clinical services, be they acute care, prevention, or health promotion, have in common the requirement that patients to be involved in their care (Dickey & Kamerow, 1994). Focusing on patient participation within the provider-patient encounter, regardless of the type of service, reinforces the broad philosophy of individual empowerment.

THE CONTEXT OF CLINICAL PRACTICE

Prevention practice (in its more usual definition) by clinicians is no simple matter, particularly within the constraints of the medical care delivery system. There are an ever-increasing number of prevention-oriented strategies to be considered. These include screening tests (e.g., prostate-specific antigen), prophylactic medications (aspirin, estrogen), immunizations (varicella, hepatitis B), and counseling interventions (HIV risk-reduction, smoking) (Dickey & Kamerow, 1994). Even the most philosophically committed clinicians are challenged to stay well-informed, to establish working protocols within their practices and to institute tracking systems to monitor patients' preventive services needs, as well as manage acute illness and symptom presentation. In view of the difficulties in providing the more commonly understood prevention services, provider commitment to the more so-

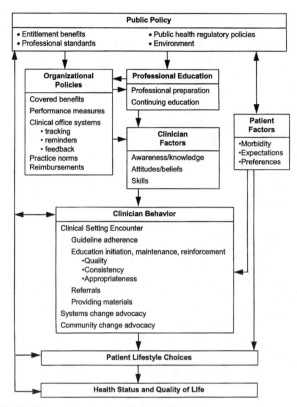

Figure 6.1. Health Promotion in the Clinical Setting

cially and developmentally focused health promotion services is even more difficult.

Certainly, physician knowledge and attitudes are a factor in attention given to prevention and health promotion. However, it is clear that many attributes of the health services system affect the content of clinical practice (see Figure 6.1). Goel and McIsaac nicely articulate several factors in the practice environment that enable or hinder prevention-oriented practice. These include reimbursement and practice organization. Kottke et al. (1993) observe that a physician's current professional practice environment is a meaningful predictor of professional behavior and that it can overcome a physician's propensity and intentions to provide certain services or practice in a certain style. Numerous studies highlight the role that reminder systems have in significantly increasing physicians' performance of selected activities, including those related to prevention (McPhee, Bird, Fordham, Rodnick, & Osborn, 1991). Organization of the practice "system" is particularly important, in that preventive care is no longer an annual physical exam or a periodic health assessment. The debate of the importance of the complete periodic health assessment versus integrating preventive services in all types of medical encounters will need revisiting (Jaén, Stange, & Nutting, 1994) as will the reimbursement for such visits. Physician and patient preconceptions about what preventive strategies, including counseling, are adopted does seem to be determined in part by the type of visit. However, they are also affected by what is viewed as worthy of payment or reimbursement. Recognition of noninvasive and nonprocedural skill as important clinical services has been slow in coming.

Although physician reimbursement schemes are a topic beyond the scope of this brief discussion (Casalino, 1992) it must be acknowledged that certain proposals, for example, the Resource-Based Relative Value Scale (Hsiao, 1988) offer more or less incentives to focus on nonprocedural services.

THE EMPIRICAL EVIDENCE

Another trend in clinical practice, is the growing emphasis on "evidence-based" medicine (Evidence-Based Medicine Working Group, 1992; Sackett, Rosenberg, Gray, Haynes, & Richardson, 1996). This emphasis is firmly entrenched in recommendations for preventive practices. The Canadian Task Force on the Periodic Health Examination (1979) and the U.S. Preventive Services Task Force (USPSTF, 1996) both adopted a clinical-epidemiological approach to making recommendations. The choice of targets for preventive interventions was based on current morbidity and mortality profiles, the performance characteristics of early detection procedures (e.g., tests, procedures, counseling), and the effectiveness of preventive interventions. Effectiveness was graded according to strength of scientific evidence, notably randomized clinical trials (Battista & Fletcher, 1988).

The pressure to practice according to "evidence" will continue. Consider, however, that health promotion interventions are by nature complex. Primary prevention interventions require high levels of cognitive and interpersonal communication skills; they require multiple administrations and reinforcement; they need to be flexible and individually tailored to be effective. Interventions requiring such dynamics do not lend themselves well to clinical trials. We can anticipate that the "poverty cycle" of "no evidence" that health promotion "works" will perpetuate. More positively, the perception that secondary prevention "works" and is "worth it" is quite strong (Dignan et al., 1990; White, Urban, & Taylor, 1993). We must continue to advocate for randomized trials and other strong quasi-experimental studies to continue to demonstrate the potential impact of coordinated clinic-based intervention on patients' health behavior (Heywood et al., 1996; Ockene et al., 1991; Taylor, Houston-Miller, Killen, & Debusk, 1990). In addition, however, we must also assert that insufficient scientific bases for many medical decisions require some combination of expert judgment and scientific judgment to formulate practice guidelines (Wall, 1993). This includes guidelines that emphasize counseling and shared decision making.

Implications

Influencing personal, environmental, and social health requires a multi-level intervention model (Simons-Morton, Simons-Morton, Parcel, & Bunker, 1988). The medical care sector is one important setting for health promotion, and clinicians must be active proponents and participants.

Health promotion proponents appropriately encourage a holistic approach to patient care. This widening of the boundaries of clinical practice has the effect of forcing clinicians to face difficult choices about where to focus their energies, given the constraints of the medical/health care environment. There must be a point along the continuum between the view that doctors be "healers" only (Oppenheim, 1980) and the view that physicians assume responsibility for the holistic person, as well as a healthy society.

Given the confusion and variability of the operational definition of health promotion and the fundamental difference in the medical and public health paradigms, perhaps the common ground is not advocacy for demedicalization but, rather, integration of, and respect for, cognitive screening (i.e., discussion of lifestyle risks) and counseling. In addition, emphasis could be placed on the following:

- Within medical school curricula, continue to refine inclusion of fundamental elements of community health, including epidemiological principles and "patient-centered" models of care (Fulmer, 1974; White, 1991). Much needs to be learned about the difficult challenges of effective clinician-patient communication (Waitzkin & Britt, 1993).

- Promote public, payer, and organizational policies that include guidelines for prevention services, including counseling and education (USPSTF, 1996).

- Emphasize the role of the clinician in providing lifestyle counseling as a clinical preventive service. Although immunizations and screening procedures remain important prevention services, the most promising role for prevention within current medical practice may lie in modifying personal health behaviors (USPSTF, 1996). Focus on lifestyle issues comes nearer to the philosophy of health promotion.

- To be sure, there are personal and health system variables that enhance or inhibit emphasis on certain philosophy and services. Although removing financial barriers is inadequate for ensuring that preventive services will be encouraged and delivered (Lurie et al., 1987), it is also unreasonable for physicians to subsidize prevention and health promotion services; finding time may be as difficult as ensuring an appropriate physician compensation system. Thus, continued attention must be given to creating practice environments with available resources that make service provisions efficient (e.g., reminder systems, referrals).

- Redirect emphasis on shared decision making between patients and clinicians. In this era of technological predominance, there is an increasing need to have patients fully informed about all potential consequences of a treatment or screening strategy. This extends to the broader issues of patient empowerment and responsibility, an essential health promotion tenet.

- Realize that for some issues, community-level interventions are more appropriate than clinical interventions. These include school-based curricula, regulatory and legislative initiatives, and multilevel community interventions (Simons-Morton et al., 1988).

- In addition, encourage clinicians' role as community leaders. Given the public respect they hold, they can promote prudent public policy, encourage healthful activities, and mobilize human and financial resources. This role, which can potentially affect the social, economic, and cultural determinants of health, complements the clinician's role in focusing on individual determinants within the clinic encounter.

In summary, the medical care sector is one, but only one, important setting for health promotion activities. The different (albeit overlapping) clinical and public health paradigms and the increasing constraints of the medical services delivery system make emphasis on health promotion difficult. The challenge is to find common ground, as illustrated by the suggestions above, so that health promotion goals can be incrementally addressed.

REFERENCES

Anonymous. (1986). A discussion document on the concept and principles of health promotion. Health Promotion, 1(1), 73-76.

Battista, R., & Fletcher, S. (1988). Making recommendations on preventive practices: Methodological issues. American Journal of Preventive Medicine, 4(4, Suppl.), 53-67.

Canadian Task Force on the Periodic Health Examination. (1979). The periodic health examination. Canadian Medical Association Journal, 121, 1194-1254.

Casalino, L. (1992). Balancing incentives: How should physicians be reimbursed? Journal of the American Medical Association, 267(3), 403-405.

Dickey, L., & Kamerow, D. (1994, July/August). Seven steps to delivering preventive care. Family Practice Management, 33-37.

Dignan, M., Beal, P., Michielutte, R., Sharp, P., Daniels, L., & Young, L. (1990). Development of a direct education workshop for cervical cancer prevention in high risk women: The Forsyth County project. Journal of Cancer Education, 5, 217-223.

Evidence-Based Medicine Working Group. (1992). Evidence-based medicine, a new approach to teaching the practice of medicine. Journal of the American Medical Association, 268, 2420-2425.

Freidson, E. (1970). *Professional dominance: The social structure of medical care.* New York: Atherton.

Fulmer, H. (1974). An approach to the teaching of epidemiology. In R. L. Kane (Ed.), *The challenges of community medicine.* New York: Springer.

Green, L., & Kreuter, M. (1999). *Health promotion planning: An educational and ecological approach* (3rd ed.). Mountain View, CA: Mayfield.

Hanlon, J., & Pickett, G. (1984). *Epidemiology and disease control: Public health administration and practice* (8th ed., pp. 265-266). St. Louis, MO: Times Mirror/Mosby College.

Heywood, A., Firman, D., Math, M., Samson-Fisher, R., Mudge, P., & Ring, I. (1996). Correlates of physician counselling associated with obesity and smoking. *Preventive Medicine, 25,* 268-276.

Hsiao, W. (1988). Results, potential effects, and implementation issues of the resource-based relative value scale. *Journal of the American Medical Association, 260,* 2429-2438.

Jaén, C., Stange, K., & Nutting, P. (1994). Competing demands of primary care: A model for the delivery of clinical preventive services. *Journal of Family Practice, 38*(2), 166-171.

Kottke, T., Brekke, M., & Solberg, L. (1993). Making "time" for preventive services. *Mayo Clinic Procedures, 68,* 785-791.

Lurie, N., Manning, W., Peterson, C., Goldberg, G., Phelps, C., & Lillard, L. (1987). Preventive care: Do we practice what we preach? *American Journal of Public Health, 77*(7), 801-804.

McPhee, S., Bird, J., Fordham, D., Rodnick, J., & Osborn, E. (1991). Promoting cancer prevention activities by primary care physicians. *Journal of the American Medical Association, 266*(4), 538-544.

Ockene, J., Kristeller, J., Goldberg, R., Amick, T., Penelope, P., Hermer, D., Quirk, M., & Kalan, K. (1991). Increasing the efficacy of physician-delivered smoking intervention: A randomized clinical trial. *Journal of General Internal Medicine, 6,* 1-8.

Oppenheim, M. (1980). Healers. *New England Journal of Medicine, 303,* 1117-1120.

Sackett, D., Rosenberg, W., Gray, J., Haynes, R., & Richardson, W. (1996). Evidence based medicine: What it is and what it isn't. *British Medical Journal, 312,* 71-72.

Simons-Morton, D., Simons-Morton, B., Parcel, G., & Bunker, J. (1988). Influencing personal and environmental conditions for community health: A multilevel intervention model. *Family Community Health, 11*(2), 25-35.

Stone, D., & Steward, S. (1996). Screening and the new genetics: A public health perspective on the ethical debate. *Journal of Public Health Medicine, 18*(1), 3-5.

Taylor, C., Houston-Miller, N., Killen, J., & Debusk, R. (1990). Smoking cessation after acute myocardial infarction: Effects of a nurse-managed intervention. *Annals of Internal Medicine, 113,* 118-123.

U.S. Preventive Services Task Force. (1996). *Guide to clinical preventive services* (2nd ed.). Baltimore: Williams & Wilkins.

Waitzkin, H., & Britt, T. (1993). Processing narratives of self-destructive behavior in routine medical encounters: Health promotion, disease prevention, and the discourse of health care. *Social Science Medicine, 36*(9), 1121-1136.

Wall, E. (1993). Practice guidelines: Promise or panacea? *Journal of Family Practice, 37*(1), 17-19.

White, E., Urban, N., & Taylor, V. (1993). Mammography utilization, public health impact, and cost-effectiveness in the United States. *Annual Reviews of Public Health, 14,* 605-633.

White, K. (1991). *Healing the schism: Epidemiology, medicine, and the public's health.* New York: Springer-Verlag.

World Health Organization. (1986). Ottawa charter for health promotion. *Health Promotion, 1*(4), iii-v.

7

Community as a Setting for Health Promotion

Marie Boutilier

Shelley Cleverly

Ronald Labonte

Community is a more problematic setting than others considered in this text. Whereas family, workplace, school, institution, and even the state have reasonably fixed boundaries, no such precision is possible with community. In social theory, the term is sometimes invoked to describe anything that falls within the rather large gap between individual and society (Lyon, 1989). This definitional space includes families, friendship networks, neighborhoods, political jurisdictions (e.g., the town, the city), interest groups, and formal government and nongovernment organizations. Moreover, the experience of community is less about the physical space in which people interact than the pattern and nature of relations that exist between people (Lyon, 1989). Practically, the inherent contingency of peoples' experiences of community requires that health promotion practices vary to accommodate the unique and dynamic qualities of each community setting (Toronto Department of Public Health, 1994).

AUTHORS' NOTE: This work was supported by the North York Community Health Promotion Research Unit, funded by the Ontario Ministry of Health, Health Systems Linked Research Units Program. This document does not necessarily reflect the opinions of the Ontario Ministry of Health.

This chapter begins with a brief discussion of community's recent policy prominence in the health sector and locates health promotion and its community orientation within a number of critical social theories. It then turns to specific health promotion practices; it cannot review all that has been written about community health promotion but uses a classic typology of community development strategies, with three conceptualizations of "community," to facilitate discussion of several projects that represent broadly differing health promotion practice models. Discussion of community as a setting, or any professional practice within it, is incomplete without an analysis of the nature of social power relations; our chapter thus closes by considering the role of health promoters in communities from the analytical vantage of "empowered" social relations.

THE EMERGENCE OF COMMUNITY IN HEALTH PROMOTION

In the health sector, community has received policy and practice prominence since at least the 1970s. The Alma Ata declaration argued for community participation in health care by stating, in part, that "people have the right and duty to participate individually and collectively in the planning and implementing of their health care" (World Health Organization [WHO], 1978, p. 20). Government reports in most first-world countries (e.g., Lalonde, 1974) extended these rights and duties beyond health care by uncoupling health from biomedicine and assessing the impact that behavioral risk factors had on morbidity and premature morality. These reports gave rise to numerous community-based interventions to lower risk factors for heart disease, cancer, and other chronic illnesses, incorporating social marketing, education, community mobilization, and policy strategies (e.g., COMMIT, ASSIST). The European Regional Office of WHO expanded the envelope of risk factors by arguing that health is affected primarily by policy decisions in nonhealth areas, including housing, transportation, and food distribution (WHO, 1984). WHO called for an intersectoral model of community development, necessitating the cooperation of institutions such as schools, workplaces, and governments to create and/or improve on conditions required for an optimal level of health. This approach served as the conceptual basis for the WHO-sponsored Healthy Cities project initiated in 1986 (Ashton, Grey, & Barnard, 1986), premised on joint planning and action on a broad range of health determinants by citizens and local governments.

The release of the Ottawa Charter (WHO, 1986) in 1986 lent further support to the legitimacy of community development as a health promotion strategy. The Ottawa Charter rejects the approach to community involvement used by traditional public health programs, which regard community members as passive recipients of interventions developed by professionals (Terris, 1992). It calls for an active role for the public through concrete and effective community action in

setting health priorities, making decisions, planning strategies, and implementing them to achieve better health; "people cannot achieve their fullest health
potential unless they are able to take control of those things which determine
their health" (WHO, 1986, p. 1). The Ottawa Charter marks a shift from strictly
medical and behavioral health determinants, to health determinants defined in
psychological, social, environmental, and political terms (Labonte, 1993a;
Minkler, 1990). At the heart of this "new" health promotion is "the empowerment of communities, their ownership and control of their own endeavors and
destinies" (WHO, 1986, p. ii) or, as Minkler (1990) expresses, a process of assisting communities in setting goals, mobilizing resources, and developing action plans for addressing shared public health concerns.

PROBLEMS IN USE OF THE TERM *COMMUNITY*

Most health promotion policy initiatives fail to define *community* explicitly and
infer its existence as a geographic space. They also infer communities to be relatively stable with homogeneous values, in which consensus is not only possible
but desirable and easily achieved (Boutilier, Cleverly, Marz, Sage, & Badgley,
1992); there is little or no acknowledgment of conflict or power struggles among
community members (Farrant, 1991). The imprecision of defining who or what
is community in health policy extends to common bureaucratic use, in which
community is often used simply as an adjective (e.g., health programs become
community health programs) or is implied to be a solution to health problems
(e.g., "We just need to work more with the community"). Lyon (1989) contends
that this abstract quality gives the term its power (in evocation) and its appeal (in
practice). Interpreted generously, the idealized community is something toward
which we reach, embodying traditional spiritual wisdoms that emphasize the reciprocal responsibilities people have for each other (Ornstein & Sobel, 1987;
Spretnak, 1991). However, key concerns arise from this abstract or idealized notion of community in two arenas: (a) the realities of citizen participation and
(b) the use of community rhetoric as a tool to manage the state's fiscal crisis.

   Imprecise or idealized notions of community that imply inclusivity and full
community participation in project decision making and implementation are often not embodied in the realities of participation. Social groups constitute themselves partly by defining boundaries of exclusion (Weber, 1946). Also, not all
human groups wish kindness on each other, and some (such as polluting industries or violent racist organizations) are hardly the types that health promoters
would encourage (Labonte, 1989). Moreover, romanticized notions of community also fail to recognize the value of social conflict between groups as an important stratagem in social change and shifting unhealthy practices of power
(Mondros & Wilson, 1994; Ward, 1987).

Zakus and Hastings (1988), in their broad review of the literature on issues of governance, planning, and policy, conclude that participation is predominately by the middle-class elite with the educational, class, and economic resources that enable participation. This raises two questions: (a) In what, exactly, are communities being invited to participate? (b) Which groups would be supported in their participation? Encouragement of participation by less powerful or more marginalized social groups thus requires that health promotion initiatives identify and counterbalance social and economic barriers that restrict "full" community participation (Labonte & Edwards, 1995).

Imprecise or abstract notions of community also serve political agendas in the contemporary management of government deficits. Interpreted from the vantage point of political economy, the idealized concept of community "is sanctified, attributed with qualities it does not possess, and treated as the remedy for problems which originated in the inadequacy of community provision of welfare" (Pinker, 1982). This romantic vision of community denies the potential for local parochialism and erases the history of centralized social welfare policies that emerged partly because local communities were unable or unwilling to assume responsibility for all of their members' welfare.

It is not accidental that community rhetoric has arisen with the fiscal crisis of the state (Miliband, 1973; O'Connor, 1973; Offe, 1984) and the ascendancy of neoliberal ideology (Baum, 1993; Farrant, 1991; Labonte, 1989; Wilson, 1977). Feminist critics have argued that the idealized community of government policy reports, particularly when referring to the devolution of authority for health and social service programs from central governments to local communities, serves as justification for a decline in state welfare programs. This has the effect of re-privatizing human caring services back to the "family" community, where responsibility for services still falls predominately on women (Bullock, 1990; Walker, 1990). Much North American community discourse supports such a devolution by presuming that a fundamental cause of contemporary social malaise lies in a loss of civic values, seen to be brought on by acculturated dependencies on bureaucratically inefficient (and now deficit-producing) welfare programs and the disempowering practices of those professionals who deliver them (Etzioni, 1993; Illich, Zola, McKnight, Caplan, & Shaiken, 1977; McKnight, 1994).

Some accounts of a recent "population health" approach in Canada specifically critique health care and other state social service expenditures as "unproductive" and call for a decrease in such spending to produce growth in the "tradable goods and services sector" of the economy (Evans & Stoddart, 1990; Mustard & Frank, 1994). There is little analysis or critique of capitalist economic practices as unhealthy (apart from the tobacco industry and to lesser extents the alcohol and fast-food industries), and the advice offered to the state differs little from the neoliberal agenda, which includes less government, lower debt through social spending cuts, and freer trade and market practices (Labonte, 1995). This relative silence on the negative health effects of economic practices derives from the state's contradictory location within economy and civil society relations; it relies on the economy for its revenue and on civil society (citizens, organized groups in "community") for its legitimacy (Offe, 1984). Government policy statements on health promotion thus often appear to announce broad social health agendas while simultaneously directing attention away from what may be economically systemic sources of personal and collective ills. Invocation of the idealized community plays a role in this deflection.

In Canada, for example, health promotion programming has been widely influenced by the 1986 federal statement, *Achieving Health for All: A Framework for Health Promotion* (AHFA; Epp, 1986). AHFA refers to health problems as they are experienced at the local or personal levels, such as income-related disease (e.g., tuberculosis, infant mortality, and stress-related tranquilizer use). Although the document acknowledges the need to "reduce inequities" in health, its articulation of health issues as local community or individual problems overlooks their broader social determination. Strategies for remediation are to be implemented through specific "mechanisms," a depoliticizing notion that suggests that health inequities (and by inference, social inequities) can be addressed through mechanistic or "technical" solutions rather than through significant political and economic changes. These health problems may occur nationally, but because they are experienced personally and locally, they are implied to be a local responsibility to which an idealized local community would respond. Poverty is identified as an important health issue because poor individuals have unhealthier behaviors, lower self-esteem, and higher unemployment. Community initiatives on some of these discrete causes are urged, but the national and transnational economic order that may induce poverty is not subject to scrutiny.

As Baum (1990, 1993) argues, health promotion in the 1980s defined itself primarily as a critique against the individualism, economic rationalism, and power-over tendencies of capitalist economy, the state, and "disabling professions" (Illich, 1975). Health promotion is both a set of programmatic interventions and a counterhegemonic ideology emphasizing holistic, communitarian approaches to social well-being (Pederson & Signal, 1994). It is also a state response to the knowledge challenges of social movements such as feminism, environmentalism, social justice, and antiracism (Labonte, 1994; O'Neill & Pederson, 1994). Thus, the primary location of health promotion in state structures places it in the difficult position of putting contradictory ideology into practice (Stevenson & Burke, 1991). Although not impossible (Labonte, 1996), the difficulty can be obscured by invocation of the unproblematic "community."

COMMUNITY-BASED/COMMUNITY DEVELOPMENT PROGRAM APPROACHES AND THE PROBLEM OF EMPOWERING HEALTH AGENCY/COMMUNITY GROUP RELATIONS

The emphasis that health promotion places on "the empowerment of communities" (WHO, 1986, p. ii), and the primary location of practitioners within state health agencies (as state structures), distills its practice to a basic question: How can relations between government health institutions and community groups, as mediated by health promotion workers, become more empowering for community groups, at least insofar as health issues are concerned? This is a complicated question. Empowerment, for example, describes a process in which individuals, groups, and institutions experience shifts in their relations of power (Labonte, 1996). Some aspects of this shift are psychological and include improvements in a person's self-efficacy, self-esteem, and so on (Wallerstein, 1992). Other aspects concern group dynamics and refer to improved abilities to communicate, demonstrate respect, analyze, and act collectively (Wallerstein, 1992). Still other aspects describe broader social changes in policies, beliefs, and political governance, such that there is more equity in the distribution of authority, status, wealth, and influence among individuals and groups (Labonte 1993a). Moreover, this empowering process both is health promoting in itself and increases groups' and institutions' abilities to act on specific health problems (Labonte, 1993a; Wallerstein, 1992). Finally, the breadth of health issues announced by the Ottawa Charter as legitimate concerns (i.e., peace, shelter, education, food, income, a stable ecosystem, social justice, and equity) challenges earlier health promotion practices that restricted health problems to those defined in behavioral terms.

Two quite distinct community-oriented health promotion practices now exist, representing its more biomedical and disease prevention orientation and its more phenomenological and socially critical socioenvironmental orientation (Labonte, 1993a). In the first instance, community becomes a venue for health behavior programs. In the second instance, community becomes a locus for organizing efforts to shift broader public and private socioeconomic policies and practices. Most health promotion programs, including even Healthy Cities/ Healthy Communities projects, tend to orient to either or both of these practices. Drawing from Felix, Chavis, and Florin (1989), these distinctions are summarized in Table 7.1 as "community-based" and "community development" approaches.

Although the two practices are best conceived of as ideal types that can coexist, they also exert real effects on practitioners in how they construe community, define and legitimate health problems, define and evaluate program outcomes,

Table 7.1 Key Differences Between Community-Based and Community Development
            Approaches

Issue	Community Based	Community Development
Community organizing model	Social Planning	Locality development; social action
Root metaphor	Individual responsibility	Empowerment
Approach/orientation	Weakness/deficit Solve problem	Strength/competence Capacity building
Definition of problem	By agencies, government, or outside organization	By target community
Primary vehicles for health promotion and change	Education, improved services, lifestyle change, food availability, media	Building community and control, increasing community resources and capacity, economic and political change
Role of professionals	Key, central to decision making	Resource
Role of participation by target community members and institutions	Providing better services, increasing consumption and support	To increase target community control and ownership, improve social structure
Role of human service agencies and formal helpers	Central mechanism for service delivery	One of many systems to respond to needs of a community's members
Primary decision makers	Agency representatives, business leaders, government representatives, "appointed" community leaders	Indigenous elected leaders
View of community	Broad, site of the problem, technically and externally defined, consumers	Specific, targeted, source of solution, internally defined subjective, a place to live
Target community control of resource	Low	High
Community member ownership	Low	High

SOURCE: Based on Felix, Chavis, and Florin (1989).

and address (or ignore) power relations between health professionals/institutions and community groups (Labonte, 1993a). Some of these effects are addressed in our review of community-organizing models and discussion of health promotion examples below, but before proceeding, we think it is important to clarify our understanding of health promotion "practice."

PRACTICE IN HEALTH PROMOTION

The broadly accepted definition of "practice" is the application of knowledge (theoretical or technical) in the exercise of a profession and encompasses a range of discipline-related activities and applications of knowledge. However, as Schon (1983) points out, "practice is an ambiguous concept" that also encompasses an element of repetition to learn and perfect one's performance (p. 60). Schon contends that the repetitive element of practice fosters learning and enhances performance, to the extent that it is reflected upon. Within health promotion, practice is not fixed by any rigorously defined discipline and is said to be practiced by individuals in diverse organizations, trained in a multiplicity of disciplines. Thus, what actually constitutes practice in health promotion will differ according to the practitioner's institutional location and discipline-related training—that is, his or her "arena" of practice. Three key arenas of practice impinge on community as a setting for health promotion:

1. Health and social services (including the disciplines of nursing, nutrition, community development, medicine, social work, education, and health education)

2. Research (defining research as a practice itself: the repetitive application of theoretical and technical knowledge that is discipline based and applied to health promotion—e.g., the practice of epidemiological or participatory research in health promotion)

3. Policy, usually as the practice of state employees (thus, policy-making is a form of health promotion practice—e.g., attempts to formulate and implement healthy public policy)

Within the community setting, the health promotion practice of each is often inextricably influenced by that of the other two. In this chapter, however, we emphasize health promotion practice rooted in health and social services rather than in research or policy—that is, the health promotion practice in which the practitioner meets directly with members (usually unpaid) of "target" groups (whether self-identified or selected by the practitioner) to work on health issues.

COMMUNITY-ORGANIZING MODELS

There are no theories of community development per se (Lyon, 1989), but there have been multiple attempts to model different forms of practice (e.g., Christenson & Robinson, 1989; Craig & Mayo, 1995; Mondros & Wilson, 1994; Popple, 1995). One of the most influential within social work, and subsequently within public health (e.g., Fawcett et al., 1995; Hoffman & Dupont, 1992; Labonte, 1996; Minkler, 1990; Rosenau, 1994), has been the community-organizing triptych developed by Rothman and Tropman (1987).[1] A more recent typology developed by Dixon and Sindall (1994) addresses differences in community health promotion programs from the vantage point of their "underlying logics of change and rationality."[2]

The social planning model of community organizing (Rothman & Tropman, 1987) defines the relationship between the state and community groups along resource and service dimensions. It emphasizes top-down consultation with, rather than bottom-up participation from, individual community members. Community, in turn, becomes construed in broad demographic terms (e.g., the poor, women, people of certain ethnoracial background, smokers, the unfit, people with silent hypertension, or even the notion of a whole "population"), which may not always correspond with how people come to form their own group identities. Problems are usually defined for communities in service sector terms (e.g., as lack of housing, lack of health care, lack of food) or disease-specific terms (e.g., heart health, cancer prevention—often what we have earlier called community-based programming). Defining the particular problem is based on extensive fact gathering and formal needs assessment that rely heavily on quantitative data. The social planning model also tends toward the discourse of market relations. The state is provider and civil society is consumer, although ultimately the community must "buy into" and eventually "own" responsibility for state-initiated behavior change programs. Community developers are variously market analysts, social marketers, public relations officers, or technical experts whose job it is to ascertain consumer preferences and ensure the "value for money" of the provider's investment (Warner, 1989). Overall, the process tends to be professionally and bureaucratically dominated (Fawcett et al., 1995; Rosenau, 1994), in which practitioners assume the role of technical assistants who bring a wide variety of special knowledge or skills that help the community mobilize both internal and external resources to meet their service or educational needs. These skills and knowledge may include grant writing, program planning and management, budgeting and accounting, knowledge of where and how to obtain external resources, and program evaluation and accountability. Community theorists sometimes refer to horizontal and vertical relations within and between community groups (Lyon, 1989); the former is more process oriented, inward looking, and focused on emotional bonding, whereas the latter is more task oriented, outward looking, and focused on changes to be made in the external environment. Social planning emphasizes vertical relationships between groups and institutions.

The locality development model (Rothman & Tropman, 1987) embodies the ideals of self-help and mutual aid common to the discourse of the idealized or romanticized community—for example, friends support friends, local businesses support community projects. Practitioners invoking this model try to involve a broad cross section of people in determining and solving problems that they share in common. They emphasize consensus approaches to decision making and seek collaboration with existing institutions of power. In addition, practitioners committed to this model support local residents to define their own concerns and how they will address them. The practitioner's role in the group-organizing process is primarily one of adult educator and small-group facilitator. The task leader, the person (or persons) who plays the most important role in defining the community's action-oriented goals, should be someone who lives in the neighborhood itself. The locality development model emphasizes building horizontal relations. People discover a greater sense of their own power, partly through strengthening their social support systems and interpersonal relationships (Wallerstein, 1992). Some Healthy Cities/Healthy Communities are explicitly or implicitly committed to the locality model; however, like many community developers, many others "talk" locality development but "walk" a social planning model.

Rothman and Tropman (1987) delineate the social action model of community organizing as concerned foremost with shifts in social power relationships, using conflict or confrontation as an organizing style. Practitioners working from this model generally define relatively powerful private or public institutions as external targets of action and build on smaller local community groups within particular neighborhoods. This model locates the creation of communities in organized, collective struggles against structured conditions of inequality (Russell-Erlich & Rivera, 1987). The issues themselves are often specific, local, and urgent with an explicit equity or power dimension. This conceptualization of community and social action, at least in North American practice, is derived principally from the work of Alinsky (1971). Although Alinsky argued against organizers bringing in their own outside ideology to community groups, similar to the classic health education aphorism to "start where the people are" (Nyswander, 1957, cited in Minkler, 1989), this itself can be seen as an ideology. Other writers on social action organizing argue that the practitioner's responsibility lies, in part, in bringing a political vision to community development and initiating a program for change in local communities (e.g., Mondros & Wilson, 1994; Russell-Erlich & Rivera, 1987; Ward, 1987). The strong "traditional" knowledge of people's own lives and situations are combined with the organizer's political knowledge (Kling & Posner, 1990). The underlying premise, that both organizers and community members bring differing knowledge to the organizing effort, is roughly similar to Habermas's (1984) arguments that technical rationality (the political/technical expertise of the practitioner) and life-world experiences (people's own wisdom of their lives) should meet under "ideal speech situations" in which both are shared to develop a "best" knowledge of what problems exist and how they might be remedied.

As discussed earlier, health promotion theory and practice are paradoxically located largely within state-funded organizations, yet engaged in struggle against the power-over tendencies embodied within the state, professions, and economic practices. This places practitioners in the difficult position of ambiguity around defining practice goals, strategies, and the direction of accountability (i.e., to the community group or to the employers.). In an earlier review of case studies in community health promotion (Boutilier et al., 1992), we found very few examples of the social action model. Although this is usually argued to be a result of the low priority afforded documentation by practitioners working within this model, it is also likely that the professional dilemmas faced by practitioners inhibit adoption of the model as a guide to health promotion practice. Thus, to be serviceable to health promotion, the social action model requires some refinement that acknowledges both the practice dilemmas and the type of challenge to power relations that are possible within health promotion.[3]

Health promotion practitioners working with a social action model often take on or support an advocacy role with community groups on issues that are local and urgent. Similar to Alinsky's later work, practitioners will often adopt a redistributive rather than a transformative politic (Kennedy, Tilly, & Gaston, 1990), in which redistributive changes in material forms of power (income, resources) are more important goals than transforming more complex ideological and communicative power relations between groups. Usually, practitioners try to create a new umbrella community organization that will fight politically for new services or resources, supporting the legitimacy of community interest groups in negotiations. Strategies address power inequities and amelioration of inequity on the specific issue but do not necessarily focus on broader underlying relations of power, such as between labor and capital.

Within this model, the state (as the largest employer of community organizers) negotiates with community groups to develop a more integral and shared agenda. Where it differs from the social planning model is in the state's recognition of the need to negotiate agendas with community groups rather than simply encourage the latter to "buy into" a preexisting agenda. Such negotiation steers away from direct conflict and confrontation that challenges the underlying relations of power yet invariably makes power relations a central concern. Unlike most locality development projects, in which the project generally begins and remains at the local level, the social action model's concern with power relations creates the potential for such projects to broaden their scope beyond local, specific issues, as often exemplified by the formation of coalitions that target higher-level government or private sector policies and practices.

CASE EXAMPLES

To this point, our discussion has been theoretical. Our thesis has been that community is best considered a phenomenon of group identity, involving complex sets of relationships within and between groups, more formal organizations, and state and nongovernmental institutions. Community as a setting for health promotion more particularly involves the relationship between health agencies (usually but not exclusively government) and individuals, groups, or organizations in civil society. This relationship is structured around actions aimed at improving health and is rooted in resource transfers (knowledge, human, financial) between the health agency and those groups with which it seeks partnership. As discussed earlier, there is a plurality of health promotion practices, in part because health and its determinants have multiple interpretations and explanatory logics (e.g., epidemiological, political, sociological, feminist, ecological) and different forms of power are inherent in the actors (with government usually possessing more). The case examples offered here draw both on the literature on well-known initiatives and on local projects with which we have some direct experience and greater access to the "grey literature" of project reports. These local examples permit us a richer examination of practice dynamics than might be permitted by a review limited to published literature; such literature tends to focus on health outcomes rather than on implementation issues. We offer one caveat to these case examples: As discussed earlier, these models of community organizing represent "ideal types"; in reality, therefore, no case example will fit the model perfectly.

Social Planning

The North Karelia Project, Finland. Along with the Stanford study (Farquhar et al., 1977), the North Karelia Project is seen as a pioneer effort in the application of scientific knowledge to communitywide initiatives (Puska et al., 1985). The North Karelia Project began in 1971 when, in response to being identified as having among the world's highest morbidity and mortality rates due to cardiovascular disease (CVD), the Finnish government was pressed by local citizens to act. Puska and colleagues (1985) report that the project was not research initiated, but a community-based program with a "quasi-experimental design." The specific objectives were both treatment and prevention of heart disease by reducing risk factors such as smoking, serum cholesterol, and blood pressure. Strategies included preventive services, education, behavioral change programs, skills training, social support, environmental change, and "community organization" (in this case, community organization is reported as consisting of weekend training programs for local informal leaders to act as role models for others) (McAlister, Puska, Salonen, Tuomilehto, & Koskela, 1982). The community mobilization program included activities such as communal cooking lessons and dinners, increasing access to heart-healthy foods, leaflet distributions, and poster campaigns (Farquhar et al., 1977; McAlister et al., 1982). The 10-year evaluation showed substantial reductions in key biological risk factors for CVD among men, with similar trends among women (Puska et al., 1985).

The research component of the North Karelia Project was intended to make a contribution to help program planners/practitioners who were frustrated by the "lack of a unifying theory" (Puska et al., 1985, p. 158). Overall, however, researchers could not tell why or how change occurred, only that it did occur (Puska et al., 1985). In contrast to predictions that changes in health would be due to increased health knowledge or attitude change, the project found that change was associated with community organization. In cases of successful persuasion and education to change behavior, the key component was found to be the credibility of the source of information rather than content per se (Puska et al., 1985). This led researchers to conclude that to achieve broad diffusion of the North Karelia model, local cultural barriers would have to be addressed (Shea & Basch, 1990a, 1990b). The importance of the local nature of the social factors that influence change also suggests, however, that when the classic social planning model imposes (rather than negotiates) an agenda, its lack of sensitivity to local nuance and idiosyncrasy can exacerbate power inequity and tension between health promoters and the groups to be served.

The North Karelia model has since been replicated internationally (e.g., in Minnesota, Stanford, and Pawtucket; Shea & Basch, 1990a, 1990b), and has generalized to the notion of "community mobilization" in health promotion practice (Health and Welfare Canada, 1992). Heart health programs internationally, PATCH (Planned Action Towards Community Health) programs in the United States and Canada, and various antismoking and chronic disease prevention programs around the world, share common assumptions with the social planning approach to community organizing. Among these are selection of measurable targets based on epidemiological or risk factor survey data and formation of broad community/agency coalitions to plan and implement actions on the "evidence-based" health priorities. Although there are important practical problems associated with managing this form of community health promotion practice (Francisco, Paine, & Fawcett, 1993), our concerns with this approach pertain more to its implicit assumptions about what are "important" health problems and the effects this has on community/agency power relations.

First, reliance on survey data, without first including community members in a critical discussion of what health issues or concerns should be studied (and how), defines as important health issues only those selected a priori by health agencies (Labonte & Robertson, 1996). These issues are usually defined in health behavior terms and contain few or no questions concerning the broader health determinants identified by the Ottawa Charter. This does not pose a practice or power problem where these behavioral concerns are shared by community members, which may have been the case in North Karelia. But this is often not the case in many of those communities where the North Karelia model has been replicated (Goodman, Steckler, Hoover, & Schwartz, 1993; Labonte, 1995; Poland, Taylor, Eyles, & White, 1995). Second, power resides more with health professionals and agencies than with citizens and community groups. Health promoters attempt to get community members to "buy into" the program and eventually "own" it, by encouraging them (usually with small grants) to participate in choosing some of the program strategies. In some instances, technically complex needs assessment surveys were found to overwhelm community members, reinforcing health professionals' expertise and authority (Goodman et al., 1993). Such surveys have also been used to convince community participants that their concerns over the health effects of poor housing, racism, or violence were "opinions," whereas the survey findings documenting health behaviors and disease rates were "facts." Not surprisingly, community participation beyond volunteers from other health agencies (e.g., heart or cancer foundations, lung associations) often declines.

Although people may not realize the impact of certain diseases on certain neighborhoods or group members and this information can serve as a "wake-up call" as it appears to have done in North Karelia, issues of poverty, unemployment, drugs, violence, racism, and so on may be more pressing and systemic health problems. Attempting to mobilize community leaders around heart disease or cancer prevention, in order to place these issues "higher up on community leaders' agendas" (Shea, Basch, Lantigua, & Wechsler, 1992) can weaken local forms of political organizing, unless health agencies simultaneously accept as legitimate health issues and support leaders' concerns over more underlying causes of unhealthy living conditions (Labonte & Robertson, 1996). Problems with the social planning/community-based approach can be overcome but only to the extent that health promoters and their agencies are able to move beyond the disease prevention/risk factor "silos" with which they might begin their community work, including developing the flexibility and willingness to support actions on other community issues of importance to participants. This, in turn, requires acceptance of new approaches to research knowledge (e.g., participatory action research) and more flexibility in how community groups account for project funding (Labonte & Robertson, 1996).

Locality Development

The Tenderloin Senior Organizing Project (TSOP). This project in San Francisco's Tenderloin district is an oft-cited exemplar of the locality development approach to community health promotion. Although Minkler (1990) notes that different aspects of all three community organization models informed the project and described its dynamics at different times, its origin in a specific neighborhood and its emphasis on local agenda setting and decision making are characteristic of locality development as an ideal type. Recognizing the poor health, social isolation, and powerlessness of the low-income elderly population who live in single-room occupancy hotels in the area, a group of health educators and graduate student volunteers worked to develop a climate of social support and social action among elderly residents (Minkler, 1990). Although the organizers still initiated the intervention and its broadly stated goals (which is more often the case in locality development approaches to health promotion than the somewhat idealized notion of groups spontaneously organizing themselves around health concerns), what distinguishes this approach from the social planning model are the efforts made by organizers to adapt and negotiate their agendas with local community members. Such people no longer represent "target groups"; they become citizens more or less systematically disenfranchised from political power. Thus, the two primary goals of TSOP were these:

> (1) improving physical and mental health by reducing social isolation and providing relevant health education and facilitating through dialogue and participation, a process through which residents were encouraged to work together to identify common problems and seek solutions to these shared problems and concerns. (Minkler, 1990, p. 275)

Starting in one hotel, student volunteers encouraged resident interaction, forming a core group that met weekly. As trust and rapport developed, group members began to discuss concerns such as crime, loneliness, rent increases, and powerlessness. The students used Freirian problem-posing methods, health education methods, and Alinksy's (1971) techniques to create dissatisfaction with the status quo and to channel frustration into concrete action; social support theory stimulated promoting social interaction opportunities to address social needs (Minkler, 1990). Using similar techniques, seven other groups were eventually established. As the groups evolved, they recognized that they wanted to link with each other and work on shared problems. With this, a coalition was formed and members developed the Safehouse Project in which 48 neighborhood businesses and agencies became refuges and offered help in emergencies for the elderly residents. Other activities of the coalition have included lobbying the mayor during an election year to increase the police service to the neighborhood; the establishment of minimarkets, a cooperative breakfast program, the renovation of a basement room into a congregate dining area, and leadership training courses for TSOP members (Minkler, 1990). Over time, TSOP members decreased their reliance on staff and volunteers, who became resources to the project. This redefinition of roles over time allowed the key mechanism for organizing and taking action to become tenant associations rather than the facilitated support group techniques used earlier (Minkler, 1990; Minkler & Cox, 1980).

TSOP is an example of the empowering actions possible in health promotion that can evolve out of locality development projects and of the fluidity of the definition of the model itself. Because the project was initiated out of an external reading of community "need" and began with the process of highly educated, generally middle class "outsiders" entering the neighborhood, it shares elements of the social planning approach. Its strategies, however, began with the maxim of community development to "start where the people are" and incorporated techniques that acknowledge power and political realities (as delineated in the social action model and based on techniques of Alinsky, 1971, and Freire, 1968) (Minkler, 1990). With the success of the community-organizing strategies implicit in the locality development approach (Brown, 1991), specific community-identified, local, urgent issues (e.g., policing and crime) emerged and were owned by the community residents. Local practitioners outside the project, however, did not always respond in a way that empowered the residents (Brown, 1991; Minkler & Cox, 1980). Rather, many neighborhood agencies and practitioners whose practice fell within top-down approaches viewed TSOP participants with suspicion, supporting them with only a "false generosity"— enough to promote their own professional or agency interests but too little to advance the empowerment perspective of the project (Minkler & Cox,1980, p. 320). It may be that key contributions to the success of such projects that practitioners and their sponsoring organizations can make are flexibility in response to local issues, commitment to collaboration (with each other and with community members), and ensuring that interagency politics do not undermine the organizing initiatives of citizen participants.

TSOP no longer exists. As may happen in locality development projects, formalization into a funded organization led to a decrease in active citizen participation. As citizens are better able to negotiate with the state (e.g., they acquire more funding and resources and develop more authority over problems) they often formalize into organizations and employ staff; they become more of a service agency, and the direct, more politicized and energetic voluntarism of the early days dissipates or moves on into other issues with the expectation that the service now created will be responsive, respectful, and helpful.

Advice for Big and Small (ABS). This project, initiated by a small group of isolated mothers in a multicultural subsidized housing project in Toronto, surfaces other practice tensions in the locality development approach to health promotion. In keeping with the ideal typical community-led principle of this approach and unlike the professionally initiated TSOP, ABS originated in discussions among mothers who realized that they could minimize risks for child abuse by reducing their own and other mothers' isolation. They were also distrustful of "helping professionals," many of whom, such as social workers, exercised state authority over their lives via welfare and child protection legislation. They also believed that reducing isolation would be achieved most effectively by and with other neighborhood mothers like themselves, without professionals being present (Boutilier et al., 1995). Professional support, however, was not absent altogether. The women approached a local community development agency for assistance in finding resources. A small government grant allowed the group to incorporate and establish a parent-helping-parent support program, employing three local mothers as "home visitors" (Boutilier & Advice for Big and Small Steering Committee, 1994). The partner organizations included the local public health department, a children's mental health facility, and a health promotion research unit. Training in child development and parenting and ongoing support for home visitors was provided by the partner organizations, but professionals themselves did not visit neighborhood family homes. In addition to providing emotional and parenting support, the home visitors showed mothers how to connect with resources (such as English classes, schools, food banks, and health care, including how to use public transportation) and arranged for mothers to meet each other and their neighbors, as well as occasionally facilitating connections with cultural groups from the mothers' countries of origin.

What ABS illustrates perhaps better than TSOP are some of the means by which vertical relations between state funders and professionals more typical of the social planning model are not absent in a locality development model but assume a different and more equitable form. Management-level professional participation in decision making was limited, and no professionals entered women's homes without an explicit invitation and having a home visitor present. This challenged and inverted the previous norm of professionals initiating their own "client" visits, for example, to determine if such persons retained strict eligibility for welfare benefits, a power-over practice associated with disempowering effects for "clients" (Bloor & McIntosh, 1990; Labonte, 1996). In fact, establishing more equitable relations with professionals and their employing agencies became an explicit goal of the project; it became part of the women's work. Unlike the stereotype of self-sufficiency, in which community-led initiatives are thought to work best when wholly dependent on their own internal resources, ABS members recognized their interdependent relations with state institutions and exercised self-reliance, in which they became able to negotiate more empowered terms of those relationships (a process also noted by Labonte, 1993b). This negotiated partnership extended to the research/evaluation relationship, a relationship important not only for the knowledge assistance it provided ABS members but also for the credibility and resources it helped to create for their work. Professionals and researchers, in turn, needed to accept and work from explicitly participatory models of practice and research (Boutilier et al., 1995). Control over all project decisions was initially retained by a steering committee composed of a few frontline professionals but with a majority being those women who initiated the project and those hired as home visitors; the local resident members made all financial decisions.

Typical of small locality development projects, however, funding for ABS was short-term, and like TSOP, larger and more secure funding was eventually obtained. This allowed the project to improve its service delivery but reshaped it from a small-scale locality development initiative to a social planning project defined in specific "siloed" terms—that is, a "practical community based approach to (reduce) conditions of risk for children . . . who face greater-than-normal risks of poor health, disability or injury" (Brighter Futures, 1992, p. 1). The shift to a social planning approach included central organizational control. The home visitors continue to work in the project, but the local residents no longer control the funding, administration, or research; the local steering committee disbanded in 1995, several years after the mothers' group first began meeting on their own initiative.

Whether this represents a "natural" progression of state institutionalization of needed and progressive service resources that originate in community demands or whether it represents a co-optation of such initiatives is a frequently argued but moot point. In a social planning approach, this concern is rarely explicit, because the intent is often to move the state agenda into the "community." In locality development, the intent is often to organize or support community groups so that, in part, they may use the state as an opportunity structure for funding, human, and ideological resources (Labonte, 1996). In doing so, however , the state may absorb the "community" agenda as its own and bureaucratize or conservatize it. The result may be more helpful services but fewer helpful supports for grassroots organizing or political action (Labonte, 1996). To the extent that this process is explicitly recognized by community members and mediated by critically reflective frontline practitioners supported by similar-minded managers, the absorption may be more, rather than less, empowering and hence more, rather than less, health promoting.

Social Action

As discussed earlier, within health promotion, social action may target state policies and practices, placing practitioners in a professionally ambiguous position. This does not preclude professionals from participating in such a practice, but the partnerships they create are based on a critique of past disabling state policies and a commitment to transform them, as well as support for enabling community group practices and processes. Obviously, this risks marginalizing such workers from their own institutions to a greater degree than the previous two approaches.

The example of The Meeting Place (Toronto, Ontario, Canada) exemplifies some of these practice risks. The project originated as a health promotion project within a social planning framework (it attempted to pilot health behavior programs to underhoused or "street" persons) until a critical review reoriented the project toward social action (Equity in Action Report, 1994). The staff role shifted from trying to make changes in the participants' health status and health behaviors to programming around five concerns: dental health care, substance abuse, housing, nutrition, and social justice (Equity in Action Report, 1994). Providing education and information became less important than creating a "safe" space for homeless and underhoused people to meet so that they might develop a sense of belonging, build social and life skills, and determine specific social actions to ameliorate their conditions of poverty and homelessness. Although the transient and crisis-ridden nature of many members' lives meant that consistent attendance for most participants was unlikely, skilled facilitation enabled many participants to contribute and benefit from small-group involvement as well as more politicized forms of social action (Equity in Action Report, 1994). Some of these actions targeted provincial and local housing policies, and discriminatory attitudes by health care providers in hospital emergency rooms, using public forums, media events, political lobbying, and other advocacy tactics; others attempted to generate income through community economic development initiatives; several pertained to direct services such as providing food, shelter, cooking, and shower facilities; free dental services; and substance abuse counseling (Equity in Action Report, 1994).

The shift from a narrow health behaviorism to a broad social health orientation was supported by government program funders who, in turn, were buttressed by policy statements adopting the Ottawa Charter's social justice rhetoric and models of health determinants that explicitly identified inadequate housing, poverty, and various forms of social discrimination as important causes of disease. Despite this initial support, however, the funding period expired and was not renewed. This leads us to speculate on the processes among our case examples: As ABS obtained significant funds by adapting to a social planning framework, The Meeting Place may have lost funds by shirking it. The technical-rational accountability systems of state agencies often constrain program success to narrowly defined outcomes congruent with social planning assumptions (Labonte, 1994, 1996); social action approaches are harder to defend because until recently, their goal ("empowerment") has not lent itself easily to discrete measures, although considerable effort has been expended to make this possible (Eng & Parker, 1994). This difficulty in evaluative defense often leads social action attempts to the margins of state relationships, eschewing large grants or other institutional supports to maintain greater practice autonomy.

Street Health (Toronto, Ontario, Canada), a community-run project that provides primary health care services to homeless and underhoused people, has a social action approach oriented primarily against disempowering and discriminatory health care practices toward the underhoused. Street Health had its origins in planning meetings about rent-geared-to-income housing, which were attended by a minister and the homeless people who used the church's (All Saints' Church) low-cost clothing store and its two drop-in centers. During these meetings, a recurring tangent emerged: the community's concerns with the inadequate and discriminatory health care they had received. From this, another group consisting of 14 homeless people, a community organizer, and a nurse who had been volunteering clerical support to the church began to meet and focus on health care issues (Ambrosia, Baker, Crowe, Hardill, & Jordan, 1992; Crowe & Hardill, 1993).

> Street Health's mandate is threefold: (a) to provide "hands-on" nursing care to clients in an environment that is comfortable to them, (b) to assist clients to gain access to appropriate care in the mainstream health system, and (c) to lobby the existing health care system to become responsive to the needs of the homeless people. (Ambrosia et al., 1992, p. 1)

Street Health opened its first of several nursing stations for homeless and underhoused people in 1986. In an effort to be responsive to the homeless community (which moves around), it has never had a fixed site. Drop-in centers and shelters are typical locations to set up nursing stations. In keeping with its mandate, Street Health also carries out research intended to be useful to the homeless community and their advocates and designed to address the absence of data about homeless people (largely because survey techniques rely on respondent telephones or mailing addresses, which excludes homeless people from sampling frames) (Ambrosia et al., 1992; Crowe & Hardill, 1993). The Street Health Report, a study of the health status and barriers to health care of homeless women and men in the City of Toronto (Ambrosia et al., 1992), included qualitative and quantitative survey findings and specific recommendations directed toward 10 municipal- and provincial-level governance and service agencies.

The complexity of the health promotion response to address equity issues such as poverty and homelessness as a social determinant of health leads to equally complex professional and agency/community group relationships. First, and in common with the locality development components, direct service remains an important facet of work. As one of the Street Health nurses commented in an interview, "Nursing is at a crossroads where it must go in two directions at once, one step backwards to clinical care, one step forwards to community action" (Labonte, 1994, p. 226). Many poorer groups engage first in social action around issues of service delivery, its appropriateness and accessibility, and the way in which service providers treat them. Moreover, trust in small-group processes is often slow to build and is based initially on developing trust with a "helping professional." As self-competence increases in groups, outward-looking social actions targeting policy and political decision making become more feasible (Hoffman, 1989; Labonte, 1995; Labonte & Edwards, 1995; Mondros & Wilson, 1994). Second, considerable professional flexibility is required as group members shift their goal orientation from inward looking to outward acting. In The Meeting Place, this did not lead to an abandonment of their health education objectives and small-group activities but to an expansion of activities and fundamental shift in overall project goals. No longer were specific health behaviors or outcomes the goals; rather, more proximate goals of group empowerment, political capacity, and resource mobilization became important.

Professional flexibility, in turn, demands organizational flexibility. In the case of Street Health, the actual location and nature of services continued to change with the physical movements and needs of the homeless themselves—from emergency hostels, to 24-hour coffee shops, to church drop-ins, to more permanent housing projects that arose, in part, from the organizing efforts of groups such as Street Health and The Meeting Place. In the case of The Meeting Place, organizational flexibility lay in the sponsoring agency's (a neighborhood-based, multiservice, nongovernmental organization) willingness to support changes in staffing and staff roles. The flexibility was further supported by state funders' willingness to shift fundamentally the project's goals (and, consequently, accountability criteria) midway through a grant period.

DISCUSSION: POWER AND PRACTICE

We must say again that the two ideal-types of community-based and community development health promotion, and their three corresponding models of community organizing, often blur in practice. Yet still we maintain that differing understandings of power relations (between professional and "client," health institution, and community group) are inherent within them. For nonprofessional community members (i.e., civil society), the conflict that can emerge in power relations may contradict the goals and vision of health promotion, as articulated in the Ottawa Charter. In such instances, community members and supportive practitioners may attempt to use the political or professional power interests of powerful others to achieve their own community agenda, work with or "around" that power, withdraw from the initiative, or confront and struggle against that power. The latter option, which represents a win-lose approach, was not evident in our review, although the first three strategies were present:

1. *Using others' power.* When, during an election year, the participants in TSOP appealed to the mayor of San Francisco for a local policy response to their concerns, they used the political power interest of a powerful outsider to advance their own health promoting initiative.

2. *Working around power.* The achievement of participation that recognizes contradiction yet avoids overt conflict by working around power was seen in Advice for Big and Small. Recognizing that professionals and their organizations would be greeted with hostility or evasion in their neighborhood, rather than confronting professionals' power head-on, the mothers set up their own health promotion project, with the help of practitioners who acted as resources rather than experts.

3. *Withdrawal from the initiative.* From community members' perspective, it is more likely that once contradiction becomes evident, overt conflict is avoided through withdrawal or nonparticipation in health promotion initiatives rather than expressed in overt power struggles, although this may be somewhat modified within organizations and other formal structures. Withdrawal may also occur if the initiative unfolds to a social planning or service provision model. As participants see the project develop into a formal structure, the energetic voluntarism in the early stages of organizing may dissipate, or activists may move on to other issues.

A detailed case-study of the Toronto Department of Public Health, which has a well-deserved record for supporting a range of community development health promotion activities, defined some of the professional and organizational characteristics that permit such a practice (Labonte, 1996). We conclude our chapter with a brief discussion of these. Although we recognize the limitations of the case study methodology on which they are based, we believe they may be instructive for health promoters wishing to engage their practice in community as a "setting."

Practitioners Skilled in Communication, Social Analysis, and Critical Reflection

The community development relationship, empowering or otherwise, is created between people and, through people, between groups, organizations, and institutions. The community developer is the fulcrum on which these relationships balance. The skills necessary for empowering community development are many but consist primarily of analytical and communicative prowess. Analytical skills help to overcome a group's localism and its potential conservatism or undemocratic practices and to motivate its members to political action. Com-

municative skills, those involving effective listening, group facilitation, and respectful interpersonal relations, allow the community developer to share his or
her knowledge, and that of the health agency, without imposing it on or negating
the knowledge generated by the group. Such a practice, however, is not merely
an exercise of technical skills. It requires what came to be referred to as an "ethical stance," one in which practitioners acknowledged their own initial power-
over (their often higher incomes, professional status, organizational and political legitimacy, and ability to influence the agendas of political authorities higher
up the institutional hierarchy) and made it available for use by community
groups. Following from Wartenberg's (1990) arguments, these "power-overs"
become transformative only when those who exercise them do so with the intent
that others in a relationship with them accrue more of these forms of power as a
consequence. In doing so, community developers actualize the oft-cited cliché
of "working themselves out of a job."

Supportive Peer Relations and Organizational Norms

The primary support that the community developer receives in maintaining
some critical reflexivity in this transformative process is from his or her own
peers. This support requires organizational norms that value a spectrum of practice styles. Not all health professionals can or should be expected to engage in
community-organizing practices, nor do community members always want to
be "empowered" but require, instead, direct services offered in caring and respectful ways. Failure to recognize and value different (and differently useful)
forms of practice can lead to intra- and interdisciplinary status rivalries over
higher- or lower-esteemed practices. Supportive peer relations also requires
cross-disciplinary "hand-offs" in organizing work, as different practitioners encounter situations that exceed their discipline-specific skills or knowledge base.
Peer support requires problem-posing approaches to staff meetings, team-
building retreats focused specifically on power relations and power-sharing, and
knowledge development workshops in which power-relational issues pertaining
to gender, race/ethnicity, class, or other social "determinants" of positive health
are analyzed.

Community Development-Oriented Managers

Flattening organizational hierarchy is a necessary, although not necessarily
sufficient, prerequisite to an organizational culture supportive of community development, because hierarchy brings with it the greater exercise of power-over.
But some hierarchic structures will continue to characterize both state institutions and formalized community groups. Managers knowledgeable of, if not
also competent in, community development practice are thus essential. Such

managers are able to protect the community developer when his or her twin systems of accountability—to community groups and to the state—create controversy or excessive personal strain. In turn, community developers need to understand the dual accountability systems faced by their managers, that of maintaining a degree of civil service autonomy while "managing" the organization's accountability to higher-level state and political authorities. Managers' abilities to develop community developers can be enhanced to the extent that they arise from the frontline ranks of the disciplines involved in community development. This managerial recruitment from within is one of the conditions that strengthens practitioners' claims to "professional" legitimacy and autonomy that, in turn, allows them to make their power-over available to community members.

Enabling Internal Policies

A degree of civil service autonomy is possible, and part of its possibility rests on the momentum created by its own policies. Health agency policies, although potentially restrictive of practitioner autonomy, can also be enabling, protecting innovative and politically "risky" practice while constraining practices that have been disempowering in the past. Several important elements of these policies are identified. They must contain specific social analyses and models that (a) locate personal troubles in political systems, (b) recognize community development goals as processual rather than static, (c) recognize community development both as a philosophy involving all practitioners and a practice specific to some practitioners, (d) define community development as a practice that supports social actions around structural conditions of power/powerlessness, (e) support accountability methods that most embody the ethical stance and social analyses that inform the institution's policies on community development, and (f) develop explicit criteria for supporting specific individuals, groups, or organizations that are public and publicly defensible.

An Expansive and Legitimating Rhetoric

Finally, state institutions themselves require their own expansive and legitimating rhetoric, one that can be used in their own struggle to forestall partisan political interference contradictory to empowerment and to generate public support for their intentions and actions. Health promotion provided such a rhetoric. Central in this process was the Ottawa Charter (WHO, 1986) and, to a lesser degree, the Achieving Health for All framework (Epp, 1986); the former in particular carried with it the nominal authority of the World Health Organization, the Canadian Public Health Association, and Health and Welfare Canada. This rhetoric is currently being eclipsed in Canadian health promotion policy circles by that of "population health," which embodies more neoliberal assumptions about the nature of the relationship between government, community, and the economy (Labonte, 1995). Recognizing this, Canada's health promotion community is currently engaged in efforts to repromote the more socially critical and empowering ideals of the Ottawa Charter.

SUMMARY

The underlying theme of this chapter has been the problematic use of the term *community*, its applications in health promotion, and the complexity of interests and relationships surrounding community health promotion. We began this chapter with a synopsis of the emergence of the concept of community in health promotion, defined practice, reviewed defining characteristics of "empowering" and "individual responsibility" metaphors for practice, delineated three models of community organizing (Rothman & Tropman, 1987), and outlined several community health promotion projects as case examples. Throughout this chapter, our reflections have, implicitly or explicitly, raised the issue of power relations in health promotion practice. As a setting for health promotion, the community encompasses the complex set of relationships that both determine and promote health. Practice in the community setting will encounter power imbalances and issues of equity related both to the determinants of health and to professional/agency and client/community group relationships.

Although the "welfare state" is now in a period of neoliberal and neoconservative attack and decline, partly supported by the imprecise invocation of the idealized community discussed earlier, it is unlikely to disappear in the near future or cease to play a powerful, and hence potentially power-transformative, role in many peoples' lives. It is this power-transformative role that lies at the heart of conceptualizing community as a health promotion setting.

NOTES

1. There is lack of clarity surrounding several of the terms frequently used with *community* as its modifier—for example, community organizing, community mobilization, community development. For purposes of our argument, *community organizing* refers to some outsider (e.g., a health promoter) attempting to create a new group or organization; *community mobilization* describes attempts to draw together a number of such groups or organizations into concerted actions around a specific topic, issue, or event; *community development* incorporates both but retains a philosophical commitment to broad changes in the structure of and power relations in society (Health and Welfare Canada, 1992; Sanders, 1975).

2. Dixon and Sindall's typology is more explicit on program evaluation issues; Rothman and Tropman's is more helpful for deeming the practitioner's role. Both typologies are ideal-typical, and both comprise useful heuristics for the analysis of different health promotion practices that follows. Space limitations preclude any focus on Dixon and Sindall's model here; however, it has both strategic and explanatory potential and may prove more influential in the future.

3. Within the different arenas of health promotion practice, challenges to power and inequity will take different forms. For example, within research as an arena of health promotion practice, the adoption of a participatory action research approach will address inequities in knowledge-based relationships while posing particular dilemmas for academy-based researchers (Boutilier, Mason, & Rootman, 1996; Fineman, 1981).

REFERENCES

Alinsky, S. (1971). *Rules for radicals.* New York: Random House.

Ambrosia, E., Baker, D., Crowe, C., Hardill, K., & Jordan, B. (1992). *The street health report: A study of the health status and barriers to health care of homeless women and men in the City of Toronto.* Unpublished manuscript.

Ashton, J., Grey, P., & Barnard, K. (1986). Healthy cities: WHO's new public health initiative. *Health Promotion, 1*(3), 319-324.

Baum, F. (1990). The new public health: Force for change or reaction? *Health Promotion International, 5*(2), 145-150.

Baum, F. (1993). Healthy cities and change: Social movement or bureaucratic tool? *Health Promotion International, 8*(1), 31-40.

Bloor, M., & McIntosh, J. (1990). Surveillance and concealment. In S. Cunningham-Burley & N. P. McKeganey (Eds.), *Readings in medical sociology.* New York: Tavistock/Routledge.

Boutilier, M., & the Advice for Big and Small Steering Committee. (1994). *Advice for big and small.* Unpublished report to Ministry of Housing, Ontario.

Boutilier, M., Cleverly, S., Marz, C., Sage, L., & Badgley, R. F. (1992, November). *Community action and health promotion: An overview.* Paper presented at the annual conference of the Ontario Public Health Association, Toronto.

Boutilier, M., Cressman, W., Scarcello, S., Munro, D., Khanam, S., Harrison, L., & Ahmed, N. (1995, June). *Equal participation in health promotion: Success and ongoing issues from the community's perspective.* Paper presented at the Canadian Public Health Association Annual Meetings, Charlottetown, Prince Edward Island.

Boutilier, M., Mason, R., & Rootman, I. (1997). Community action and reflective practice in health promotion research. *Health Promotion International, 12*(1), 69-78.

Brighter Futures. (1992). *Canada's action plan for children.* Ottawa, Ontario: Health and Welfare Canada.

Brown, E. R. (1991). Community action for health promotion: A strategy to empower individuals and communities. *International Journal of Health Services, 21*(3), 441-456.

Bullock, A. (1990). Community care: Ideology and lived experience. In R. Ng, G. Walker, & J. Muller (Eds.), *Community organization and the Canadian State* (pp. 64-82). Toronto: Garamond.

Christenson, J., & Robinson, J. (Eds.). (1989). *Community development in perspective.* Ames: Iowa State University Press.

Craig, G., & Mayo, M. (1995). *Community empowerment: A reader in participation and development.* Atlantic Highlands, NJ: Zed.

Crowe, C., & Hardill, K. (1993, January). Nursing research and political change: The street health report. *Canadian Nurse,* 21-24.

Dixon, J., & Sindall, C. (1994). Applying the logics of change to the evaluation of community development in health promotion. *Health Promotion International, 9*(4), 297-339.

Eng, E., & Parker, E. (1994). Measuring community competence in the Mississippi Delta: The interface between program evaluation and empowerment. *Health Education Quarterly, 21*(2), 199-220.

Epp, J. (1986). *Achieving health for all: A framework for health promotion.* Ottawa, Ontario: Health and Welfare Canada.

Equity in Action Report. (1994). *Equity in action: A report of the interview findings with local action projects: Case studies.* Ottawa, Ontario: Premier's Council on Health, Well-being and Social Justice.

Etzioni, A. (1993). *The spirit of community.* Toronto: Simon & Schuster.

Evans, R. D., & Stoddart, G. L. (1990). *Producing health, consuming health care.* Vancouver: University of British Columbia, Health Policy Research Unit.

Farquhar, J., Maccoby, N., Wood, P., Alexander, J., Breitrose, H., Brown, B., Haskell, W., McAlister, A., Meyer, A., & Nash, J. (1977). Community education for cardiovascular health. *The Lancet, 1,* 1192-1195.

Farrant, W. (1991). Addressing the contradiction: Health promotion and community health action in the United Kingdom. *International Journal of Health Services, 21*(3), 423-439.

Fawcett, S., Paine-Andrews, A., Francisco, V., Schultz, J., Richter, K., Lewis, R., Williams, E., Harris, K., Berkley, J., Fisher, J., & Lopez, C. (1995). Using empowerment theory in collaborative partnership for community health and development. *American Journal of Community Psychology, 23*(5), 677-697.

Felix, M., Chavis, D., & Florin, P. (1989, May). *Enabling community development: Language, concepts, and strategies.* Presentation sponsored by Health Promotion Branch, Ontario Ministry of Health, Toronto.

Fineman, S. (1981). Funding research: Practice and politics. In P. Reason & J. Rowan (Eds.), *Human inquiry: A sourcebook of new paradigm research* (pp. 473-484). Chichester, UK: Wiley.

Francisco, V. T., Paine, A. L., & Fawcett, S. B. (1993). A methodology for monitoring and evaluating community health coalitions. *Health Education Research: Theory and Practice, 8*(3), 403-416.

Freire, P. (1968). *Pedagogy of the oppressed.* New York: Seabury.

Goldsmith, C. H., Cameron, R., Zanna, M., & Poland, B. (1995). *Critique of the COMMIT study based on the Brantford experience.* Unpublished manuscript.

Goodman, R., Steckler, A., Hoover, S., & Schwartz, R. (1993). A critique of contemporary community health promotion approaches: Based on a qualitative review of six programs in Maine. *American Journal of Health Promotion, 7*(3), 208-220.

Habermas, J. (1984). *The theory of communicative action* (Vol. 1). London: Heinemann.

Health and Welfare Canada. (1992). *Community mobilisation.* Ottawa, Ontario: Health and Welfare Canada.

Hoffman, K., & Dupont, J. M. (1992). *Community health centres and community development.* Ottawa, Ontario: Health Services and Promotion Branch.

Hoffman, L. (1989). *The politics of knowledge in medicine and planning.* Albany: State University of New York Press.

Illich, I. (1975). *Medical nemesis: The expropriation of health.* London: Penguin.

Illich, I., Zola, E., McKnight, J., Caplan, J., & Shaiken, H. (1977). *Disabling professions.* New York: Marion Boyers.

Kennedy, M., Tilly, C., & Gaston, M. (1990). Transformative populism and the development of a community of color. In J. M. Kling & P. S. Posner (Eds.), *Dilemmas of activism: Class, community and the politics of local mobilization.* Philadelphia: Temple University Press.

Kling, J. M., & Posner, P. S. (1990). *Dilemmas of activism: Class, community and the politics of local mobilization.* Philadelphia: Temple University Press.

Labonte, R. (1989). Community empowerment: The need for a political analysis. *Canadian Journal of Public Health, 80*(2), 87-90.

Labonte, R. (1993a). *Health promotion and empowerment: Practice frameworks.* Toronto: Centre for Health Promotion/Participation.

Labonte, R. (1993b). Partnerships and participation in community health. *Canadian Journal of Public Health, 84*(4), 237-240.

Labonte, R. (1994). Birth of program, death of metaphor. In A. Pederson, M. O'Neill, & I. Rootman (Eds.), *Health promotion in Canada.* Toronto: W. B. Saunders.

Labonte, R. (1995). Population health and health promotion: What do they have to say to each other? *Canadian Journal of Public Health, 86*(3), 165-168.

Labonte, R. (1996). *Community development in the public health sector: The possibilities of an empowering relationship between the state and civil society.* Unpublished doctoral dissertation, York University, Sociology Department, North York, Canada.

Labonte, R., & Edwards, R. (1995). *Equity in action: Supporting the public in public policy.* Toronto: Centre for Health Promotion/Participation.

Labonte, R., & Robertson, A. (1996). Delivering the goods, showing our stuff: The case for a constructivist paradigm for health promotion research and practice. *Health Education Quarterly, 23*(4), 431-447.

Lalonde, M. (1974). *A new perspective on the health of Canadians.* Ottawa, Ontario: Health and Welfare Canada.

Lyon, L. (1989). *The community in urban society.* Toronto: Lexington.

McAlister, A., Puska, P., Salonen, J., Tuomilehto, J., & Koskela, R. (1982). Theory and action for health promotion: Illustrations from the North Karelia Project. *American Journal of Public Health, 72*(1), 43-50.

McKnight, J. (1994). *Community and its counterfeits.* Toronto: CBC Ideas.

Miliband, R. (1973). *The state in capitalist society.* London: Quartet.

Minkler, M. (1989). Health education, health promotion and the open society. *Health Education Quarterly, 16*(1), 17-30.

Minkler, M. (1990). Improving health through community organization. In K. Glanz, F. Lewis, & B. Rimer (Eds.), *Health behavior and health education: Theory, research and practice.* San Francisco: Jossey-Bass.

Minkler, M., & Cox, K. (1980). Creating critical consciousness in health: Applications of Freire's philosophy and methods to the health care setting. *International Journal of Health Services, 10*(2), 311-322.

Mondros, J., & Wilson, S. (1994). *Organizing for power and empowerment.* New York: Columbia University Press.

Mustard, J. F., & Frank, J. (1994). The determinants of health. In M. V. Hayes, L. Foster, & H. Foster (Eds.), *The determinants of population health: A critical assessment* (Western Geographical Series 29). Victoria, BC: University of Victoria.

O'Connor, J. (1973). *The fiscal crisis of the state.* New York: St. Martin's.

Offe, C. (1984). *Contradictions of the welfare state.* Boston: MIT Press.

O'Neill, M., & Pederson, A. (1994). Two analytical paths for understanding Canadian developments in health promotion. In A. Pederson, M. O'Neill, & I. Rootman (Eds.), *Health promotion in Canada.* Toronto: W. B. Saunders.

Ornstein, R., & Sobel, D. (1987). *The healing brain.* Toronto: Simon & Schuster.

Pederson, A., & Signal, L. (1994). The health promotion movement in Ontario: Mobilizing to broaden the definition of health. In A. Pederson, M. O'Neill, & I. Rootman (Eds.), *Health promotion in Canada.* Toronto: W. B. Saunders.

Pinker, R. (1982). *Models of social welfare: Theory and ideology in the making of social policy.* Text of Address, Social Policy in the 1980's Conference, Melbourne, Australia.

Poland, B. D., Taylor, S. M., Eyles, I. D., & White, N. F. (1995). Qualitative evaluation of community mobilization for smoking cessation: The Brantford COMMIT Intervention Trial. In K. Slama (Ed.), *Tobacco and health: Proceedings of the 9th World Congress.* New York: Plenum.

Popple, K. (1995). *Analyzing community work.* Philadelphia: Open University Press.

Puska, P., Nissinen, A., Tuomilehto, J., Salonen, J., Koskela, K., McAlister, A., Kottke, T., Maccoby, N., & Farquhar, J. (1985). The community-based strategy to prevent coronary heart disease: Conclusions for the ten years of the North Karelia Project. *Annual Review of Public Health, 6,* 147-193.

Rosenau, P. V. (1994). Health politics meets postmodernism: Its meaning and implications for community health organizing. *Journal of Health, Politics, Policy and Law, 19*(2), 303-333.

Rothman, J., & Tropman, J. (1987). Models of community organization and macro practice perspectives. In F. M. Cox, J. L. Erlich, J. Rothman, & J. E. Tropman (Eds.), *Strategies of community organization* (4th ed.). Itasca, IL: Peacock.

Russell-Erlich, J., & Rivera, F. (1987). Community empowerment as a non-problem. *Community Development Journal, 22*(1), 2-10.

Sanders, I. (1975). *The community.* Chicago: University of Chicago Press.

Schon, D. (1983). *The reflective practitioner: How professionals think in action.* New York: Basic Books.

Shea, S., & Basch, C. E. (1990a). A review of five major community-based cardiovascular disease prevention programs: Part I. Rationale, design and theoretical framework. *American Journal of Health Promotion, 4*(3), 203-213.

Shea, S., & Basch, C. E. (1990b). A review of five major community-based cardiovascular disease prevention programs: Part II. Intervention strategies, evaluation methods and results. *American Journal of Health Promotion, 4*(4), 279-287.

Shea, S., Basch, C., Lantigua, R., & Wechsler, H. (1992). The Washington Heights-Inwood Healthy Heart Program: A third-generation community-based cardiovascular disease prevention program in a disadvantaged urban setting. *Preventive Medicine, 21,* 203-217.

Spretnak, C. (1991). *States of grace: The recovery of meaning in the postmodern age.* San Francisco: Harper.

Stevenson, H. M., & Burke, M. (1991). Bureaucratic logic in new social movement clothing. *Health Promotion International, 6*(4), 281-290.

Terris, M. (1992). Concepts of health promotion: Dualities in public health theory. *Journal of Public Health Policy, 13*(3), 267-276.

Toronto Department of Public Health. (1994). *Operational plan for community development and advocacy.* Toronto: Department of Public Health.

Walker, G. (1990). Reproducing community: The historical development of local and extra-local relations. In R. Ng, G. Walker, & J. Muller (Eds.), *Community organization and the Canadian state* (pp. 31-46). Toronto: Garamond.

Wallerstein, N. (1992). Powerlessness, empowerment and health: Implications for health promotion programs. *American Journal of Health Promotion, 6*(3), 197-205.

Ward, J. (1987). Community development with marginal people: The role of conflict. *Community Development Journal, 22*(1), 18-21.

Warner, P. (1989). Professional community development roles. In I. Christenson & I. Robinson (Eds.), *Community development in perspective.* Ames: Iowa State University Press.

Wartenberg, T. (1990). *The forms of power: From domination to transformation.* Philadelphia: Temple University Press.

Weber, M. (1946). Class, status, party. In H. H. Gerth & C. Wright Mills (Eds.), *From Max Weber: Essays in sociology.* Oxford, UK: Oxford University Press.

Wilson, E. (1977). *Women and the welfare state.* London: Tavistock.

World Health Organization. (1978). *Health for all: Alma-Ata Declaration.* Geneva: Author.

World Health Organization, Regional Office for Europe. (1984). *Health promotion: A discussion document on the concepts and principles.* Copenhagen: Author.

World Health Organization. (1986). *Ottawa charter for health promotion.* Ottawa, Ontario: Author.

Zakus, J. D. L., & Hastings, J. E. F. (1988). Public involvement in health Promotion and disease prevention: A comprehensive literature review and analysis. In *Health services and promotion branch working paper* (pp. 88-100). Ottawa, Ontario: Health and Welfare Canada.

COMMENTARY

John Raeburn

The chapter by Boutilier, Cleverly, and Labonte represents a thoughtful, sociologically oriented analysis of modern community-located health promotion thinking and work. In particular, it points out what a difficult area this is, both conceptually and practically, and how its terminology and action can readily be subverted by politicians and others with disempowering agendas. There are very important messages here, especially because they come from people who are immersed on a daily basis with the exigencies of community action.

I guess my main reservation about the chapter is that it is perhaps overly cautious about the field and somewhat pessimistic and intellectual in its tone, whereas I believe this area is one of "heart" and optimism. This seems connected with a main theme of the chapter—the danger and inappropriateness of romanticized or idealized concepts of community. As will be seen, I believe a passionately held vision of community is essential for this enterprise.

The chapter opens with a discussion of the concept of community within the health and health promotion sectors. What we got in the early "behavioral" days of health promotion was a concept of community the opposite of what we today would regard as an empowered view. This view seemed to portray "community" as passive groupings of largely ignorant people who were ruining themselves through inappropriate lifestyle habits and who had to be made to change their errant ways. As a consequence, the community—that is, people viewed as residents of relatively discrete large (e.g., national) or medium-sized (e.g., regional) geographical areas—were either targeted with mass media behavior change messages or were subjected to some of the big research/demonstration projects of the type mentioned here—the North Karelia Project, the Stanford Heart Project, and so on. At best, the results of these projects were ambiguous, and one can question whether they deserve to be regarded as community endeavors at all. That is, they were professionally driven juggernauts, with little or no community consultation. Where "community people" were actively involved, the term *community participation* was used, which mainly involved getting people to support predetermined agendas.

Then, as Meredith Minkler points out in her excellent chapter (Minkler, 1990), another view of community started to emerge in health promotion rhetoric. This was the view associated not with professionals but with more grassroots and social justice movements. In the Third World, these movements came to the fore during the 1960s and 1970s, in the form of economic and social community development projects for which the guiding principle was self-determination rather than professional control. From this Third World movement came what for me represents the bottom line for any truly empowering community development endeavor—namely, "community control." This is where the community runs the enterprise in all its dimensions, as well as controlling the resources and agendas.

In the West, a more deprofessionalized view of community action became evident with some of the North American sociopolitical movements of the 1960s onward—those involving black power, feminism, gay rights, and so on. However, a major difference between these movements and the Third World approach was that the "communities" involved were issue based rather than locality based.

Increasingly, then, the view of community in both the Third World and Western trends was changing from that of passive recipient of professionally controlled programs to one in which community had power, influence, and political clout. Ideals of self-determination, justice, and "people power" were very much part of this "new" view of community. This more "empowered" view of the community became, at least for some of us, the dominant way of thinking about community in the context of health promotion, and it is this view we see embodied in the Ottawa Charter. At the same time, much practice in health promotion still seems to remain back in the old lifestyle view of community.

As one might expect from a sociologically oriented analysis, issues of structure and power are central in the Boutilier et al. chapter. In particular, emphasis is put on the unscrupulous use of the concept of community by politicians, bureaucrats, and others to bring about what amount to anticommunity ends. This is a good point, and there is no doubt that politicians and others will continue to use the term *community* in a manipulative way. Also, there is no doubt that communities are at the mercy of all sorts of macrostructural forces, many of which arise from international, national, or local political and economic ideologies that many of us find repugnant. Notwithstanding that, I believe that the power of community itself remains very strong. Regardless of external or structural circumstances, people have to go on living their lives, and there is tremendous psychological and health benefit to be gained by the power of community, regardless of circumstances. We are undoubtedly living in an imperfect world, and I am not suggesting we stop trying to improve the world. But there is also important work that can be done now by people in controlling and bettering the lives of themselves and their communities.

What is especially significant about a community perspective, in my view, is that it occupies the "middle ground" between the extremes represented by psychology and sociology. It is more than an individual perspective but less than a national-societal or large-population perspective. It acknowledges macrostructural influences but also capitalizes on the power of ordinary people to influence things and be proactive. It is not driven by crisis or short-term interventions but takes a medium- to long-term developmental view, where change is measured over (say) a 5-year period.

From this middle-ground perspective, the term *community* represents the everyday living and working context. It is the setting in which we customarily act, associate with others, learn about life, and express our values. It is here that we most strongly interact with our culture and with others' cultures. To me, it represents the optimal perspective for health promotion, especially because it typically includes workplaces, schools, and families—the major settings covered by this book. Having said this, it is also conceded that many or most modern urban communities, with their alienation, transitoriness, fragmentation, communication systems, and other forces acting against a cohesive local sense of community, may not fit the "ideal." Nevertheless, we all do have an ecological niche into which we fit, whether successfully or not, and we all relate to others on a geographical basis to some extent. I see some of the important "work" of health promotion to be the fostering of a sense of local community, regardless of the starting point.

This then brings us to the question of how best to "do" health promotion from a community perspective, and here the authors present the familiar Rothman and Tropman (1987) breakdown of approaches to what they characterize as "community organization," which to an outsider like me seems a peculiarly American term. Boutilier et al. do not distinguish between community organization and community development, nor do they attempt to define the latter. I say this, because for me, the premium approach in considering community as a setting for health promotion is what I understand by the term *community development.* Furthermore, again stating my own preference, "true" community development is what Rothman and Tropman call "locality development," whereas the other two categories are more what I would call "community organization."

That is, if the central issue in community-located health promotion is "empowerment"—and many would agree that it is—then there is some question about the extent to which the two nonlocality development approaches of Rothman and Tropman qualify as being empowering. As Boutilier et al. say,

the "social planning model" is a top-down approach and is hence by definition nonempowering. As for the social action model, not only do the authors
say "we found very few examples," but it is also often professionally driven
rather than community driven. That is, the social action issues are frequently
selected by practitioners rather than the community, and the community
may first be required to "have its consciousness raised" to be persuaded by
the practitioners to accept their political or other views. Also, the social action approach tends to be predicated on anger and on an assumption of social oppression. The energy of anger is often an important ingredient for mobilizing a community. But the reality is that many communities, in New
Zealand anyway, prefer a more peaceful and community-building approach
to their development. This is not to say communities will shrink from
adrenaline-charged social action when this is clearly needed. Marches, peti-
tions, sit-ins, and so on do happen and can be very effective. But they do not
constitute the ongoing core of a developmental community approach to
health promotion, in my view. And in a democracy, people generally prefer
to be democratic and negotiatory rather than continuously confrontational.

So, clearly, I place myself primarily in the consensus or locality development camp of community development. At the same time, I do not deny the
reality of the current world, where one sees the destructiveness, greed, and
basic malevolence of the agendas of some New Right governments and
their deliberate attempts to dismantle the welfare state and to create a disenfranchised and impoverished underclass. But the question is, How does one
best approach this from a community perspective? Is it all-out war? Or can
one deal with it in a democratic, community-building, and empowering
way? I believe the latter is generally to be the preferred route, except in the
most extreme of politically oppressive situations.

Boutilier et al.'s outline of the nature of locality development is an excellent one. As they say,

> [Locality development] embodies the ideals of self-help and mutual aid . . . for
> example, friends support friends, local businesses support community proj-
> ects. Practitioners invoking this model try to involve a broad cross section of
> people in determining and solving problems that they share in common. They
> emphasize consensus approaches to decision making and seek collaboration
> with existing institutions of power. . . . Practitioners committed to this model
> support local residents to define their own concerns and how they will address
> them. The practitioners' role in the group organizing process is primarily one
> of adult educator and small-group facilitator. The task leader, the person (or
> persons) who play the most important role in defining the community's
> action-oriented goals, should be someone who lives in the neighborhood it-
> self. The locality development model emphasizes building horizontal rela-
> tions. People discover a greater sense of their own power, partly through
> strengthening their social support systems and interpersonal relationships.

This passage defines, for me, the actualization of empowerment as I understand that term—the community itself in charge of its own affairs, defining its own agendas and concerns, taking its own action, having the organization and issues under its own control, and growing in strength, power, self-determination, and well-being through the process.

So what do the authors say is wrong with this approach? Well, the first "..." in the quotation above contained a reference to "the discourse of the idealized or romanticized community." That is, the full sentence reads: "The locality development model (Rothman & Tropman, 1987) embodies the ideals of self-help and mutual aid common to the discourse of the idealized or romanticized community—for example, friends support friends, local businesses support community projects."

Earlier in the chapter, the authors take issue with a view of "idealized or romanticized community." Indeed, they see such a view as a major reason why concepts of community become corrupted and are used by unscrupulous politicians and institutions for their own ends.

> Interpreted generously, the idealized community is something toward which we reach, embodying traditional spiritual wisdoms that emphasize the reciprocal responsibilities people have for each other ... However, key concerns arise from this abstract or idealized notion of community in two arenas: (a) the realities of citizen participation and (b) the use of community rhetoric as a tool to manage the state's fiscal crisis.
>
> Imprecise or idealized notions of community that imply inclusivity and full community participation in project decision making and implementation are often not embodied in the realities of participation. ... Imprecise or abstract notions of community also serve political agendas in the contemporary management of government deficits ... [such as when] the devolution of authority for health and social service programs from central governments to local communities serves as justification for a decline in state welfare programs.

So what we have here is a critique implying that idealized concepts of community are "bad," and that therefore by inference, locality development is "bad," or at least under suspicion, because it is predicated on concepts of idealized community.

It is this, more than anything else, that I would like to take issue with in this chapter, especially because it seems to be a key point that the chapter is attempting to make. For the rest of what I am going to say here, I would like to defend what the authors call an idealized view of community, and also the locality approach, and to support this by examples. (The examples given of locality development by the authors only marginally meet the criteria for such an approach, I believe. There are other examples that could better illustrate the effectiveness and power of this approach.)

For me personally, a "romantic" vision of community has been a driving force for over 20 years. This harks back to when, in my early years, I could not find a label for what I was trying to do in the community and discovered the 19th-century sociologist (yes! a sociologist!), Tönnies, and his breakdown of community into Gemeinschaft (old-fashioned generic, locality-based community) and Gesellschaft (the new, industrial concept of community based on association rather than locality). Tönnies (1995) bewailed the loss of Gemeinschaft, as did community psychologist Seymour Sarason in his book *The Psychological Sense of Community* (Sarason, 1974), and it could be argued that at some level we all, as social/tribal animals, yearn for a "return" to this old sense of community based on locality and that many of our human ills arise from the dislocation of "old" community.

Nobody would argue that with modern urban development, industrialization, transport systems, and communication technology, we should return to the "old" forms of village pump community in their classic sense. However, what has driven me for 20 years is the desire to bring some aspects of Gemeinschaft back into modern urban communities, no matter how raw, dislocated, or conflictual they might be—and no matter how they may have been disempowered by New Right politics, of which we are very aware in New Zealand, I can assure you. How does one do this? Partly, it is a matter of determining the motivation in a community for "community building." In our experience, most New Zealand suburban and other communities have a powerful underlying desire for community, as determined by surveys, even if this is not immediately apparent from what people are currently doing or saying. (Our surveys typically show 70%-90% of the residents of a community want more opportunity to interact with local people, to participate in community activities, to "develop a sense of community," to "contribute to the community," etc.). Our experience is that when this information is used intelligently and sensitively by the community itself to set up appropriate participatory action, projects take off, grow, and endure. The results are measurable improvements in health, mental health, and social indicators, plus high levels of expressed satisfaction with what is going on.

Another inspiration for the romantic/generic/cooperative/locality-based view of community is the vision or sense of community evident among many indigenous people and in many Third World countries. In Canada, it is clear that First Nations people see community first and foremost in terms of land and the people's connection with that land. In New Zealand, the Maori people (who call themselves *tangata whenua* or "people of the land") have a similar view—that their identity as a people and as a community is in terms of their tribal land. We are lucky in New Zealand to have this view widely promulgated, because Maori people make up 15% of the population and are now strong politically. These values are linked to *whanau* (family), community, land, and *aroha* (love). This view is a spiritual one—it goes to the deepest essence of existence. Health, in the Maori world, is an indivisible "whole" of mind, body, family, and spirit. Therefore, any health promotion for Maori has to incorporate these elements. To quote directly from Maori health workers,

> Taha Whenua [the land] is our footstool or turangawsewee [place to stand]. It is our personal, familial and tribal locator. Without it, we are bereft, rootless, landless and tribeless. Our relationship with the Earth-Mother is perfunctory, superficial and callous. She who has suckled us. She who has sheltered us. She who will embrace us. (Te Roopu Awhina o Tokanui, 1986, p. 1)

To dismiss this as "romantic" is, I think, to miss the point. Similarly, the Third World is rich in examples of health promotion and quality of life endeavors based on community development of a locality nature (Durning, 1989). My favorite example here is the Buddhist-based Sarvodaya project in Sri Lanka (Ariyaratne, 1985), which involves 10% of the rural area of that country and hundreds of community-controlled village development projects, where the values are peace, justice, nonviolence, cooperation, community, and enlightenment.

The question is, Can these "romantic" ideals be translated into a modern urban context? Maybe Toronto is beyond redemption—I don't know. But certainly here in New Zealand, we have managed to do so. In the first locality-based project with which I personally was involved, the level of participation was over 10,000 in a new, suburban community of 14,000 people. The issues covered (based on extensive and repeated needs/wishes assessments, the key to this approach in my view), were extremely "generic"—covering all dimensions of life and, certainly, covering all sectors of the population and all age groups, not just white, middle class adults. This resulted in measurable increases in quality of life in that community and its going from being one of the most at-risk and disliked areas of Auckland, to the most liked (by its residents) in only 5 years, with commensurate improvements in many health, mental health, and social indicators (Raeburn, 1986). Since then, we have engaged in many similar projects, including communities of poverty, where residents have been most affected by New Right policies.

There are impressive examples in other developed countries in both urban and rural settings of outstandingly successful (and inspirational) generic, locality-based health and quality-of-life promotion projects. In the United States, three examples are Bertha Gilkey's Cochrane Gardens Project in St. Louis (Boyte, 1989), the urban block organization projects described by Chavis and Wandersman (1990), and the Florida Modello and Homestead Gardens Project, based on what is called the Health Realization approach (Mills, 1990). In Canada, I find the Alkali Lake First Nations self-determined project one of the most moving and successful of any health promotion projects in the world (Health and Welfare Canada, 1985). The secret of all these projects is to define a community that is of "intermediate" scale—one that is large enough to have good people resources and the ability to develop complex networks on a generic basis but small enough to be a definable "locality" with which people can identify. There is no question for me that these issues can be tackled by a well-organized community development project. This is not to say that the dislocating and fragmenting effects on communities of both internal conflicts between groups and external governmental and other forces are not extremely important for any consideration of community development. As Boutilier et al. point out, they are. But I believe they are not insurmountable, with good community development practice. However, a powerful "vision" of community as a unified cooperative entity is vital for this. Perhaps finding an overarching or "spiritual" basis for bringing a dislocated community together may be the ultimate art and purpose of community development.

The issue here, I believe, is not one of romanticism versus reality. The issue is having a vision that inspires a community and those working with it. This vision needs to ensure that community control, people values, and empowerment are built into every aspect of the project, which then proceeds to work in an all-out way to meet comprehensively the overall needs of that community. I believe it is not the concept of locality development that is at fault but, rather, that it is difficult and slow to take that approach and that it requires a great deal of vision, skill, and commitment to make it succeed.

Obviously, my comments here have been based primarily on a locality development approach to community. The reader could well ask how this applies to issue-based communities such as the gay community or the elderly. And what about communities that do not appear to identify strongly with a locality, such as homeless youth? Clearly, these groupings are extremely important for health promotion. My response is that issue-based groupings, especially those with a political agenda, may perhaps be more fruitfully considered in terms of "group development" or "organizational development." As for groups such as homeless youth—well, even they are usually located in specific areas of cities—a locality has their allegiance at least for the time being. That being the case, one can proceed in a locality development manner with regard to such groupings. In short, then, I see locality development as primary, embodying as it does the archetypal or fundamental ideals of what is meant by "community development."

In summary, then, I feel that Boutilier, Cleverly, and Labonte have provided us with a thoughtful, intelligent chapter, which makes many good points. My major point of difference is with its criticisms of a "romantic" view of community and of locality development. Clearly I feel these have their place in health promotion practice. Locality development is certainly a difficult way to work and is very demanding for those facilitators and community leaders involved. It can easily be subverted as well—I grant that. But once up and running, I believe it is one of the most powerful forces for good in the modern world. No intellectual analysis of its faults will dissuade me from believing that working this way is perhaps the ultimate health promotion activity and a calling of the highest nature.

REFERENCES

Ariyaratne, A. T. (1985). *Collected works* (Vol. 3). Sri Lanka: Sarvodaya Shramadana.

Boyte, H. C. (1989). People power transforms a St. Louis housing project. *Utne Reader, 34,* 46-47.

Chavis, D. M., & Wandersman, A. (1990). Sense of community in the urban environment: A catalyst for participation and community development. *American Journal of Community Psychology, 18,* 55-81.

Durning, A. B. (1989). Grass roots groups are our best hope for global prosperity and ecology. *Utne Reader, 34,* 40-49.

Health & Welfare Canada. (1985). *The honour of all* [Video]. Ottawa, Ontario: Ottawa Health & Welfare.

Mills, R. C. (1990). *Substance abuse. Dropout and delinquent prevention: The Modello/Homestead Gardens Public Housing Early Intervention Project.* Coconut Grove, FL: RC Mills & Associates.

Minkler, M. (1990). Improving health through community organization. In K. Glanz, F. M. Lewis, & B. K. Rimer (Eds.), *Health behavior and health education* (pp. 257-287). San Francisco: Jossey-Bass.

Raeburn, J. M. (1986). Toward a sense of community: Community houses and comprehensive community projects. *Journal of Community Psychology 14,* 391-398.

Rothman, J., & Tropman, J. E. (1987). Models of community organization and macro practice perspectives: Their mixing and phasing. In F. M. Cox, J. L. Erlich, J. Rothman, & J. E. Tropman (Eds.), *Strategies of community organization: Macro-practice* (4th ed., pp. 3-26). Itasca, IL: F. E. Peacock.

Sarason, S. B. (1974). *The psychological sense of community: Prospects for a community psychology.* San Francisco: Jossey-Bass.

Te Roopu Awhina o Tokanui. (1986, September). *Cultural perspectives in psychiatric nursing: A Maori viewpoint.* Paper presented at the Australian Congress of Mental Health Nurses, Twelfth National Convention, Adelaide, Australia.

Tönnies, F. (1955). *Community and association.* Translated and supplemented by C. P. Loomis. London: Routledge and Kegan Paul.

COMMENTARY

Beyond Community Action: Communication Arrangements and Policy Networks

Evelyne de Leeuw

My response to the chapter by Boutilier, Cleverly, and Labonte is not so much a critique as it is an expansion on some of their points and a call for a

AUTHOR'S NOTE: I would like to thank my colleagues Matthew Commer and Marleen Goumans for their help, assistance, and sometimes harsh criticisms on earlier drafts of this piece and Blake Poland for his editorial skills and astute comments.

shift in perspective. First, the notion of *community* will again be problematized. For semantic, etymological, and cultural reasons, I will argue that communities are "communication arrangements," and should be dealt with as such. The introduction of this new conceptualization for the notion of community is not only important to overcome ethno/lingocentrism, but it also more unequivocally links community organization principles with local policy-making endeavors.

The second premise of my commentary is to provide some insights into issues around policy-making in settings for health promotion, with specific reference to communities. Current theoretical insights into policy-making will be briefly described and examined within the framework of the community-organizing models presented by the three authors. Some key barriers in community health policy development will be identified, problems that I argue are particularly relating to fin de siècle communication arrangements in Western industrialized nations.

WHERE IS COMMUNITY?

In their description of problems associated with the use of the term *community*, Boutilier, Cleverly, and Labonte quickly jump to a closely related term: *participation*. They successfully challenge the already somewhat dated notion that (community) participation is a value-free concept with benefits to all. In the following, I will argue that participation does not necessarily constitute the core of community action; in my view, policy, political, and organizational orientations form quintessential characteristics. There is, however, another issue that should be recognized first. This issue is of a semantic nature—that of Anglo-Saxon sociocultural imperialism.

The concept of "community" is hard to translate into many languages. In Dutch, for instance, the most direct and correct translation for the notion expressed by "community" would be *gemeenschap*. However, *gemeenschap* can also mean "sexual intercourse," and is therefore generally avoided in the realm of community health professionals. They try to sidestep the issue by either using the English words ("community projects") or using words that, they feel, best reflect the concept in the Dutch context. Thus, "community" health promotion becomes (a) *buurtgericht gezondheidswerk* (neighborhood health work) or simply (b) *volksgezondheid* (public health)! Evidently, Dutch "communities" are described in terms of localities or in professional terms. The locality-oriented conception (a) is by definition limiting, whereas professional perspectives (b) might not do justice to community dynamics. Similarly, neither German or Finnish, nor many other languages, can properly identify with the Anglo-Saxon conceptualizations around "community."[1]

One might wonder whether communities therefore do not exist outside the Anglo-Saxon world. Certainly they do, but they can have quite different dimensions from those described by Boutilier, Cleverly, and Labonte. The closely knit communities of the past (centering around race, religion, sometimes even sex—the Castro District in San Francisco being a case in point—professional affiliations, miners' villages, etc.) have evolved into less-obvious prominence in Western European welfare states and will, no doubt, become less visible elsewhere, too. These are often replaced by new types of living arrangements, identification networks, peer groups, or whatever these may be called.

The increasing individualization and new communication modalities of the late 20th century in Western societies have created "communities" that challenge the conceptualizations and intervention types that have traditionally been associated (throughout the spectrum described by Boutilier, Cleverly, and Labonte) with "community action."

Either as a consequence of a deliberate wish not to be confined within narrow norms and values of traditional "communities" (think of the emergence of yuppies and dinks in the 1980s—individuals hardly participating in traditional "community" life defined in locality terms) or as a less fortunate consequence of a disrupting social fabric (social exclusion of, e.g., political refugees; single parents without adequate support structures), individualization has put considerable pressure on traditional "community" life. I argue that in the 1990s it is not just living (in the sense of dwelling) arrangements (in terms of spatially defined localities) that determine "communities," but, rather, ways in which people relate to each other.

People have found (and technology has created) new ways to communicate and associate with certain kinds of "communities." Whether television and new media (fax, Internet) are the cause or consequence of new communication patterns within "communities" remains unclear. However, television has created new senses of "community" that cannot be ignored: One Dutch television station (TROS—the Television and Radio Broadcast Corporation) even markets its product with the slogan "The Biggest Family of The Netherlands!" Although this example may remain just a slogan, televised church services in the United States have indeed created nonspatial religious communities. New "communities" pop up on the Internet: Bulletin Boards, listservs, and chat boxes have established sites where users share more than they do within traditional locality-defined "communities." Up-to-date health education endeavors take account of these developments. The move toward individually tailored health education messages (Skinner, Strecher, & Hospers, 1994; Strecher et al., 1994) does not contradict the current adagium that "community" organization is the (only) way forward. This development clearly shows that in the health promotion domain two approaches remain dominant: the "community" approach (whatever kind of "community" is meant) and the individual approach. Here, I do not want to enter into the debate of whether "community" or "individual" approaches are either morally or effectively superior to one another. It is, however, my position that both approaches can be complementary if current social developments are taken into account and if the pitfalls described by Boutilier, Cleverly, and Labonte are avoided.

One successful example of linking individualized health advice with a community perspective is found in Tokyo. To counteract decreasing mobility of the elderly (for a range of reasons: fear of going out, physical limits, reduced family ties, etc.), Tokyo Healthy City established, together with an association of elderly people, a program by videophone (telephone with view screen). Each day, a group of elderly people contacts a Tokyo Healthy City office for a chat and physiotherapeutical exercises. The physiotherapist, using this new technology, can address the group as a whole but also participants individually. In this way, the benefits of group work (a "community!") are combined with individual support and counseling.

To conclude this section, here is yet another, but crucial, semantic observation. Television religious parishes, Internet sites, and the like, are often referred to as "virtual communities." To the people participating in these "communities," however, these contacts are very real. *Virtual*, when used in this sense, almost acquires a derogatory connotation. It should be recognized by health promotion academics and practitioners that these communication arrangements are as real and challenging as more traditional arrangements (Milio, 1996); in the light of modernity, they are a natural evolution. To many "virtual communities," nothing is more real! The distinction between "real" and "virtual" communities thus turns out to be superficial. A "community" can be established as being "real" as soon as it affects the thoughts and behavior of those who feel they belong to that "community"—even in cyberspace.

It is worth noting that the etymological roots of *community* and *communication* are the same. To communicate is to pass on, to share and exchange, and to connect. If these verbs constitute the reasons people identify with a certain "community," whereas at the same time the word *community* itself is such a difficult concept in languages other than English, and virtual "communities" are indeed real communities, it is my proposition to simply define *community* as "communication arrangement." So what, one is tempted to comment, yet another obscure delineation . . .

I believe that "communication" is semantically a more unequivocal notion than "community." If understood as a process beyond (social) psychological interaction but as a function of group dynamics, "communication" seems to do justice to all notions of traditional, "real," "virtual," spatially, or belief-grounded communities, without having to use the specific Anglo-Saxon concept. Furthermore, *arrangement* would refer to some kind of (self-) organized order that Boutilier, Cleverly, and Labonte justly imply to be associated with community action.

The introduction of communication arrangement to replace the more ambiguous community is further supported by comments by McLeroy, Bibeau, Steckler, and Glanz (1988). They find that communities are (a) mediating structures or face-to-face primary groups, (b) relationships among organizations and groups within a defined area, and (c) geopolitical constructs, but they fail to introduce a unifying concept for the three distinct meanings of community.

POLICY FORMULATION FOR "COMMUNITY ACTION"

The sustainability of community organization is problematic. Simplifying to the extreme, projects die when academics and professionals leave (social planning approaches) and empowerment is lost due to institutionalization (locality development models). Social action perspectives require an uncommon flexibility and recognition of social dynamics, specifically on the part of (but not limited to) funding agency and staff.

The question is whether fixed-term projects can evolve into longer-term policies. The central idea is that most health promotion endeavors suffer from "projectism" (Goumans, 1997). However well intended and effective most health promotion projects are or could be, they hardly constitute bases for well-rooted public or private policies,[2] because they remain projects, with a fixed beginning, a fixed ending, specified funding for the project period, and prerequisite conditions that do not necessarily contribute to integration and institutionalization into broader policy frameworks (apart from the obligatory rhetoric by most governments that health promotion and disease prevention form constituent parts of the [national] health policy package). Broad implementation, based on conscientious policy considerations, of interventions that have been proven effective and lasting is still rare (e.g., Paulussen, 1994).

The Ottawa Charter for Health Promotion specifically includes the development of Healthy Public Policies. Although health education and health promotion professionals and academics pay their obligatory lip-services to policy development, their understanding of the intricacies of policy-making is generally naive and does not take into account the wealth of theory development in the realm of political and policy science (I would point to Mullen et al., 1995, as an example of such naïveté, insofar as their article treats policy development as a mere phase in the health education planning process).

A theme issue of *Health Education Quarterly* devoted to policy advocacy (Schwartz, Goodman, & Steckler, 1995) even fully lacks any reference to the broad body of knowledge developed in the academic domain of political science.

The main thesis of this chapter is that a more compelling view of policy-making places it at the heart of community action. Milio (1986) asserts that public policy sets and limits the options for individuals, groups, and communities to lead a healthy life. A decade later, she continues the argument, clarifying the involvement of individuals, groups, and communities in policy development (Milio, 1996). Generally problematic issues in policy development are constituted by one major question: Who determines which policy is to be formulated?

The WHO Healthy Cities Project has recognized this question. Tsouros (1994) asserted, "The WHO Healthy Cities project is a long-term international development project that seeks to put health on the agenda of decision-makers in the cities of Europe and to build a strong lobby for public health at the local level." WHO obviously assumes that agenda status would lead to policy development and lasting political attention for health. The social action agenda presented by Boutilier, Cleverly, and Labonte would contribute to this objective through its "more proximate goals of group empowerment, political capacity and resource mobilization."

Although Boutilier, Cleverly, and Labonte recognize that "the health promotion practice of each [of the three arenas of practice] is often inextricably influenced by that of the other two," their argument does not do justice to the role of policy formulation and implementation in community action. It is my position that (at least debates around) policy issues are at the core of community action.

Policy development is traditionally seen as a top-down, linear, and planned endeavor. Even authors with the best intent to strengthen community action for health have regarded policy-making as essentially a role of the health promotion professional (McLeroy et al., 1988). According to them, the professional should act as a policy developer, policy advocate, and policy analyst. This view of such an also esoteric and elitist process does not necessarily lead to community involvement in policy development.

Fortunately, policy and political scientists now recognize that this process is more intricate, dynamic, and iterative. Recent studies on policy agendas (Kingdon, 1995; Laumann & Knoke, 1987) and policy-making configurations (Goumans, 1995a, 1995b; Marin & Mayntz, 1991; Scharpf, 1990) show a remarkable match with processes occurring in social action programs. In the following, this compatibility and its challenges will be described in some detail.

Some modern political scientists have observed that (the public and official perception of) the role of the state in policy formulation has been transformed. Various new phrases have been coined to describe this transformed role; governments themselves now talk of "public-private partnerships" or "retreating government"; philosophers take "constructivist" or "neocorporatist" perspectives; and policy academics have started to talk of "policy networks."

Whatever the role of a retreating government or the configuration in which policy is debated (top-down, bottom-up, hub-wheel, web, or network), "communities" play a role in policy development. Apart from being potentially important political constituencies, they also constitute the quintessential domain in which social agendas are formed. In the following, I will also briefly review shifts in policy development theories. My purpose is to show that "community" organization shares important phases and elements with the policy process, and that acknowledgment of these shared values may shed light on the advancement of communication arrangement programs.

AGENDA BUILDING

Why do some issues become problematic and others not? Why are some "communities" better able to structure the policy agenda than others? Why are some policies formulated almost matter-of-factly, whereas it takes others years of debate to materialize? These questions are addressed by policy scientists interested in agenda building.

Three perspectives can be distinguished: I would label them the more romantic (Cobb & Elder, 1983), the more cynical and power oriented (Laumann & Knoke, 1987), and the pragmatic/social interactionist (Kingdon, 1995). Cobb and Elder (1983) regard agenda building (the question of why some issues are considered problematic and require policy solutions) as essentially a democratic exercise in which public perceptions of problems, and the expansion of these problematic perceptions from smaller identification groups to larger publics, determine agenda access. The strategy, they propose, to move an issue from the systemic (societal) to the institutional (political) agenda (called issue expansion), is to present it as equivocal, with high social relevance, without historical precedents, relevant over a longer period, and as a nontechnocratic one. This is generally done through the use of symbolism and metaphors. One should bear in mind that issues are never "objectively" problematic, but always perceived to be such: They are constructed and manipulated by stakeholders to mobilize other publics. "Communities" depending on their degree of organization and capabilities to identify with problematic issues, play important roles in agenda building toward policy status.

Laumann and Knoke (1987) take another starting point. Policy-making, in their view, is largely a corporate endeavor. In their study of policy developments in the U.S. energy and health domains, they found that the better corporate actors are able to monitor each other's and government's actions, the better they are able to influence the policy agenda to their advantage. Laumann and Knoke see hardly any relevance in "community" action when it comes to policy development, although their argument may have power-based implications at the "community" level.

The most recent insight into agenda building is provided by Kingdon (1995). This perspective, in my view, is the most realistic and yet the least tangible of the three. Kingdon proposes that in each policy realm there are three more or less independent streams: problems, policies, and politics. Problems are always there, he maintains, and are only there to be found by their solutions. Policies, and attempts to produce policies, are in constant flux as well. Politics are determined by elective terms and continuity of political positions. Finally, there are all kinds of visible and less visible participants in problems, policies, and politics. The trick is to open a "window of opportunity" between the three. Generally, this is done by a (small group of) social entrepreneur(s) (Duhl, 1995) capable of linking a preferred solution to a set of problems, policies, and participants. The social entrepreneur, then, is able to show the "opportunistic" advantages involved in effective agenda building. Goumans (1997) has shown that this is exactly the reason why city administrations have joined the international Healthy Cities movement; it is rarely "health" that has put Healthy City on the municipal agenda but the capability of one social entrepreneur to move existing problems, policies, and participants toward the Healthy City ideology as an opportunistic way of dealing with a number of issues, ranging from environment and employment to housing and community development.

In Table 7.2, some characteristics of community organization models and agenda-building perspectives are summarized. I have attempted to take critical elements in agenda building, and confront three theoretical perspectives with the three community organization models. Naturally, this is a crude analysis because there is no academic or practical documentation available in which community organization endeavors have been developed while consciously using any of these theoretical perspectives. Also, the empiricism provided by Boutilier, Cleverly, and Labonte had to be translated, somewhat superficially, into agenda-building elements.

However, it is obvious that there is only a limited match between the social planning model and either of the three agenda-building perspectives. On the other hand, the pragmatic view of agenda building (Kingdon) seems to best connect with both locality development and social action models. My (tentative) finding is, therefore, that current theoretical and empirical insights into agenda building indicate that locality development and social action organization schemes best reflect political and policy realities.

Table 7.2 Some Core Characteristics of Community Organization Models and Policy Agenda-Building Perspectives

| | Community Organization Model | | | Agenda-Building Authors | | |
	Social Planning	Locality Development	Social Action	Cobb & Elder	Laumann & Knoke	Kingdon
Element						
Initiation of agenda-building process by . . .	Authority	Authority and client	"Community"	"Issue identification group"	Corporate actor or government agency	Social entrepreneur
Strategy to expand program from primary stakeholders to others:	Academic ("expert") centered	Client, facilitated by "expert" consultation	"Community" politicizing issues	Symbolic communication aimed at perception change	Counterpart communication monitoring; preserving power base	Opportunism: seizing the moment
Implementation	Guided and predetermined	Interactive within prerequisite general frame	Social-interactive	Through expansion from inner to outer "publics"	Through proactive corporate risk reduction	Through reconceptualization and linkage of actors and events

295

An issue that might seem rather confronting is that the corporate power perspective of agenda building does not, as yet, seem to find a match with any community organization model. There is a challenge here. Community organizers would have to recognize that talk of public-private partnerships, civil society, and building new alliances (WHO, 1996) in fact creates new opportunities for communities. Taking account of the findings by Laumann and Knoke (1987) may well increase the efficacy of community activities; this would mean that social entrepreneurs (or community leaders or those with "vested" interests in communication arrangements) would recognize the need for, and opportunities in, partnerships with corporate actors.

POLICY NETWORKS

Policy science in the past has involved itself mainly in *why* and *what* questions and less in *who* issues (de Leeuw, 1993). The reason for this limited view was the idea that, in essence, government was considered a black box that would direct policy-making in a unilateral and temporally linear way. Making policy was regarded by political scientists, but particularly by local and national governments, as a process of establishing goals and objectives, setting time frames, and determining the instruments that could be employed to achieve these goals within the time frame (de Leeuw, 1989). Of course, the primary actor was the policymaker par excellence: the government bureaucracy. It was assumed that through clever deployment of instruments that government had available (regulatory, facilitative, and communicative control and steering), policies could be made effective. Partly because of better insights into the art of policy-making by academia, partly because of—almost paradigmatic—shifts in the perception of the role of government, the *who* question became more prominent.

Kenis and Schneider (1991) present the assumptions of the policy network approach:

> The mechanical view of the world established the idea of linear causality explaining social states and events as determined by external forces. The big-organic perspective shaped the notion of functional causality in which societal subsystems contribute to prerequisites and needs of a global social organism. Both the mechanical and biological world pictures conceived systemness and societal control as something beyond individual actors. Essentially, this perspective is changed in the network perspective of society. The core of this perspective is a decentralized concept of social organization and governance: society is no longer exclusively controlled by a central intelligence (e.g., the State); rather, controlling devices are dispersed and intelligence is distributed among a multiplicity of action (or "processing") units. The co-ordination of these action units is no longer the result of "central steering" or some kind of

"pre-estabilished harmony" but emerges through the purposeful interactions of individual actors, who themselves are enabled for parallel action by exchanging information and other relevant resources.[3] (p. 26)

Table 7.3 summarizes some core characteristics of the community organization perspectives and policy-making views. Again, I do not hope to provide a rigorous analytical framework here, because, once more, community organization models have not been documented in terms of these policy model elements. Yet juxtapositioning these ideas will provide insight into the potential roles of communication arrangements (and various models in communication arrangement organization) in policy development theories.

When confronting the different models, it is clear that the social planning model follows lines that Kenis and Schneider would have labeled mechanistic and "big-organic" and that are not consonant with policy perspectives of the 1990s.

It should be noted, however, that many local political administrations have not yet recognized (or have limited capacities to associate themselves with) the networking perspective. The traditional policy model clearly has a fit with social planning, whereas networking perspectives are not necessarily incompatible with either of the three community organization models. Nevertheless, in more ideological (and idiosyncratic) terms, policy networking clearly is more easily associated with the more libertarian and empowering perspectives of locality development and social action. In the conclusion, I will further argue that the networking view yields promising prospects for the further development of communication arrangements.

CONCLUSION: COMMUNITIES AND POLICIES

I have identified "communities" as communication arrangements. The discussion of agenda-building and policy-making perspectives shows that such a juxtaposition opens up new opportunities in forging more unequivocal links between community organization and policy making.

Effective strategies for health and social change, we have found, constitute a link between particularly (a) locality development and (b) social action models within community organization on the one side, and (a) the social-interactive view of agenda building and (b) policy networks on the other. Theoretically, the most important feature of the policy perspectives that I have provided is their emphasis on communication. In agenda building, communication is used either to convince wider realms of "publics" that an issue is legitimate or—more blatantly—to monitor actions and intents of (competitive) stakeholders in the domain. The social-interactive model even entirely relies on flexible and relevant communication patterns.

TABLE 7.3 Some Core Characteristics of Community Organization Models and Policy Development Perspectives

	Community Organization Model			Policy Model	
Element	Social Planning	Locality Development	Social Action	Traditional	Network
Problem statement in operational terms established by . . .	Authority	Authority and client	"Community"	Authority	Network
Intervention development by . . .	Academic ("expert")	Client, facilitated by "expert"	"Community," determining need for involvement of "expert"	Authority, using operational "agents" (academic, other)	Multilateral network linkages
Funding by/ through . . . , Consequences	Authority, under specific conditions	Miscellaneous sources, unstable	Low or zero budget, internal generation of monies	Authority, under specific conditions	Network partners
Sustainability of action	Limited, often none as soon as "experts" leave	Limited, depending on degree of social empowerment and community identification with issue	Uncertain, depending on social and political skills acquired	Limited, depending on political terms of office and agendas	Depending on degree of shared institutionalizaiton and identification with program

The network perspective on policy development assumes that network actors are enabled for parallel action by exchanging information and other resources. Adequate communication and meting out of intelligence have thus become essential. In the policy network, we would find communication arrangements ("communities"), but other types of actors as well (corporate players, institutionalized nongovernmental agencies, partisan but nongovernment related action committees, etc.). They will compete for access to the network. If communication capabilities are truly determining effective participation in policy networks, then organization models for "communities" should more rigorously and in a planned manner focus on the importance of communication.

It is worth noting that these findings are fully consistent with core characteristics of the Ottawa Charter. Its crucial action modalities are mediation, advocacy, and enablement. These three require an understanding and application of horizontal communication (as opposed to vertical communication—"telling people what to do," in educational science also referred to as "frontal learning" as opposed to "problem-based learning"). My observations on the importance of communication capabilities seem to validate the legitimacy of the Ottawa Charter and its perspective on health promotion. "Health promotion" is still perceived in many circles as "turbo health education" (traditional health behavior modification), whereas the Ottawa Charter has attempted to broaden the perception of health promotion into organizational, political, environmental, and health services domains. My review of policy approaches and "community" organization has presented arguments for such an extended view. Policymakers, social entrepreneurs, local politicians, and even academics should more consciously employ this view. Their role in the organization and development of communication arrangements is crucial, but not decisive: Ultimately, the participants in communication arrangements would have the opportunity and responsibility to control determinants of their health and quality of life. A policy perspective on that process is a helpful asset.

NOTES

1. Because this contribution by necessity should be phrased in English, I will continue using *community,* but in quotation marks to denote the problematic nature of the word. The argument will continue to deal with various old and new "community" conceptualizations.

2. Policy is the expressed intent of an institution (government, corporation, volunteer group, etc.) to act strategically toward the attainment of specified goals.

3. Although space does not allow us to enter into the debate on whether the network perspective is yet another "belief system" or paradigm that does or does not do justice to the realities of social action in general, and to policy-making in particular, it is noteworthy that the perspective within a decade had acquired a large following, both in academia as well as in policy-making circles and politics, for whatever reasons.

REFERENCES

Cobb, R., & Elder, C. (1983). *Participation in American politics: The dynamics of agenda building.* Baltimore: John Hopkins University Press.

de Leeuw, E. (1989). *Health policy.* Maastricht, The Netherlands: Savannah.

de Leeuw, E. (1993). Health policy, epidemiology and power: The interest web. *Health Promotion International, 8*(1), 49-52.

Duhl, L. (1995). *The social entrepreneurship of change.* New York: Pace University Press.

Goumans, M. (1995a). An ecological perspective on the health of a city—The Healthy City project of the WHO. In European Academy of the Urban Environment (Ed.), *Prospects for climate-oriented planning in European cities* (pp. 19-24). Berlin: EAUE.

Goumans, M. (1995b). Putting concepts into (health) policy practice. In N. Bruce, J. Springett, J. Hotchkiss, & A. Scott-Samuel (Eds.), *Research and change in urban community health* (pp. 327-338). Brookfield, VT: Aldershot.

Goumans, M. (1997). *Structuring unstructured policy processes: Healthy cities in the Netherlands and Britain.* Doctoral dissertation, University of Limburg, Maastricht.

Kenis, P., & Schneider, V. (1991). Policy networks and policy analysis: Scrutinizing a new analytical toolbox. In B. Marm & R. Mayntz (Eds.), *Policy networks: Empirical evidence and theoretical considerations* (pp. 25-59). Boulder, CO: Westview.

Kingdon, J. (1995). *Agendas, alternatives and public policies* (2nd ed). New York: Harper Collins College.

Laumann, E., & Knoke, D. (1987). *The organizational state.* Madison: University of Wisconsin Press.

Marin, B., & Mayntz, R. (Eds.). (1991). *Policy networks. Empirical evidence and theoretical considerations.* Boulder, CO: Westview.

McLeroy, K. R., Bibeau, D., Steckler, A., & Glanz, K. (1988). An ecological perspective on health promotion programs. *Health Education Quarterly, 15*(4), 351-377.

Milio, N. (1986). *Promoting health through public policy.* Ottawa, Ontario: Canadian Public Health Association.

Milio, N. (1996). *Engines of empowerment: Using information technology to create healthy communities and challenge public policy.* Ann Arbor, MI: Health Administration Press.

Mullen, P. D., Evans, D., Forster, J., Gottlieb, N. H., Kreuter, M., Moon, R., O'Rourke, T., & Strecher, V. J. (1995). Settings as an important dimension in health education/promotion policy, programs, and research. *Health Education Quarterly, 22*(3), 329-345.

Paulussen, T. G. W. (1994). *Adoption and implementation of AIDS education in Dutch secondary schools.* Utrecht: National Centre for Health Education & Promotion.

Scharpf, F. W. (1990). *Games real actors could play: The problem of connectedness* (MPIFG Discussion Paper 90/8). Köln, Germany: Max-Planck-Institut fur Gesellschaftsforschung.

Schwartz, R., Goodman, R., & Steckler, A. (Eds.). (1995). Policy advocacy interventions for health promotion and education [Special issue]. *Health Education Quarterly, 22*(4).

Skinner, C. S., Strecher, V. J., & Hospers, H. J. (1994). Physician recommendations for mammography: Do tailored messages make a difference? *American Journal of Public Health, 84,* 43-49.

Strecher, V. J., Kreuter, M., Den Boer, D. J., Kobrin, S., Hospers, H. J., & Skinner, C. S. (1994). The effects of computer-tailored smoking cessation messages in family practice settings. *Journal of Family Practice, 39,* 262-268.

Tsouros, A. (1994). *The WHO Healthy Cities Project: State of the art and future plans.* Copenhagen: WHO/EURO/HCPO.

World Health Organization. (1996). *The ninth general programme of work.* Geneva: Author.

ADDENDUM

Social Capital, Social Cohesion, Community Capacity,
and Community Empowerment: Variations on a Theme?

Blake D. Poland

In recent years, much of the same conceptual terrain invoked by concepts of community and by practices of community development has been elaborated in constructs such as social capital (Berger, 1998; Caledon Institute, 1996; Evans, 1996; Furstenberg & Hughes, 1995; Kawachi, Kennedy, & Lochener, 1997; Kawachi, Kennedy, Lochener, & Prothrow-Stith, 1997; Kennedy, Kawachi, Prothrow-Stith, & Gupta, 1998; Leeder, 1998; Lomas, 1998; Mustard, 1996; Putnam, 1993, 1995, 1996; Putnam, Leonardi, & Nanetti, 1993), social cohesion (Jenson, 1998; Organization for Economic Cooperation and Development [OECD], 1997), community capacity and community competence (Cottrell, 1983; Dedrick et al., 1994; Eng & Parker, 1994; Freudenberg et al., 1995; Goeppinger & Baglioni, 1985; Jackson et al., 1997; McKnight, 1987), and community empowerment (Eng et al., 1992; Israel, Checkoway, Schulz, & Zimmerman, 1994; Wallerstein, 1992). These are often ambiguous, even contested, concepts, which have risen in prominence since Boutilier, Cleverly, and Labonte first drafted their chapter. Only the most cursory of introductions to each is offered below, to build on the thorough discussion they have already provided regarding the community as a setting for health promotion.

The construct of "social capital" is most often associated with the work of Robert Putnam (Putnam, 1995, 1996; Putnam et al., 1993). In detailed empirical comparison of northern and southern Italy (Putnam et al., 1993), social capital was conceptualized in terms of density of associational membership (or civic engagement/civic participation), levels of interpersonal trust, and norms of reciprocity (mutual aid). Social capital, although frequently measured at the individual level (survey research), can be distinguished from the social capital accumulated as a resource by individuals as described by Coleman (1988) or Bourdieu (Wacquant, 1996). To quote Kawachi, Kennedy, Lochener, and Prothrow-Stith (1997), "The aspect of social capital that makes it a classic public good is its property of nonexcludability; that is, its benefits are available to all living within a particular community, and access to it cannot be restricted" (p. 1496). The possibilities for understanding

AUTHOR'S NOTE: I would like to acknowledge the contribution of the Critical Social Science in Health Group in the Department of Public Health Sciences, University of Toronto, for ongoing group discussion, which has contributed to my thinking about these issues.

the intricate interrelationships between social capital as a public good (as understood in the literature cited above) and social capital as an individual or social group/social class asset (as understood by Bourdieu and others) do not appear to have been extensively explored by those in the health field interested in social capital. Bourdieu's concept of "habitus," his extensive field research on the elaborate exchange systems of the Kabyla in North Africa (arguably rich in social capital in a Putnamian sense), and his conceptualization of social capital as a resource in the struggle by social groups to claim distinction (a form of social exclusion) offer some intriguing opportunities for a more rigorous sociological understanding of the concept of social capital and the relationship between individuals, social groups, and "the community."

Putnam's research led him to believe that social capital is an essential lubricant for effective social and political institutions and for economic prosperity. He has subsequently also argued that social capital is on the decline in the United States (Putnam, 1995, 1996), although this has been disputed by others (Greeley, 1997; Strengal, 1996; see also Harriss & de Renzio, 1997; Heying, 1997; Lemann, 1996; Levi, 1996; and Tarrow, 1996, for critical reviews of Putnam's work). The concept of social capital has been invoked by Ichiro Kawachi, Bruce Kennedy, and Richard Wilkinson to explain the association between income inequality and aggregate mortality rates (Kawachi, Kennedy, & Lochener, 1997; Kawachi, Kennedy, Lochener, & Prothrow-Stith, 1997; Wilkinson et al., 1998). Specifically, they claim that "disinvestment in social capital appears to be one of the pathways through which growing income inequality exerts its effects on population-level mortality" (Kawachi, Kennedy, Lochener, & Prothrow-Stith, 1997, p. 1495).

Kawachi et al. use the terms *social capital* and *social cohesion* interchangeably as if they were more or less synonymous. Elsewhere, it is argued that "social cohesion is the outcome of robust social capital" (Maxwell, 1996, cited in Jensen, 1998, p. 27). Jensen (1998) maintains that the constituent dimensions of social cohesion include belonging/isolation, inclusion/exclusion, participation/noninvolvement, recognition/rejection (of difference), and legitimacy/illegitimacy (of public and private institutions that mediate value conflicts or provide a space for this to happen). Noting the widespread definition of social cohesion as "shared values and commitment to a community," she questions the necessity of either shared values (i.e., consensus, as opposed to capacity to manage dissensus) or commitment to a community (civic pride or nationalism, depending on the scale at which community is defined) to a definition of social cohesion. In her comprehensive and insightful "mapping" of the conceptual terrain, she argues that recent interest in social cohesion must be understood in the context of fears and concerns about the disintegration of civic society in an era of globalization and neoliberal social and economic policy, which broadly mirror historically cyclical concerns with social order in periods of rapid social (economic) upheaval. Drawing on the relevant work of functionalist (consensus-oriented) and conflict theorists, she demonstrates the divergent orientations of those whose emphasis is on the well-being and conduct of individuals in local settings and those whose emphasis is on the nature of broader social structures and interests. The policy and intervention implications of these divergent interpretations can be far-reaching.

Like social capital, the concept of community capacity is meant to refer to aspects of civic society that enable individual and collective action (community development). Framed in terms of aggregate resources, skills, knowledge, and abilities to act, capacities are seen as embodying the positive attributes of communities—the latent strengths on which communities (and those hired to work with communities) can draw to effect change, while avoiding the pitfalls of naming communities by their deficits, which is so often the result of traditional exercises in "needs assessment" (McKnight, 1987). Kretzman and McKnight (1993) have developed a mapping exercise to create an inventory of "skills information," "community skills," and "enterprising interests and experience" as a basis for community work (for application examples, see Dedrick et al., 1994). Jackson et al. (1997) define community capacity as comprising community capabilities (aggregate of individual endowments plus community-level endowments) and socioenvironmental conditions that include facilitating factors and barriers to the realization of community capabilities as capacities (funding, negative labeling by others, presence of supportive public or private institutions, etc.). In seeking to specify clearly the conditions under which community capacities are realized and flourish or are suppressed, this model has the advantage of avoiding some of the victim blaming that can accrue from models that construe capacity primarily in terms of individual and collective attributes.

Some of the literature on capacity building draws on the closely related concept of community competence (Eng & Parker, 1994; Iscoe, 1974) and the work of Cottrell (1976), in which eight dimensions of community competence are identified: participation, commitment, self-other awareness and clarity of situational definitions, articulateness, conflict containment and accommodation, management of relations with wider society, machinery for facilitating participant interaction and decision making, and social support. Another closely related term, *community empowerment* (as distinct from individual empowerment) has been defined as a social action process that promotes participation of people, who are in positions of perceived and actual powerlessness, toward goals of increased individual and community decision making and control, equity of resources, and improved quality of life (Wallerstein, 1992; see also Mondros & Wilson, 1994).

It can be said that, in the final analysis, each of these constructs is concerned with the strength and vibrancy of civic society. This in turn reflects ongoing interest in the maintenance of social order (Jensen, 1998). Critical differences of opinion reflect, in part, the extent to which the "problem of social (dis)order" is seen as resting primarily on the "civic-ness" of citizens (social trust, civic engagement, norms of reciprocity, shared values) and on what conditions foster civic-mindedness. The issue of social capital can be cast in terms of a moral economy of interdependence (see Robertson, 1998, 1999), or in terms of the creation and maintenance of moral order in the tradition of the "communitarian" writings of Etzioni (1993), or Lerner's "politics of meaning." These and other commentators differ in the extent to which they view civic society as being (more or less) distinct from the market or the state, although the precise nature of the relationships between these three broad entities are seldom fully explicated, including the relationship of local to extra-local structures and processes. Specifically, they differ in the extent to which they acknowledge the central importance of the institutions of the state (see Evans, 1996; Heller, 1996; Jensen, 1998) and of the market itself in setting the conditions in which social cohesion flourishes, community capacities are realized and built on, and social capital is accumulated—or conversely, setting the conditions under neoliberal discourse in which divestment of social capital is accelerated in the name of supplicating to economic globalization. These conditions can be said to include (but are not limited to) the mediation of (value and resource) conflicts in an increasingly pluralistic society (Jensen, 1998), the provision of "guarantees embedded in the social safety net" (Maxwell, 1996, p. 14-15, cited in Jenson, 1998), and more generally support for, and the vibrancy of, the "commons" or public sphere (see Boggs, 1997; Fisher, 1996). To the extent that the role of the state (and the market) is overlooked in this regard, it is likely that attention to social cohesion, social capital, community capacity, and community empowerment will result in calls for a variety of community development initiatives intended to (re)build civic society, at the expense of adequate attention being given to the fundamental processes of social exclusion embedded in neoliberal economic and social policy and in capitalism itself, which create and sustain the growing inequities which in turn are thought to be destructive of social capital, social cohesion, and community capacity. This underscores the observation that seemingly progressive concerns about social capital and social cohesion, community capacity and community empowerment—insofar as community is romanticized and a localized response advocated to what are arguably much broader social, economic, and political forces—may contain powerful regressive implications by focusing attention away from issues of equality and social justice and by shifting responsibility for economic development, health, and social care to the voluntary/third sector, to be mostly absorbed by poorly paid or unpaid female labor (see Bullock, 1990; Dixon, 1989; Jensen, 1998). This is not to deny the fundamental importance of citizen participation in meaningful grassroots initiatives but, rather, to question the implicit social ontology and social analysis underlying recent enthusiasm for concepts such as social capital and social cohesion—as well as the political (and economic) agendas that are served, intentionally or otherwise, by particular framings of the issues. It is, in short, a call for a deepening of the social (and political) analysis vis-à-vis the questions, Why these concepts? Why now?

REFERENCES

Berger, P. (Ed.). (1998). *The limits of social cohesion: Conflict and mediation in pluralist societies: A report of the Bertelsmann Foundation to the Club of Rome.* Boulder, CO: Westview.

Boggs, C. (1997). The great retreat: Decline of the public sphere in late twentieth-century America. *Theory and Society, 26*(6), 741-780.

Bullock, A. (1990). Community care: Ideology and lived experience. In R. Ng, G. Walker, & J. Muller (Eds.), *Community organization and the Canadian state.* Toronto: Garamond.

Caledon Institute of Social Policy. (1996). *Sustainable social policy and community capital* (Session proceedings). Ottawa, Ontario: Author.

Coleman, J. S. (1988). Social capital in the creation of human capital. *American Journal of Sociology, 94,* S95-S120.

Cottrell, L. S. J. (1976). The competent community. In B. H. Kaplan, R. N. Wilson, & A. A. Leighton (Eds.), *Further explorations in social psychiatry.* New York: Basic Books.

Cottrell, L. S. (1983). The competent community. In R. Warren & L. Lyon (Eds.), *New perspectives on the American community.* Homewood, IL: Dorsey.

Dedrick, A., Mitchell, G., & Roberts, S. (1994). *Community capacity building and asset mapping: Model development.* Edmonton, Alberta: Community Development Caritas.

Dixon, J. (1989). The limits and potential of community development for personal and social change. *Community Health Studies, 13*(1), 82-92.

Eng, E., & Parker, E. (1994). Measuring community competence in the Mississippi delta: The interface between program evaluation and empowerment. *Health Education Quarterly, 21*(2), 199-220.

Eng, E., Salmon, M. E., & Mullan, F. (1992). Community empowerment: The critical base for primary health care. *Family and Community Health, 15*(1), 1-12.

Etzioni, A. (1993). *The spirit of community: The reinvention of American society.* Toronto: Touchstone.

Evans, P. (1996). Government action, social capital and development: Reviewing the evidence on synergy. *World Development, 24*(6), 1119-1132.

Fisher, R. (1996, September). *Community and public life in a private world.* Paper presented at the Conference on Defining Community, Reexamining Society, University of Michigan—Flint.

Freudenberg, N., Eng, E., Flay, B., Parcel, G., Rogers, T., & Wallerstein, N. (1995). Strengthening individual and community capacity to prevent disease and promote health: In search of relevant theories and principles. *Health Education Quarterly, 22*(3), 290-306.

Furstenberg, F. F., & Hughes, M. E. (1995). Social capital and successful development among at risk youth. *Journal of Marriage and the Family, 57,* 580-592.

Goeppinger, J., & Baglioni, A. J. (1985). Community competence: A positive approach to needs assessment. *American Journal of Community Psychology, 13,* 507-523.

Greeley, A. (1997). *The strange reappearance of civic America: Religion and volunteering.* Retrieved July 8, 1999, at http://www.agreeley.com/articles/civic.html

Harriss, J., & de Renzio, P. (1997). "Missing link" or analytically missing? The concept of social capital. *Journal of International Development, 9,* 919-937.

Heller, P. (1996). Social capital as a product of class mobilization and state intervention: Industrial workers in Kerala, India. *World Development, 24*(6), 1055-1071.

Heying, C. H. (1997). Civic elites and corporate delocalization: An alternative explanation for declining civic engagement. Retrieved July 8, 1999, at http://www.upa.pdx.edu/Faculty/Heying/civelite.htm

Iscoe, I. (1974, August). Community psychology and the competent community. *American Psychologist, 607-613.*

Israel, B. A., Checkoway, B., Schulz, A., & Zimmerman, M. (1994). Health education and community empowerment: Conceptualizing and measuring perceptions of individual, organizational and community control. *Health Education Quarterly, 21*(2), 149-170.

Jackson, S. F., Cleverly, S., Poland, B., Robertson, A., Burman, D., Goodstadt, M., & Salsberg, L. (1997). *Half full or half empty? Concepts and research design for a study of indicators of community capacity.* North York, Ontario: North York Community Health Promotion Research Unit.

Jensen, J. (1998). *Mapping social cohesion: The state of Canadian research.* Ottawa, Ontario: Canadian Policy Research Network.

Kawachi, I., & Kennedy, B. P. (1997). Health and social cohesion: Why care about income inequality. *British Medical Journal, 314,* 1037-1040.

Kawachi, I., Kennedy, B. P., & Lochener, K. (1997, November-December). Long live community: Social capital as public health. *The American Prospect, 35,* 56-59.

Kawachi, I., Kennedy, B. P., Lochener, K., & Prothrow-Stith, D. (1997). Social capital, income inequality, and mortality. *American Journal of Public Health, 87*(9), 1491-1498.

Kennedy, B. P., Kawachi, I., Prothrow-Stith, D., & Gupta, V. (1998). Social capital, income inequality, and firearm violent crime. *Social Science and Medicine, 47*(1), 7-17.

Kretzman, J., & McKnight, J. (1993). *Building communities from the inside out: A path toward finding and mobilizing a community's assets.* Evanston, IL: Northwestern University, Center for Urban Affairs & Policy Research, Neighborhood Innovations Network.

Leeder, S. (1998). *Social capital and its relevance to health and family policy.* Retrieved July 8, 1999, at http://www.pha.org.au/social.htm

Lemann, N. (1996). Kicking in groups. *Atlantic Monthly.* Retrieved July 8, 1999, at http://www.theAtlantic.com/atlantic/issues/96apr/kicking/kicking.htm

Lerner, M. (1996). Twelve points of unity for the politics of meaning. *Tikkun, 11*(4), 26-32.

Levi, M. (1996). Social and unsocial capital: A review essay of Robert Putnam's *Making Democracy Work. Politics & Society, 24*(1), 45-55.

Lomas, J. (1998). Social capital and health: Implications for public health and epidemiology. *Social Science and Medicine, 47*(9), 1181-1188.

McKnight, J. (1987). *The future of low-income neighborhoods and the people who reside there: A capacity-oriented strategy for neighborhood development.* Evanston, IL: Northwestern University, Center for Urban Affairs & Policy Research, Neighborhood Innovations Network.

Mondros, J., & Wilson, W. (1994). *Organizing for power and empowerment.* New York: Columbia University Press.

Mustard, F. (1996). Health and social capital. In D. Blane, E. Brunner, & R. Wilkinson (Eds.), *Health and social organization: Towards a health policy for the twenty-first century* (pp. 303-313). New York: Routledge.

Organization for Economic Cooperation and Development. (1997). *Societal cohesion and the globalizing economy: What does the future hold?* Washington, DC: Author.

Putnam, R. D. (1993). The prosperous community: Social capital and public life. *American Prospect, 13,* 35-42.

Putnam, R. (1995). Bowling alone: America's declining social capital. *Journal of Democracy, 6*(1), 65-78.

Putnam, R. (1996). The strange disappearance of civic America. In R. Kuttner (Ed.), *Ticking time bombs: The new conservative assaults on democracy* (pp. 263-282). New York: New Press.

Putnam, R. D., Leonardi, R., & Nanetti, R. Y. (1993). *Making democracy work: Civic traditions in modern Italy.* Princeton, NJ: Princeton University Press.

Robertson, A. (1998). Critical reflections on the politics of need: Implications for public health. *Social Science and Medicine, 47*(10), 1419-1430.

Robertson, A. (1999). Health promotion and the common good: Theoretical considerations. *Critical Public Health, 9*(2), 117-133.

Strengal, R. (1996, July 22). Bowling together: Civic engagement in America isn't disappearing but reinventing itself. *Time,* pp. 35-36.

Sullivan, T. (1996, January/February). Civic society and state reform in Canada: Bowling alone? *Canada Watch,* pp. 66-68.

Tarrow, S. (1996). Making social science work across space and in time: A critical reflection on Robert Putnam's *Making Democracy Work. American Political Science Review, 90*(2), 389-397.

Torjman, S. (1997). *Civil society: Reclaiming our humanity.* Ottawa, Ontario: Caledon Institute of Social Policy.

Wacquant, L. J. D. (1996). Reading Bourdieu's *Capital. International Journal of Contemporary Sociology, 33*(2), 151-170.

Wallerstein, N. (1992). Powerlessness, empowerment, and health: Implications for health promotion programs. *American Journal of Health Promotion, 6*(3), 197-205.

Wilkinson, R. G., Kawachi, I., & Kennedy, B. P. (1998). Mortality, the social environment, crime and violence. *Sociology of Health & Illness, 20*(5), 578-597.

8

The State as a Setting

John N. Lavis
Terrence J. Sullivan

Governments, like people, make decisions that have unforeseen effects. We present in this chapter a paradoxical example of this phenomenon: Past efforts by government to improve health have created constraints to undertaking a new approach to improve health. This new approach, which we call "population health" (Frank, 1995), involves (but is not restricted to) developing or modifying public policies for which health is a consequence, not the primary objective. We focus on policy because it is one of the primary mechanisms available to the state for implementing (or preventing) change. Public policies that affect the level of unemployment or the experiences of those who are unemployed, for example, are not designed for the primary purpose of improving health. Yet labor market experiences such as unemployment can have a profound impact on health (Dooley, Fielding, & Levi, 1996; Jin, Shah, & Svoboda, 1995).

We argue that some of the constraints that hinder the use and influence of health-related arguments in the development or modification of public policies are the unanticipated outcome of well-meaning policies designed to increase access to and quality of health care. To provide an analytic base on which to build our argument, we draw on recent thinking on policy feedback. This approach posits that policies, once enacted, frame the choices of the government elite, interest groups, and the public. Policies frame choices by creating resources and incentives for these political actors and by influencing their efforts to interpret the social world (Pierson, 1993). We refer to these framing effects as policy legacies.

308

Two objectives led us to adopt a policy feedback framework. First, we sought to link innovations in theory with innovations in practice. Policy feedback, as part of a theoretical paradigm called "historical institutionalism," represents a recent innovation within political science, and we wanted to explore the insights this theoretical development can provide for practice (Steinmo, Thelen, & Longstreth, 1992). Second, we sought to highlight a previously neglected component of the political environment—past actions by the state—that might contribute to explanations for the limited use and influence of health-related arguments in the development or modification of public policies. Past research has tended to look for explanations in institutional fragmentation (Milio, 1986) or in the distribution of power between political actors and their interpretations of the social world (Marmor, Barer, & Evans, 1994). We wanted to take a different approach, to explore how policies developed by the state in the past can act as constraints in the present and future.

In emphasizing the importance of past policies and how these policies influence political actors and their interpretations of the social world, we do not mean to imply that past policies are necessarily the crucial constraint. Like past research in this area, our research design does not allow us to compare the relative importance of policies and other components of the political environment in explaining the limited use and influence of health-related arguments in policymaking. Instead, we highlight the ways in which policy feedback acted as a constraint. Powerful health-care provider groups, for example, can act as a constraint, but a policy feedback framework allows us to explore in part why they became opposed to population health.

In this chapter, we restrict our analysis to a single level of government, which we call the state. By state we mean both the national level of government and the constituent political units of federations (such as provinces, states, or *Länder*). In a previous chapter, other authors considered communities and local levels of government. We maintain this important distinction between levels of government because the policy levers available, such as labor law or policy, differ between levels. Also, the policy-making process itself can differ between levels. For example, state-level policy-making affords fewer opportunities for the direct participation of affected constituencies than does policy-making at the local level.

We motivate our discussion with examples drawn from the literature on the links between labor market experiences and health. By labor market experiences we mean, for example, unemployment, involuntary part-time employment, or involuntary self-employment. Faced with a reduction in demand for its product, a firm could choose to lay off some workers, reduce the amount of working time for all workers, or change the status of many employees from permanent staff to contract workers who can be retained or let go on little notice. We chose to focus on labor market experiences because they provide a good example of how arguments that invoke the negative health consequences of these experiences could be used to influence the development and modification of public policy. A state could choose, for example, to influence those choices that firms make through labor laws and policies, or it could choose to better respond to their social costs through, for example, targeting assistance to those whose labor market experiences are associated with the most severe health consequences.

OVERVIEW OF THE CHAPTER

We explore the effects of policy legacies in health through a case study. We focus our attention on efforts in Canada to improve health through or with the involvement of the state. Occasionally, we also draw on experiences in the United Kingdom and the United States. Moreover, we complement our analysis of policy feedback in health with reference to policy feedback in environmental protection, a cause that shares many similarities with the new approach to improving health. Public policies that affect a firm's choice of technology, for example, may not be designed for the primary purpose of improving health. Yet pollution arising from some technologies can have a profound impact on health.

We present the story of policy feedback in health and its implications in four parts. We begin by outlining a framework that will allow us to identify the many dimensions of policy feedback. We provide examples of each of these dimensions, but these examples are not critical to the flow of argument and can be skipped by those primarily interested in our core argument. Next, we provide the historical context for our case study, sketching out past and proposed efforts to improve health through the state. We then highlight the mechanisms through which past policies have hindered the new approach to improving health. Finally, we outline the conditions that we believe would favor political change and draw out the implications of these conditions for policymakers, researchers, and others interested in moving beyond current efforts to improve health through the state.

To summarize the argument that we will develop, our analysis suggests that policies designed to increase access to and quality of health care have had three main effects. First, these policies led government officials to develop experience in health program administration and fostered a tendency among these officials and allied interest groups to respond to health-related problems by developing more health-related programs or by advocating their development. Yet the new approach to improving health through the state calls less for new "population health programs" within the Ministry of Health than for a new perspective within other areas of government, such as the Ministry of Labor.

Second, health care policies (and policy reactions to them) created resources and incentives for interest groups that have a primary focus on health. These groups could (and sometimes do) fulfill an important role in lobbying on behalf of the new approach to improving health. However, despite their good intentions, they are not necessarily best suited to undertaking this new approach alone. Resources and incentives might be better provided to groups who recognize the importance of considering health outcomes when articulating trade-offs in public policy and who have direct experience in the development or modification of such policy.

Third, health care policies in most Western industrialized nations were designed such that their consequences, like medical cures for disease, would be clear and easily associated with government action in health care financing and delivery. This design may have been politically advantageous when health care was seen as a panacea and potential investments in it appeared finite. Now that the limitations to this view have been recognized (Organization for Economic Cooperation and Development [OECD], 1995), the government elite and some interest groups have sought to reduce public commitments to health care. One means to this end is to present expenditures related to public policies with health consequences as an alternative to expenditures related to health care policies. Without the policy legacies associated with health, we may have seen neither this false competition between health care and the new approach nor the intensity with which the battle is currently fought in some jurisdictions.

In highlighting the importance of policy feedback, we do not mean to suggest that it alone drives policy formulation and hence that political change cannot happen. Policy legacies can be overcome, and in our view, three conditions would favor change. As a first condition, the government elite and interest groups should move beyond the view that health care and population health compete directly with one another. Population health can take its appropriate place alongside health care as a complementary approach to improving health through the state.

As a second condition, "healthy public policy," the one explicitly elaborated vision of how to develop and modify public policy for which health is a consequence, not the primary objective, should be focused for use at the state level. The implementation of the population health approach, as we view it, need not await a multisectoral policy-making process or the direct participation of affected constituencies. As many advocates of healthy public policy might agree, these features, although perhaps attractive and certainly more feasible at the local level, unnecessarily restrict the range of options available. Finally, as a third condition, efforts to improve health should seek to reframe the choices of the government elite, interest groups, and the public. In the conclusion to this chapter, we propose two possible means to this end.

THE DIMENSIONS OF POLICY FEEDBACK

Having provided a brief description of our destination, we can now begin to chart our course. Here, the question of whether policies matter assumes less im-

Table 8.1 The Dimensions of Policy Feedback

	Actors Affected by Feedback Mechanism		
Type of Mechanism	Government Elite	Interest Groups	Public
Resource & incentive effects	Administrative capacities	"Spoils" Organizing niches Financing Access	"Lock-in" effects
Interpretive effects	Policy learning	Policy learning Visibility/traceability	Visibility/traceability

SOURCE: From Pierson (1993).

portance than the question of how they matter. Several scholars have (implicitly or explicitly) introduced plausible mechanisms through which policies, once enacted, can frame choices, but only recently has an attempt been made to provide a unifying framework within which these mechanisms can be sorted. We draw on a framework developed by Pierson (1993) to guide our analysis and explore its applicability in a new policy arena.

According to this framework, policy feedback can operate through two principal mechanisms and across three distinct types of actors. As one mechanism, policies can affect the resources and incentives available to political actors. We interpret resources and incentives broadly and include, for example, economic resources such as direct funding, administrative incentives such as advancement within the government bureaucracy, and political resources such as privileged access to policymakers. (In focusing on resources and incentives, we do not mean to imply that political actors cannot be motivated by other factors such as altruism.) Secondly, policies can also have interpretative effects, affecting individuals' efforts to interpret the social world. Both of these mechanisms can affect the government elite, interest groups, and the public. We use these three types of actors because they provide convenient groupings, although we recognize that the types of subgroups within them will differ in their ability to exert political influence.

As shown in Table 8.1, these two mechanisms operating across three types of actors generate six categories of policy feedback. We illustrate below each of these potential categories with examples drawn from the literature. In describing these examples, which can be skipped without interrupting the flow of argument, we highlight only the role of policy feedback. Other factors, such as the distribution of power among political actors, also play important roles, but policy feedback emerges in each of these examples as a crucial constraint. These examples provide a flavor of the types of policy legacies that we will be looking for in health. All of the categories except one—resource and incentive effects for the public—have direct relevance for our analysis.

Resource and Incentive Effects

As one type of policy feedback, policies can provide resources and incentives that affect the government elite. Accordingly, efforts to implement these policies can transform the administrative capacities of the state, in turn affecting the administrative possibilities for future policy. Given the capacities developed in response to past policy initiatives, some policy options will appear more "doable" than others. The contrasting responses of Sweden and the United Kingdom to the Great Depression illustrate this effect (Weir & Skocpol, 1985). Sweden had an established public works program that provided a "bridge" to the development of Keynesian policies such as job creation. The United Kingdom lacked experience with a public works program but had developed the administrative capacity to operate an unemployment insurance program. Instead of pursuing a Keynesian agenda, the United Kingdom responded to the Great Depression by expanding unemployment benefits.

Policies can also provide resources and incentives that inhibit or facilitate the formation or expansion of interest groups. Pierson (1993) has identified four ways in which the activity of interest groups can be affected by public policies. First, policies can create "spoils" that provide an incentive for beneficiaries to mobilize to resist programmatic retrenchment or support programmatic maintenance or expansion. As an example of this mechanism, Skocpol (1992) cites the case of Civil War pensions in the United States and the organization and mobilization of veterans' groups to demand the expansion of benefits. Second, policies can create niches for political entrepreneurs who may take advantage of these incentives to help interest groups form, organize, and mobilize. For example, the market-based regulatory approach to health care policy in the United States, with its associated lack of comprehensive health care benefits for the elderly, created a niche for the American Association of Retired People. This organization provided health care insurance as a selective incentive to joining and subsequently became a powerful elderly lobby group (Pierson, 1993). Third, policies can affect the resources available to interest groups, as when Sweden delegated authority over unemployment funds to unions, thereby giving them a selective incentive to offer workers and contributing to the development of powerful labor confederations (Rothstein, 1992). Finally, policies can affect the ability of groups to bring their resources to bear on policymakers by influencing their access to them. Corporatist arrangements provide an example of this mechanism: These policies, adopted by many Scandinavian countries, brought business associations and labor confederations directly into the decision-making process.

But resource and incentive effects are not restricted to the government elite and interest groups. The general public can also be affected. Pierson (1992) argues that one potential mechanism for these effects is that policies encourage individuals to "lock in" to a particular path of policy development. For example, the maturity of the American public pension plan hindered Reagan's efforts to restructure old-age pensions. With a retired generation that had made irreversible commitments based on a public pension system, changing to a private system would have created a double-payment problem whereby current workers would have to finance both their own retirement and that of the previous generation. Thatcher, who faced no mature public pension system in the United Kingdom, was able to move toward a more private system.

Interpretative Effects

Policy feedback can also operate by influencing how political actors interpret the social world, in part by affecting how they make sense of their environment. This mechanism, called policy learning, typically involves individuals or groups at or near the center of the policy-making process, such as the government elite and interest groups. Also, policy learning typically occurs in areas of complex policy-making where expertise is critical (Pierson, 1993). Heclo (1974), for example, found in his study of the British and Swedish welfare states that a technique such as social insurance, once adopted in one social policy arena, tends to be readopted in other social policy arenas. In addition to building on past "successes," policies may reflect lessons learned from past "mistakes." For example, Skocpol (1992) argues that federal social expenditures in the United States were not increased in the pre-New Deal era because the introduction of Civil War pensions was viewed (negatively) by policymakers as an example of patronage politics.

Political actors' views can also be shaped by the distribution of information about their environment. Some policies are visible, such as those that produce concentrated benefits (or costs) or those that affect a network of people who share information. That is, the consequences of these policies will not go unnoticed, and any changes in these policies may generate a response from interest groups and the public. Income taxes, for example, are highly visible, whereas excise taxes are not. Policies also vary in the extent to which their consequences can be linked to government action or in what Arnold (1990) calls their traceability. The length of the causal chain between policy and outcome determines, at least in part, a policy's traceability. For example, consumers may not like the food prices in their local grocery store, but these consumers are unlikely to attribute high prices to the government's trade and agriculture policies. Hence, changes in trade and agricultural policies are unlikely to generate a widespread public response.

THE HISTORICAL CONTEXT:
HEALTH IMPROVEMENT AND THE STATE

With these potential feedback mechanisms in mind, we can now turn to the historical context for our discussion of policy legacies in health. Efforts to improve health through the state have evolved over the last century, responding in part to changes in what were perceived to be the pressing (and "treatable") health problems of the day. We describe here two shifts in emphasis—one realized, the other proposed. The policy legacies from the first shift have profound implications for the second.

In describing these shifts in emphasis, we will refer to three models for improving health and three types of public policies that have come to be associated with these models. The differences between the first two models, which we will call the public health and biomedical models, are substantial. The public health model adopts a multicausal and ecological perspective that allows for reciprocal associations among variables. Its focus is groups of people, usually communities, and its goal is health promotion and disease prevention. The biomedical model "typically refers to a unidirectional, biological cause-and-effect relationship between an agent and host" (Runyan, 1985, p. 605). Its focus is individuals and its goal is the medical cure of disease.

The approach of practitioners whose activities are predicated on the public health and biomedical models and the public policies that have built on these models can be readily distinguished in theory, if not always in practice. Public health practitioners and public health policy seek to promote health and prevent disease through, for example, occupational health and safety or immunization programs. Health care providers, on the other hand, seek to cure disease once it develops, and health care policy addresses the regulation, financing, and/or delivery of that care. In some countries, such as the United States, the line between them has occasionally become blurred as public health practitioners have found themselves providing services to individuals, such as behavior modification counseling, rather than administering programs for groups.

The third model attracts more controversy (see Frank, 1995, and Labonte, 1995, for one set of competing perspectives on this model). Although we have chosen to call the model population health, we recognize that other scholars use different labels to refer to a similar concept. We use the label population health when discussing the development or modification of public policies for which health is a consequence, not the primary objective. This model shares with public health an analytic framework, in that it focuses on populations, not individuals. With few exceptions, however, public health policy has come to take health as its primary objective.

Researchers in many countries have begun to develop a research base that can inform the development or modification of public policy. This research on the modifiable social determinants of health draws on a range of disciplinary perspectives, from economics to epidemiology. A number of edited volumes have recently been published that weave together the different threads within this field of inquiry (see, e.g., Amick, Levine, Tarlov, & Walsh, 1995; Marmor, Barer, & Evans, 1994). Population health research has found, for example, that labor market experiences, income distribution, and social networks can have profound health consequences (Hertzman, Frank, & Evans, 1994).

Given population health's focus on public policy with health consequences, not health objectives, there is no such thing as "population health policy." Instead, there are, for example, labor market experiences whose negative health consequences could be reduced by influencing the choices that firms make or by better responding to their social costs. The state could choose to make health-improving changes in public policy, such as developing or modifying labor laws or policy that affect job strain. Alternatively, the state could choose to reduce the negative health consequences of public policy: It could redistribute some of the gains that accrue from trade liberalization by developing training and adjustment programs to help those workers whose jobs were lost to other jurisdictions as a result of trade.

Only one vision of how to develop and modify public policy for which health is a consequence, not the primary objective, has been explicitly elaborated. This vision, called "healthy public policy," was first formally articulated in the Ottawa Charter for Health Promotion (World Health Organization, 1986). Healthy public policies, according to Pederson, Edwards, Marshall, Allison, and Kelner (1988), "are those which are developed through a multisectoral and collaborative process which endeavours to ensure participation by the affected constituencies and which are unique for having an explicit awareness of their health implications" (p. 5). As we will argue later, as one of the conditions for political change, we believe that this vision of how to develop and modify public policies with health consequences should be better focused for use at the state level.

From Public Health to Health Care

The first shift in emphasis by the state in its effort to improve health was from public health policy alone to a combined approach involving both public health and health care policies. By the late 1960s, this shift had occurred in all Western industrialized nations. Two health-related developments provide part of the background for this shift. First, by the early to middle part of the 20th century, the architects of what came to be known as public health policy had successfully addressed many of the pressing health issues of their day, such as poor water quality. Second and concurrently, scientists informed by the biomedical model had begun to find cures for disease, true cures that were (for the first time) both safe and effective. Perhaps most important among the advances were the discovery of antiseptic surgical technique and then antibiotics, both of which made possible dramatic improvements in health. No longer was the cure worse than the disease.

Policy legacies from public health policy were not inimical to an expansion of state activity into health care policy and might even have been supportive of it. For example, public health policy had been primarily a community-based undertaking, in implementation if not always in development. State-level government elites, who had no opportunity to develop particular administrative capacities or approaches to addressing new health-related problems, had no reason to seek to influence the transition. As another example, public health policies, given that they tended to be locally implemented, had not created resources or incentives for statewide interest groups that had a primary focus on health and may have sought to influence the shift in emphasis. Moreover, this transition was seen as a positive-sum game, so little competition arose between approaches. With little competition, neither the differences in visibility of the consequences of public health and health care policies for the public nor the ease with which these two types of policies could be associated by the public with government action played an important role in the transition.

Although public health policies did not hinder the development of policies designed to increase access to and quality of health care, the particular array of public health policies may explain in part the particular pattern of organizational arrangements that characterize each Western industrialized nation's health care system. However, policy legacies related to public health are not the focus of this chapter. In the remainder of this section, we outline the health care arrangements relevant to our later discussion of how policy legacies related to health care policy hindered efforts for the proposed transition to a more comprehensive approach involving public health, health care, and population health. We will motivate our description with examples drawn from Canada.

Provincial governments in Canada developed large bureaucratic structures—usually called the Ministry of Health, although the Ministry of Health Care Services would have been a more appropriate name—to develop health care policy and administer health care programs. These bureaucratic structures were set up to run in parallel with other structures such as the Ministry of Labour. Within the Ministry of Health, responsibility was delegated along programmatic lines, with most resources flowing to (and hence administrative capacity developed in) the programs dealing with hospital funding, physician reimbursement, and drug benefit payments. In response to the perceived successes or failures of old policies, the government elite would modify these policies or develop new ones. For example, to contain costs, provincial governments introduced limits on hospital expenditures, and to improve quality of care, they introduced hospital accreditation bodies.

Health care policies (and policy reactions to them) also created resources and incentives for interest groups that have a primary focus on health. With the state acting as the single payer for insured health care services, the Ministry of Health became the predominant source of income for physicians and the arbiter of the conditions under which they worked. Provincial medical associations, already strong, became entrenched as monopoly negotiators on behalf of their physician members and developed tougher, more sophisticated bargaining techniques (Naylor, 1986) as well as the public affairs divisions needed to build public support for their views. In one province, Ontario, the payment of membership dues by physicians to their medical association was made mandatory and the medical association was given a privileged position as copartner with the Ministry of Health in a planning body charged with steering the future course of the health care system.

Ministries of Health also provided a combination of organizing niches, financing, and privileged access to health groups that could provide a countervailing influence to those interest groups that had been particularly advantaged by health care policies. Public health associations, for example, took advantage of these offers to become some of the few voices calling for attention to the social determinants of health. Because membership in these groups was drawn almost exclusively from those working in the health field, these associations tended to look to the Ministry of Health for new programs and developed the technical expertise relevant to debates conducted within the Ministry of Health.

Health care policies in Canada were designed such that their consequences would be clear and easily associated with government action in health care financing and delivery. Removing financial barriers to medical care meant that more people could benefit from medical cures and treatments for disease. Acting as a single payer for health care services meant that governments could use general tax revenues to remove these financial barriers. The government elite wanted the credit for saving lives and they designed health care policy such that they would receive the credit.

The United Kingdom and the United States have experienced a generally similar pattern of accommodation to health care policies designed to increase access to or quality of health care. Some important differences do exist, however. For example, the involvement of the British government in health care delivery, as well as in health care financing, has accentuated the focus by the government elite on health program administration. The American system, with its blend of state and private sector involvement, has diminished the ease with which the consequences of health care policies can be associated with government action. But by and large, when it comes to policy legacies in health, we are all in the same boat.

From Health Care to Population Health

The second shift in emphasis by the state in its effort to improve health, one that has as yet only been proposed, is from public health and health care policies to a combined approach involving public health, health care, and population health. These proposals have been given formal expression over the past decade by policymakers, researchers, and others interested in the new approach to improving health, such as public health associations. As with the previous shift, two health-related developments provide part of the background for this shift.

The first pressure for change comes from a recognition of the limits to health care policy. As one illustrative example among many, despite differences in health care expenditures across political jurisdictions, we do not see a corresponding pattern of differences in health status, regardless of which measure of health status is used. In 1990, for example, Japan spent only 6.8% of its gross domestic product on health care, whereas Canada spent 10.0% and the United States spent 13.2% (Schieber, Poullier, & Greenwald, 1993). Yet the pattern of life expectancy and infant mortality was the reverse of what one would expect based on this pattern of health care spending. On average in 1990, women in Japan could expect to live 81.9 years, whereas Canadian women could expect to live 80.4 years and American women 78.8 years. More striking were the differences between countries in infant mortality rates: 4.6 infants died for every 1,000 live births in Japan, compared with 6.8 deaths in Canada and 9.1 deaths in the United States (Schieber et al., 1993).

The second pressure for change comes from gradually accumulating evidence that the determinants of health extend beyond health care. Having meaningful work, a reasonable income in comparison with one's peers, and a social network have all been found to correlate with improved health (Evans, 1994). Several attempts have been made to provide a conceptual framework within which these determinants can be sorted and better understood (Bunker, Gomby, & Kehrer, 1989; Evans & Stoddart, 1990; Hertzman, Frank, & Evans, 1994; Lalonde, 1974). Common to all frameworks is the central importance of social environments—our work, our incomes, our social networks, for example— which are or can be shaped in part through the state.

These findings suggest a potential role for developing or modifying public policies for which health is a consequence, not the primary objective. For example, the experiences of those who are unemployed, as mentioned earlier, can be affected by labor market policies. Also, our incomes and how they compare with the distribution of income in our state are determined in part by fiscal and social policy. Wilkinson (1992) has estimated that if Britain were to adopt an income distribution more like the most egalitarian European countries, about 2 years might be added to the population's life expectancy (see Judge, 1995, and Wilkinson, 1995, for a debate on the validity of this type of research).

Table 8.2 Policy Feedback in Health

Type of Mechanism	Actors Affected by Feedback Mechanism		
	Government Elite	Interest Groups	Public
Resource & incentive effects	Developed health program administration capacities	Provided "spoils," organizing niches, financing, & access to health groups	
Interpretive effects	Develop health programs in response to problems	Develop health programs in response to problems	
		Made health care policies visible & traceable	Made health care policies visible & traceable

STUDIES IN CONTRAST: POLICY IN HEALTH AND THE ENVIRONMENT

Despite such pressures for change, policy feedback in health has created constraints to undertaking the new approach to improving health. In this section, we describe how health care policies have hindered the population health approach. Many of these mechanisms are those suggested by Pierson (1993). We also contrast the case of policy legacies in health with policy legacies in environmental protection, a cause that shares many similarities with the new approach to improving health.

Policy Legacies and Political Constraints: The Case of Health

Policies designed to increase access to and quality of health care have primarily affected the political behavior of the government elite and interest groups, creating resources and incentives for these political actors and influencing how they interpret the social world. Building on the framework developed by Pierson (1993), which we introduced earlier in the chapter, we have summarized in Table 8.2 the mechanisms through which health care policies, once enacted, have affected these political actors. To facilitate discussion, we have grouped these effects into three arguments about how past efforts by government to improve health have created constraints to undertaking the new approach to improving health.

First, health care policies fostered the development of particular administrative capacities by the government elite and fostered policy learning by both the government elite and interest groups. In response to resources and incentives, the government elite gained experience in developing health care policy and in administering health care programs. When funds were plentiful, this elite chose new areas in which to invest health care dollars. More recently, as funds have become scarce, they developed expertise in articulating trade-offs in health care. Over the past decade, more money in Canada has been spent on home care services, for example, and less on hospital care. Changes have also occurred in program administration. Initially, many of the programs in a Canadian provincial Ministry of Health simply involved "paying the bills." Over time, however, Ministry officials found themselves overseeing increasingly complex programs dealing with, for example, hospital funding or physician reimbursement.

Both the government elite and interest groups learned from their experiences with health care policy. The government elite tends to respond to health-related problems by doing what has worked in the past: developing more health-related programs or modifying existing ones. As health care policymakers became aware of the limits to health care policy and the evidence that the determinants of health extend beyond health care, they responded by developing "health promotion" programs within the Ministry of Health. Allied interest groups, such as public health associations, have learned similar lessons and advocate more or modified programs within the Ministry of Health.

Like the responses of Sweden and the United Kingdom to the Great Depression (Weir & Skocpol, 1985), which we described earlier, the government elite in health has responded to pressures for change by building on existing administrative capacities. And like the tendency in Sweden and the United Kingdom at other periods in their development to readopt a policy design that proved successful in the past (Heclo, 1974), the government elite and interest groups in health have responded to health-related problems by developing new health programs in the Ministry of Health. These administrative capacities and learned responses to health-related problems undoubtedly led to better public policies for which health is the primary objective.

But the new approach to improving health through the state involves developing or modifying public policies for which health is a consequence, not the primary objective. The approach calls less for new programs or a new focus within the Ministry of Health than for a new perspective within, for example, the Ministry of Labour. The government elite within neither the Ministry of Health nor the Ministry of Labour have developed the expertise to consider explicitly health outcomes when articulating trade-offs in labor law or policy. Decisions with profound health consequences are made in Ministries like Labour. Yet the "health experts" in the Ministry of Health have no arguments with which to inform these deliberations and no experience in framing these arguments in ways that invoke the language of those other Ministries and their associated "issue networks." These issue networks are, in fact, defined by the common technical expertise that binds their participants together (Heclo, 1978).

Our second argument about policy feedback in health relates to how health care policies (and policy reactions to them) created resources and incentives for health groups. Provincial medical associations responded to the "spoils" provided through health care policy by developing sophisticated public affairs divisions that can mobilize resistance to any perceived threats to these spoils. These associations (sometimes rightly given the rhetoric of some population health researchers and public health associations) have seen population health as a foray into their territory, interpreting potential investments in the population health approach as being made at the expense of investments in health care and hence in their livelihood. Not surprisingly, these groups have made use of their public affairs divisions to mobilize resistance to real or threatened reductions in health care spending, reductions that have often been justified using population health rhetoric.

Other health groups, such as public health associations, also responded to the resources and incentives made available to them by Ministries of Health. These health groups developed proposals primarily for the Ministry of Health, an environment with which they were familiar and for which they had relevant technical expertise. Also, these associations, whose vision of how to develop and modify public policy grew out of community-based initiatives, embraced the notion of a multisectoral and participatory approach to policy-making. With such approaches rare in Canadian state-level politics, public health associations were left to inform debates in other Ministries even though they lacked experience in framing health-related arguments in ways that invoke the language of those other Ministries and their associated "issue networks."

Our third and final argument about policy feedback in health relates to how health care policies were designed such that their consequences would be clear and easily associated with government action in health care financing and delivery. As the government elite in Canadian Ministries of Health recognized that health care was not a panacea and that potential investments in health care were not finite, they sought to "get the hyena off the foot"—that is to limit health care spending. The new approach to improving health appeared to offer a justification for this decision. If differences in health care expenditures across political jurisdictions bear little relationship to differences in health status and research finds that the determinants of health extend beyond health care, then population health could be used as a rhetorical device to justify spending limits. This way of thinking needlessly placed health care and population health in direct competition.

A population health approach is a complement to, not a substitute for, health care policy. Even if a population health approach could replace in some way an approach premised on a biomedical model, the particular design of health care policies would hinder such an undertaking. In Canada, health care policies were intentionally designed such that their consequences, like medical cures for disease, would be clear and easily associated with government efforts to remove financial barriers to access. Any effort by government to invest in population health at the expense of health care would therefore face significant resistance.

Policy Vacuums and Political Opportunities: An Aside on the Environment

A very brief outline of the case of environmental protection serves as a useful contrast to our analysis of policy legacies in population health. The two approaches share many similarities. Both approaches seek to affect the development and modification of public policies across a range of policy arenas and invoke arguments about the health consequences of these public policies to do so. More specifically, a direct analogy can be drawn between labor market policies that affect a firm's choice of job and organizational design and public policies that affect a firm's choice of technology. In both cases, public policy can be used to reduce the negative externalities (in this case, the health consequences) that flow from firm choices.

Thirty years ago, advocates of environmental protection did not face a similar set of policy legacies to those that currently face advocates of the new approach to improving health. Whereas a Ministry already "had" health, no Ministry "had" the environment in the 1960s. The government elite had not developed particular administrative capacities in this area; the government elite and interest groups had not learned particular responses to environmental problems; and interest groups and the public had not been influenced by highly visible environmental protection policies. Business groups, however, represented a formidable obstacle, for they had developed sophisticated lobbying abilities.

We can draw two observations from the case of environmental protection. First, compared with population health advocates, environmental protection advocates faced a "policy vacuum." This context meant that political actors faced a less constrained set of choices about how to implement the environmental protection approach. Second, because they faced fewer constraints, environmental protection advocates were able to move directly to articulating trade-offs in public policy and were not sidelined by a futile competition between falsely competing approaches. Policy vacuums create political opportunities.

OVERCOMING POLICY LEGACIES

Our account of policy feedback in health, especially when compared with policy feedback in environmental protection, may seem overly deterministic. But past efforts by government to improve health have only created constraints to imple-menting a new approach to improve health; they have not created insurmount-able barriers. Policy legacies can be overcome, and in this (penultimate) section we outline three conditions that would be conducive to political change and pro-vide one example of a successful effort to bring about change. The first two con-ditions require us to revisit notions related to population health: both the rela-tionship between health care policy and public policy for which health is a consequence, not the primary objective, and the currently accepted vision of how to develop and modify public policy for which health is a consequence. The last condition suggests a role for a cross-sectoral political advisory body or a po-litical entrepreneur in reframing the choices of the government elite, interest groups, and the public.

Condition 1: Rethinking the Place of Population Health

As the first condition conducive to political change, we believe that the place of population health within the armamentarium of approaches to improve health should be rethought. As we have suggested throughout the chapter, the biomedi-cal model, like the public health model, remains central to our efforts to improve health. The notion that the population health model competes directly with the biomedical model is misplaced. We will always require a systematic approach to the treatment of disease. The potential offered by the biomedical model may have been overemphasized in the past, and a more realistic portrayal of its strengths and limitations may be needed. We have begun to recognize the dimin-ishing marginal returns to health from health care spending (Lavis & Stoddart, 1994). But these diminishing marginal returns refer, by definition, to the last (or next) dollar spent. On average, taking all dollars spent, the biomedical model still serves a critical purpose in underpinning our efforts to improve health.

The same argument can be made for the public policies that build on these models. Health care policy, like public health policy, remains central to our ef-forts to improve health through the state. Public policies informed by a popula-tion health model will never replace those informed by a biomedical model. Even if governments implemented all of the public policies proposed by popula-tion health researchers and public health associations, individuals would still get sick, and both they and (in most caring societies) their fellow citizens would still look to the state to regulate, finance, and/or deliver their health care. Using insights from population health research, we can perhaps help people live longer, healthier lives. We cannot prevent them from ever having to use the health care system.

The progression in model or policy from health care to population health, like that from public health to health care, is nonlinear. A contrast with mac-roeconomic policy is instructive. Unlike the many states who threw off the trappings of one way of thinking for another when they moved from a macroeconomic policy predicated on Keynesianism to one predicated on a new (monetarist) view, the same cannot be done for efforts to improve health. These approaches to improving health through the state are complements, not substitutes; they each have something to offer. In theory, investments in health care are made at the expense of investments in public policies that may have health consequences, not objectives. But the decision to incorporate health-related arguments in public policy development is made separately from a decision to increase or decrease investments in health care.

Condition 2: Better Focusing the Vision of "Healthy Public Policy"

As the second condition conducive to political change, we believe that the vision of "healthy public policy"—the only explicitly articulated vision of how to use health-related arguments in the development or consideration of public policy for which health is a consequence—should be better focused. We believe that the community-based perspective from which this vision grew led its proponents to embrace a multisectoral and participatory approach to policy-making, an approach that has both intuitive and practical appeal at the community level. However, multisectoral and participatory policy initiatives occur rarely at the provincial or national level in Canada (or at the state level in most other Western industrialized countries). Opportunities to invoke health-related arguments in the development or modification of public policy need not await these rare events. A more comprehensive vision should allow for a broader range of ways in which advocates of the new approach can work to influence public policy development. We describe our own proposal for this broader vision in this and the following section.

The public health base from which many healthy public policy advocates come might explain their implicit acceptance of health as a superordinate objective in public policy. Health, as distinguished from the broader notion of well-being, need not be the only consideration or even necessarily one of the more important considerations in developing public policy with health consequences. Health, like income or leisure time, is only one determinant of our well-being. The electorate may be willing to sacrifice health for some other advantage brought by public policy (or the absence of public policy) or to avoid some disadvantage. As suggested by the example of overtime, short-term gains in income may be valued more highly than long-term gains in health. The goal for advocates of the new approach to improving health should not be to argue for health at all costs. Instead, these advocates should seek to better articulate the health consequences of public policy and how these consequences can inform trade-offs in public policy, where health is narrowly defined and is objectively measurable. Electorates can then provide the values and priorities with which governments can make these trade-offs.

Condition 3: Reframing Choices
Through a Cross-Sectoral Political
Advisory Body or a Political Entrepreneur

If the population health approach is a complement (not a substitute) for public health and health care policies and it can be helpful in articulating trade-offs in public policy, then advocates of the population health model can begin to reframe constructively the choices of the government elite, interest groups, and the public. We believe that there are two principal ways through which choices can be reframed: a cross-sectoral political advisory body and a political entrepreneur. Both approaches recognize that Ministry-specific policy formulation tends to ignore outcomes perceived to be the domain of other Ministries.

With few exceptions, most developed countries have delegated responsibility for each of trade, labor market, fiscal, social, and health policy to separate Ministries or departments. This fragmentation of political and bureaucratic authority created the specialized organizations necessary to govern effectively amid increasing economic and social complexity (Chubb & Peterson, 1989). However, creating Ministry-specific lines of authority has profound implications for those seeking to bring about health-improving change in public policies for which health is a consequence, not the primary objective (Milio, 1986). As long as these Ministries develop and modify policy in isolation, the prospects for reframing choices are limited. Even states with parliamentary governments and a cabinet, such as Canada or the United Kingdom, would find it difficult to reframe choices once presented with Ministry-specific arguments.

The challenge to reframe choices, then, lies not in Ministries of Health but in the other decision-making branches and central agencies of government. Ministries of Health have developed the administrative capacities to administer health programs and develop public health and health care policy; other Ministries have developed the administrative capacities to develop public policies relevant to their policy arena. Our formulation of the population health approach suggests that advocates of the new approach to improving health should seek to influence policy development in other Ministries, and we propose two means to this end in the following two subsections. Many considerations other than health motivate policy development in other Ministries and these advocates must be prepared to advance health-related arguments that can effectively compete with these other motivations.

We may also seek to address the health consequences of one Ministry's policy through another Ministry. For example, the gains from trade liberalization are probably very significant. On average, we are better off with cheaper products of the same or higher quality. Yet the distributional consequences of trade agreements are profound and we may seek to minimize them through Labour Ministry-sponsored retraining programs for those whose jobs are lost because of firm relocations. The population health approach can help to better articulate such trade-offs by highlighting the health consequences of such changes and the alternative ways of either influencing these changes directly or living with the social costs that follow from these changes.

Of course, the Ministry of Health could play a role in these efforts. To provide a dramatic example of how the agenda of one department can influence the agenda of another department, consider the case of the Ministry of Finance in Canada. This central agency, through its control of the government's purse, effectively controls the range of options available to other Ministries. The Ministry of Finance need not always exert its influence directly because knowledge of its financial leverage leads to anticipatory reactions on the part of other Ministries. Of course, the Ministry of Health cannot exert financial leverage over other Ministries like the Ministry of Finance, but it can make better use of its "ownership" of health, a highly salient issue for many Canadians.

A cross-sectoral political advisory body, as the healthy public policy advocates suggest, can provide one way to reframe the choices that governments face. Although it can take many forms, typically, such a body comprises officials within semiautonomous sites of political and bureaucratic authority, such as Ministries or departments. Membership could also include experts and representatives from interest groups and the public. This body could allow preferences for health and other often-ignored outcomes such as environmental quality to be explicitly incorporated into public policy. A Ministry of Health representative could help to reframe choices, but also representatives from other jurisdictions would feel an obligation to move beyond jurisdiction-specific arguments and instead frame issues more broadly.

Many state-level governments have experimented with a cross-sectoral political advisory body. The motivations for these innovations have been mixed: greater rationality in public sector planning for some, like the British Labour government in the 1970s, or more coordination (read doing more with less) in social policy-making for its more market-oriented replacement under Mrs. Thatcher in the 1980s (Challis et al., 1988). Regardless of motivation, such an institutional innovation presents population health advocates with a significant opportunity to reframe issues.

One example, drawn from Canada, illustrates the potential offered by a cross-sectoral political advisory body. This example involves the Premier's Council on Health Strategy and the Premier's Council on the Economy and Technology, two advisory bodies that were convened by the Ontario Liberal Government under Premier David Peterson in the late 1980s. Both councils were established with broad-based representation from senior policy-makers, experts, interest groups, and the public (see Signal, 1994, and Spasoff, 1992, for a more detailed description of the Premier's Council on Health Strategy). These bodies contributed to an important policy innovation in the province of Ontario: the development of a training and adjustment program for workers, the Ontario Training and Adjustment Board. We chose this example because it represents one of the few cases with which we are familiar where explicit consideration of health outcomes contributed at the margin to the development of public policy for which health is a consequence, not an objective.

As one of two parallel processes that led to this policy innovation, the Premier's Council on Health Strategy successfully engaged senior policymakers in discussion about the health consequences of public policy. A committee of the council conducted a series of workshops and follow-up interviews with senior politicians and bureaucrats from across government to develop an inventory of policies that could improve health (Signal, 1994; Sullivan, 1991). In a widely circulated document, titled *Nurturing Health* (Gerstein et al., 1991), the committee identified several policy domains as priority areas for government action. One of these priority areas was "adult adjustment and labour market adjustment policy," and two of the four recommended strategies in this priority area involved training.

The joint chairmanship of the councils by the Premier and the cross-appointments of several Cabinet Ministers and one expert ensured that the work of the Premier's Council on Health Strategy would inform the work of the Premier's Council on the Economy and Technology. The latter council identified the need for a skilled, flexible, and adjustable workforce in Ontario, and in a report titled *People and Skills in the New Global Economy* (Premier's Council, 1990) called for the development of a training and adjustment program to address the "skills gap" in the province. In their concurrent deliberative process, members of the Premier's Council on the Economy and Technology moved beyond jurisdiction-specific arguments and instead framed issues more broadly, citing health consequences as one justification for their proposal (Premier's Council, 1990). The decision to create the Ontario Training and Adjustment Board came shortly after the release of this council's report.

A cross-sectoral political advisory body is not, however, a recipe for success. The central message of a comprehensive review of cross-sectoral initiatives was simple: "Co-ordination does not just happen because ministers or top civil servants say that it should. It means creating the right kind of framework and providing the right kind of incentives for the individual actors who alone can make it work" (Challis et al., 1988, p. xi). To this warning we can add that health-improving changes in public policy or reductions in the social costs of public policy do not just happen because a cross-sectoral political advisory body is created. But institutional innovation can provide for the possibility that population health advocates are sitting at the table when choices are framed.

A political entrepreneur provides a second way to reframe the choices that governments face. The highly specialized nature of each Ministry's policy domain encourages the involvement of only those policymakers and interest groups who are familiar with its language and policy details. The incentives for population health advocates are no different. As argued previously, population health advocates tend to direct their lobbying or research transfer efforts to the Ministry of Health, even though this jurisdiction may not offer the most promise for improving health through public policy or reducing the social costs of public policy. The Ministry of Industry and Trade or the Ministry of Labour likely offer more potential.

Yet population health advocates are not adequately trained to invoke health-related arguments in the development of trade or labor market policy. These jurisdictions are the domain of politicians and experts, not well-meaning but technically naive amateurs. In the absence of a cross-sectoral political advisory body or (better yet) even with such a body, those interested in improving health through the state should learn to frame issues in ways that can be understood by policymakers and interest groups in policy arenas other than health care and by the public. Here lies the opportunity for a political entrepreneur, an individual with an understanding of a policy arena and its health consequences and who can reframe choices in language understandable to those who develop or modify public policy in that arena.

CONCLUSION

It is possible for the state to overcome policy legacies in health and undertake a new role in improving health. We believe that three conditions favor political change: (a) rethinking the place of population health, (b) reformulating the concept of healthy public policy, and (c) reframing choices through a cross-sectoral political advisory body and/or a political entrepreneur. These conditions have implications for policymakers, researchers, and those interested in contributing to this new role for the state.

Policymakers in Ministries of Health can make an important contribution to the population health approach by nurturing its development in other Ministries. Technical support can be provided to other Ministries, both to develop and modify public policies and to support policy evaluation. Ministries of Health can also provide resources and incentives to groups who recognize the importance of considering health outcomes when articulating trade-offs in labor market policy and who have direct experience in the development or modification of such policy.

Researchers can contribute to this new approach by conducting research that is more relevant to the trade-offs faced by Ministries other than the Ministry of Health and by evaluating public policies developed or modified in other Ministries to determine their health consequences. For example, much research has been done on the links between unemployment and health. Yet there are many other labor market experiences, such as underemployment or contingent employment, that may have less profound consequences for health. At present, researchers can safely say that unemployment is bad for your health (Jin et al., 1995). They cannot say whether an attempt to reduce unemployment by moving to a more flexible employment pattern (such as contingent employment) has more or less negative health consequences. Also, researchers cannot say whether advance notification of pending lay-off increases or decreases these negative health consequences.

Health promotion practitioners can also contribute to this new approach. Practitioners can (continue to) lobby for the approach and for a cross-sectoral political advisory body. Also, they can work with experts in other policy arenas, nurture the development of a policy entrepreneur or develop a career as a policy entrepreneur in a specific policy arena. The final goal of all these efforts should be to help better articulate trade-offs in public policy. The elements of the healthy public policy vision may serve an important purpose at the community level. By adopting a broader vision of how to implement this new approach at the state level, practitioners and advocates may influence policy development or modification and thereby help to bring about significant change.

REFERENCES

Amick, B. C., Levine, S., Tarlov, A., & Walsh, D. C. (1995). *Society and health.* New York: Oxford University Press.

Arnold, D. (1990). *The logic of congressional action.* New Haven, CT: Yale University Press.

Bunker, J. P., Gomby, D. F., & Kehrer, B. H. (1989). *Pathways to health: The role of social factors.* Menlo Park, CA: Henry J. Kaiser Family Foundation.

Challis, L., Fuller, S., Henwood, M., Klein, R., Plowden, W., Webb, A., Whittingham, P., & Wistow, G. (1988). *Joint approaches to social policy: Rationality and practice.* Cambridge, UK: Cambridge University Press.

Chubb, J. E., & Peterson, P. E. (1989). American political institutions and the problem of governance. In J. E. Chubb & P. E. Peterson, *Can the government govern?* Washington, DC: Brookings.

Dooley, D., Fielding, J., & Levi, L. (1996). Health and unemployment. *Annual Review of Public Health, 17,* 449-465.

Evans, R. G. (1994). Introduction. In R. G. Evans, M. L. Barer, & T. R. Marmor (Eds.), *Why are some people healthy and others not? The determinants of health in populations.* New York: Aldine de Gruyter.

Evans, R. G., & Stoddart, G. L. (1990). Producing health, consuming health care. *Social Science and Medicine, 31*(12), 1347-1363.

Frank, J. W. (1995). Why "population health." *Canadian Journal of Public Health, 86*(3), 162-164.

Gerstein, R., Labelle, J., MacLeod, S., Mustard, F., Spasoff, R., & Watson, J. (1991). *Nurturing health: A framework on the determinants of health.* Toronto: Premier's Council on Health Strategy.

Heclo, H. (1974). *Modern social politics in Britain and Sweden.* New Haven, CT: Yale University Press.

Heclo, H. (1978). Issue networks and the executive establishment. In A. King (Ed.), *The new American political system.* Washington, DC: American Enterprise Institute.

Hertzman, C., Frank, J., & Evans, R. G. (1994). Heterogeneities in health status and the determinants of population health. In R. G. Evans, M. L. Barer, & T. R. Marmor (Eds.), *Why are some people healthy and others not? The determinants of health in populations.* New York: Aldine de Gruyter.

Jin, R. L., Shah, C. P., & Svoboda, T. J. (1995). The impact of unemployment on health: A review of the evidence. *Canadian Medical Association Journal, 153*(5), 529-540.

Judge, K. (1995). Income distribution and life expectancy: A critical appraisal. *British Medical Journal, 311,* 1282-1285.

Labonte, R. (1995). Population health and health promotion: What do they have to say to each other? *Canadian Journal of Public Health, 86*(3), 165-168.

Lalonde, M. (1974). *A new perspective on the health of Canadians.* Ottawa, Ontario: Government of Canada.

Lavis, J. N., & Stoddart, G. L. (1994, Fall). Can we have too much health care? *Daedalus,* 43-60.

Marmor, T. R., Barer, M. L., & Evans, R. G. (1994). The determinants of a population's health: What can be done to improve a democratic nation's health status? In R. G. Evans, M. L. Barer, & T. R. Marmor (Eds.), *Why are some people healthy and others not? The determinants of health in populations.* New York: Aldine de Gruyter.

Milio, N. (1986). *Promoting health through public policy.* Ottawa, Ontario: Canadian Public Health Association.

Naylor, C. D. (1986). *Private practice, public payment: Canadian medicine and the politics of health insurance 1911–1966.* Kingston, Ontario, & Montreal, Quebec: McGill-Queen's University Press.

Organization for Economic Cooperation and Development. (1995). *Health reform in seventeen countries* (OECD Health Policy Studies No. 5). Paris: Author.

Pederson, A. P., Edwards, R. K., Marshall, V. W., Allison, K. R., & Kelner, M. (1988). *Coordinating healthy public policy: An analytic review and bibliography* (Working paper 88-1). Ottawa, Ontario: Health Services and Promotion Branch Working Paper.

Pierson, P. (1992, Fall). "Policy feedbacks" and political change: Contrasting Reagan and Thatcher's pension-reform initiatives. *Studies in American Political Development, 6,* 359-390.

Pierson, P. (1993, July). When effect becomes cause: Policy feedback and political change. *World Politics, 45,* 595-628.

Premier's Council. (1990). *People and skills in the new global economy.* Toronto: Queen's Printer for Ontario.

Rothstein, B. (1992). Labour market institutions and working-class strength. In S. Steinmo, K. Thelen, & F. Longstreth (Eds.), *Structuring politics: Historical institutionalism in comparative analysis.* Cambridge, UK: Cambridge University Press.

Runyan, C. W. (1985). Health assessment and public policy within a public health framework. In P. Karoly (Ed.), *Measurement strategies in health psychology.* New York: John Wiley.

Schieber, G. J., Poullier, J. P., & Greenwald, L. M. (1993, Summer). Health spending, delivery, and outcomes in OECD countries. *Health Affairs,* 120-129.

Signal, L. N. (1994). *The politics of the Ontario Premier's Council on Health Strategy: A case study in the new public health*. Unpublished doctoral dissertation, University of Toronto Department of Behavioural Science.

Skocpol, T. (1992). *Protecting soldiers and mothers: The political origins of social policy in the United States*. Cambridge, MA: Belknap.

Spasoff, R. (1992). A new approach to health promotion in Ontario. *Health Promotion International, 7,* 129-133.

Steinmo, S., Thelen, K., & Longstreth, F. (Eds.). (1992). *Structuring politics: Historical institutionalism in comparative analysis*. Cambridge, UK: Cambridge University Press.

Sullivan, T. J. (1991). Strategic planning for health: How to stay on top of the game. *Health Promotion, 30,* 2-8, 13.

Weir, M., & Skocpol, T. (1985). State structures and the possibilities for "Keynesian" responses to the Great Depression in Sweden, Britain and the United States. In P. Evans, D. Rueschemeyer, & T. Skocpol (Eds.), *Bringing the state back in*. Cambridge, UK: Cambridge University Press.

Wilkinson, R. G. (1992). Income distribution and life expectancy. *British Medical Journal, 304,* 165-168.

Wilkinson, R. G. (1995). Commentary: A reply to Ken Judge: Mistaken criticisms ignore overwhelming evidence. *British Medical Journal, 311,* 1285-1287.

World Health Organization. (1986). Ottawa charter for health promotion. *Health Promotion, 1*(4), iii-v.

COMMENTARY

Marshall W. Kreuter

The following response to the Lavis and Sullivan chapter comes from the perspective of one who is calling on his experiences as a health promotion practitioner/administrator within the public health sector at the state and national levels in the United States. I apologize in advance to scholars outside the field of public health for using examples specific to my field, but that is where my experience lies. The response begins with a brief overview of the points I found central to the thesis presented by Lavis and Sullivan, followed by a commentary inspired by their recommendations, which I concur with and support. The latter segment includes a few simple ideas that health promotion leaders at the provincial, state, or national levels may find useful as they attempt to translate the recommendations of Lavis and Sullivan into action.

GENERAL REACTION

Whatever their theoretical or conceptual differences, health promotion academicians and practitioners seem to find common ground in the reality that policy strategies constitute a critical focal point for health promotion research and practice. Lavis and Sullivan point out what should be obvious to anyone paying attention: that a large portion of a community's health status can be attributed to social and economic determinants. They go on to take the position that the "population approach"[1] to health offers the most coherent strategy to address those important determinants.

Based on their application of a policy feedback framework,[2] Lavis and Sullivan argue that in the absence of a strategy to address the social and economic determinants of health, categorical approaches to health policy-making paradoxically work *against* the development of innovative population approaches that try to address the root causes of unnecessary death, disease, and disability.

More specifically, policy feedback analyses reveal that a wide variety of actors involved in the policy formulation learn certain patterns of policy-making called "legacies." One example of such a "legacy" would be that special interest groups learn how to use their public affairs departments to mobilize resistance to real or threatened reductions in health spending in an effort to protect their categorical interests. Another example is manifested by the emergence of a competitive, "we/they" mentality where, for instance, acute care and clinical services are pitted against prevention or public health as they both seek economic support from a common resource pool. As these "legacies" become integrated in the policy-making process, according to Lavis and Sullivan, policymakers tend to lose sight of important population health goals and, thus, to work as a frequently unintended barrier to "population health" approaches.

The authors repeatedly suggest that the key to overcoming policy legacies that are detrimental to the concept of population health concept is finding ways to frame health as a *consequence,* not a primary objective, of the policies. This idea is consistent with one of the fundamental principles of the Precede/Proceed model for health promotion planning—specifically, that planners and practitioners should view health as an *instrumental,* not an ultimate, value, the rationale being that by embracing this principle, planners will be more likely to frame health as something that will benefit the primary interests of those outside the health sector.[3] For example, business leaders are not likely to support health promotion programs because of the inherent goodness of health per se; rather, they will be supportive because of the belief that such programs may (a) lower the rate of absenteeism, (b) reduce hospital and medical claim costs, or (c) enhance work performance; in short, health promotion would be seen as good business.

COMMUNICATING A COHERENT
VISION OF POPULATION HEALTH

Lavis and Sullivan describe three conditions that might result in an increase in the number of policies where the *consequences of health* are specifically incorporated as an important element: (a) rethinking the place of population health, (b) better focusing the vision of healthy public policy, and (c) reframing choices through a cross-sectoral political advisory body. What can state-, provincial-, and national-level health promotion leaders do to make these conditions a reality? I believe that an essential first step is to develop a plan to communicate a coherent and inspiring vision of population health—a vision designed to connect simultaneously with political decision makers and the general population they are supposed to serve.

Geoffrey Rose (1992)[4] has offered us this wisdom:

> Political decisions are for the politicians. Their agenda is complex, and mostly hidden from public scrutiny. This is unfortunate, because often the public would give higher priority to health than those who formulate political policies. Anything that stimulates more public information and debate on health issues is good, not just because it may lead to healthier choices, but also because it earns a high place for health issues on the political agenda. In the long run, this is probably the most important achievement of health education. (p. 123)

In the present context, Rose's message to health promotion leaders is clear: Place less emphasis on talking to one another and direct more time and attention to communicating a vision of population health to those outside your immediate circle. As population health advocates begin to act on that message, they may find some use in the lessons learned from a recent study conducted by Macro International and funded by the National Centers for Disease Control and Prevention (CDC).[5] The study offers an example of how the principles of marketing theory and research[6] were used to ascertain the extent to which the American public understood the goals, purpose, and value of public health. The results of focus group interviews of both political leaders and the general public confirmed the experience of public health pundits: that the decision makers and average citizens have little comprehension of either the scope or the significance of public health. For example, when asked, "What comes to mind when I mention public health?" responses included the following:

"Public health is restaurant inspections."

"Free immunizations."

"Doctors for the poor."

"The ugly pink building downtown."

More specifically, the study identified several misperceptions and attitudes that, if unaddressed, would tend to undermine efforts to create support for public health. These included the following:

- Limited awareness of public health's scope and significance

- Strong and exclusive association of public health and health departments as delivering services for the poor

- Misplaced confidence that public health functions can be and will be performed by others (the National Guard is one example!)

- Concern about the intrusiveness of lifestyle messages

- Resentment of public health's regulatory role

- Generic antigovernment sentiment—public health is yet another waste of tax dollars

However, the study also revealed that appreciation for public health could be readily stimulated by these approaches:

- Calling specific attention to the benefits from actions that are often taken for granted, such as clean water, environmental protection, and immunizations—respondents expressed appreciation for the value of public health

- Making clear how all people benefit from public health, even if they never set foot in the health department

- Providing local examples—for respondents, the most compelling evidence in highlighting the benefits and value of good public health, which confirms the conventional wisdom of looking to your own backyard first for those examples

The notion that decision makers are more likely to shift their views once they become more cognizant of relevant circumstances and/or consequences was dramatically demonstrated recently in the United States. Most political pundits were surprised by the Republican party's failure to hold the political gains made in the 1994 off-year elections through it's "Contract With America" strategy. On the basis of results from their 1994 national survey of American political attitudes, Lock, Shapiro, and Jacobs (1996) concluded that the reversal of fortune occurred when voters, especially Republican voters, realized that the strategy left out programs they valued and cared about, such as Medicare, Social Security, and environmental protection, at great risk. Thus, as state, provincial, and national health promotion leaders begin to formulate strategies to communicate the social and health benefits of population health, they should recognize that a critical first step must be to gather information regarding the specific misperceptions that decision makers may hold about the concept of population health. That step, in turn, is followed by a second task: creating "message concepts" designed to address those specific misperceptions. Here are some examples of effective message concepts that were developed based on data obtained from the Macro/CDC study. What are the analogues for population health?

Public health works. This idea highlights public health's many accomplishments and counters negative views of wasteful, ineffective bureaucracies. Public health is cost-effective.

Prevention works and is a good investment. Prevention services encompass everything from immunization to health education to restaurant inspections that prevent food-borne pathogens. This message acknowledges that when decision makers invest, they want two things: *profit* and *value.* An investment in health improvement that emphasizes prevention will achieve both. "Profit" will manifest itself in greater productivity and improved quality of life. "Value" will occur because for a large portion of contemporary health problems, effective prevention yields positive health outcomes at less cost than awaiting treatment (Tolsma & Koplan, 1992).

Public health has a mandate to address the health of everyone in your community. This message reinforces the protective aspect of public health and applies to entire communities as well as to individuals and families. It also captures the essential role of monitoring health status and documenting progress in combating diseases, injuries, and disabilities.

The approach taken in the Macro/CDC study, as well as the recommendations from Lavis and Sullivan, are consistent with counsel previously offered to health promotion planners:

> Those who enter the political arena do so because they have a stake in policy and must engage the conflict . . . to pursue their policy agenda. Your purpose in diagnosing the politics of policy is to anticipate the political sides, the political actors, and the power relationships that will line up for and against the policies you or someone else must promote to bring about the enabling support, regulation, and organizational or environmental changes required for a given program. With sides, actors, and relationships identified, the remaining task is to propose a set of exchanges that will enable each of the sides or actors to gain something in a win-win, rather that a win-lose transaction. (Green & Kreuter, 1999)

INTEGRATING HEALTH CONSEQUENCES
INTO PUBLIC POLICY

Without question, health promotion advocates must be active participants in the formulation of policies that address the priority health problems threatening the quality of life of those they serve. But Lavis and Sullivan have reminded us that we have an additional leadership challenge: to develop viable strategies ensuring that relevant aspects of health, with special emphasis on the social and economic determinants of health, are inferred in all public policy. Are there precedents we can draw on as we take up this challenge?

Nutrition offers one of the most dramatic examples of population health benefits resulting from actions taken by nonhealth sectors. Although the initiation of the dramatic shift toward the consumption of healthful foods in advanced economies may be credited to health advocacy based on nutrition research, its rapid diffusion is unquestionably the result of food manufacturers responding to consumer demands. Thus, state, provincial, and national health leaders seek ways to systematically activate consumer demand. Based on his 25 years experience with the famous longitudinal North Karelia cardiovascular disease prevention program, Puska (1996) observed that most politicians are quite sensitive to what they hear from the people and from media and industry leaders. By comparison, they don't listen much to experts.

In some instances, the organizational mechanisms, or at lease some parts thereof, for inferring the consequences of health into public policy, are already in place. In the United States for example, the Office of Disease Prevention and Health Promotion (ODPHP) within the Department of Health and Human Services (DHHS) has responsibility for maintaining policy consultations and reviews with all federal-level agencies, not just those in DHHS. And in both Australia and the United States there has been an increase in philanthropies and foundations dedicated to a wide range of health improvement initiatives. Some of these foundations have used their leverage and resources to go beyond the boundaries of traditional health care to create cross-sectoral partnerships for health. For example, Healthway, the Western Australian Health Foundation in Perth, Western Australia, has maintained its credibility through research affiliations with local universities (University of Western Australia and Curtain University), while forging productive alliances with, among other groups, public schools, professional athletic teams, the music industry, food producers, the arts, and numerous businesses. In each instance, *health consequences* are the major focus of programs and policies tied to these partnerships.[7]

SOME FINAL THOUGHTS

As leaders advance the philosophic and policy intent of population health, especially as it is articulated within the context of the Ottawa Charter for Health Promotion (World Health Organization, 1986), I urge them to express those tenets with clarity and precision. Such clarity of expression should include a clear reminder that social justice remains a core value in democratic governance. That said, advocates beware! As is readily noticeable in all market economies, those with strong conservative interests are facile in their ability to juxtapose the principle of social justice *against* the principle of freedom, artfully framing the former as a threat to freedom by claiming that it diminishes opportunity—opportunity to choose and compete in the marketplace without interference.

The following quote by Milton Friedman (Friedman & Friedman, 1962), the supply-side economist whose theories have so influenced contemporary conservative political thinking, offers a good example of such rhetoric: "Few trends could so thoroughly undermine the very foundations of our free society as the acceptance by corporate officials of a social responsibility other than to make as much money for their shareholders as possible" (p. 26).

Not only does it tie the drive to make "as much money as possible" to the powerful moral value of freedom, it also argues that the connection between economic gain and freedom would be compromised if corporate leaders were inclined to assume social responsibility. This is the economic perspective that has served as the primary force behind the global move to privatize government, including public health. As the privatized proportion of government has increased, so too has the sentiment expressed by Friedman (that social responsibility undermines freedom); we have been generally ineffective in contesting that position. Within the context of a participatory democracy where individual freedoms are balanced against the common good, the expression of moral indignation over Friedman's logic is insufficient; more care should be taken to show that his thesis is empirically faulty. A free society is not undermined by taking on social responsibility, even at the possible expense of corporate profits; on the contrary, as history demonstrates, it is undermined when civic responsibility is dismissed and greed celebrated.

As the cause is taken up for what Lavis and Sullivan refer to as a "new approach," care should be taken not to let legitimate criticism over limitations in some aspects of public health be interpreted as a wholesale dismissal of the entire discipline. Many of the key aspects of population health have been made, and should continue to be made, within the boundaries of public health. Winslow's (1923/1984) much referenced 1923 definition of public health serves to illustrate the point:

> Public health is the science and the art of preventing disease, prolonging life and promoting physical health through organized community efforts for the sanitation of the environment, the control of community infection, the education of the individual in the principles of personal hygiene, the organization of medical and nursing services for the early diagnosis and preventive treatment of disease and the *development of the social machinery which will ensure to every individual in the community a standard of living adequate for the maintenance of health.* (p. 23)

The italicized reference to the notions of *social machinery* and *standard of living adequate to the maintenance of health* is clear acknowledgment that we cannot seriously address the matter of a public's health without confronting its social and, therefore, economic determinants. The creation of new terminology such as "population health" does have the benefit of making sharper distinctions for academics and advocates. However, if such innovations are not advanced within the context of an overall scheme of health improvement, it can have the negative effects of confounding decision makers and the general public and raising barriers that separate professionals who should be allies.

Oversimplified debates that try to separate the concepts of public health and population health have already led to a familiar line of clatter. One side takes the position that there is clear evidence that preventable health problems compromise quality of life; ergo, society is obliged to address those problems. The opposing side argues that until inequities are resolved, interventions into health problems are futile exercises in blaming the victim! Such polemic causes us to lose sight of the fact that the concepts are interdependent and share common ground in the moral principles of social justice.

So the task for national- and state-level health promotion leaders is straightforward. Get the message out that inequity is the major risk factor inhibiting quality of life, and communities, indeed nations, cannot be truly healthy until that risk factor is honestly addressed (Marmot, 1996). And if visionary leadership is a prerequisite, so too is the skill and commitment to get into alignment the organizational connections and mechanisms through which the *consequences* of health are inferred, across the board, into public policy.

NOTES

1. In this context, "population health" is the extension of health promotion as described in healthy public policy and so on.

2. "Policy feedback" describes a kind of learning process that policymakers experience. Policy feedback "frames" the context in which government officials, interest groups, and the general public discover how resources are created and are influenced by various political and economic incentives. Lavis and Sullivan refer to actions taken as a result of this framing process as "policy legacies."

3. See Green and Kreuter (1999, pp. 52-56) for a detailed discussion on why health promotion practitioners and researchers would benefit from viewing health as an *instrumental value* rather than an ultimate value.

4. See *The Strategy of Preventive Medicine* (Rose, 1992). In this classic 125-page paperback, the late Professor Rose combines his command of science with his sensitive humanity to give public health workers insights they can apply every day. It should be a part of every practitioner's personal library.

5. *Marketing Core Public Health Functions: Summary of Focus Group Findings and Implications for Message Concepts.* Macro International, Inc., and Westat Inc., August 1994. Contract study with the Centers for Disease Control and Prevention #200-93-0653. Practitioners will find this straightforward description to be a useful resource.

6. For a practical descriptions of communications and media advocacy methods in a similar context, see Kreuter, Lezin, Kreuter, and Green (1998).

7. For more information about Healthway, contact Healthway, PO Box 1284, West Perth, WA 6872, Australia. For e-mail: healthway@healthway.wa.gov.au

REFERENCES

Friedman, M., & Friedman, R. D. (1962). *Capitalism and freedom.* Chicago: University of Chicago Press.

Green, L. W., & Kreuter, M. W. (1999). *Health promotion planning: An educational and ecological approach* (3rd ed.). Mountain View, CA: Mayfield.

Kreuter, M. W., Lezin, N., Kreuter, M., & Green, L. W. (1998). *Community health promotion ideas that work: A field book for practitioners.* Sudbury, MA: Jones & Bartlett.

Lock, S., Shapiro, R. Y., & Jacobs, L. R. (1996, April). *Public discontent: Reminding the public what the federal government does: An experiment.* Paper presented at the annual meeting of the Midwest Political Science Association, Chicago.

Marmot, M. (1996). The social pattern of health and disease. In D. Blane, E. Brunner, & R. Wilkinson (Eds.), *Health and social organization.* London: Routledge.

Puska, P. (1996). Development of public policy on the prevention and control of elevated blood cholesterol. *Cardiovascular Risk Factors, 6*(4), Lippincott-Raven Publishers.

Rose, G. (1992). *The strategy of preventive medicine.* New York: Oxford University Press.

Tolsma, D. D., & Koplan, J. P. (1992). Health behaviors and health promotion. In J. M. Last & R. B. Wallace (Eds.), *Maxcy-Rosenau-Last: Public health and preventive medicine* (13th ed., pp. 701-714). East Norwalk, CT: Appleton & Lange.

Winslow, C. E. A. (1920). The untilled fields of public health. *Science, 51,* 23.

World Health Organization. (1986). Ottawa charter for health promotion. *Health Promotion, 1*(4), iii-v.

9

Reflections on Settings for Health Promotion

Blake D. Poland
Lawrence W. Green
Irving Rootman

This concluding chapter offers the opportunity to reflect on the insights and suggestions of each of the contributors to this volume. In particular, we pose three questions emerging from the key themes in the chapters of this book. First, what can we deduce about the nature of settings from the diverse perspectives represented, concerning their differences and similarities within and across types of settings? Second, what challenges face those who would undertake a settings approach? Third, what are the likely future directions in research and practice that will shape the development of settings approaches most productively for health promotion?

THE NATURE OF SETTINGS

The first question has two parts. What makes classification by settings distinct enough to warrant separate attention to its special features in planning health promotion for its occupants, residents, or participants? Second, for those seeking to make sense of, and to apply, a settings approach to health promotion, are settings sufficiently alike within categories of settings (e.g., educational, occupational, communities, health care settings) to be able to identify essential features of these categories of settings as a basis for a systematic approach to practice? The assumption implicit in the prevailing organization of training, planning, policy, research, and evaluation for most health promotion development would indicate that such homogeneity within categories and distinctions between categories in fact justify these dominant organizing themes of the field.

Yet settings differ significantly both within categories (e.g., different types of workplaces) and across categories of settings (e.g., the home versus the school as a setting). Clearly, "total institutions" such as hospitals, clinical practice settings, workplaces, and schools are different environments from settings that have less formalized organizational structures and procedures, such as homes and communities. Thus, a first feature of settings to justify the use of this rubric to organize conceptual thinking and strategy in health promotion is that the specification of setting immediately connects the practical and humanistic project of health promotion with the theoretical and scientific literature, the historical and cultural traditions, and the contemporary trends and customs associated with the type of setting in question. Hospitals and other clinical settings, for example, have an administrative and management literature that guides the training and conduct of administrators in those settings in ways that distinguish them from school administrators and educational planners in their worldview, their preparation for practice, and their values and assumptions. Yet both bodies of literature and research draw on a common body of more generalizable knowledge, more basic research, and organizational theory from sociology, political science, and economics. Thus, the applied sciences have tended to branch away from their basic science roots along lines that often correspond with specific types of settings. So have policy and practice.

Settings also differ according to stakeholders, the people who pay for health promotion and the people who should benefit from health promotion. For example, for hospitals, health promotion may represent a "lucrative new market" (Chapter 5) for third party reimbursement, whereas in the workplace it may be seen as an additional expense with uncertain benefits. In schools, it might seem a frill in an era of back-to-basics education or a way to improve attendance and student alertness so that educational goals can be more efficiently achieved. A second justification for using settings as an organizing framework for research and development in health promotion, then, might be to link health promotion more effectively to the goals and aspirations of stakeholders who will support it and sustain it.

As noted in Chapter 1, a critical social science perspective reminds us that all social relations are contingent on the unique confluence of personalities and other social, economic, and political influences in time and space. This suggests a third justification for organizing the health promotion field's theory and practice according to settings—namely, that settings provide a time-and-space specificity to the interpretation of social and psychological processes, their economic and political influences. This allows the organization of data and observations according to consistent characteristics in setting-specific environments.

Notwithstanding differences in theoretical and scientific grounding, stakeholder interests, and the contingent nature of social processes in specific categories of settings, some similarities and core features can be identified as cutting across settings for health promotion. Several contributors in this volume seek to identify these core features of a setting. Soubhi and Potvin (Chapter 2), for example, argue that the home as a setting comprises four principal components: physical structure and layout, temporal patterning of behavior, material milieu, and social milieu. Much the same could be said of each of the other categories of settings, so one might start with these as the essential building blocks of a settings approach to health promotion. Several authors point to the significance of the physical or built environment of the setting as a determinant of health in its own right (e.g., potential for injuries in the home, school, or workplace or the availability of green space in school grounds, work environments, or community settings). They also cite the effects of the built environment on social relations (e.g., impact of distance between workstations on social interaction in the workplace). These relationships in turn exert an influence on health.

Most also point to the setting as a psychosocial environment, as a shared social reality. The relatively well-defined patterning of social interactions is based largely on the setting-specific definition (and allocation) of social roles and resources. Certain shared cultural assumptions accompany the social roles, for example, of parent, teacher, physician, and state legislator, and these shape the nature of social interaction within settings such as the home, school, hospital, and workplace. In addition, these settings themselves have unique expectations or norms regarding "how one acts." Behavioral norms in one type of setting differ from what is expected in another type of setting. On the other hand, aspects of broader social relations, such as those based on race, gender, age, and occupation, cut across and are also reflected in specific settings. The psychosocial environment of the setting includes the quality and level of intimacy of relationships, degree of participation and control (i.e., hierarchy, power relations), organizational arrangements (such as management style, in the case of formal institutions), and history of internal politics. All of these more or less systematic psychosocial variations make settings a useful unit of analysis and unit of planning for health promotion intervention.

KEY CHALLENGES AND
OPPORTUNITIES FOR PRACTICE

One of the implications of taking the psychosocial environment seriously is that the whole is more than the sum of its parts; the family is not reducible to individual family members any more than the workplace is reducible to individual supervisors or employees or the community is reducible to individual community groups or neighborhoods. Indeed, this is fundamental to an ecological perspective on settings, as outlined in Chapter 1. In his commentary on Chapter 2, Larry Fisher argues that this means interventions ought to be directed at relationships, not individuals; but that to the extent that they do address individuals, they should focus on those who have power in that setting, lest that power be used to block change. It is also clear that the routinization of social relations within settings—and the sense of being taken for granted and social stability that it engenders—acts as a powerful conservatizing force that resists change. This is sometimes highlighted when it becomes clear that making the setting a target of health promotion risks destabilizing existing taken-for-granted social relations.

The preceding discussion bears directly on a long-standing debate in social theory that has implications for health promotion practice—namely, the relative emphasis one places on agency (individual action) or structure (social and material environment) in the making of human history (Eakin, Robertson, Poland, Coburn, & Edwards, 1996; Poland, 1992). Recent contributions in both behavioral and social theory overwhelmingly stress the dialectical nature of agency and structure. People shape their environments consciously through directed action and less consciously through repeated actions that reproduce taken-for-granted aspects of the status quo. Just as surely, they are influenced in their thoughts and actions by the social and material environment in which they operate. Critical theorists (e.g., Habermas, 1973) and advocates of critical pedagogy (e.g., Freire, 1990) argue that a more reflexive stance vis-à-vis the taken-for-granted can contribute significantly to (and indeed is a prerequisite for) more intentionally self-directive and emancipatory individual and collective action aimed at making settings more healthful environments for daily living.

This has been echoed, in many ways, by calls for more active involvement of people in settings in the planning and evaluation of health promotion efforts. Evidence also suggests that such participatory approaches are more likely to result in sustained and meaningful change (Green et al., 1995). Indeed, many would argue that such participation is congruent with the notion of "enabling" in health promotion, which requires that people be given the resources, power, and knowledge to create and support change. It also appears congruent with shifting and newly emerging modes of governance in the form of decentralized control, privatization, and community participation, which have produced newly fractured and reconstituted lines of accountability and partnerships (see O'Malley, 1996). But clearly, the practices that flow from a rhetorical appeal to the benefits of participation span a continuum with respect to the level of grassroots decision-making power and control, from token consultation through negotiated partnership to complete grassroots control (Arnstein, 1969; Labonte, 1993; Rifkin, 1985).

This issue has been debated by several contributors to this volume. On the one hand, McLaren, Leonardo, and Pérez (commentary on Chapter 3) hold that for health promotion to truly be enabling and self-emancipatory, it must relinquish technocratic management of individuals and of settings to promote health. It should, instead, enable the self-actualization of the critical citizen, they argue. On the other hand, in her commentary on Chapter 3, Perry argues that large multicomponent and theory-based interventions by definition require top-down development by "experts." In large measure, what differentiates these perspectives is the perspective of the authors with respect to things such as the objectivity of "science," the way in which social theory informs practice, how broadly health and well-being are defined, and the ultimate goals of intervention. These must be recognized as influences on practice regardless of the settings to which health promotion is applied, although clearly settings also contain their own perspectives and leanings in these regards that also influence practice.

It would appear that if the institutionalization of the promotion of health in settings is to be complete, it will require a transformation in the perspectives, values, and training of the majority of people in that setting. Health cannot remain the exclusive purview of health promotion and other professionals working in relative isolation. Indeed, one would hope that the longer-term goal is to ensure that the consideration of health and promotion of health be well ensconced in the routine practices of that setting. This is discussed perhaps most clearly by Lavis and Sullivan in Chapter 8, but it applies elsewhere as well. Yet curiously, the expectation of integrating health promotion across a wide spectrum of settings and routine institutional practices (as has been proclaimed necessary within hospitals and clinical general practice, by contributors to this book), has not carried over into the workplace or other settings in which health is not seen as the primary raison d'être. The experience even in settings where health is the primary focus suggests that the implementation of practice guidelines has not been sufficient to ensure adequate health promotion. Changes must also be made at the organizational level.

The organizational change literature is clear about the way in which new organizational structures (reporting relationships, reward structures, etc.) are required to support (or even catalyze) the desired behavior change. Beer, Eisenstat, and Spector (1990), for example, indicate that strong central leadership and vision must be coupled with decentralized and autonomy-supportive implementation. In other (noncorporate, community) circles, it is argued that the visioning also needs to happen at the grassroots level (Hancock, 1990; Raeburn, commentary on Chapter 7). The centralized versus decentralized debate in health promotion reduces, like most such debates, to a recognition of the need for both. Some centralized support if not leadership is needed, and some bottom-up initiative and control is also needed.

With respect to community development in health, Boutilier, Cleverly, and Labonte (Chapter 7) argue that a supportive organizational context includes "supportive peer relations and organizational norms"; knowledgeable, experienced, and supportive managers; "enabling internal policies" (regarding flexibility, accountability, ethical stance, political analysis of health problems), and "an expansive and legitimating rhetoric." Many of the projects described by contributing authors as making up the leading edge of health promotion in various settings are characterized by terms such as *integrated, comprehensive, multifaceted, participatory, empowering, partnership, responsive,* and *tailored.* Although descriptive of the gist of their intent, these terms need to be unpacked to understand the range of practices they conceal, as well as both their intended and unintended consequences.

Shifting institutional cultures with respect to health promotion will require support for staff training. Few teachers, physicians, hospital workers, bureaucrats, or parents are trained in health promotion. Nor are they trained to see practices and policies in terms of their influence on health, to see opportunities for enhancing health, and to have the broad range of analytic and communicative skills to make it happen. But such training should also be mindful of the potential for the ever-expanding medicalization of daily life. Although health can provide a helpful focal point and impetus for galvanizing action on issues affecting the well-being of citizens, practitioners should be mindful of the need to frame health in terms of broad personal and social/community mental, spiritual, and physical well-being. It cannot be left simply as the avoidance of disease ensconced in a discourse of "risk avoidance" and "risk management." In their commentary on Chapter 3, McLaren et al. argue that this discourse of risk management may do more to create moral and social distance between the "well" and the "unwell" than to foster solidarity and collective action on issues of social justice.

Despite the search in some circles for complex, evidence-based, multifaceted interventions that can be packaged and exported to most settings, a one-size-fits-all approach (the use of identical protocols in similar settings) is often ineffective or inappropriate. The recent reports on complex intervention trials at the community level (e.g., Farquhar et al., 1990) demonstrate the need for some local autonomy not only in the implementation and adaptation of set strategies but also in the assessment of needs (e.g., Bailey, Rukholm, Vanderlee, & Hyland, 1994) and setting of priorities and objectives (e.g., Zanna et al., 1994). This is the essential understanding in the application of participatory planning approaches to the development of health promotion programs (Green & Kreuter, 1999; Green et al., 1995; Kok, 1992).

Indeed, a review of the contributions to this book suggests that much of the success of health promotion initiatives in all settings depends on a careful reflexive reading of the particular setting and one's role in it. This could include the following:

- The institutional or organizational culture

- The expectations, attitudes, and beliefs of key players (workers and management, patients and physicians, students and teachers, parents and children, community groups and state officials)

- The nature of the practice environment (e.g., incentives and disincentives for undertaking health promotion such as reward structures, pace of work, competing demands, skepticism regarding the value or relevance or effectiveness of health promotion, training of key staff)

- Historical developments in that setting (trends in the organization of work, in the composition of the family, or in the organization of health care)

- Internal politics, leadership (formal and informal), past successes and failures

- Who controls access to the setting; who has influence within the setting

- Broader social, economic, and political context (nonsetting influences)

Settings may have multiple roles or functions. For example, a hospital, in addition to being a particular kind of acute and chronic care institution for patients, also functions as a workplace for its employees and a home for those who are terminally ill (and for residents of longer-term care facilities). Workplaces provide a locus for productive activity but also serve as a primary social setting for many workers, a source of personal identification, and even the site for child care, health education, and physical exercise in those worksites where the employer has pursued a progressive policy of supporting employee health. Home or residence serves basic biological needs for shelter, food preparation, and rest but also a place for privacy, intimacy, esthetic expression, and self-actualization and, increasingly, a place for income-generating work. Each type of setting, then, may perform some of the functions of the other types of settings.

In Chapter 2, Soubhi and Potvin issue a challenge to health promotion professionals to employ an integrated model that would specify health promotion at three levels: that of the individual, that of the setting, and across settings (the external environment, related settings, the resources available to members, and how these are distributed among members and across specific settings, for example). This acknowledges the need in health promotion to develop ecological approaches to program development (Green, Richard, & Potvin, 1996; Kickbush, 1989; McLeroy, Bibeau, Steckler, & Glanz, 1988; Richard, Potvin, Kishchuk, Prlic, & Green, 1996). The coordination of efforts across settings, and the integration of interventions in multiple settings, is advocated by several authors in this volume. This is based in part on the recognition that people move in and out of settings in the course of their daily routines, so their lives are not as compartmentalized as a settings approach might lead us to believe. Second, a call for a more coordinated approach is also based on the recognition that interventions in other settings can have synergistic impacts or work at cross-purposes to what health promotion is trying to achieve in a particular setting. Large, community-based, cardiovascular risk reduction intervention trials demonstrate the synergistic effects of coordinated efforts at the community level and within several sites (schools, workplaces, etc.) at the same time. Third, many problems that are experienced in one setting (e.g., schoolyard bullying) have their origins in other settings (e.g., in the home). In her commentary on Chapter 4, Joan Eakin argues that this presents an opportunity for health promotion to tackle health issues (such as stress) that have their roots in several settings, thereby helping to spread the blame as needed so that management is not too threatened, but which leaves open the possibility of moving from an initial focus on stress management (as individual coping) to contributing factors in the work environment (as trust is built and participants are ready to make that shift in focus). In addition, a number of authors in this volume have challenged practitioners to consider settings not simply as locations for health promotion (using the setting as a vehicle for reaching a specific audience with lifestyle modification programming) but also as targets of intervention themselves, recognizing the contributions that the physical, organizational, and psychosocial environment of the setting (could) make to the health of its members.

UNRESOLVED QUESTIONS

What is less clear from the selection of chapters and commentaries in this book is how practitioners should decide, when they have the luxury of doing so, which setting is the most appropriate for a given health issue or problem. This will likely depend on whom one is trying to reach (who are the high-risk people, if the approach is to be directed at high-risk people), where there is political will (and resources) to work, where willing and enthusiastic partners can be found, and so forth. The likelihood of pressure being brought to bear by gatekeepers in shaping the nature of the intervention must also be considered, and it is likely that familiarity with successful interventions undertaken elsewhere will have a bearing on what is tried.

In this regard, a settings approach presents some unique challenges with respect to evaluation, compared with many other health promotion programs, especially if the focus of intervention extends beyond that of the setting as a location of health promotion to include efforts at improving the setting itself. The uniqueness of many settings limits the utility of randomized controlled trials and other experimental methods of evaluation, and in any case, such methods by themselves tell us little about why and how an intervention succeeded or failed (Poland, Taylor, Eyles, & White, 1994). In addition, changes in intermediary factors such as institutional culture or quality of family life may not be readily apparent, much less their impacts on health and well-being. We would suggest that evaluators in a settings approach must become adept at identifying intermediate outcomes that can be theoretically and practically linked to health and well-being through a plausible logic model.

FUTURE DIRECTIONS IN PRACTICE AND RESEARCH

There are many other settings—public washrooms, street corners, supermarkets, the Internet, specific institutions (e.g., prisons, public health units, nursing homes)—that are not covered in this book but that are places in which health and health experience is shaped. As the settings approach becomes more widely practiced, discussed, examined, and researched, we anticipate that some of these "nontraditional" settings will begin to receive more attention in health promotion. As a result, some marginalized groups who are excluded from mainstream settings such as the home, school, or workplace, and who have hitherto been missed by a settings approach, will have the opportunity to work with health promotion professionals to address key determinants of their health.

The emergence of new information technologies will create new opportunities and challenges for a settings approach in health promotion. On the one hand, such technologies have increased the permeability of setting boundaries, as people work from home, engage in distance education, and form social bonds with people in distant locations. As indicated in particular by Ilze Kalnins, in her commentary on Chapter 2, new information technologies also present new challenges for health promotion (with the commercialization of the Internet and the extension of its reach into the home and the schools, for example), as well as new opportunities for communicating in novel and engaging ways about the determinants of health.

With the pace of change accelerating as we enter the new millennium, we predict that a focus on understanding and managing change within and across settings will assume greater importance in its own right as a concern of health promotion. As Jane Lethbridge notes in her commentary on Chapter 5, health promotion professionals may be uniquely poised to take advantage of this opportunity, given their interdisciplinary training and scope of expertise across levels of analysis (micro/meso/macro).

We also suspect that as we gain a fuller understanding of the holistic nature of health (mind-body connections, ecological complexity, etc.), the importance of well-rounded, multilevel, intersectoral health promotion initiatives will be highlighted (e.g., Cook, Back, & Trudeau, 1996; Parcel, Simons-Morton, & Kolbe, 1988).

From a research perspective, a holistic understanding of health and of the role of settings in influencing health will require a shift in the methods required to understand fully the influence of settings on health. Specifically, we foresee increased attention on interpretive (qualitative and historical) methods as a basis for understanding the complexities and intricacies of settings, and the impact of health promotion interventions and initiatives within these contexts (Poland, 1992).

Clearly, more research is required to understand the true nature of a settings approach to health promotion, to better appreciate the range of considerations that must be brought to bear on the design, implementation, and evaluation of a settings approach.

Relative to research within settings, we know little about relationships between settings: how people move across settings in their daily routines, interactions between settings, and the role that relationships and discontinuities play in health.

REFERENCES

Arnstein, S. R. (1969, July). A ladder of citizen participation. *American Institute of Planners Journal, 35*(4), 216-224.

Bailey, P. H., Rukholm, H. H., Vanderlee, R., & Hyland, J. (1994). A heart health survey at the worksite: The first step to effective programming. *AAOHN Journal, 42*(1), 9-14.

Beer, M., Eisenstat, R. A., & Spector, B. (1990). Why change programs don't produce change. *Harvard Business Review, 44,* 1192-1202.

Cook, R. F., Back, A., & Trudeau, J. (1996). Substance abuse prevention in the workplace: Recent findings and an expanded conceptual model. *Journal of Primary Prevention, 16,* 319-339.

Eakin, J., Robertson, A., Poland, B., Coburn, D., & Edwards, R. (1996). Towards a critical social science perspective on health promotion research. *Health Promotion International, 11*(2), 157-165.

Farquhar, J. W., Fortmann, S. P., Flora, J. A., Taylor, C. B., Haskell, W. L., Williams, P. T., Maccoby, N., & Wood, P. D. (1990). Effects of community-wide education on cardiovascular disease risk factors: The Stanford 5-city project. *Journal of the American Medical Association, 264,* 359-365.

Freire, P. (1990). *Pedagogy of the oppressed.* New York: Continuum.

Green, L. W., George, A., Daniel, M., Frankish, C. J., Herbert, C. P., Bowie, W., & O'Neill, M. (1995). *Participatory research in health promotion.* Ottawa, Ontario: Royal Society of Canada.

Green, L. W., & Kreuter, M. W. (1999). *Health promotion planning: An educational and environmental approach.* Mountain View, CA: Mayfield.

Green, L. W., Richard, L., & Potvin, L. (1996). Ecological foundations of health promotion. *American Journal of Health Promotion, 10,* 270-281.

Habermas, J. (1973). *Legitimation crisis.* Boston: Beacon.

Hancock, T. (1990). Developing healthy public policies at the local level. In A. Evers, W. Farrant, & A. Trojan (Eds.), *Healthy public policy at the local level.* Boulder, CO: Westview.

Kickbush, I. (1989). Approaches to an ecological base for public health. *Health Promotion International, 4,* 265-268.

Kok, G. (1992). Quality of planning as a decisive determinant of health education effectiveness. *Hygie: International Journal of Health Education, 11*(4), 5-9.

Labonte, R. (1993). Community development and partnerships. *Canadian Journal of Public Health, 84*(4), 237-240.

McLeroy, K. R., Bibeau, D., Steckler, A., & Glanz, K. (1988). An ecological perspective on health promotion. *Health Education Quarterly, 15,* 351-377.

O'Malley, P. (1996). Post-social criminologies: Some implications of current political trends for criminological theory and practice. *Current Issues in Criminal Justice, 8*(1), 26-38.

Parcel, G. S., Simons-Morton, B. G., & Kolbe, L. J. (1988). Health promotion: Integrating organizational change and student learning strategies. *Health Education Quarterly, 15,* 435-450.

Poland, B. (1992). Learning to "walk our talk": The implications of sociological theory for research methodologies in health promotion. *Canadian Journal of Public Health, 83*(Suppl. 1), S31-S46.

Poland, B., Taylor, S. M., Eyles, J., & White, N. F. (1994). Qualitative evaluation of the Brantford COMMIT intervention trial: The smokers' perspective. *Health and Canadian Society, 2*(2), 269-316.

Richard, L., Potvin, L., Kishchuk, N., Prlic, H., & Green, L. W. (1996). Assessment of the integration of the ecological approach in health promotion programs. *American Journal of Health Promotion, 10,* 318-328.

Rifkin, S. (1985). *Health planning and community participation.* London: Croom Helm.

Zanna, M., Cameron, R., Goldsmith, C. H., Poland, B., Lindsay, E., & Walker, R. (1994). Critique of the COMMIT study based on the Brantford experience. *Health and Canadian Society, 2*(2), 319-336.

Index

About the Editors

Blake D. Poland is Assistant Professor in the Department of Public Health Sciences at the University of Toronto, Affiliate Scientist with the Centre for Addictions and Mental Health, and Director of the Masters of Health Science program in Health Promotion at the University of Toronto. He received his Ph.D. in geography from McMaster University and was a postdoctoral fellow with the Centre for Health Promotion before joining the Addiction Research Foundation in 1994. His research is informed by critical social theory and relies primarily on qualitative methods. His research interests include governmentality and processes of spatial and social exclusion and their implications for health promotion, community development as an arena of practice for health professionals, and interactions between smokers and nonsmokers in public and private spaces.

Lawrence W. Green was Director of the University of British Columbia Institute of Health Promotion Research and Professor in Health Care and Epidemiology while this book was in preparation. He is now Distinguished Fellow and Visiting Scientist in the Office on Smoking and Health of the National Center for Chronic Disease Prevention and Health Promotion, U.S. Centers for Disease Control. He has worked in health promotion at local, state, federal, and international levels, at several universities in the United States, Canada, Australia, and the Netherlands, and as a practitioner or researcher in community, school, clinical, and workplace settings.

Irving Rootman is Director of the Centre for Health Promotion and a Professor in the Department of Public Health Sciences at the University of Toronto. Prior to joining the university in 1990, he worked for Health and Welfare Canada in a number of senior positions in the Health Promotion and Non-Medical Use of Drugs Directorates. He has published widely in the field of health promotion, his most recent book being *People-Centered Health Promotion* (1998) with John Raeburn.

About the Contributors

L. Kay Bartholomew is Assistant Professor of Behavioral Sciences at the University of Texas School of Public Health and is also affiliated with the Center for Health Promotion Research and Development. For 15 years, she directed patient education at a large teaching hospital, and she has conducted research on the self-management of chronic diseases such as asthma and cystic fibrosis.

Karen Basen-Engquist, Ph.D., M.P.H., is Assistant Professor in the Department of Behavioral Science at the University of Texas M. D. Anderson Cancer Center. She received her Ph.D. in community psychology from the University of Texas at Austin and her master's degree in public health from the University of Texas School of Public Health. She conducted research on adolescent and school health for approximately 11 years and served as co-principal investigator on Safer Choices, a randomized trial of a school-based HIV, STD, and pregnancy prevention program. In addition, she is currently conducting research on the health behavior and quality of life of cancer survivors and the effect of innovative cancer-screening technologies on patients.

Robert L. Bertera is currently an independent investigator and consultant. He previously held management and research positions in health promotion and health care services at the DuPont Company. He led the company's efforts to design, implement, and evaluate health promotion and clinical preventive services for over 300,000 employees, pensioners, and family members. The C. Everett Koop Award for excellence in program design and evaluation recognized the published record of this effort. His primary research interests are the health of older workers and the evaluation of workplace and community programs that focus on health, educational, behavioral, socioeconomic, and environmental factors.

Marie Boutilier holds a status appointment as Assistant Professor in the Department of Public Health Sciences, University of Toronto. For several years, she was the Senior Research Associate in Community Action Research with the North York Community Health Promotion Research Unit, a partnership of the Centre for Health Promotion, University of Toronto, and the North York Public Health Department. Her research has focused on increasing the capacity of professionals and community members to work together on health issues. This has involved participatory action research projects with grassroots community groups, health organizations, and professionals, integrating participatory and action research into public health practice. She is currently working on a study of community action and public health across Ontario.

David Butler-Jones is the Chief Medical Health Officer for the Province of Saskatchewan and is Assistant Clinical Professor in the Faculty of Medicine, University of Saskatchewan. He is President of the Canadian Public Health Association, Vice President of the American Public Health Association, International Regent for the American College of Preventive Medicine, and Past Chair of the National Coalition on Enhancing Preventive Practices of Health Professionals. In 1992, he received the Distinguished Service Award for contributions to Public Health in Ontario. He trained at the University of Toronto and Queen's University and is a Fellow of the Royal College of Physicians, Fellow of the American College of Preventive Medicine and a Certificant of the College of Family Practice of Canada. He is married to a United Church minister, and they have three children.

Shelley Cleverly has been the Project Coordinator for a study of Indicators of Community Capacity, based at the University of Toronto and funded by the National Health Research and Development Program. For 5 years prior to this project, she was Research Officer and Co-Investigator with the North York Community Health Promotion Research Unit on other community health and action research projects, including Indicators of Empowerment in Public Health Practice and a study of the North York Community Systems Alliance as a Model for Managing Change and Supporting the Development of Communities. Between 1984 and 1991, she worked as a nurse and hospital systems analyst at the Toronto Hospital. The primary foci of her work and volunteer activities are community development, health promotion, social development, strategic planning, and advocacy for people with disabilities. Currently, she is working toward a master's of science degree in community health at the University of Toronto.

Evelyne de Leeuw has been involved in WHO health promotion endeavors since the Ottawa Conference and attended all subsequent international health promotion conferences; at the fourth one (Jakarta, 1997), she acted as conference rapporteur. Since its initiation, she has been active in the international Healthy Cities movement, from 1992 as Director of the World Health Organization Collaborating Center for Research on Healthy Cities at the University of Maastricht. Between 1992 and 1998, she served two terms as Secretary-General of the Association of Schools of Public Health in the European Region. After a master's in health policy and administration from the University of Maastricht (1985), she acquired an M.P.H. at the University of California at Berkeley in comparative health systems research (1986) and a Ph.D. on the feasibility of true health policy in the Netherlands (Maastricht, 1989). She has produced several textbooks on health promotion and health policy, published over 100 articles, and enjoys writing "lighter" material in the form of weekly newspaper columns and novels. Her current research interest focuses on the interface between health, urbanization, and globalization.

Joan M. Eakin is Associate Professor in the Department of Public Health Sciences at the University of Toronto. She is a sociologist with a general focus on the social dimensions of illness and health care and a specific focus on the relationship between work and health and work-related health promotion and prevention, particularly in the small workplace and contingent employment sector.

Lawrence Fisher, Ph.D., is Professor in the Departments of Family and Community Medicine and Psychiatry, University of California at San Francisco. He was formerly on the faculty at the University of Rochester and is the author of over 65 published papers. His most recent work addresses the family context of care in the management of chronic disease across the age range, with special emphasis on Type 2 diabetes in adult couples and Alzheimer's disease in three-generation families. He maintains an active practice based in a primary care medical setting. He received his Ph.D. at the University of Cincinnati and was a postdoctoral fellow at the University of Colorado School of Medicine.

John W. Frank is a Senior Scientist at the Institute for Work & Health, a Fellow with the Canadian Institute for Advanced Research, and Professor at the University of Toronto in the Department of Public Health Sciences. As a physician-epidemiologist with a special interest in prevention, his main area of interest is the determinants of health status at the population level. He is currently a visiting professor at the School of Public Health, University of California (Berkeley).

Vivek Goel is Associate Professor and Chair of the Department of Health Administration at the University of Toronto and Adjunct Senior Scientist with the Institute for Clinical Evaluative Sciences in Ontario. He is a community medicine physician with a master's of science in health administration from the University of Toronto and a master's of science in biostatistics from the Harvard School of Public Health. He is the Scientific Program Leader for the Health Evidence Applications and Linkages Network of Centres of Excellence. His research interests include population health status assessment and the evaluation of health services, particularly medical-screening interventions. He practices health promotion in a preventive oncology program.

Joy L. Johnson, Ph.D., R.N., is Associate Professor in the School of Nursing, University of British Columbia, and National Health Research and Development Program Scholar. She conducts research in the field of health promotion, behavior change, and disease prevention and holds a number of nationally funded research grants. Her work also focuses on examining how health professionals can best incorporate health promotion strategies into their practices. She received her Ph.D. in nursing at the University of Alberta in 1993 and has been the recipient of several research awards and prizes. She has authored numerous publications and chapters and has spoken nationally and internationally on the topics of health promotion, the reorientation of health services, and the implementation of research findings in practice.

Ilze Kalnins is Professor in the Department of Public Health Sciences, Faculty of Medicine, University of Toronto and Associate Director of the M.H.Sc. Program in Health Promotion. Her teaching, research, and professional activities encompass both basic research on children's concepts of health, health decision making, and health behavior as well as more applied work on the development and evaluation of programs that promote children's and family involvement in health promoting community development activities. As a member of the Health Behaviour in School-Aged Children: A WHO Cross-National study (HBSC), she is actively engaged in international research on children's health with a special interest in developments in Eastern Europe and the Baltic States.

Steven H. Kelder, Ph.D., M.P.H., is Associate Professor of Epidemiology and Behavioral Science, Associate Director of Design and Analysis at the CHPRD, and Director of the Outreach and Distance Education programs at the University of Texas—Houston School of Public Health. He also is a Research Fellow with the CDC working to develop an implementation assessment tool for school-based nutrition and physical activity programs and is a member of the Behavior Change Expert Panel for the White House Office of National Drug Control Policy's National Youth Anti-Drug Media Campaign (1998–2004). He has over 10 years' experience in design and evaluation of child and adolescent health promotion research. He received his Ph.D. in epidemiology at the and his master's of public heath in community health education at the University of Minnesota.

Marshall W. Kreuter was President of Health 2000, a public health consulting and technical assistance firm in Atlanta, Georgia. Now Associate Director of the division of Chronic Disease Control and Community Intervention at the Centers for Disease Control and Prevention, his current research interest focuses on measuring social capital in the context of public health programs.

Ronald Labonte is Director of the Saskatchewan Population Health Evaluation and Research Unit and Clinical Professor of Community Health and Epidemiology at the University of Saskatchewan. He also heads his own consulting firm (Communitas Consulting) and has held a variety of visiting and adjunct university appointments in Canada, Australia, and Aoteraora/New Zealand. Most recently, he was Visiting Professorial Fellow in Health Promotion at Deakin University in Melbourne. He worked as a health educator and health promoter for 18 years with provincial and municipal governments in Canada before turning his attention to consulting and academic work. He has been an adviser with the WHO, PAHO, and UNICEF and works frequently with government and nongovernmental organizations in Canada, Australia, Aotearoa/New Zealand, Europe, and the United States. His recent books include *A Community Development Approach to Health Promotion* (1998) and *Power, Participation and Partnerships for Health Promotion* (1997). Active in many professional public health and health promotion associations, he has recently turned his attention to the effects of global "free" trade and investment agreements on health, and policy options for more health-promoting forms of global regulation and governance.

John N. Lavis is Assistant Professor in the Department of Clinical Epidemiology and Biostatistics at McMaster University, faculty member in the Centre for Health Economics and Policy Analysis at McMaster University, and Scientist and Associate Research Director (Strategy) at the Institute for Work & Health. His principal research interests include the social determinants of health and the role of research in policy-making.

Zeus Leonardo earned his Ph.D. from University of California, Los Angeles, Graduate School of Education and Information Studies. He has published articles and book chapters on critical pedagogy and social theory. He is also coeditor (with Tejeda and Martinez, in press) of *Charting New Terrains in Chi-*

cano[a]/Latina[o] Education. His current work can best be described as the engagement between ideology, discourse, and school reform.

Jane Lethbridge is an independent consultant in international policy and strategy development. Most recently she was Executive Director of an international health and development nongovernmental organization working on information sharing and knowledge development. She has previously worked at a local and national level in both governmental and nongovernmental sectors. Her main interests are how international health policy can be shaped at national and local levels and in the interface between government and nongovernmental sectors.

Warren McIsaac is a family physician at the Mt. Sinai Hospital Family Medicine Centre and Associate Professor in the Department of Family and Community Medicine at the University of Toronto. He is interested in health services research in primary care. His active area of research is determinants of antibiotic rescribing by family physicians in upper-respiratory and urinary tract infections.

Peter McLaren is Professor, Graduate School of Education and Information studies at the University of California at Los Angeles. He is author of a number of award-winning books on critical pedagogy and the author, coauthor, editor, and coeditor of over 30 books and monographs. Hundreds of his articles, interviews, reviews, commentaries, and columns have appeared in dozens of scholarly journals and professional magazines. His most recent books include *Revolutionary Multiculturalism* (1997), *Critical Pedagogy and Predatory Culture* (1995), *Schooling as a Ritual Performance* (3rd ed., 1999), and *Che Guevara and Paulo Freire: An Introduction to the Pedagogy of Revolution* (1999).

David McQueen is a Senior Biomedical Research Scientist and Associate Director for Global Health Promotion at the National Center for Chronic Disease Prevention and Health Promotion (NCCDPHP), at the Centers for Disease Control and Prevention (CDC) in Atlanta, Georgia, USA. Prior to joining the Office of the Director he was Director of the Division of Adult and Community Health at NCCDPHP and Director of the Office of Surveillance and Analysis at (NCCDPHP). Prior to joining CDC he was Professor and Director of the Research Unit in Health and Behavioral Change at the University of Edinburgh, Scotland (1983-1992), and prior to that Associate Professor of Behavioral Sciences at the Johns Hopkins University School of Hygiene and Public Health in Baltimore. He has served as Director of WHO Collaborating Centers as well as a technical consultant with the World Bank.

Patricia Dolan Mullen is Professor of Behavioral Sciences and Health Education and a senior investigator with the Center for Health Promotion Research and Development at the School of Public Health, University of Texas–Houston. She has worked closely with managed-care organizations over the past 20 years—as an employee, a state regulator, a federal-level advocate for health promotion and disease prevention, and currently, as a university-based researcher conducting health promotion intervention trials.

Guy S. Parcel is Director for the Center for Health Promotion Research and Development and Professor of Behavioral Sciences and Pediatrics at the University of Texas Health Science Center in Houston. He has held faculty positions at the University of Maastricht, University of Texas Medical Branch, Penn State University, the U.S. Military Academy, and Eastern Illinois University. He is currently conducting research to develop and evaluate effective school-based health promotion programs for children and youth. His work includes addressing diet, physical activity, and smoking prevention in children, as well as studying the process of diffusing effective smoking prevention programs into schools. He was also principal investigator on a project to evaluate a school-based intervention to reduce behaviors that result in STD/HIV infection. He has directed research projects on self-management of childhood asthma, sex education for adolescents, and preschool health education. Dr. Parcel received his B.S. and M.S. degrees in health education at Indiana University and his Ph.D. at Penn State University with a major in health education and a minor in child development and family relations. Dr. Parcel has made extensive contributions to child health fields through his many scientific and other related publications. He has authored or coauthored more than 150 papers published in scientific or professional journals, book chapters, reports, or proceedings. He received the American School Health Association 1990 William A. Howe Award for outstanding contributions and distinguished service in school health.

Xóchitl Pérez is a doctoral student in the Social Science and Comparative Education program of the Graduate School of Education and Information Studies at the University of California at Los Angeles. Her dissertation work focuses on the role of U.S. teacher unions in promoting and assisting educational reforms. She is currently associated with the Teacher Union Reform Network (TURN).

Cheryl L. Perry is Professor in the Division of Epidemiology, School of Public Health, at the University of Minnesota. She began her career as a junior high and high school teacher, and junior high school vice principal in Sacramento and Davis, California. She then received her Ph.D. from Stanford University and worked with the Stanford Heart Disease Prevention Program prior to joining the faculty at the University of Minnesota in 1980. At the University of Minnesota, she served as Director of Youth Health Promotion Research and was responsible for the youth and parent component of the Minnesota Heart Health Program from 1980 to 1993. She has published over 180 articles in the peer-reviewed literature on health promotion programs with children and adolescents, including papers on health promotion theory, design, implementation, and outcomes. She was the senior scientific editor of the 1994 *Surgeon General's Report on Preventing Tobacco Use Among Young People* and was an expert witness in Minnesota's landmark trial against the tobacco industry. Currently, she serves as principal investigator of a community-based evaluation of Dare and Dare Plus, the Cafeteria 5-a-Day Power Plus study in 26 schools in Minnesota, and Project Northland, a 28-community trial to reduce alcohol use among adolescents. Her book, *Creating Health Behavior Change: How to Develop Community-Wide Programs for Youth,* was recently published by Sage (1999).

Michael F. D. Polanyi is Research Associate at the Institute for Work & Health and a doctoral student at York University in Environmental Studies. His research focuses on organizational change and its impact on health. He helped coordinate a major research project on musculoskeletal disorders among newspaper workers. He holds a master's degree in political science from the University of Toronto.

Louise Potvin, Ph.D., is Scientist, Medical Research Council of Canada, Groupe de Recherche Interdisciplinaire en Santé, Faculté de Médecine, University of Montreal. She is also Professor, Department of Social and Preventive Medicine, University of Montreal. Her research program focuses on the evaluation of community health promotion programs and on linking community and family health promotion processes with social and structural conditions.

John Raeburn is Associate Professor of Behavioral Science at the University of Auckland, New Zealand. He has had a long-term association with health promotion, and his research and teaching have been especially in the area of grassroots community approaches to health promotion. He is coauthor with Irving Rootman of the 1998 book *People-Centered Health Promotion.*

Harry S. Shannon is Professor in the Department of Clinical Epidemiology and Biostatistics and Director of the Program in Occupational Health and Environmental Medicine at McMaster University. He is seconded to the Institute for Work & Health as a Senior Scientist. He holds a Ph.D. in Applied Statistics from the University of London, England. His current research focus is on organizational factors and health, work-related injuries, and musculoskeletal disorders.

Hassan Soubhi, M.D., Ph.D., is currently a postdoctoral fellow at the Department of Health Care and Epidemiology at the University of British Columbia. His research focuses on the family as an interface between external influences from the general environment, including health promotion programs, and family members' health and health-related behavior. A former Assistant Director of a Community Health Center in Morocco, Dr. Soubhi has worked for 5 years as a family physician with families living in a shantytown in the suburban area of Casablanca. He also has a master's in public health from the School of Public Health at the Free University of Brussels, Belgium.

Terrence J. Sullivan is President of the Institute for Work & Health. He has played senior roles in a number of Ministries of the Ontario government. He maintains an external appointment at the faculty of medicine at the University of Toronto and is Adjunct Professor in the Graduate Program in Sociology at York University in Toronto. He recently edited *Injury and the New World of Work* (1999) and is coeditor with D. Drache of *Health Reform: Public Success/Private Failure* (1999).

Jane G. Zapka is Professor of Medicine in the Division of Preventive and Behavioral Medicine at the University of Massachusetts. She is a behavioral scientist with extensive experience in health policy and management teaching and research. She has expertise in primary care and prevention services, with a focus on program evaluation, quality improvement, and managed care. She is an adjunct faculty member of the Center for Quality at the Harvard School of Public Health, where she collaborates on research related to quality improvement measurement. She has coordinated community-based projects involving work with providers and public education for improving quality of, and participation in, breast cancer screening and evaluating coordinated screening programs within community health centers serving primarily Latino clients. She is interested in research related to women's health and is an investigator on the NIH Women's Health Initiative. Currently, she is involved in evaluation studies for the Massachusetts Department of Public Health-funded smoking cessation projects and Breast and Cervical Cancer Screening Program. Both projects involve educational activities within primary care settings.